HOME
GROWN

HOME GROWN

DENYS DE SAULLES

Foreword by
SARA MIDDA

MACMILLAN
LONDON

A Marshall Edition
Conceived, edited and designed by
Marshall Editions Ltd, 170 Piccadilly,
London W1V 9DD

Editor   **Carole McGlynn**
Art editor   **Daphne Mattingly**
Managing editor   **Ruth Binney**
Design assistant   **Rachel Mozley**
Research   **Jazz Wilson**

Production   **Barry Baker**
Production secretary   **Nikki Ingram**

Colour plates   **Kate Osborne**
Herb colour plates   **Lynn Chadwick**
Line illustrations   **Liz Pepperel**
     Jim Robins

Typeset by Servis Filmsetting Limited,
Manchester, UK
Originated by Newsele Riproduzioni
Fotolitografiche, Milan, Italy
Printed and bound in Spain by
Printer Industria Gráfica S.A., Barcelona
D.L.: B. 39215-1987

1 2 3 4 5 92 91 90 89 88

First published in Great Britain 1988 by
MACMILLAN LONDON LIMITED
4 Little Essex Street London WC2R 3LF
and Basingstoke

Associated companies in Auckland, Delhi,
Dublin, Gaborone, Hamburg, Harare, Hong
Kong, Johannesburg, Kuala Lumpur, Lagos,
Manzini, Melbourne, Mexico City, Nairobi,
New York, Singapore and Tokyo

British Library Cataloguing in Publication Data

De Saulles, Denys
  Home grown.
  1. Vegetable gardening   2. Fruit-culture
  3. Cookery (Vegetables)   4. Cookery
  (Fruit)
  I Title
  635   SB322

  ISBN 0-333-45221-6

CONTENTS

FOREWORD

'Sallets in general consist of certain Esculent Plants and
Herbs, improv'd by Culture, Industry, and Art of the Gard'ner.'
(John Evelyn, 1699)

In the Middle Ages vegetables were rarely eaten by the wealthy. They were relegated to fast days, or made into soups by the peasants. Fruit trees, however, were widely grown in England and even the smallest cottage garden would have probably had one. By Elizabethan times, the wealthier classes were growing many kinds of vegetable.

The age of exploration, and especially the discovery of the New World, greatly increased the variety of fruit and vegetables available to the Englishman. It was through this exploration of distant lands that James Cook first appreciated the importance of fruit to prevent disease. But it was not until this century, and the discovery of vitamins, that the great importance to our diet of fruit and vegetables came to be realized.

In Britain, under siege during the last World War, growing one's own fruit and vegetables was strongly urged by the Government under the slogan 'Dig for victory'. As a child, every radish that we grew – no matter how misshapen or nibbled by our molluscan 'friends' – was an achievement, even if it had been left to grow enormous and become almost inedible, tasting like fiery wood.

What could be more pleasing to the eye than a kitchen garden: row upon row of fruit, vegetables and herbs and the order, pattern, colours and texture of a garden that is both decorative and functional? At Villandry, a sixteenth-century château in the Loire valley of France, this was taken to an extreme. There, between the years of 1914 and 1918, the great *potager* garden was planted and continues to this day. Vegetables of many kinds, and soft fruits bordered by low-growing espaliered apple trees and conically-trimmed pear trees, make up wonderfully varied plots of symmetrical design and create a most pleasing sight just before the harvest.

On a more domestic scale, even a small city balcony can produce handfuls of fresh herbs, a two-person ration of runner beans, a cluster of wild strawberries resembling a Fabergé decoration, and, late in the year, a bowl of corn salad, all of which provide enormous satisfaction and pleasure. One can participate in a complete cycle of growth from seed to fruit, and be sure the end product is free from preservative and pesticide.

'Good huswives in summer will save their own seedes against the next yere as occasion needes' (Thomas Tusser, 1557). Today there is the excitement of a search through seed catalogues, and a quest for new and unusual varieties at the beginning of each year. By home growing, one is not limited to a single variety of limp lettuce, but can choose from the whole lettuce tribe.

As the round of seasons continues, with it comes the pleasure and involvement in growing nature's products, and in preserving and eating them at the peak of perfection.

Sara Midda

Sara Midda is an illustrator and also the author of *In and Out of the Garden*, published in 1981. She is currently engaged on a wide range of illustrative work.

PLANNING TO GROW YOUR OWN

Growing vegetables and fruit successfully demands, as many beginners can testify, more than merely having 'green fingers'. What it certainly depends on are the fundamentals of gardening – choosing the right plants for your site, growing and caring for plants according to simple instructions and, most important of all, being prepared to improve and care for the soil. It is poor, neglected soil that accounts for most crop failures and disappointments.

If you are establishing a plot from scratch, or replanning a garden, the first step is to decide where the food garden is going to be. It is worth taking some trouble over this, for no amount of effort at the growing stage will compensate for an unsuitable site.

Before consigning food crops, like outcasts, to the far end of the garden, consider whether they might form part of the decorative area – particularly if this will provide them with the most favourable growing conditions. A well-kept fruit and vegetable plot looks attractive in its own right, while trained fruit trees and bushes are both decorative and productive.

Similarly, study the needs of the crops you plan to grow (details are given, later in the book, of the preferences of individual fruits and vegetables), and give careful thought to what you might grow where. Some crops, such as tomatoes or onions, need plenty of sun while others, such as blackcurrants, raspberries or gooseberries, will grow well in a partially shaded area. Many low-growing plants, like parsnips or cabbages, will withstand a considerable amount of wind, while plants that are taller or more tender need protection and/or support.

A small area will obviously yield less than a large one, but worthwhile crops can be grown in relatively cramped surroundings. When space is limited, it is particularly important to study a variety of possibilities, and establish your priorities, before deciding what to grow, and how much. Garden size will also be a factor in determining layout, but remember to plan for pathways. Harvesting vegetables and fruit, barrowing compost, pruning fruit trees and other garden jobs means that you need easy access to plants all year round.

Before buying seeds or plants, take time to study the selections of fruit and vegetables included in this book and to thumb through suppliers' catalogues to see what appeals. Also, work out what tools and equipment you may need.

If you are a beginner, there is much to be said for starting in a fairly small way, for example by growing salad vegetables or herbs, or some quick-maturing vegetables such as courgettes. Much will depend on the condition of your soil, and your personal tastes and preferences.

When planning a food-growing plot, you may well be concerned about how much time you need. There is really no absolute answer, but in most temperate climates there will be plants needing attention and jobs to be done in the garden during most spring, summer and autumn weekends. It partly depends on what you grow – celery takes up a lot more time than cabbages, for example – as well as the condition of your soil.

As a guide, tending a greenhouse and a plot measuring about 125 square metres (150 square yards) might demand, on average, half a day's attention a week. You might well need to spend more hours in the garden and greenhouse during the spring and early summer months, but if gardening is a pursuit you find pleasurable, you will probably want to spend as much of your spare time as possible tending your plants and your plot.

**The ideal vegetable and fruit
garden** allows for planned planting
and for crop rotation. Pathways
are not only a design feature, but
allow easy access to plants. Areas
should be set aside for greenhouse,
compost heap and possibly a cold
frame too.

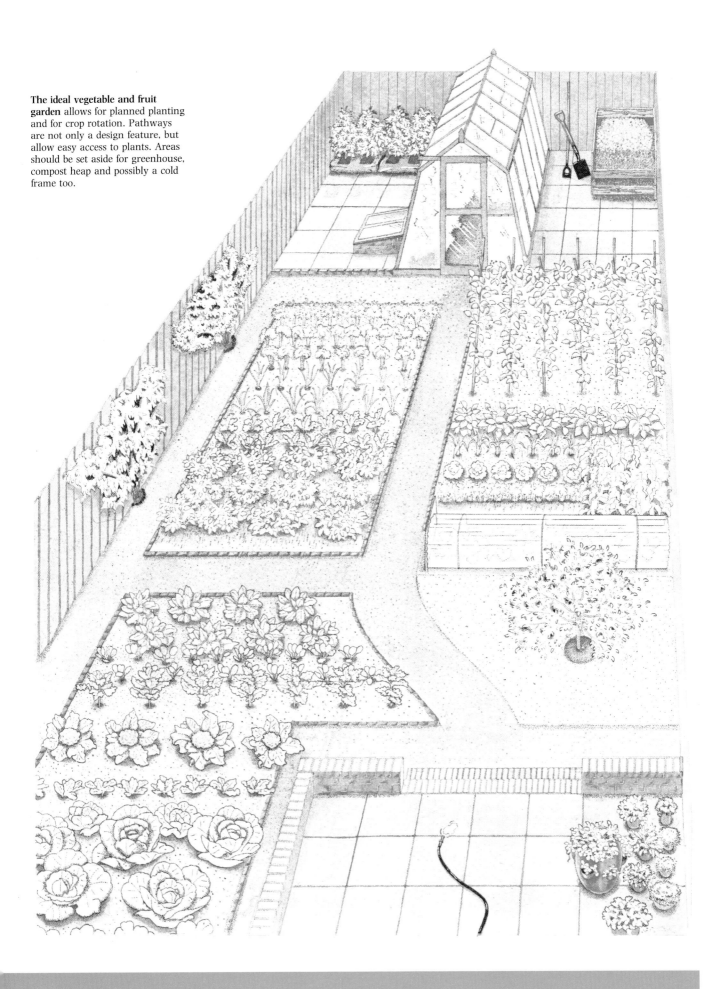

Food crops need a favoured position in your garden if they are to produce a worthwhile harvest, not least because they often have to make a lot of growth in a short time. A cabbage grows from a tiny seed to a football-sized plant in only four months, for example, while a single seed potato planted in spring should give a twentyfold increase by autumn. Fruit trees produce over a longer time scale, but an established bush apple tree, for instance, might be expected to produce 50kg (100lb) of fruit per year – every year.

SUN AND SOIL
The ideal spot for most crops is generally well-drained, open to the sky and receives plenty of sunshine. You will probably have to compromise, but avoid at all costs a patch shaded by an overhanging tree and starved by its roots. Neither vegetables nor fruits will prosper there.

You cannot do anything to increase the average number of hours of sunshine your area receives each year. But what you can do is site your food crops so that they receive the maximum your garden can offer. For example, you can grow fruit trees against a south-facing wall so that they get all the sunshine going and benefit from the extra heat stored by the wall.

If your soil is poorly drained, it is essential to improve it, as explained on page 26, since very few vegetables or fruit crops thrive in soggy ground. If the soil remains damp and sticky for long periods, perhaps with an overall greening, you have a drainage problem on your hands.

The type of soil – sandy, clay or somewhere in between – is less critical. Though each type has its merits and drawbacks (see pp.24–5), all are capable of growing crops, especially if you take steps to improve their texture and fertility. It is a question of making the best of what you have. All soils can be improved – and by much the same type of treatment.

WIND AND FROST
Whether your garden is north- or south-facing, and the degree of shelter or exposure to winds, is of even greater significance than the average amount of sunshine or rainfall.

Shelter from wind is a bonus in any garden, and almost essential on an exposed site. A living windbreak formed by a hedge causes less turbulence than a wall or solid fence, and could in itself be productive if it were, for example, a double row of raspberry canes. Restricted forms of fruit trees, such as espaliers, cordons or fans, can also be trained against solid barriers, such as walls or fences.

Frost can be a particular hazard in low-lying gardens, since cold air 'flows' downhill. A frost pocket may also be formed when a barrier, such as a fence, checks the movement of air down a slope. Other than avoiding a vulnerable site, the solutions are to plant later in spring and to make full use of cloches and frames. It is also a simple matter to choose late-flowering varieties of tree fruits and to delay spring pruning in order to retard new shoots, if you expect spring frosts.

Other protective measures against frost include the use of mulches – in the form of compost, straw, bracken or even newspapers. These are laid on the ground around plants to protect their roots until the soil warms up in spring.

MAKING THE MOST OF THE SPACE
If you are short of space, you will need to think carefully about what to grow as well as where to plant it. There are no set rules, since much depends on personal taste. Even so, some crops do give better value than others for the space they occupy and, provided they are crops you enjoy, these are the ones to grow.

Planting vegetables in beds or patches makes the most of a small plot. The much-reduced spacing between plants possible in a bed, as opposed to a row, enables many more plants to be grown in a given area. Details of bed systems are given on p.132.

MINIMUM-SPACE CROPS
Salads, including lettuces, spring onions and radishes, are all compact, rapid growers and much tastier when freshly gathered. A few well-chosen herbs can be successfully grown in pots or an odd corner: select the ones you use most, for example chives, mint, thyme, parsley.

Plants that grow vertically, such as runner beans or the climbing French varieties, increase the output of any given area. They may be grown against a wall or in the open. If there is enough space for one or two gro-bags, tomatoes will crop heavily on a sheltered patio. You may also like to experiment with peppers or aubergines, which are a little less hardy, grown in the same way.

Most root crops are ruled out if your space is restricted, but try to find space for a few early carrots which, freshly pulled, are rewarding. Likewise, most brassicas – cauliflowers, Brussels sprouts and the like – take up rather too much space, but the small, plump hearts of 'Minicole' cabbage are a worthy exception.

For an ongoing supply of tender leaves from just two or three plants, consider growing perpetual spinach (spinach beet). And bear in mind that both globe artichokes and sweet corn, though large, are attractive plants for the flower garden. A row of beetroot makes an effective edging to a flower border, as do alpine strawberries, the new red varieties of lettuce, and several decorative herbs.

PLANTS IN CONTAINERS
A window-box garden is a practical and decorative possibility. Among suitable herbs are sage, chives, mint and marjoram. The restricted root run will help to keep the plants dwarfed. Pots or even a hanging basket may be used for the same purpose.

If you have a sizeable patio, it is perfectly feasible to grow courgettes, ridge cucumbers and even melons in tubs or other substantial containers. Some of the fruits may need supporting.

Strawberries grown in barrels or tall earthenware pots crop well. Once covered with foliage, blossoms and fruits, the container makes an attractive feature in its own right, on a patio or elsewhere. As with all container-grown plants, however, watering must be regular and generous.

TRAINED FRUIT TREES
Nearly all gardens have space for a fruit tree, so long as you choose one of the trained forms – fan, espalier or cordon – and a self-fertile variety if you are growing only one tree. Such trees may be grown against a wall or fence; they take up very little room but are capable of substantial yields.

Alternatively, cordons and espaliers may be planted as dividers or screens within the garden. The trees look neat and decorative, even during the dormant season.

CLIMATE AND MICROCLIMATE

The climate map of Europe shown below is divided into zones based on the average annual minimum temperatures. All gardeners need to be aware of the expected degree of frost in their district, since this is one of the most significant considerations in choosing what crops to grow, and what, if any, protective measures to adopt.

Such a map can, however, give only the broadest categories of hardiness, and you should also take factors within your district and your garden into consideration.

The altitude of your area, whether it is in an open, rural situation or a built-up urban location, whether it is exposed to coastal winds or nestling in a sheltered valley, will all influence your choice of crops and varieties, and method of cultivation. The orientation of your garden and the microclimate within it will also govern what you can grow and where you plant it.

While you cannot change the weather patterns of the area in which you live, there are many ways in which to minimize the drawbacks and maximize the potential of a particular site. There are usually sheltered

corners within every garden that will give half-hardy plants extra protection, or walls that will shelter fruit trees.

If you have a greenhouse, you need not rule out even tender crops, wherever you live, provided you are prepared to heat it during the coldest weather; localized heat, in the form of propagators or soil-warming cables, may even be sufficient. Tender crops, such as melons, grapes and cucumbers, can all be grown under glass.

Frames and cloches can be put to good use to give extra protection – as well as to sow and raise early crops. Cloches will also help to warm up the soil ready for seeds to be sown *in situ* or hardened-off seedlings to be planted outdoors.

It is always more important to garden by the weather than by the book. In most climates the weather is variable and unpredictable from year to year. Whatever it says on the seed packet, do not sow seeds outdoors in mid-spring if the ground is still cold. Trust your judgement; give extra protection where it is necessary, and you will be able to grow successful crops.

EFFECTS OF A MICROCLIMATE

- **Type of soil** Light soil heats up and cools quicker than heavy soil.
- **Orientation** A south-facing garden makes the most of any sunshine.
- **Slope of the ground** A south-facing slope is warmest. Do not plant in a hollow; cold air flows downhill and it may become a frost pocket.
- **Walls** A wall gives shelter, stores heat, and radiates it at night. This benefits fruit trees, but the earth at their base will dry out faster.
- **Proximity of buildings** A garden surrounded by buildings is likely to be warmer and more sheltered than an open one, but buildings can cut out a lot of light.
- **Proximity of large trees** A large tree's extensive roots may starve crops of food and moisture.
- **Exposed site** Plants are at risk from strong winds; fences and hedges give them some shelter.

Annual average minimum temperatures

30° to 40°F

20° to 30°F

10° to 20°F

5° to 10°F

−5° to 5°F

−10° to −5°F

−20° to −10°F

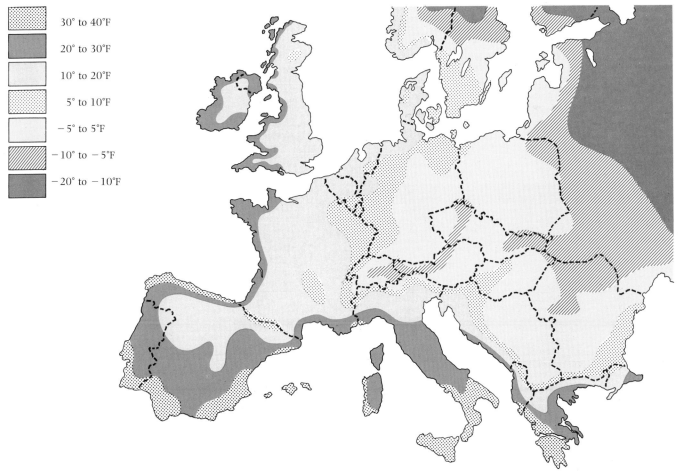

USING A GREENHOUSE, pages 12–13
MULCHING, page 43

THE FRUIT GARDEN, page 65
GROWING TREE FRUITS, pages 87–89

SPACE-SAVING METHODS, pages 132–133

The protected environment of a greenhouse offers the food gardener many advantages. If you live in a temperate, or cooler, climate zone, it enables you to grow crops that need winter protection and that can be grown outdoors only in warmer, or frost-free areas. By lengthening the gardening year, it allows you the satisfaction of growing out-of-season crops, if only by means of early seed-raising under glass. It also lets you enjoy particular crops over an extended period. You can make early sowings, before the soil has warmed up, and extend the fruiting period of crops such as tomatoes, at the other end of the growing season.

A greenhouse also protects tender plants against weather hazards such as frost, rain and chilling winds, to which they are vulnerable outdoors. At the same time it offers all plants protection against pests.

SPRING SOWINGS
Early salads are a considerable bonus for all food growers. Even in an unheated greenhouse, radishes, lettuces and spring onions will germinate and grow, well before the soil outside has started to warm up.

Several half-hardy vegetables and fruits can be raised under glass, for planting out after the spring frosts. This category includes melons, ridge cucumbers, marrows, outdoor tomatoes, pumpkins and squashes.

Runner beans and sweet corn can be given an early start by being sown in the greenhouse. Established plants can then be transplanted to outdoor positions. There is no need to raise the whole of each crop in this way. Raise enough plants to provide some early pickings before the main outdoor-sown crop matures.

SUMMER CROPS
Along with spring plant-raising, you can plant the summer crops that are grown to maturity inside the greenhouse. Most important of these are tomatoes, which provide a supply of ripening fruits from late spring or early summer until autumn. Greenhouse tomatoes are more tender than those grown outdoors and the plants will bear twice as many trusses. Cucumbers are another worthwhile greenhouse crop. Because they can be grown vertically, right up to the greenhouse roof, both cucumbers and tomatoes provide excellent returns for the ground space they occupy.

There are also a number of tender, exotic crops that can be grown in a greenhouse, including aubergines, peppers, chillis and okra, as well as fruits such as grapes, kiwi fruit and melons. Given a warm, sheltered spot, success is possible outdoors with any of these, but your chances are improved if the plants are cultivated under glass.

COLD OR HEATED?
Artificial heating brings a further advantage to the greenhouse gardener; in particular, it allows earlier sowing and planting. For growing food crops, however, it is by no means essential to heat the whole greenhouse. Localized warmth, in the form of soil-warming cables or a propagator (see p.38), is sufficient to give seedlings a good start; it is also much cheaper.

Your aim in using a partially or wholly heated greenhouse must be to time your sowings to suit the conditions that will prevail after the seedling stage. If a small propagator is your only heat source, sowing will have to be later than in a heated greenhouse. But the lengthening spring days will help delayed sowings to catch up.

GRO-BAGS AND RING CULTURE
An alternative to soil borders is to grow crops in containers. This is less trouble, and cuts down the disease problems encountered in greenhouse soil. Disease organisms multiply, and the soil becomes exhausted, in greenhouse borders that are cropped for years in succession; this often happens with tomatoes, for instance. Instead of simply replacing the soil in the borders with fresh soil, a better solution might be to grow the plants in peat bags or in pots.

Peat bags, or gro-bags as they are often

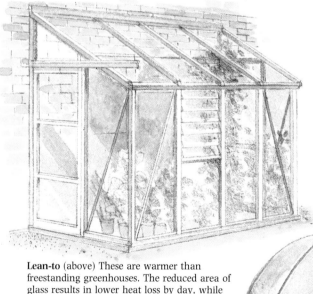

Lean-to (above) These are warmer than freestanding greenhouses. The reduced area of glass results in lower heat loss by day, while the backing wall serves, to some extent, as a storage radiator at night. A wall facing between south-east and south-west is needed.

Plastic (right) The advantages of low capital outlay must be weighed against the cost of replacing the cover. When buying, check that there is provision for controlled ventilation at both ends and that the door is substantial.

Miniature lean-to Designed for small gardens, these structures serve the dual funcion of greenhouse and cold frame. The plants, grown on shelving, are tended from outside. Their small volume makes it more difficult to maintain a stable temperature, so extra attention is needed during frosty or hot weather.

called, are about a metre long, which is large enough for a couple of cucumbers or three tomato plants. Water the mature plants daily or twice a day, depending on the condition of the peat, and start giving liquid feeds from an early stage.

CHOOSING A GREENHOUSE
Shape, size and structural material are the chief points to consider when choosing a greenhouse. Once you have a broad idea of your requirements, send for makers' catalogues to compare specification and prices.
Size A ground area of as little as 4sq m (4¾sq yd) will suffice if your object is simply to raise half-hardy plants, such as marrows, in spring, and to leave sufficient space during the summer for a few tomatoes and a cucumber. If you also wish to grow salads during the spring, followed by a greater range of summer crops, you will need a base of about 7.5sq m (9sq yd).

It is best, if space and financial considerations allow, not to start small, if only because you will quickly become aware of the many uses of the greenhouse.
Shape Although most greenhouses are rectangular and freestanding, there are a number of permutations and other possibilities (see illustrations). Consider the practical pros and cons for your site.
Materials The principal choice is between

timber (unpainted) and aluminium. Given occasional treatment with preservative, a good-quality timber greenhouse will last several decades, and may well seem more in keeping with garden surroundings.

Cedar, a favourite wood for greenhouses, has natural resistance to rot. It is easy to fit shelves, insulating sheeting, and vine eyes for plant support in a timber greenhouse.

Aluminium is strong and needs no maintenance. Though less convenient for attaching sheeting and screws, most systems have patent clamps and fittings for securing to the glazing bars. A metal greenhouse lets in more light than a wooden one, and glazing takes less time, since the panes are simply clipped into place. Condensation is heavier than in a wooden greenhouse.
Plastic greenhouses Instead of being conventionally glazed, some greenhouses are clad with polythene or PVC. This is most commonly seen in the tunnel houses widely used by commercial growers, and which are sold in smaller form for amateurs. Polythene, which deteriorates in sunlight, needs replacing every year or two. PVC has a longer life but costs more.

A disadvantage of plastic greenhouses is their rapid heat loss, with accompanying condensation. Because the main tunnel section is formed by a continuous skin, ventilation may also prove a problem.

SITING CHECKLIST
You may have no choice about where to site your greenhouse, but if there is more than one possible location, there are several points to consider in order to make the most of its benefits.
Light Choose the sunniest position available. Remember that trees and buildings cast longer shadows early in the year, when good light is important for plant growth. Keep the windows clean to maximize the light.
Shelter Make sure your greenhouse is not in an exposed position, otherwise the east wind will chill the glass and significantly reduce the inside temperature. Position the door on the side least affected by cold winds.
Access As a rule, the nearer a greenhouse is to the house, the more convenient it will be. However, it should not be in such a position that the house shades it. For a greenhouse some distance from the house, access by an all-weather path is essential.
Services A water tap in or near the greenhouse is valuable – the alternative is a hose and water butt. Consider the distance from the electricity supply for heating or for a propagator.

Span-roof Inside this conventionally shaped greenhouse, the usual arrangement is a central path, with a soil border on each side and across the far end. One side border may be covered with staging, for plant raising during at least part of the year. Some span-roof greenhouses have partially boarded side walls; others are glazed to ground level. The fully glazed type is preferable for food-growing, since the crops receive maximum light. However, the structure itself gets colder.

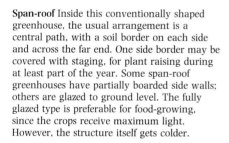

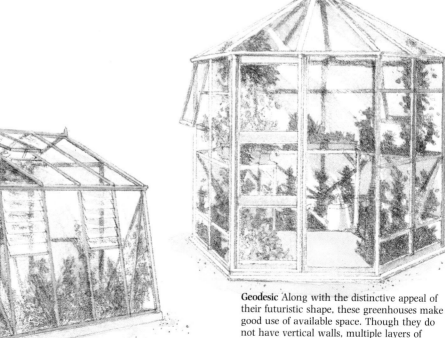

Geodesic Along with the distinctive appeal of their futuristic shape, these greenhouses make good use of available space. Though they do not have vertical walls, multiple layers of staging can be fitted and you can grow tall plants, such as tomatoes, in them.

SOWING UNDER GLASS, pages 38–39
GREENHOUSE EQUIPMENT, pages 14–15

KIWI FRUITS, MELONS AND GRAPES, pages 81–86
VEGETABLE FRUITS, pages 166–167

TOMATOES, pages 168–170

Control of the greenhouse environment is entirely in the hands of the gardener. The inside temperature, the degree of ventilation or insulation, the provision of shading, and the amount of watering are all your responsibility; they can be adjusted according to the time of year, and to suit the crops you are raising or growing under glass. Technology has come to the aid of the greenhouse gardener, however, and many of these routine tasks, which were once so time-consuming, are now automatically controlled. But while modern equipment will make your tasks easier, it cannot replace your personal care and judgement.

STAGING

Some form of greenhouse benching is needed to support seed trays and pots at a convenient working height. Most greenhouse manufacturers offer staging to fit their structures, along with the necessary fittings. Simplest of all are the wooden supporting frames with slatted tops supplied for timber greenhouses; they have good air circulation and free drainage.

A metal frame supporting a mesh top provides similar conditions. These devices are supplied by the makers of aluminium greenhouses, and may also be fitted with metal trays about 2.5cm (1in) deep. The trays make good supports for a capillary watering system (see below); turned upside down, they provide a firm working surface.

Staging needs to be removable if you plan to use the greenhouse border for summer crops. Dismantle it in late spring when the last of the seedlings or tender plants have been moved outside. Some greenhouse owners choose to have permanent staging on one side of the house, with the other side left open for crop-growing. It is possible to grow salad crops beneath the staging if that side has a sunny aspect. The legs of staging must stand on bricks or metal plates to prevent them settling into the soil in the border. Shelving fixed at a higher level will provide space for pots and small trays.

HEATING

Several worthwhile crops can be grown in an unheated greenhouse, but there are some tender fruits, such as melons, and vegetables, such as peppers, whose seeds must be sown in heat if they are to germinate. An economical alternative to heating the whole greenhouse is to provide local heat in the form of soil-warming cables or an electric propagator (see p.38).

If you do decide to extend the scope of your greenhouse by heating it, you will have a choice of sources of power.

The chief advantage of electricity is that it emits a dry heat, so does not cause extra condensation. Electric fan heaters are particularly good, since they help to avoid a stagnant atmosphere, which encourages disease. Tubular heaters, secured to the walls, take up little room. The main drawback of electric heating is its relatively high running cost. There is also a charge for having the supply installed professionally.

Main gas provides reasonably economical heating, and the carbon dioxide given off by natural (not town) gas is beneficial to green plants. There is an installation charge for the pipework but the running costs are relatively low. Heavier condensation is a drawback to consider. Bottled gas is substantially more expensive as a fuel than mains gas, but there is no installation cost.

Paraffin heating also gives rise to condensation, but it provides a convenient means of heating during spring when weather conditions are not over severe. Both its running costs and the initial outlay are moderate.

INSULATION

Only a few, costly, greenhouses are double-glazed. Heat lost through the glass in the majority of greenhouses is considerable, but improved insulation is the answer to heat preservation and lower heating bills. The best method is to secure plastic sheeting to the inside of the framework, which traps air between the plastic and the glass.

VENTILATION

Efficient greenhouse ventilation is essential throughout the year. In summer it provides a necessary means of temperature control; without adequate ventilation plants wilt and rapidly die. In winter, some ventilation is needed to prevent the development of a stagnant atmosphere, in which disease-causing organisms flourish. Winter ventilation is very important in greenhouses that suffer from heavy condensation.

Roof ventilators are the most efficient type, but many small greenhouses are inadequately supplied with these. The ideal is to have two ventilators, on alternate sides, every 2m (6ft). Side ventilators – sliding, hinged or louvred – help to increase the flow of air during warm weather. The greenhouse door can always be left open to increase the air flow.

Automatic vent openers, sensitive to heat, and thermostatically controlled, are a boon. They keep hinged lights (panes) adjusted to suit the temperature, so you can leave a greenhouse all day.

Electric extractor fans, similar to those used in kitchens, but thermostatically controlled, provide another means of automatic ventilation. The fan unit is mounted in the glass opposite the door. Small circulating fans help to maintain an even and oxygen-rich atmosphere. Some fan heaters can be used for this purpose, with the heating elements switched off.

SHADING

Sun that strikes plants directly through the glass can overheat and scorch plants, even in a well-ventilated greenhouse. Some form of shading is needed to counter this.

The simplest and cheapest form is a proprietary shading liquid which you can 'paint' directly onto the outside of the glass. Though resistant to rain, it can be rubbed off at the end of the season. Some liquids have the disadvantage that they continue to act during cloudy weather, making dull days even duller inside the greenhouse. However, some spray-on liquids are formulated to turn opaque in bright sunlight, while remaining transparent on dull days.

Roller blinds provide a more expensive but more satisfactory solution. Those fitted to the outside of the greenhouse are best, since they keep both the glass and the interior of the greenhouse cool. Inside blinds are less at risk from the weather; they shade the plants effectively but have less effect on the overall temperature.

WATERING

Hand watering of greenhouse plants is time-consuming but allows accurate control. Because your aim should be to act before plants begin to show signs of distress, you will need to water greenhouse plants at least once a day during the main growing season. The weight of trays and pots is a guide to moisture content, as well as the feel of the compost itself. Use a trowel to check the state of border soil a short way down.

A number of proprietary automatic watering systems are available. The drip watering system may be supplied directly from the mains using a pressure regulator control, or else from a container mounted at a higher level inside the greenhouse. The drip nozzle can be positioned above the capillary matting or over individual pots.

The simpler capillary system is based on capillary matting, a highly absorbent material from which compost in pots draws up moisture by capillary action. This is most suitable for plants small enough to be grown in pots on the greenhouse staging.

To set up a capillary system, lay the matting on a sheet of polythene. Turn one end of the matting over into a water-filled trough or tray; make sure that the water level is lower than the matting. A narrow 'wick' of matting linking the compost to the water will serve the same purpose.

Regular treatment with an algicide is needed to prevent the matting becoming clogged with green growth.

USING A GREENHOUSE, pages 12–13
FRAMES AND CLOCHES, pages 16–18

SOWING UNDER GLASS, pages 38–39

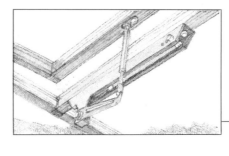

Automatic vent openers depend on heat-sensitive mineral wax in a cylinder exerting pressure on a piston which, in turn, is linked to the vent. The device can be adjusted to make the vent open when the inside temperature reaches upward of about 13°C (55°F). The weight of greenhouse vents varies, so be sure to buy an opener suitable for yours.

Exterior blinds (above) keep the glass and interior of the greenhouse cool. Though formerly made from slats or natural reeds, they are now made in weather-resistant plastic. Pleated interior shading (right) slides up and down on guide cords. A cheaper, but less flexible, alternative is to fasten material directly to the glazing bars.

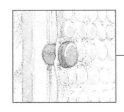

'Bubble' insulation sheeting is particularly effective in reducing heat loss. If draped over taut strings at ridge and eaves, the material can be secured with double-sided adhesive pads, drawing pins or – for aluminium greenhouses – a variety of patent fixings.

Electric tubular heaters, mounted here beneath the staging, are an efficient form of greenhouse heating if you have a mains supply. At the far end is a small paraffin heater for use when conditions are not too severe. Electric fan and mains gas heaters (left) can be controlled thermostatically.

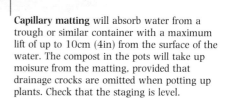

Capillary matting will absorb water from a trough or similar container with a maximum lift of up to 10cm (4in) from the surface of the water. The compost in the pots will take up moisure from the matting, provided that drainage crocks are omitted when potting up plants. Check that the staging is level.

In a cold or less than temperate climate, cloches serve as unheated miniature greenhouses to protect a variety of crops from cold and wind. Their great advantage, compared with greenhouses, is that they are easily moved about. As one crop matures, or ceases to need shelter, the cloches may be shifted to another. In a carefully-planned cropping programme cloches would be in almost continuous use.

Because the air and soil inside a cloche are warmer than outside, crops may be sown or planted earlier in the season. Subsequent growth is then much faster, so that crops raised under cloches may be harvested well ahead of their usual season. Spring salads, for example, mature several weeks sooner than they do in open ground.

Tender plants, such as runner beans, can be protected under cloches and may be sown or planted before the last of the spring frosts. Strawberries, cloched from early spring onward, will be ready for picking from late spring. Melons, planted during the spring, will benefit from cloche protection for much of the summer.

Used in this way, cloches add up to a mini-revolution in garden food-growing, and can make the whole enterprise more rewarding for those gardeners who live in cooler climates.

TYPES OF CLOCHE

Cloches are constructed from glass or from a variety of plastic materials to provide a translucent covering for a row of plants. The ends must be closed to prevent a wind-tunnel effect.

Cloches were designed originally as solitary, bell-shaped units: hence their name, from the French for bell, *la cloche*. Although the common aim of gardeners is now to form a continuous shelter, this is still, in most cases, made up of separate units (which can vary in height and width) placed end to end in a row. One exception is the polythene tunnel cloche (see below).

Glass Glass cloches are expensive, but they provide particularly good conditions for plant growth. They let in more light, and conserve more heat, than their plastic counterparts. Occasional breakages are inevitable, but they stand up well to wind.

There are two basic shapes. Tent cloches, formed from two sheets of glass secured by wires or fixed together at the top with a galvanized iron clip, are for compact crops such as lettuces. Barn cloches, made from four sheets of glass with a 'pitched roof', are designed for multiple rows and for larger plants, such as peas. Besides the 30cm-(1ft-) high barn cloche, there is a higher-sided version, about 50cm (20in), for protecting tomatoes, aubergines and peppers until they are well grown. The panes may be secured either with patent wire supports or with metal clips.

Since glass is expensive both to make and transport, many cloche manufacturers now sell only the wire supports or clips. You can either make your own cloche using offcuts of glass, or have glass cut to size; horticultural glass is cheaper than window glass.

Corrrugated PVC Cloches made from this material are light and strong and give good protection. Because they weigh so little, they need to be well anchored in the soil; always choose supporting frames that have spikes; stuck into the soil, they serve as ground anchors.

At least one design of tent cloche has netting secured under the plastic cover, giving it a dual function. With the cover in place, it serves as a normal cloche. Without it, the netting gives protection against birds.

A barn cloche is constructed from four sheets of glass, supported by a thick wire frame. There is a carrying handle at the top, and one side of the roof can be opened to increase the amount of ventilation.

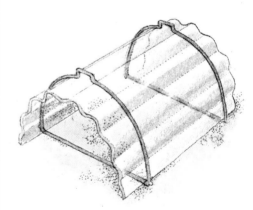

Corrugated PVC combines strength and lightness. The wire or plastic frames that hold this type of cloche in place have spikes for pushing into the soil. For ventilation, adjacent cloches may simply be moved apart.

CROPPING WITH CLOCHES

Broad beans Sow direct in late autumn or during winter/early spring. Cover until mid-spring.

French beans or runner beans Sow in spring, either direct or under glass for planting out. Cover until early summer.

Brassicas Start early cabbages under cloches in late winter/early spring. Remove when they outgrow the cloches.

Carrots Sow direct from early spring. Cover until mid- to late spring.

Cucumbers (ridge) Sow in a greenhouse or frame in spring. Plant out, then cover for part or all of the summer.

Lettuce Sow direct in autumn, winter and early spring, or in a greenhouse or frame in winter and spring for planting out. Cover until mature.

Marrows and courgettes Sow in a greenhouse or frame in spring. Plant out, then cover until early summer.

Melons Sow in a greenhouse or frame in spring. Plant out and keep covered for part or all of the summer.

Peas Sow direct in late autumn, late winter or spring. Cover until mid-spring.

Radishes Sow direct from early spring. Cover until mature.

Strawberries Cover in early spring, removing the cloches in late spring/early summer.

Sweet corn Sow direct in mid-spring, or under glass for planting out. Cover until late spring/early summer.

Tomatoes Sow in a greenhouse or frame in early spring. Plant out in mid-spring and cover until early summer.

Polythene tunnel cloches provide an inexpensive means of covering rows of any length. They are easy to erect and ventilate, but the polythene has to be replaced fairly frequently.

Cone-shaped plastic cloches give protection to single plants. Individual cloches can also be improvised, for example by using a transparent plastic umbrella, with its handle cut off and glued to the end spike. Empty plastic bottles cut off at the base may also be used.

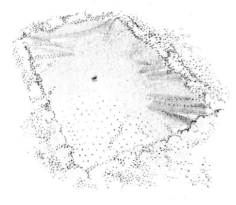

A floating cloche, so-called because the growing plants raise it clear of the ground, gives moderate protection while still allowing moisture to penetrate. The edges are held in place by a covering of soil.

Polythene A variety of individual cloches, covered with polythene in different thicknesses is sold. They are less expensive than PVC cloches, but check that the cover is easy to replace. This will become necessary every year or two. Some cloches have a secondary covering of netting to serve as a bird guard when the plastic is removed.

Condensation can be a problem with polythene-covered cloches, and this is to be avoided since such conditions encourage the spread of fungal diseases. It is important to make sure that such cloches are always well-ventilated.

Moulded polypropylene Cloches made of this material cost more than both polythene and PVC versions. Though not always fully translucent, which means that the light transmission is rather poor, they combine lightness with strength. Double-skinned polypropylene cloches also have good insulation properties. They give satisfactory results and should last for many years.

Polythene tunnels Tunnel cloches can be bought as kits and are easy to erect. The tunnel is formed by stretching a sheet of polythene over wire hoops anchored in the ground, then fixing another set of wire hoops to secure the plastic. They are a particularly good choice for fairly long rows – upward of about 6m (20ft). You can simply slide back one side of the polythene cover for access to seedlings or plants for purposes of watering or cultivation.

The plastic will probably need replacing every two years or so, since it deteriorates in sunlight and is liable to be easily ripped or damaged. It also gets very dirty, so wash and dry it before storing.

Individual cloches Cone-shaped, rigid plastic cloches are ideal for covering individual plants, such as tomatoes, peppers and aubergines. They protect the plants against frost and wind, as well as against insects and birds, until they are well established. These cones are semi-transparent, so they let in enough light without allowing a build-up of heat. They are sturdy enough to last for several years.

MAKING THE BEST USE OF CLOCHES
Although cloches are mobile, you should avoid using them in the most exposed positions in the garden. Increase the anchorage of all types of cloche if there is any danger of their being blown away.

Place the cloches in position two weeks or so before early sowings or plantings, so that the soil can warm up. Secure the end panels in place with canes driven into the ground, if necessary. Be ready to sow or to plant out,

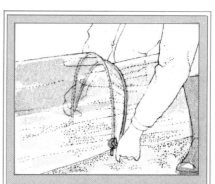

CONSTRUCTING A TUNNEL CLOCHE
Insert the supporting wires at intervals along a marker line. Stretch the plastic cover over the top, and tie its ends to pegs driven into the soil. Finally, hold it down with thin wires hooked into loops at the base of the main wires.

once the ground is sufficiently warm. For a single row, position the line along the centre of the cloches, where plants will have most headroom. Position double rows at equal distances from the sides. Scatter slug pellets around after sowing or planting.

A degree of ventilation is needed, especially with polythene, but you may find that there are enough gaps, where individual units are joined, to provide sufficient ventilation early in the season. As the weather warms up, open one side of the tunnel cloche or space individual cloches a little further apart.

Remove the cloches before watering seedlings or small plants. Use a watering can with a rose attached. In good soil, there should be no need to remove cloches before watering established crops during a dry spell. Water percolating from the edges of the cloche generally supplies sufficient moisture. If in any doubt, check the soil a little way down in the centre of the cloche.

FLOATING CLOCHES
These are not cloches in the true sense, but consist simply of a rectangular sheet of perforated polythene laid directly over the seedbed or plants to speed up their growth. The perforations serve both for ventilation and to allow rainwater to penetrate. The system is best suited to fairly wide blocks of plants rather than individual rows. Secure the edges of the sheet by covering them with soil. The perforations also permit some expansion of the sheeting, which is gradually lifted or 'floated' off the ground by the developing crop.

It is important to remove the sheeting at the right time, so keep a close watch for signs that a crop is getting cramped.

MELONS, pages 54–55
STRAWBERRIES, pages 68–69

A garden frame is a low, glazed structure which has many uses in the food garden. It is more permanent than a cloche and usually remains in a fixed position. Since it can be heated by means of electric soil-warming cables, a frame can become a small version of a greenhouse in some respects and widens the gardener's scope further than cloches can. Frames can be bought or made at home.

An unheated frame can provide an invaluable halfway house for plants raised in artificial heat, in a greenhouse or on a windowsill indoors. A spell in the frame, during which the ventilation is gradually increased, will acclimatize seedlings before they are planted out in the garden. This is known as hardening off (see p.39).

A frame is a good place, too, for raising seeds of cabbages, cauliflowers and other brassica plants for growing outside. It can also be used for lettuces and more tender plants such as runner beans and sweet corn. Brassicas, in particular, tend to make sturdier growth in a frame than when raised in a greenhouse.

The frame may also be used for growing salad crops to maturity. Autumn-sown lettuces are ready early in the spring when grown in a frame. Radishes, spring onions, beetroot and carrots may all be sown and harvested well before outdoor crops.

Even in summer, the frame need not be left vacant. Ridge cucumbers and melons fruit more reliably with this form of protection, especially in exposed gardens. Peppers and chillis grown in pots can be covered for at least part of the summer.

Using electric soil-warming cables, the timing of early crops and plant raising is brought forward even further. The cables are easy to install if you follow the manufacturer's instructions, and electrically heated frames are economical to run.

TYPES OF FRAME

A traditional garden frame is a shallow wooden 'box', with walls that slope to the front. A glazed top, called a light, is mounted on the low sides. It slides or is lifted to open. This type of frame can be constructed at home quite easily, using offcuts of wood and spare pieces of glass. Make sure the sides are not so high that they exclude a lot of light.

Most proprietary frames now have a metal framework (generally aluminium) and glass or plastic sides and roof; they are both lightweight and maintenance-free. The walls can be deeper without affecting plants adversely, though more heat will be lost than through wooden sides. A deeper frame provides more space for cucumbers, peppers and other tender plants.

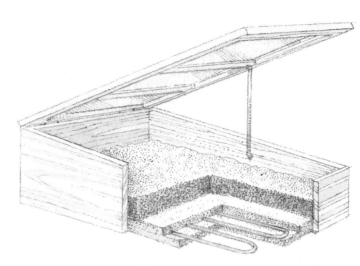

Roof lights may be hinged or sliding, single or multiple. The most important consideration is that they are sturdily made, and will not come adrift in windy weather.

SITING AND USING A FRAME

The ideal position for a frame is a sheltered spot in the garden, so you can ventilate plants without causing cold draughts. A sunny position is essential, especially with timber-sided frames; a single, sloping light should be positioned to face south. If these criteria can be met, and the frame can be sited close to the greenhouse, this is desirable, since many operations involve moving plants from greenhouse to frame.

If the frame has sliding lights, make sure there is sufficient space at the sides or rear to accommodate them. A firm standing is needed in front of the frame, to enable you to tend the plants inside.

Before growing crops in a frame, improve the soil that will be inside it, if necessary. Soil should be well-drained and contain plenty of organic matter; you may have to buy in fresh soil or move some from another part of the garden. The addition of manure and peat will ensure that the ground is sufficiently moist for overwintering crops, which should not be watered until they start to develop in spring. Scatter slug pellets over the soil after sowing or planting.

Keep the glass or plastic clean at all times to admit maximum light. When necessary, cover the frame at night with old carpet or sacking to help retain warmth.

A little daytime ventilation is required at most times; this need increases rapidly as spring advances. Remove the lights altogether during hot weather.

A **home-made frame** constructed of chipboard or timber will give long service if treated with a preservative safe to plants. Use glass or rigid plastic for the top, and hinge this at the back. Soil-warming cables may be installed.

Proprietary timber frames are often made of cedarwood, an attractive and durable timber. Some designs, based on the commercial Dutch light system, have low sloping sides and large, single-sheet glass tops – ideal for early crops.

Aluminium frames, with glass or plastic sides and ends, admit maximum light and are immune to rot. They come in many shapes and sizes, the largest offering a growing area comparable with a small greenhouse.

Every food gardener has to make a decision about whether or not to stick to natural, or 'organic', means of nourishing crops and of preventing and combating pests and diseases. Indeed, the main reason that some people decide to grow their own crops is in order to have more control over the amount of chemicals used on the fruit and vegetables that they eat.

'Organic' means derived from living organisms; it has a number of connotations in gardening. Organic gardening is cultivation of food plants without recourse to any artificial fertilizers or chemical pesticides. (Organic methods of pest and disease control are discussed briefly below and, in more detail, overleaf.)

Organic dressings include bulky materials, such as manure, peat and garden compost, and also concentrated fertilizers of plant or animal origin, such as bonemeal and fishmeal (see pp.28–9). In contrast, inorganic fertilizers are the product of chemical manufacture and have no direct origins in plant or animal life. Two common examples of these are superphosphate and nitrate of soda.

So, is there anything wrong with these chemical products? Whether or not they do actual harm is open to debate. Some chemical products are, of course, more toxic than others, but many people dislike the idea of food products being tainted with chemicals of any description, since they will, in turn, enter their bodies when the foods are eaten.

As experienced gardeners will have discovered, inorganic fertilizers can give crops a considerable boost, if used with care. They have a tonic effect, which is quite dramatic when plants have been undernourished. But there are two major drawbacks. First, as with most tonics, their effect is generally short-lived. The other, more serious drawback is that chemical fertilizers do little or nothing for the long-term fertility and structure of the soil, both of which are vital for the continuing healthy growth of plants. This is because plants are able to make immediate use of chemical fertilizers, without the soil itself gaining any benefit.

ORGANIC DRESSINGS
The nourishment provided by organic manures and fertilizers has to be 'unlocked' by the complex action of earthworms and the minute bacteria and fungi in the soil. Since this is a relatively slow process, most organic dressings have a long-lasting effect.

The benefit is cyclical, too, since this vast army of microscopic workers depends on adequate dressings of organic material for maintaining soil fertility and a soil structure that is favourable both to plant growth and to easy working. Their action, in turn, results in the fine, dark material known as

humus, which aids both drainage and moisture-retention, and serves as a storage reservoir for plant foods.

The benefits of bulky organic dressings are therefore incontrovertible. Without the use of manure, well-rotted garden compost or peat, it is impossible to grow good crops year after year on the same ground.

In addition, more concentrated dressings will be needed from time to time. True organic gardeners will use only those derived from plant or animal materials. Some will use a judicious mixture of organic and chemical fertilizers. Either course of action can bring good results, but only if the bulky dressings are maintained.

PESTS AND DISEASES
The longer and more widely any crop has been growing in a particular area, the more firmly established are the pests and diseases associated with it. Several of the newer, and less popular, fruits and vegetables, such as globe artichokes, Florence fennel, scorzonera and asparagus peas, are relatively free of pests and diseases and it is worth trying at least one or two of these.

Chemical sprays and dusts may be the easiest and most direct method of preventing or eradicating known pests and diseases, but their use is shunned by organic gardeners. The more toxic chemicals are not only of potential danger to humans but they have an indiscriminate effect on beneficial insects, including bees, and other wildlife in the garden. Their use nevertheless remains widespread.

If you choose to employ chemical sprays, be sure to time your spraying to minimize the possible damage to other forms of life. Derris, for example, is relatively safe because it is not persistent. If plants are sprayed in the evening, once bees are back in the hive, the derris will have lost its toxicity by the following morning.

An alternative solution is to use safer sprays. A number of those particularly

recommended by the Henry Doubleday Research Association, are given on p.21.

There is also some scope for preventing unwanted damage by adopting various tricks of timing or by taking alternative forms of preventive action. For instance, if broad beans are sown in autumn, their overwintered stems and foliage should be tough enough to resist spring attacks by blackfly. Hoverflies, whose larvae decimate aphid colonies, can be attracted by sowing a patch of the hardy annual *Convolvulus tricolor*. This is an excellent food source for the adults.

Rather than spreading poisonous slug pellets, slugs and snails can be lured to their death by means of traps based on diluted, sweetened beer. If you do use metaldehyde slug pellets, prop a tile or slate over the bait so that animals and birds cannot eat it and risk being poisoned.

The sections on Pests and Diseases of Fruits (pp.108–11) and Pests and Diseases of Vegetables (pp.172–5) give further details of such methods.

You must expect minor damage to some crops if you do not use chemical sprays at all. It is a price that organic gardeners are prepared to pay for their more natural form of gardening. The compromise is to use such sprays when all else fails, but always with consideration for other living creatures.

WEEDS
Chemical weedkillers exist in a wide variety of forms. Managing without these is not a great problem in most gardens, provided perennial weeds were eradicated at the outset. Others can be dug out by hand as they appear, and regular hoeing will take care of annual weeds. Well-fed soil makes weeding easier too, since full-grown 'healthy' weeds are easier to pull out and do not run to seed as quickly as those on poor, dry soil. Further advice is given on pp.45–7, together with information on weedkillers for those with a particularly persistent problem to overcome.

ORGANIC METHODS OF CULTIVATION: A SUMMARY

- Improve the texture and fertility of your soil with organic dressings – manure or garden compost.
- Where hand weeding is difficult, such as around soft fruit bushes, weeds can be effectively controlled by mulching (see p.43).
- Practise a rigid rotation of vegetable crops to control soil-borne pests and diseases (see p.25).
- Encourage natural predators. Fork

over the plot in mid-winter to enable birds to eat the chrysalids of cabbage, carrot and onion flies, and fork around raspberry canes to turn up the larvae of raspberry beetle. Have a pond for frogs and toads, which feed on slugs.
- Choose disease-resistant vegetables and certified virus-fee fruits.
- Use safer, organic pesticides and fungicides such as pyrethrum, derris and nicotine that are non-persistent and non-systemic.

Many gardeners, as well as scientists and concerned laymen, are uneasy about the widespread use of chemical sprays and powders for the control of pests and diseases. Some contain highly toxic substances that are slow to break down in the soil and potentially dangerous to humans and wildlife. Furthermore, several of them kill beneficial insects, such as bees, that are responsible for pollination and others that prey on the insects regarded as pests. In this respect, and because resistant strains eventually develop, chemical means of pest control are to some extent self-defeating. They are also quite expensive.

Yet, there is no denying their effectiveness. Without them it is almost impossible to keep crops free from pests and diseases; during the first year or two of organic gardening plants are particularly at risk in this respect. Many gardeners settle for a compromise, using commercial sprays only when less drastic measures (see below) have failed, and always with due care. They resign themselves to accepting a certain amount of damage to crops rather than expecting everything to be blemish-free.

Well before the spraying stage, though, there is plenty that can be done to reduce the risk of attack from pests and diseases. Plant diseases, in particular, are much easier to prevent than to cure. Of prime importance as a preventive measure is the build-up of soil fertility.

PREVENTING PESTS AND DISEASES
Well-nourished crops are less likely to develop ailments. When they grow sturdily and rapidly, plants are better able to cope with attacks by insect pests. Humus-rich soil, the result of ample organic dressings (see p.28), provides the surest basis for such growth.

It is important, too, that sowings and plantings take place with regard to soil and weather conditions as well as the calendar. Plants recovering from a slow start caused by cold, wet soil are particularly susceptible to disease and pests.

Overcrowding is another hazard, especially where diseases are concerned. Sow seeds thinly, and remove surplus seedlings as soon as they are large enough to handle. Allow sufficient space for plants to develop; if they are jammed together, they are more prone to fungus troubles.

Crop rotation (see p.25) helps to counter the build-up of pests and diseases associated with particular classes of crops. Club root, a fungus which affects the cabbage family, is an example. Growing brassicas on the same piece of land only one year in three reduces the risk of the spores infecting the soil permanently.

Slugs and snails are much more troublesome on a weed-grown plot or where there are weeds and dense grass around the edges. These night feeders must have cover during the day, so regular weeding will deter them. Similarly, a range of both pests and diseases either breed or find sanctuary in the neglected corners to be found in many gardens, amongst the rubbish and rotting wood. A clean-up can do much to keep them at bay, as well as improving appearances.

Make use of disease-resistant strains of vegetables where you can. 'Avoncrisp' and 'Avondefiance' lettuces, for instance, are highly resistant to root aphids and mildew. 'Maris Bard' first-early potatoes are virus-resistant. 'Desirée' runner beans seldom suffer from bean mosaic virus, just as 'Avonresister' parsnips are unlikely to suffer from canker.

THE GARDENER'S FRIENDS
The garden is a jungle, where one species depends upon another for its living. Among ground-dwelling insects, the fast-moving kinds are often the predators, consuming the slower, plant-eating sorts. Study the illustrations on this page so that you know, at least, which to spare.

Remember that birds have insatiable appetites for insect pests, from greenfly to leatherjackets. Attract birds to the garden with food in winter and nestboxes from late winter onward. Any damage they themselves may do is relatively easy to control (see p.44).

Frogs, toads and hedgehogs are also to be encouraged, since all consume large quantities of grubs and insects. Frogs and toads prefer cool, damp conditions. It is said that saucers of milk and water left out overnight will encourage visiting hedgehogs to stay, as will cat foods with a fishy flavour.

SAFER FUNGICIDES
Organic gardening enthusiasts are reluctant to recommend any sprays or dusts as completely safe. The following, though, are some of the types given tentative approval by the Henry Doubleday Research Association, a leading organization in the organic field. Control may not always prove as decisive as with some modern chemicals, but neither is resistance likely to develop. **Bordeaux mixture,** obtainable as a proprietary powder or liquid, is a general-purpose, copper-based fungicide and a long-established preventive spray against potato blight.
Burgundy mixture, which is more powerful, is recommended as a winter wash for fruit trees and bushes. To make your own, stir 90g (3oz) of copper sulphate into 4.5

Lacewing
The adult and its grubs have a considerable appetite for aphids and red spider mites

Centipede
This fast-moving creature, with a flattened, orange body, eats insects and small slugs

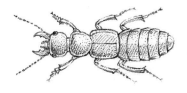

Devil's coach horse
This active predator, easily distinguished by the way it turns its tail up, eats soil insects

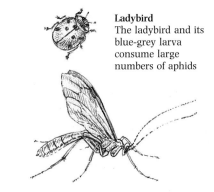

Ladybird
The ladybird and its blue-grey larva consume large numbers of aphids

Ichneumon
As well as consuming aphids, this insect lays its eggs in the bodies of caterpillars

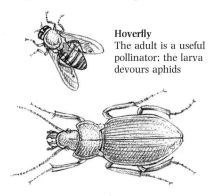

Hoverfly
The adult is a useful pollinator; the larva devours aphids

Ground beetle
Both the adult and the larva of this common creature live on insects, grubs and slugs

litres (1 gallon) of hot water, using a plastic bucket. In a similar container, dissolve 110g (4oz) of washing soda in 4.5 litres (1 gallon) of cold water. Wait for a few hours for the copper sulphate to dissolve thoroughly, then mix the two liquids together and use at once.

Washing soda controls downy mildew, including American gooseberry mildew. Dissolve 90g (3oz) of washing soda in 4.5 litres (1 gallon) of hot water and stir in 30g (1oz) of soap flakes. Allow to cool before use.

Potassium permanganate For powdery mildew, troublesome on both vegetables and fruit, stir 15g ($\frac{1}{2}$oz) of this chemical into 13 litres (3 gallons) of cold water. Use the mixture at once, wetting both sides of the leaves.

Elder leaves Another fungicidal spray, claimed to be effective against mildew, is prepared by placing half a kilo (1lb) of elder leaves and young, smooth-barked shoots into an old saucepan, along with 3.5 litres (6 pints) of water. After bringing to the boil, simmer for 30 minutes, topping up as necessary. When cold, strain through muslin and use undiluted.

Carbolic acid Mildew, too, is the target for a spray made by adding a dessertspoonful of carbolic acid to 4.5 litres (1 gallon) of cold water, then stirring in 60g (2oz) of soap flakes.

SAFER PESTICIDES

Derris is particularly useful, since it is harmless to animals and humans, bees and hoverfly larvae. It kills ladybirds, however, and is poisonous to fish. Use it in spray form to kill aphids and caterpillars; as a dust to control flea beetles. Both liquid and powder are sold in proprietary packs.

Pyrethrum is harmless to humans and animals but kills insect predators along with the pests. If sprayed at dusk, plants will be safe for bees by the following morning. This pesticide is moderately effective against aphids and caterpillars. Crops may be treated right up until harvest time.

Nicotine, available as a soapy wash, is poisonous to humans and also to bees. However, it is said not to be persistent and is thought to break down in the soil within four days. Though harmless to ladybirds and several other predators, it gives good control of caterpillars, bean weevils and red spider. It is advisable to wash your hands after using it, to keep it off your skin as far as possible and to stick a prominent 'Poison' label on bottles containing the liquid.

To make a spray solution, simmer 110g (4oz) of filter tip cigarette ends in 1 litre (2 pints) of water for half an hour. Strain the liquid, diluting it with four times the quantity of water before spraying. Reduce the

dilution if pests prove persistent. Add 30g (1oz) of soap flakes to each litre (2 pints) of the mixture when spraying in the autumn against cabbage caterpillars.

Rhubarb leaves can be made into a safe and reasonably effective spray against aphids. Simmer half a kilo (1lb) of sliced rhubarb leaves in a litre (2 pints) of water for half an hour. Dilute the liquor with 2.3 litres (4 pints) of cold water and use within 24 hours. Elder leaves can be used in the same way as rhubarb leaves.

Quassia chips, obtained from the wood of a Caribbean tree, kills aphids and most small caterpillars but does not harm bees or ladybirds. Prepare the concentrate by boiling 110g (4oz) of chips in 4.5 litres (1 gallon) of water for half an hour. For spraying, dilute the concentrate, which will keep indefinitely, with three times as much water, adding 60g (2oz) of soap flakes to every 4.5 litres (1 gallon). Do not spray crops that are to be eaten within two weeks, as it leaves a bitter taste.

ALTERNATIVE METHODS

Sprays and dusts apart, there are other courses of action designed to discourage the pests that attack crops. These are mainly applicable to vegetables and are referred to in the individual entries for relevant crops. The following are a few examples:

Blackfly on beans Pinch out the tips of autumn-sown broad beans in early summer once four trusses of pods have formed.

Cabbage root fly Hang strips of paraffin-impregnated blanket or sacking from canes to prevent the flies from scenting young plants and coming to lay their eggs on them.

Carrot fly Try the impregnated blanket, as above, or spread lawn-mowings thinly between the rows. Again, the fly's scent glands are confused.

Whitefly Marigolds (*Tagetes*) or nasturtiums planted as a border to the vegetable plot outdoors, or in a greenhouse, will attract whitefly and thus help to keep your crops clear of them.

CARE WITH CHEMICALS

Even when following the best growing methods, there is still some risk of invasion by pests or diseases. If 'safe' sprays or dusts do not give adequate control you will have to decide whether to accept a degree of damage or to use a proprietary chemical product.

Details of what product to use against particular pests or diseases are given on pp. 108–111 (for fruits) and pp. 172–175 (for vegetables).

If you decide to use a proprietary spray, try to minimize the possible side-effects by taking a few sensible precautions. In addition to the environmental safeguards listed below, make sure you keep all chemicals where children cannot reach them. Store liquids, whether diluted or not, only in the manufacturer's clearly labelled bottles.

■ Follow the manufacturer's instructions in every detail.

■ Use at the safest time of day. Try to spray during the late evening, when bees and other pollinating insects have stopped flying. They are also less active during dull weather. Do not spray when it is raining, or while you have a sprinkler watering the garden.

■ Avoid spraying during windy weather, when the droplets will drift over a wider area.

■ Keep the spray well away from ponds or other water.

■ Spray as lightly as possible. A fine misting over the foliage is more effective than a drenching that will simply run off in droplets.

DOWN TO EARTH

The returns you get from your food garden depend to a large extent on the amount of care and attention you devote to your soil. Other aspects of gardening, including sowing, planting, pruning and weeding are important, but without good soil your results are bound to be disappointing, however conscientious you are.

The section that follows treats the basics of gardening in the order in which they should be tackled. It starts by explaining what soil is and shows how it can be improved – by composting, digging, draining and feeding. Details of sowing, planting, watering, crop protection and weeding then follow each other in logical progression, and you will quickly discover that most techniques of crop-growing are both straightforward and easily mastered, even if you are a complete beginner.

Gardening activity follows a pattern that is repeated from year to year. As you work and get to know your soil, and become attuned to the ways of the weather, you will gradually learn which crops do best in your garden, and which respond best to the 'microclimate' of your garden.

In the first few seasons make a real effort to link cause and effect. If you do this you may be able to conclude that your soil responds well to a specific treatment, that a particular pest can be thwarted by a certain strategy or that the prevailing climate in your area makes your plot 'earlier' or 'later', as regards sowing, planting and harvesting, than the averages that are generally quoted.

To keep track of your progress, and to help you work out what influences your garden from year to year, you may find it helpful – and entertaining – to keep a gardening diary. Note in it the work you do on the soil, such as digging and fertilizing, the most troublesome pests, weeds and diseases, and, of course, the weather, including temperature and rainfall. After a few years you will see a definite pattern emerging which will be a great help in improving your efforts and your output. Above all, it will help you learn by your mistakes.

As you become more experienced you will learn which garden practices work best for you. The same is true of equipment. A nucleus of a few good tools, each of which performs well for you personally – that has the correct weight and balance and is easy and comfortable to use – is far better than a plethora of expensive but ill-suited gadgets.

Care of the soil in your garden is critical to all aspects of raising and growing crops, and the tools and other equipment you choose will be devoted to this end. All soil needs to be dug, enriched with organic matter, weeded, watered and, in cooler climates, warmed beneath cloches.

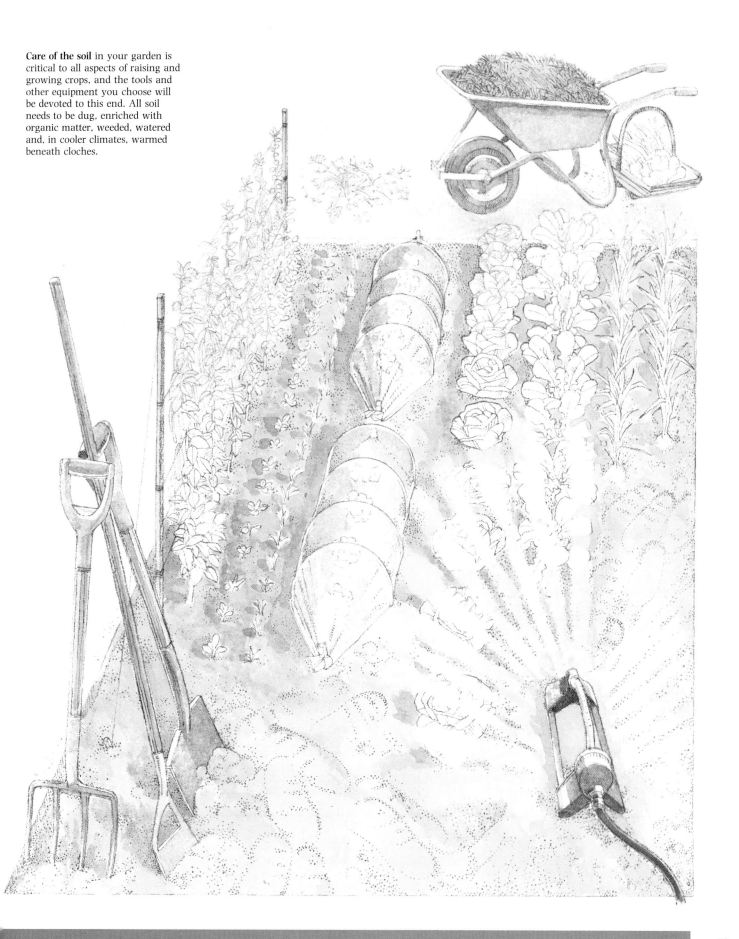

Soil consists mainly of fragmented rock, ground down over centuries by weathering agents such as rain, frost and sunshine into minute particles. Each particle is surrounded by a film of moisture in which plant nutrients are dissolved, and the juxtaposition of the particles helps to force water, and therefore food, up to the plant roots. It is the size of these particles that determines the nature of the soil. Only by understanding your soil can you get the best out of it.

TOPSOIL AND SUBSOIL

In addition to the rock particles, each type of soil contains organic matter. This is concentrated in the shallow layer of surface soil on which all plant and human life depends. Termed the topsoil, it may vary from trowel depth to below that of a spade.

Beneath this, and distinguishable by its paler colour, is the generally infertile subsoil. Its depth varies according to the hardness of the underlying rock and the amount of erosion it has suffered. Though the subsoil may contain some nutrients useful to deep-rooting plants, most efforts to improve the soil should be concentrated on the upper layer.

It is essential, especially when levelling uneven ground, to maintain a consistent depth of topsoil and not to mix it with the subsoil. The only way to do this is to remove all the topsoil first, then level the subsoil before replacing it. If you are correcting uneven ground, aim to have a layer of topsoil at least a spade depth (about 25cm/10in deep).

SOIL TYPES

Sandy soil is a light soil, made up of coarse particles. It feels gritty when rubbed between finger and thumb and does not readily form lumps. It remains crumbly and workable even after rain.

Light soils warm up early in the spring, because of the easy flow of air between the large particles, and they are easy and rewarding to cultivate. They dry out rapidly, though, and are 'hungry' in the sense that plant foods soon wash through them.

Clay soil, at the other extreme, consists of minute, finely-ground particles that stick together in a putty-like mass. Water drains only slowly through this type of soil, air is excluded and the soil remains cold until well into spring. Clay soils, which are difficult to work, are termed heavy – with good reason.

Clay soils are, nevertheless, naturally well supplied with nutrients; since there are a greater number of particles to a given area, more water adheres to them. But these nutrients are not always available to the plants, since in a compacted soil they may be blocked from reaching the plant roots. However, dressed with ample organic matter to improve their texture, clay soils will grow fine crops.

Loams, which include the best of garden soils, consist of a mixture of sand and clay. The proportions may vary – hence the terms light loam and heavy loam – with a medium loam being the elusive ideal.

Chalky soils, grey in colour, are alkaline and free-draining, though they may be sticky after rain. Some are very shallow, presenting a considerable challenge to the gardener to increase the depth of the topsoil by creating humus. The deeper soils are easier to cultivate, so long as acid-loving plants are avoided.

Peat is derived from plant materials. When it is found in a marshy area, peaty soil is rich in nutrients and easy to work. In contrast, the peaty soil in moorland areas is shallow, acid and lacking in nutrients. It can be improved by liming and draining, but the process takes time.

ACID OR ALKALINE?

Soils vary in their degree of acidity or alkalinity. Most vegetables and fruits have a broad measure of tolerance but it is sensible to avoid extremes. There are, however, some plants – and these are mentioned, where appropriate, in the individual descriptions – that have definite preferences for, or aversion to, acid or alkaline conditions.

Simple kits are sold for home soil testing. These indicate the soil's pH value; pH is the standard scale for measuring acidity. A reading of pH 7.0 denotes a neutral soil. Above this the soil is alkaline, and below this it is acid.

Most crops grow best in slightly acid soil, with a pH reading of about 6.5. Excessive acidity may be reduced by spreading lime (see p. 29).

1 To test the pH level of your soil with a simple kit, first gather a small sample from 5–8cm (2–3in) beneath the surface. Do not touch it with your hands. If the soil is wet, let it dry naturally. When it is reasonably dry, crumble it finely on a plate and remove any stones or other pieces of debris.

2 Fill a test tube about a quarter full with some crumbled soil. Use a spoon to avoid touching it with your hands. Next, pour in the lime-test solution until the tube is half full. With the stopper inserted, shake the tube thoroughly to mix liquid and soil. Allow the soil to settle to the bottom.

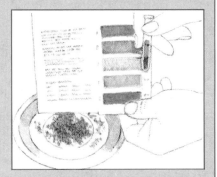

3 The pH level of the soil can now be checked by comparing the colour of the liquid with the bands on a gradated shade chart. A simple table in the instruction booklet explains what to add to your soil, and in what quantity, to raise or lower the pH level in one-point stages to meet the needs of your crops.

There are several ways in which you can improve the texture and condition of your soil, apart from feeding it (for details see pp.28–9) and watering it when necessary (see p.42). The principal means are by digging and at the same time adding various dressings, and by growing your crops in such a way that the soil benefits from the way you rotate them. (The techniques of digging are covered in detail on pp.34–5).

Certain soils have special needs but all soils are improved by the addition of bulky organic matter, usually in the form of compost (see pp.30–31). Eventually reduced by micro-organisms to humus, this helps light soils to retain moisture as well as nutrients by giving more bulk to the soil.

Digging in organic matter not only improves the fertility but also opens up heavy soils, making them more crumbly and less sticky. Shredded newspaper can also be dug in, or buried in a trench, to help break up a clay soil. Similarly on chalk and on acid peat, repeated dressings will add precious depth to the topsoil.

IMPROVING A HEAVY SOIL

Waterlogging is a common problem on uncultivated clay soils. If water lies on the surface after rain, or collects in a trench during digging, the soil is waterlogged and crops are unlikely to prosper. Waterlogged soil is cold and airless, the reverse conditions to those needed for healthy root growth. Clay soil also sets hard when it dries and has a tendency to crack, subjecting plant roots to another danger.

Leave a clay soil alone while it is wet and sticky: the structure will be harmed if you attempt to cultivate it. Early winter is usually the best time to dig a heavy soil, adding organic material at the same time. Leave it in rough clods for the frost to work on; as the ground dries in spring, rake it into a crumbly, seed-sowing tilth.

Heavy soils can be further opened up, and drainage thereby improved, by adding grit or sharp sand while digging. This will remain in the topsoil indefinitely. Where an impervious subsoil is preventing water from draining away, artifical drainage is the only answer (see p.26) and other attempts at soil improvement would be wasted without it.

IMPROVING A LIGHT SOIL

Late winter or early spring is the time to dig organic matter into light soil. Autumn digging inevitably results in some nutrients being washed away during the winter.

Mulching (see p.43) helps to keep light soils moist during dry weather. Be prepared to feed plants generously with fertilizers (see p.28): potash, in particular, is often in short supply.

CROP ROTATION

Maintaining the soil's fertility is one of the reasons for growing a given crop in a different part of the plot in successive years. This is because certain crops make special demands on available nutrients, which may become depleted if there is no movement, or 'rotation'. Legumes, one of the three vegetable groups, take little out of the soil and may in fact put back some nitrogen from their root nodules.

Grouping crops with similar needs facilitates their cultivation and enables organic material, often in short supply, to be used to best advantage. All root vegetables, for example, need a deep tilth.

The other benefit of moving plants around the plot is that it helps to break pest and disease chains, such as club root to which all brassicas are prone.

For all of these reasons it is helpful to group vegetables into three broad categories (below), and to devote a section of the garden to each one in turn, for a year.

A LEGUMES (peas and beans)
B BRASSICAS (cabbages, sprouts etc.)
C ROOT VEGETABLES, including potatoes

This grouping omits all the salad crops, onions, sweet corn, tomatoes and other vegetables which have no particular problems or advantages and whose positioning is therefore not critical. Add them to whichever group you wish, aiming to fill about a third of the total area with each basic group. Unless you grow a great many legumes, this will probably mean adding most of the remaining vegetables to Group A.

A more or less permanent position will have to be found for perennial vegetables, such as asparagus, and for soft fruit.

To put this scheme into action, divide the plot into three equal parts. Each year, follow the same manuring/liming programme. For Group A crops (legumes), dig in as much manure or compost as you can spare. For Group B (brassicas), spread lime after digging, then fertilizer at sowing or planting time. On a chalky soil, you should omit the lime dressing and apply manure or compost instead, if available. For Group C (roots), use fertilizer only.

Year by year, rotate the crops in the same order. That is, in the second year of the cycle plant brassicas on what had been the legume patch, sow roots where brassicas had been, and grow legumes in place of the roots – and so on, through successive years on a three-year cycle.

Year 1	A. Legumes	B. Brassicas	C. Roots
Year 2	B. Brassicas	C. Roots	A. Legumes
Year 3	C. Roots	A. Legumes	B. Brassicas

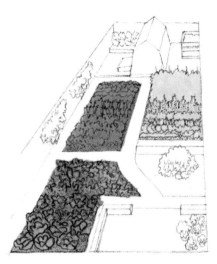

First year Brassicas are in the foreground, roots behind them and legumes on the right.

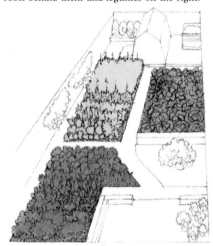

Second year Brassicas are now in the plot heavily manured a year ago for legumes.

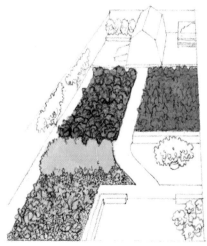

Third year Roots are always grown in land not manured recently, as this could cause them to 'fork', in their search for nourishment.

FEEDING THE SOIL AND PLANTS, pages 28–29
DEALING WITH WEEDS, pages 45–47

Good drainage is essential to the condition of your plot and the health of your crops. Not only is a waterlogged soil hard to cultivate, but it is also cold and airless, making the plant roots cold and unhealthy. There may be several ways in which you can improve the drainage of your plot without going to the trouble and expense of installing a full drainage system.

A compacted surface alone will prevent water draining from heavy soil, for example, but digging will be enough to cure this. As mentioned earlier (see p. 24), digging organic material into a heavy clay topsoil will help to open it up and improve natural drainage.

If the land remains waterlogged, check that there is not an impervious layer of compacted subsoil or rock just below spade depth – something that is by no means uncommon. The solution in this case is to loosen the bottom of each trench as you dig, using a fork, crowbar or pickaxe.

A quite different approach to a badly drained soil is to grow at least some of your vegetables – preferably shallow-rooted ones – in beds raised above ground level, with a brick or stone edging. A good example would be one about a metre (3ft) off the ground on a free-draining base of rubble, and with gravel added to the soil; the problem would thus be largely circumvented. You will, of course, have to find additional soil for raising the level of the bed.

If all else fails, however, you will need to lay some form of pipework in the soil. On a small-scale, a rubble-filled trench could be laid instead of pipes, but this would be almost as much trouble and might soon become clogged with soil. In laying a system of drainage pipes, it is the outlet that creates the chief difficulty, for few gardens have drainage ditches. The answer is to dig a soakaway pit at the lower end of the drainage system. A capacious soakaway should prevent or reduce waterlogging for much of the year, though it is likely to fill up during wet spells.

DRAINAGE SYSTEMS

Until recently, almost the only method of draining soil has been to lay plastic or earthenware pipes in trenches, surrounding the pipes with gravel. The trenches need to be sufficiently deep for the pipes to lie below spade depth. The joints between pipes are uncemented, allowing water to percolate through. They are laid at a gentle but even angle to provide a flow toward the outlet (see below).

This method is still very common, but an alternative is now available in the form of a continuous plastic core surrounded by a tough but porous fabric. This is easier to lay and does not require the normal back-filling of gravel. Nevertheless, on clay it is advisable to mix sand and peat with the soil when refilling the trench to improve the flow toward the drain.

PLANNING THE LAYOUT

Whichever system you choose, the layout of the drains can take much the same form. On a small, narrow plot a single drain will suffice. Otherwise, a main drain is laid down the centre, with well-spaced side drains leading into it from each side. The side drains are set at an angle to the main run, giving the layout its distinctive herringbone pattern.

The spacing between the side drains depends on the nature of the soil. It varies from about 4.5m (15ft) on clay to 12m (40ft) on sandy soil. Suggested spacings for the plastic patent system are provided in an instruction booklet. Both forms of drainage must be laid with a fall toward the outlet. Take advantage of a natural fall if there is one; otherwise, a slope of 1 in 90 is the minimum.

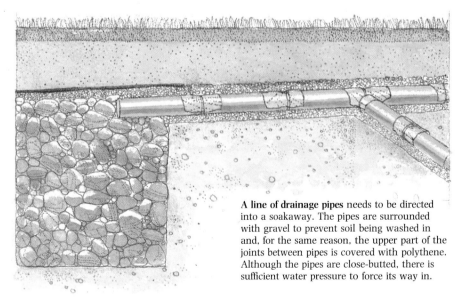

A line of drainage pipes needs to be directed into a soakaway. The pipes are surrounded with gravel to prevent soil being washed in and, for the same reason, the upper part of the joints between pipes is covered with polythene. Although the pipes are close-butted, there is sufficient water pressure to force its way in.

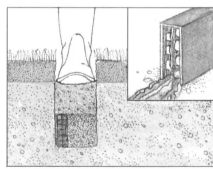

Patent drainage tubing, supplied in continuous lengths many metres long, is easy to lay. A spade-width trench is dug and the tubing laid along one side of the base. On heavy soil it is an advantage to add free-draining sand or gravel immediately around it. Direct the outlet into a ditch or soakaway.

If you are starting with a long-neglected, weed-grown jungle, it may take a year or two to achieve a productive garden. Shorter-term neglect may be remedied more quickly. Assess the nature of the problem first and then work to a well thought out plan.

CLEARING THE WEEDS

Before you clear weeds, determine what sort they are. If your plot is knee-high with weeds it may be worth using a strimmer first; this will take off the top of the growth so that you can at least see what you are doing at ground level.

A short period of neglect, resulting in a covering of annual weeds, is hardly a problem at all, since digging will destroy them. A fresh batch of seedlings will probably follow but hoeing will take care of these.

Perennial weeds are more serious: digging will multiply them by chopping their roots; a new plant will grow from a very short piece of root. If there are just a few, dig them out individually with a fork or trowel, removing all the roots. If they are numerous, and especially if the ground is overgrown with persistent types such as couch grass, convolvulus or ground elder, this is a good reason for using a systemic weedkiller or a cultivator.

During spring or summer, when the weeds are in active growth, a weedkiller based on glyphosate would be suitable. This will work right through the plant systems, without affecting the soil. Ammonium sulphamate, another weedkiller, could also be used quite early in the season before growth has really got under way. Do not use it indiscriminately, however, because it works through the soil, killing any tree or shrub roots in its path, and it persists for two or three months. It is also important not to inadvertently tread this weedkiller about over areas you want to keep untouched.

An alternative to weedkillers is to cut down and remove the weeds, then till the ground at frequent intervals throughout the first spring and summer with a rotary cultivator, which you can buy or hire. As long as the weather remains dry, this will kill most of the perennial weeds, as well as successive batches of germinating annuals.

The roots and woody stems of perennial weeds cut and gathered before the soil is cultivated should be put on a bonfire rather than composted. Only the hottest of fermenting heaps can be relied upon to kill all their seeds and roots. Weeds destroyed with a weedkiller should also be burned.

AFTER THE WEEDS

Builder's rubble, stones or other debris may have to be removed from the ground in a new or neglected garden. If you have the space, store it: it can be recycled eventually for foundations, lining drainage trenches and so on.

Once the ground is clear, dig some random holes to check the depth of the topsoil (see p.24). This is often inadequate where a builder has been at work. It is even possible that you will find a substantial area of topsoil buried under the subsoil. If it has been subjected to drastic upheaval, the subsoil itself, as well as the topsoil, may have to be levelled in order to produce an even depth of topsoil. This will involve a certain amount of digging and barrowing. In extreme cases, bought-in topsoil may be needed.

Once the ground is relatively smooth and level, you will need to dig in plenty of bulky organic matter before you can consider growing even a few crops.

THE FIRST GROWING SEASON

The soil in a hitherto neglected garden is unlikely to be in very good condition. You will need to use fertilizers, preferably organic, during the early days of growing crops to build up soil fertility. Lime, too, may be needed (see p.24); if so apply it as soon as practicable but do not use fertilizers for a few weeks afterwards.

Potatoes are an excellent crop to grow on a reclaimed plot during the first year; their wide-spreading foliage will discourage weed growth, as will the earthing up process. If you do decide to grow potatoes, do not dress the soil with lime. Alternatively, make a border in which to plant some radishes, lettuces or other short-term crops.

USING A CULTIVATOR

Use a cultivator to turn over neglected ground from spring onward or to make a seedbed on land left untouched since the previous year. When using it as a means of killing perennial weeds, which may take some months, frequent cultivating is the key to preventing re-growth. By the end of summer the roots will have died from starvation.

On most domestic cultivators the rotating tines serve the dual purpose of breaking the soil and drawing the machine forward. Forward speed is controlled by pressure on the handlebars; this also controls the depth of cultivation. When first using a cultivator, set the depth skid quite low to ensure that it does not run away with you. Allow it to move forward only a short distance at a time, while letting the blades dig down to the depth required.

A **hood** attached to the lance of a sprayer will prevent the droplets from drifting.

A **petrol-powered brushcutter** can cut back even dense and quite woody growth.

A **motor cultivator** will turn undug ground and keep germinating weeds under control.

The fertility of your soil has a direct bearing on the quantity and quality of the crops grown in it. Because all plants derive nutrients from the soil, the soil's food reserves need to be replenished regularly. All soils need annual treatment, with bulky organic dressings, such as compost and farm manure, and with both chemical and organic fertilizers. Through their combined use, you will create a well-fed soil which will in turn nourish the crops you choose to grow in it.

The three main requirements for the nutrition of plants are nitrogen, phosphate and potash. They are absorbed through the plant roots in a dilute form and are essential to all plant growth.

Nitrogen is the principal growth promoter, stimulating the development of stems and leaves. A shortage of it in your soil is revealed by yellow leaves and stunted growth of plants, as well as by small fruits or tubers. Nitrogen is readily washed out of the soil and needs to be replaced every year.

Phosphate contains phosphorus, which aids root growth and is especially valuable for root vegetables such as carrots and turnips. A lack of it results in stunted, discoloured foliage, small or misshapen flower buds and sour-tasting fruits.

Potash contains potassium. This chemical helps to build up resistance to stress and disease. It is also valuable for the development and ripening of soft fruits and tomatoes, as well as building up starches and sugars in vegetables such as potatoes, beetroot and sweet corn. A deficiency manifests itself as stunted growth, brown-edged or blotched leaves, curling foliage or early fruit drop.

Potash and phosphates remain in the soil for longer than nitrogen when applied in an organic form – generally for about two or three years.

Bulky organic dressings, such as compost or manure, can provide a good proportion of the nutrients that plants need. On a heavily cropped vegetable plot, though – and especially on light soil – fairly massive dressings would be needed to provide sufficient nutrients by this means alone. For continuing heavy yields, additional plant foods, in the form of concentrated fertilizers, are generally required. There are organic and inorganic forms of these fertilizers. Guidelines for how much to apply are given under the entries for specific crops where they need a particular fertilizer. Otherwise follow the manufacturer's instructions on the container.

BULKY ORGANIC DRESSINGS

The virtue of organic soil dressings are many (see pp.24–5), but finding sufficient material may appear to be the main difficulty, especially in town gardens. But even in cities there are sources from which you can obtain suitable organic material at very little cost, if not free.

First and foremost is garden compost, which can be made from garden waste such as grass cuttings and annual weeds, supplemented by vegetable waste from the kitchen. Shredded newspaper can also be added in small amounts. You should always return all spent compost from containers and seedboxes to the soil, as long as the plants grown in it were disease-free.

Farm manures

If you live in or near the country, animal manures are the most obvious choice. There are also riding stables in most towns which will gladly give or sell you sacks of horse manure. Check the classified directory for addresses.

Horse manure is the richest, followed by that from pigs and cattle. All animal manures need to be stacked and rotted down in a heap for several weeks or months before use. They are too concentrated when fresh and would provide an overkill of nutrients which would damage plants. Unless they already contain a lot of straw, add some more to increase the bulk. Pig manure, especially, needs this treatment as it is particularly strong and caustic on its own.

Fresh poultry manure is also highly concentrated and, initially, smells rather unpleasant so is best stacked well away from the house. Once composted with plenty of straw, it provides a rich dressing and, when dried, forms a nitrogen-rich, concentrated fertilizer. It may be beneficially mixed with peat.

This stacking and rotting process applies to every other sort of animal manure too, including goat, rabbit and pigeon. Try to turn the heap at least once while it decomposes, shifting the outside to the inside.

Garden compost

This valuable source of organic matter is available to all gardeners. Made and used sensibly, it is a prime source of improved soil condition and garden fertility. For further details see pp.30–31.

Mushroom compost

The spent compost on which mushrooms have been grown is excellent for the soil as well as being easy to handle. It contains ground chalk, which makes it of particular value on acid soils. Check in the classified directory to see whether there is a mushroom farm in your district; share with a neighbour if the farm's smallest load is too much for you. You can also buy mushroom compost in sacks from a garden centre, though it is more expensive purchased in this way.

Spent hops

Hop waste, which can be purchased in plastic sacks, makes good manure, since it has usually been mixed with other fertilizer. If you live near a brewery you might be able to buy spent hops direct, and much more cheaply; they will improve the texture of the soil but would need to be mixed with a general fertilizer since they have a low nutrient content.

Seaweed

Once it has rotted down, which it does quite readily, seaweed improves the soil structure and is a rich source of plant foods, especially nitrogen and potash. Collect as much as you can if you live near the sea, and either stack it separately or mix it with garden compost. Leave it for a month, or until the rain washes the salt out, before you use it. If you do not do this, the salt will disrupt the internal chemical balance of plants.

Leafmould

To supplement your own leaf sweepings, ask the local park-keeper if you may collect some of his autumn harvest, or visit a local wood after the leaves have fallen, provided you have the space to stack them. Taken home in plastic sacks, the leaves provide a rich source of humus after they have been stacked for a couple of years. They need this long period to rot thoroughly.

Peat

Though rather expensive, peat provides a ready source of humus and is especially useful for small town gardens. It may be dug into the topsoil or spread as a weed-suppressing mulch (see p.43).

ORGANIC FERTILIZERS

True organic fertilizers are concentrated plant foods made of processed materials such as bonemeal or dried blood. Just like bulky organic dressings, organic fertilizers depend on the action of micro-organisms in the soil to convert them into sources of plant food. By stimulating this activity they aid soil fertility, as well as feeding the plants, though they do little toward creating humus.

The majority of organic fertilizers are a good deal more expensive than their inorganic counterparts. Though they act more slowly, their effects are longer-lasting so they would need applying less often.

Most organic fertilizers come in powder form. The main types are:

Bonemeal Animal bones, coarsely or finely ground, make a long-lasting phosphatic fertilizer, usefully applied when planting fruit trees or bushes, as well as vegetables. Its effects last about three years.

Hoof and horn releases nitrogen slowly, over two years, but it is costly and not always readily obtainable.

Fishmeal contains nitrogen and phosphorus and is effective for two years. An inorganic form of potash is usually added to make a balanced fertilizer, so you could end up paying a high price for a product that is not truly organic.

Dried blood provides a fast-acting nitrogenous tonic for plants. It comes in the form of powder or a liquid feed.

INORGANIC FERTILIZERS

The value of inorganic fertilizers is that they can be absorbed immediately by plants and can quickly remedy known deficiencies. However, they make no lasting contribution to the soil's fertility.

If you suspect, from the symptoms of your plants, that your soil is deficient in one of the main nutrients, you can confirm this with the aid of a proprietary testing kit, rather like the kit which measures the pH level in the soil. Instructions with the kit would also tell you how to remedy a specific deficiency in order to create a more balanced soil. Potash, for instance, is often in short supply in light soils. A 'straight' or single-chemical fertilizer would be called for to remedy a particular shortage.

Unless you know your soil to be deficient in a particular chemical, a general or 'compound' fertilizer is the best choice. That is, an inorganic formulation (NKP) containing a balanced mixture of the three main nutrients – sulphate of ammonia, superphosphate of lime and sulphate of potash – in the proportions needed by most soils, as well as traces of minerals such as iron.

The compound fertilizer may take the form of granules, liquid or powder. Granular fertilizers, the most common form, can be applied either to bare ground, a fortnight or so before sowing or planting, or as a top dressing around growing plants. Many quick-maturing crops, for example radishes, benefit from the former, called a base dressing. Top dressings are particularly useful as a boost for crops that remain in the soil for a number of months, such as sprouts. Work both forms of dressing into the soil surface, using a rake on unplanted ground and a hoe between plants.

Liquid formulations, both balanced and single-purpose, need to be diluted before use. They are applied as a top dressing watered into the soil and are quickly absorbed by the plants.

Foliar feeds are those that are applied directly to the foliage of plants by spraying; the leaves are able to absorb the nutrients immediately. During a dry spell these feeds give quicker results than soil dressings. Some foliar feeds are designed to correct a shortage of one or more trace elements, essential chemicals that plants need in only minute quantities. They are most likely to be lacking in soils that are low in organic matter, resulting in stunted plant growth.

There is also a range of 'straight' or single-purpose fertilizers sold for garden use. These 'one chemical' inorganic fertilizers act faster than their organic equivalents but are readily washed out of the soil, leaving no enduring benefits.

Sulphate of ammonia, a major source of nitrogen, is very fast acting but it has an acidifying effect on the soil. It can be raked in prior to sowing or used as a top dressing for growing crops, especially brassicas and salad vegetables.

Nitro-chalk is another rapid-action nitrogenous fertilizer to be used as a top dressing, but it does not make the soil more acid.

Nitrate of soda, also fast acting, tends to make clay soils more intractable.

Superphosphate of lime is the most popular inorganic source of phosphate. Used before sowing or planting, it remains effective for a season or two.

Sulphate of potash is a safe source of potash for all plants. Use it as a top dressing, especially for fruit trees and bushes and for tomatoes.

Muriate of potash is a more concentrated proprietary high-potash liquid fertilizer than sulphate of potash. It may damage soft fruits and tomatoes.

LIME LORE

Most vegetables grow best in a slightly acid soil, so a dressing of lime is the answer if your soil is too acid. Lime is good for certain crops too: onions, brassicas and lettuces in particular.

Lime is available in two forms: ground limestone and hydrated lime. An average dressing of ground limestone for a light soil is about 250g per sq m (8oz per sq yd), and double this amount on clay. If you use hydrated lime, reduce the amounts by a third.

Spread lime on the soil surface after digging. Do not dig it in. Try not to spread lime after manuring the soil.

Excessive alkalinity, produced by too much lime in the soil, is less likely to be a problem but can be reduced by the liberal use of peat. A dressing of sulphate of ammonia, at 35g per sq m (1oz per sq yd) also helps.

GETTING TO KNOW YOUR SOIL, pages 24–25
MAKING GARDEN COMPOST, pages 30–31

Compost is a term loosely used to describe any bulky organic dressings made from animal or vegetable waste. You can buy some forms ready-made or make garden compost yourself. The value of organic dressings is indisputable; they are fundamental to the soil's well-being. Many gardeners, however, have a problem finding sufficient material to make their own compost: those with access to plenty of farm manure are in a minority. Possible alternatives, such as peat-based planting mixtures, can be costly.

Garden compost, by contrast, is free and, despite a certain mystique surrounding it, is not difficult to make. Most vegetation will rot down of its own accord, without assistance. What the gardener can do is speed up the process and make sure that the finished product is evenly and thoroughly decomposed.

Making good compost, rapidly, is all about keeping bacteria happy. These micro-organisms convert garden waste into the rich, moist, crumbly material that greatly enriches the soil. To do this they must have sufficient – but not too much – air, water and, at least initially, warmth.

COMPOST MATERIALS
A wide variety of waste is suitable for composting. Most leafy waste can be used, from the garden or the kitchen. Avoid diseased garden material, though, and also perennial weeds with tough, persistent roots. Typical of these are docks, horsetails, couch grass and ground elder. Though the heat in the centre of a well-made heap will destroy the leafy part of such weeds, they should nevertheless be burned, since the woody stems will not rot down and the roots may survive. Take care also not to include plants suffering from club root infection. Burn them instead.

Vegetable peelings and trimmings provide good compost material, but avoid any waste that might attract rats, such as plate scrapings; bones will not decompose. Tough, fibrous material such as cabbage stalks may be placed near the centre of the heap if you are confident of it heating well but it is essential to hammer or chop them thoroughly first, in order to start the breaking down process. Better still, with long-term compost-making in mind, invest in a garden shredder to process these and other tough materials. An average family does not usually generate enough vegetable waste to provide, alone, sufficient compost for a sizeable plot. One answer is to collect vegetable trimmings from a greengrocer or from neighbours.

Another invaluable supplement is lawn mowings, easily the most plentiful garden 'waste' for at least half the year. Mixed with plenty of straw, which both prevents their compaction and increases their bulk, they rot down beautifully. But added to the heap on their own, they will form a dense mass, the very opposite of good compost.

COMPOSTING: THE ESSENTIALS
The compost heap itself – that is, the vegetation – needs to be contained in some form of structure, known as the bin (see the illustrations on this and the facing page).

The right conditions are most easily provided in a compost heap that has upright sides and adequate depth (minimum of 1–1.5 metres/3–5 feet). Compared with a sprawling mound, this shape prevents excessive wetting and drying and, most important, aids the heating process that results from bacterial action. It does not matter whether the heap is square or circular, but the mound of rotting vegetation must be contained in some way.

A purpose-made compost bin looks neat and, if made from metal or plastic, will not rot. But get the largest size you can: many proprietary bins are too small to allow the contents to heat and decompose rapidly or to contain all you have to put in them. They work, but the process takes rather longer than it need. Inadequate ventilation is another disadvantage with some models, depriving the bacteria of air. If this looks like being a problem, stand the container on bricks and leave the top uncovered.

A home-made timber compost bin, with slatted sides and front, can be as large as you wish and will have adequate ventilation. Make it with sides at least 1.2m (4ft) long and wide, and of a similar height. A bigger bin is an advantage if there is likely to be plenty of material. Design is not critical; the

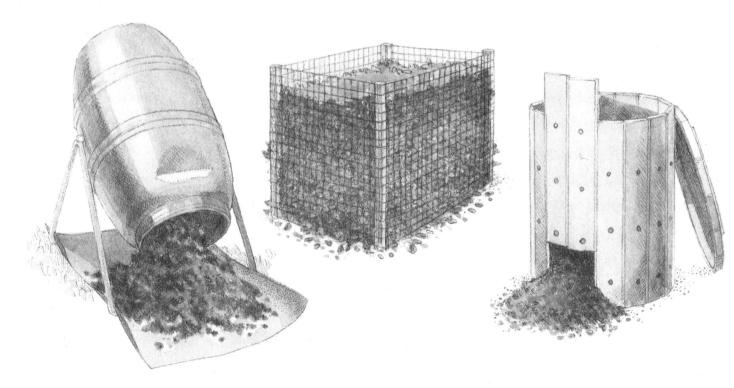

main feature is a front that can be fitted or removed in stages during filling and emptying. You could line a slatted bin with fine-mesh plastic netting to prevent material from falling through the spaces.

The price of new timber means that a home-made bin can cost almost as much as one bought at a garden centre. Broken pallets are a possible cheap source of wood, as are offcuts from a timber yard. Treat the timber with an anti-rot preservative first.

It is a great advantage to have at least two compost bins so that one can be left to mature while the second is being filled. Should you become really compost-minded you will find that three or more are needed.

BUILDING THE HEAP
Some gardeners build their compost heap on a base of open, stemmy material, with or without bricks beneath, to help aerate it. This is a good idea if the bin containing it has fully enclosed sides, but less important if there are gaps for ventilation.

Bacteria thrive on a mixed diet, so fill the bin accordingly. In particular, mix soft and fibrous material together, rather than adding unmixed layers of either. Spread the stuff evenly, leaving it loose. It will soon consolidate on its own.

Mix in a little manure at intervals, if it is available. Failing this, use a proprietary compost activator. The purpose is to stimulate bacterial action, which is often slow to get going in winter or in a heap where soft, leafy material is in short supply.

Water the heap, and then keep it covered with polythene sheeting if it shows signs of drying out during warm weather. There is no need to water it during changeable weather. If you wish, empty and refill the completed bin after a few weeks so that the outer, slow-to-rot material can be replaced on the inside. Alternatively, simply add it to another bin when emptying the material for use. Rotting down takes about three months in the summer, and twice as long in winter.

Keep the bin covered once the compost is ready for use. Even in winter, try to have a fresh heap of compost on the go at all times to make use of every scrap of waste.

READY-MADE BINS
Far left Tumbler bins, turned daily to assist aeration, are designed to speed up the process of compost-making.
Centre Wire mesh bins are relatively inexpensive but the compost may be slow to generate heat and to decompose.
Left Sliding panels allow small amounts of rotted compost to be taken from the base of this metal bin before the rest is ready.

MAKING YOUR OWN COMPOST BIN
The available space in your garden will dictate the size of compost bin to a large extent. But bear in mind that bins smaller than about 1.2m (4ft) sq do not heat up quite as readily as large ones. You may be able to use cheap offcuts from your local timber merchant. Even if they are a little shorter than this, they will still make a serviceable bin.

Planks about 19mm ($\frac{3}{4}$ in) thick and 10cm (4in) wide will make a reasonably strong bin. They may, of course, be thicker or broader. The corner uprights need to be a minimum of 5cm (2in) sq – somewhat thicker, for preference. Buy them long enough to bury 30cm (1ft) in the soil.

1 First construct the two sides of the bin, nailing the slats to the corner uprights. Then stand the sides on end and connect them with the slats that will form the back of the bin.
2 Stand the three sides of the bin in position, with the foot of each corner upright set 30cm (1ft) into the soil. Now

Pressure-treated fence posts are ideal. Old railway sleepers, sometimes offered for sale, are another possibility. They will form extremely strong and stable bins, though they cannot be joined by nailing. Use angle-iron stakes, driven into the ground at the corners on the inside and the outside, instead.

Protect untreated timber with wood preservative, painting this on liberally after cutting the wood but before construction. Choose a preservative that is not based on tar-oil, for preference, though even creosote will have little or no effect on the compost once the timber has dried out.

Use galvanized nails throughout for fastening the slatted sides.

position the removable front slats, cutting a notch in each to hold it secure.
3 A pair of bins, built side by side, is a great advantage. One can be filled while the other is maturing. Alternatively, the first heap, partly decomposed, can be turned into the second one to complete the process.

Well-made tools are a good investment since they should last you a lifetime. It is, therefore, worth spending time choosing them carefully. Their cost is not the only consideration. Apart from the design, and the quality and suitability of the materials used, you should check the weight and balance of all tools carefully before you buy. If they are too heavy and cumbersome for you, even simple chores may prove a trial.

Those illustrated here are the basic tools required by all gardeners who are growing their own fruit and vegetables. If both you and your partner garden, you may well find that you need to duplicate some of the essential tools. There are other, more specialized tools to help with specific tasks, such as long-armed secateurs for pruning tall fruit trees, but these will clearly depend on the particular crops you grow.

SPADES
Consider whether you are strong enough, or your soil light enough, for a full-size blade, which is about 29cm (11½in) long and 18cm (7in) wide. A smaller one, called a border spade (23cm by 14cm/9in by 5½in) may be more suitable, particularly if you have heavy soil. A spade with a flat tread is less tiring to use if you are digging for a prolonged period, and it will not damage your footwear. If you are carrying out a single task, such as planting an apple tree, the non-treaded spade is fine.

Choose a model with a smooth, slightly angled shaft and a D-shaped handle, preferably made from polypropylene, which is lighter than wood. The shaft should be long enough to enable you to drive the blade into the soil with the minimum of bending.

Stainless steel blades retain their mirror-like finish; this makes for easier digging, especially on heavy soil, since soil does not cling to them. They are relatively expensive, though, and an ordinary forged steel blade can always be kept rust-free by cleaning and greasing after use. (Treaded blades are not generally available in stainless steel.)

FORKS
Choose a fork with square tines and overall dimensions about the same as those of a spade, or even slightly larger. Forks with flat tines are intended mainly for potato lifting. Stainless steel forks are available, though their advantages are less marked than with spades.

Among their several uses, forks are invaluable for breaking down lumpy soil, for breaking up the subsoil layer in double digging, for loosening a compacted surface between plants and for shifting manure, piles of weeds and garden rubbish.

RAKES
A rake is an essential tool for seedbed preparation and levelling. It is used to break the soil down to a fine tilth after digging. Choose the kind with a one-piece forged head and about a dozen gently curved teeth.

Lightness is an advantage, since part of the weight should be supported by the lower hand. If it is not, the soil will be drawn into ridges instead of forming a level bed.

HOES
Regular hoeing is the key to controlling annual weeds, provided that you act as soon as there is a hint of the plot greening over. That way, minimum effort is needed because weeds never get a chance to become established. There are several other gardening tasks for which a hoe of one kind or another is suitable.

A draw hoe, with its blades set almost at right angles to a long handle, is used with a scraping or chopping action. Though suitable for dealing with heavy weed growth, small weeds tend to get buried and may continue to grow. Two other important uses are for drawing soil up around potatoes, known as earthing up, and for forming seed drills.

A Dutch hoe has one main purpose. When pushed forward, in a series of short, jabbing motions, its flat blade severs annual weeds without burying them.

An onion hoe is a short-handled draw hoe. It is effective for thinning out rows of seedlings and for close, accurate, hoeing around small plants. The gardener has to bend low, however, so it is tiring to use.

There are, in addition, a number of patent hoes, for the most part based on the Dutch hoe principle. Some, with flattened blades sharpened at front and rear, are used with a push-pull action.

CULTIVATORS
A tool with three or five hooked tines, a cultivator is invaluable for breaking up lumps on a heavy soil. If land was dug in

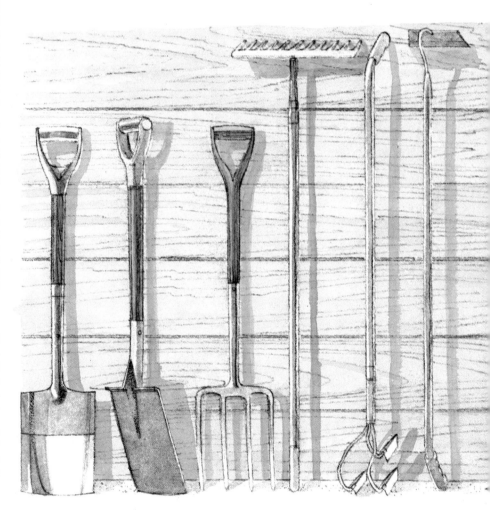

early winter, one or two passes with a cultivator in spring, followed by a light raking, gives a splendid seedbed.

Cultivators are also useful for loosening compacted soil at any time of year. When drawn through the soil in a series of parallel passes, the curve of the tines helps the cultivator to penetrate the densely compacted earth.

MEASURING ROD AND LINE

A flat batten about a metre (3–4ft) long is useful for accurate spacing between rows and plants. Use black paint to mark thick lines across the batten at about 30cm (1ft) intervals, with additional half-width lines every 15cm (6in).

A cord mounted on a reel is a more accurate and convenient way of marking seed drills than making do with pegs and string. With the free end secured to a steel pin, the line should be strong enough and remain taut enough to guide the hoe when opening drills.

DIBBERS

Some plants, brassicas in particular, require firm planting. A dibber is the ideal tool; you can first use its pointed end to form the planting hole, and then, inserting it again alongside the plant, to press the soil hard against its roots.

A purpose-made dibber has a steel tip to reduce friction. But should you have a broken or discarded spade, you can cut off the top 15cm (6in) of the wooden shaft and trim it to a point to make a dibber.

TROWELS

A trowel's main use is for planting. For plants with little or no stem, such as lettuces, a trowel is the only tool to use. Failing a dibber, a trowel is also quite effective for planting brassicas. The knack is to form a slit just wide enough to take the roots, without removing any soil.

Trowels are also essential for removing perennial weeds individually, and for any close work around plants.

SECATEURS

You will need secateurs if you are growing fruit, but they are also useful for a variety of tidying up jobs in the garden. There is little to choose between the two basic designs, those that cut with a scissor action and the others with a single blade cutting against an anvil. Make sure the blades cut cleanly and keep them sharp, either with professional help or by using a sharpening device.

WHEELBARROWS

Unless the garden is very small, go for a substantial barrow, preferably one with a pneumatic tyre. Throughout the year it will make your work much easier, particularly in tasks that involve shifting soil, manure, compost materials or garden rubbish. A flimsy barrow with a small wheel may need replacing within a short time.

Apart from the garden tools listed above, each with a specific use, there is a miscellany of small, general-purpose items which you will find invaluable in the vegetable garden. Keep a penknife on hand for general trimming jobs, and a sharp knife for trimming vegetable crops such as brassicas.

Have a supply of bamboo canes in assorted sizes for using as stakes and supports. A ball of string and a supply of 'plant ties' (lengths of plastic-covered wire) will be needed for tying plants to their supports or back against a wall. Plastic markers are useful for identifying rows of seeds or individual plants; write on them with a special waterproof marker pen.

It is worth keeping in your tool shed a supply of empty yogurt pots and plastic containers to supplement purpose-made plant pots and trays. They are perfectly satisfactory for seed-sowing and for pricking-out seedlings.

From left to right: untreaded spade; spade with a tread; garden fork; rake; cultivator; draw hoe; Dutch hoe; patent hoe (Swoe); push-pull weeder; onion hoe; anvil-type secateurs; reel and line; dibber; trowel; measuring rod; pneumatic-tyred wheebarrow.

> ### CARING FOR TOOLS
> ■ Clean all tools after use, in particular removing earth.
> ■ Either smear blades with grease or spray them with an anti-rust aersol.
> ■ Store tools in a dry shed or garage; never leave them outdoors.
> ■ Remember to oil bearings and pivots.
> ■ Use a coarse file to sharpen hoe blades.

DIGGING THE PLOT, pages 34–35
PLANTING VEGETABLES, page 40

It may seem odd that you need to turn your garden upside down at regular intervals; wild plants manage well enough without such an upheaval. So is digging really necessary?

The answer, unfortunately, is 'yes', unless your soil is already in a quite superb state of rich, crumbly fertility. The fruit and vegetable gardener asks a great deal of the soil, in terms of returns, and digging enables you to put something back – to mix in plenty of organic matter, bury weeds, let in life-giving air and relieve the compaction caused by frequent treading. Heavy soil in particular benefits from digging done at the right time of year.

For the most part, digging applies only to the topsoil, that precious fertile layer which supports plant life. 'Single digging', by far the most common practice, involves loosening and turning this layer without disturbing the inorganic subsoil beneath. From time to time, though – and particularly if you are aware of an extra hard 'pan' below the topsoil – it is worth loosening the subsoil as well.

WHEN TO DIG
Full-scale digging is not practicable until the end of the growing season, when only a few winter and spring vegetables remain. If you need to loosen the soil between harvesting one crop and planting another, this is best done with a fork.

Autumn and early winter are the easiest times to dig heavy soil, which may be too dry and hard earlier in the year. At the same time, however, you should aim to finish digging heavy soil before the soil becomes saturated with winter rains. Left until mid-winter, the work will be twice as hard and the structure of the soil may be harmed or fail to improve.

The exception is light soil, where early winter digging is less important. Indeed, if manure or compost is to be dug in, the job is better left until late winter, so reducing the risk of plant foods being washed away. It is easy enough to get a fine tilth on light soil, with or without the help of frost.

If dug soil is left in unbroken lumps, the combination of rain and frost during the winter will yield a crumbled surface by the following spring, creating a manageable soil more effectively than any amount of hard labour with tools. In spring, you simply need to rake or lightly fork the surface to prepare it for sowing or planting.

Always avoid digging ground that has a frozen crust or a covering of snow, especially toward the end of the digging season. Either will chill the soil unnecessarily, sometimes remaining unmelted until well after the surface has thawed.

PREPARING TO DIG
Annual weeds are best dug into the soil and buried, and this will happen automatically as you dig your plot. If the same treatment is given to perennial weeds, though, many will survive to grow again the following year. Some will actually be increased by the chopping action of the spade. If you are unsure about distinguishing perennial weeds from annual ones, turn to pp.45–7 for help in identifying them.

The solution is either to dig out the perennial weeds individually, roots and all, or else to kill them with a weedkiller in advance of digging (see pp.46–7). Persistence does eventually pay off with perennial weeds: if you are meticulous about removing their roots, they do come back less quickly. Once they are dead, rake long-rooted, perennial weeds into a pile and burn them.

SINGLE DIGGING
1 The first task is to dig out a trench at one end of the plot. This will provide space for soil to be thrown forward as digging proceeds. In this way you maintain an open trench to the far end of the plot. Barrow the soil from the first trench to just beyond the end, ready for filling in as the final stage of the operation.

2 With the soil barrowed away, move to one end of the trench and start on the first row of actual digging. Chop the spade in at right angles to the trench, marking and loosening a spade-width 'spit' of soil. Now press the blade in with your foot about 10cm (4in) from the edge, lift the soil just clear of the ground and throw it forward.

3 As you throw the soil forward, twist the shaft of the spade with your upper hand so that the earth, and any manure or compost on it, is inverted. This will also bury annual weeds, but you must take care to remove the roots of perennial weeds. Scrape manure from near the edge of the trench on to the newly-turned face. Carry on digging the next row.

HOW TO DIG

Assuming that you are digging in some organic matter, first barrow this to the plot and empty it out into evenly-spaced heaps. Spread the material over the ground but leave bare a narrow strip along one edge where you will begin.

Dig out a fairly broad trench, about the depth of a spade, along the edge of the plot (the strip you left bare). Throw the soil from it into a wheelbarrow, then barrow this soil to somewhere just beyond the far end of the plot, where you will need it for filling in the final trench.

Carry on with digging, trench by trench, keeping the spade as vertical as possible. Throw the soil forward to fill the previous trench; try to keep an open trench all the time. Either turn the manure under with each spit of soil, or else flick it forward across the face of the previous spadeful.

In a new or recently replanned and altered garden it may be necessary to dig up a turfed area. In this case, make the first and subsequent trenches a little wider so that turf stripped from the surface can be placed upside down on the bottom of the trench. Cut and invert a spade-width strip of turf at a time, chopping it into easily-lifted pieces. If you have recently cleared a piece of ground and have a pile of annual weeds, these can also be put into the trench.

DOUBLE DIGGING

'Double digging' involves penetrating the subsoil: the compacted and generally infertile layer immediately below the topsoil. It is coarser in texture and paler in colour than the topsoil itself. Double digging will improve overall drainage and increase, gradually, the depth of the upper, fertile layer. Plants benefit from the moisture and, sometimes, the few nutrients to be found at a lower level.

Double digging is slow, hard work. The best plan it to tackle only a limited area at a time, marking the point to which you have double dug, as a guide for the following season. When double digging, it is important not to mix the upper, fertile layer of topsoil with the subsoil beneath. It is especially useful to double dig an area where you intend to plant deep-rooted vegetables, such as parsnips or runner beans.

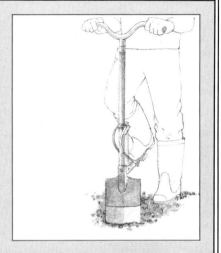

DIGGING WITHOUT STRAIN
If you are unused to digging or after a long break from gardening, take it in easy stages and do not try to hurry. The risk of back strain is increased by attempting too much too soon. Half an hour a day may prove long enough until your spine and back muscles are used to the unfamiliar movements.

Buy a good spade, and make sure that it is not too heavy for you to use comfortably. Lift small amounts of soil at a time rather than the maximum that the blade will carry. Avoid digging when the soil is sodden or frozen.

Let the weight and momentum of the spade, and your own weight pressing on the blade, do most of the work. Free each spadeful by driving the blade in at right-angles to the trench. Lift the soil just clear of the ground, tilting the blade as you do so with a rhythmic action.

An automatic spade could be a good investment if you have a weak back. This works with a lever action, virtually eliminating lifting and bending. The blade is hinged to a foot-plate, so that a pull on the handlebars throws the soil forward into the trench, inverting it at the same time.

An alternative would be to hire or buy a motor cultivator (see p. 27); these machines are especially effective on light and medium soils. However, though they avoid the strain of lifting and bending, handling a motor cultivator calls for a degree of strength on hard or stony soil.

DOUBLE DIGGING
1 First take out a spade-depth trench, about 60cm (2ft) from front to back, across one end of the plot. Move the topsoil you have just removed in a barrow to just beyond where the digging will finish. After loosening the bottom of the trench by forking, add some manure or compost. This may be left as a layer or forked lightly into the surface of the subsoil.

2 Fill the trench by throwing the soil forward from the next 60cm (2ft) strip. This will create a new trench, ready for loosening and manuring in the same way as the first one. Double digging is of most value when the lower layer is compacted.

Most vegetables and some herbs are grown as annuals and raised from seed each year. Seeds should therefore be sown in soil or seed compost which is warm and damp, and not too deeply.

Most vegetables *can* be sown directly in the ground. But whether you sow your seeds outdoors or under glass will depend on the climate zone in which you live and on how early a start you wish them to have. There are also some tender vegetable fruits, such as aubergines, peppers, cucumbers and tomatoes, which need fairly high temperatures to germinate and which must therefore be sown in a greenhouse (see pp. 38–9) or a warm room indoors; they can either be grown permanently in the greenhouse or else moved outside once the weather has become milder.

SELECTING SEEDS

Study the seed catalogues and make your selection of plants and varieties. Buy seeds well ahead of the sowing season in case sought-after varieties become scarce.

When choosing the varieties to grow, you will see that some are termed F1 hybrids. These are the result of crossing two carefully selected parent strains and they produce exceptionally vigorous and uniform plants. There are generally fewer F1 hybrid seeds to a packet.

Pelleted seeds are individual seeds, each one coated with soluble clay, which makes them easier to sow at regular spacings. They reduce or cut down the need for thinning and are an excellent idea for crops, such as carrots or lettuces, that are difficult to thin after germination. Be sure to keep the ground moist when sowing them, otherwise the coating will not be softened and germination will be impaired.

Each year brings a batch of new varieties announced by the seedsmen in their catalogues; some of them are illustrated in the colour catalogues, pages 112–128 and 176–192. You must decide whether to try these or to stick to reliable old favourites, whose results have been proved on past experience, or which have been recommended by books or fellow gardeners.

On balance, it probably pays to stay with known good performers for most of your crops. However, it is always interesting to try something fresh, and it is a good idea to experiment with at least one or two likely-sounding newcomers each year. Some may well become your long-term choices.

PREPARING FOR MAIN SOWINGS

Many plants, particularly root crops, must be sown in the place where they are to grow and mature, since they cannot be successfully transplanted.

Getting the soil ready for sowing and planting is one of the main spring jobs in the food garden. Whatever the time of sowing indicated on the seed packet, you should pay as much attention to the condition of the soil as to the calendar. Never make a start while the land is still sticky, but wait until it is dry enough to be walked on without the soil sticking to your boots. Also, it should have been given time to warm up.

If the soil has already been dug over the previous winter, light soil will need no more than raking. This is the time to spread a base dressing (see p.29) if the soil, or the crop, requires it. Heavy soil that has been dug should crumble if it is lightly forked or stirred with a cultivator first; you can then use a rake. Take care to disturb only the loose surface soil.

If you did not dig the plot the previous winter, light and medium soil will respond to being turned with a fork, with the addition of well-rotted manure, where appropriate. Heavy soil may need to be worked repeatedly with a fork and/or a cultivator to coax a tilth. It is important that you start work on clay soil when it has dried out but before it sets hard. A motor cultivator can be a considerable help (see p.27).

If the ground is very dry at sowing time, soak the bottom of the drill with a watering can immediately before distributing the seeds of your chosen crops.

SOWING IN SEEDBEDS

Some vegetables, notably brassicas and leeks, are sown in a seedbed and moved to their final positions when partly grown. The plants tend to be 'leggy' if they are sown where they are to grow.

The seedbed may be in any sunny, well-drained corner of the plot. First prepare the ground and form the drills as described for main sowings, and as shown in the illustrations. However, instead of a line and pegs, use a straight batten as a guide for the hoe. Space the rows 15cm (6in) apart and label each one as you sow the seeds.

Some crops, such as summer cabbages, can be given an earlier start by preparing the seedbed under glass, perhaps in a cold frame or under cloches. The method is the same, but you would need to put cloches in position two weeks before sowing to warm up the soil. Remember to ventilate the frame if the weather turns warm.

When the soil is loosened, use a rake to complete the preparation of a fine seedbed (above). Once you have raked in one direction, finish by raking the seedbed crossways.

A cultivator (left), with three or five prongs, is invaluable for loosening compacted soil, either between rows of plants or as the first stage in seedbed preparation. Drawn behind in a series of passes, it causes a minimum of back strain.

THE LIFE OF SEEDS

Seeds gathered from the previous year's crop are not usually a sound proposition. Many vegetables, notably brassicas, will cross-pollinate, with unpredictable and disastrous results. Possible exceptions are peas and beans, provided they have been grown separately from other varieties of the same crop.

As long as they are carefully stored, many vegetable seeds remain viable for several years. Seal the opened packets with adhesive tape and keep them in a dark, cool place in a closed tin or jar. Write the year of purchase on the packet if it is not printed on it. Two exceptions are onions and parsnips, which will probably fail to germinate with any reliability after about a year; parsley is also risky.

SOWING THE SEEDS

Vegetables may be grown either in well-spaced rows or, with closer spacing, in beds (see below and p.132). The sowing method is essentially the same in each case, though when sowing a bed, a batten placed crossways is sufficient guide for drawing the seed drills. The line method, described here, is for well-spaced rows on a conventional plot.

Measure the correct spacing between rows with a measuring rod, then insert the pins or pegs at each end of a row to hold the line taut. Form the seed-sowing furrow, called a drill, with the corner of a draw-hoe blade; rest the blade lightly on the line as you draw it backward in short, easy movements. Make the drill as deep as indicated for the particular plant; this will vary from 10–12mm (up to $\frac{1}{2}$in) for the smallest seeds,

such as carrots, turnips and lettuces, to 5cm (2in) for the largest seeds, such as those of beans. Peas are one exception: they require a flat trench, formed with the whole blade.

Take a pinch of seeds between finger and thumb and sow them thinly along the drill as you walk forward. As you finish each pinch of seeds, make a mark in the soil as a guide to where to start sowing again.

Cover the seeds by walking backward from the far end of the drill, brushing soil into it from each side with your hands, or use the upturned head of a rake. Finish by walking forward once more, firming the replaced soil lightly with one foot, or, on a seedbed, with the back of your hand.

If you prefer, you can use one of the patent seed sowers that simply need pushing along the drill; they save a little time.

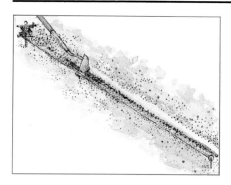

To form a seed drill, first fasten the line and make sure that it is taut. Holding a draw hoe at an angle against the line, pull it toward you in a series of movements to form a V-shaped groove. As a rough guideline, the larger the seed the deeper it needs to be sown.

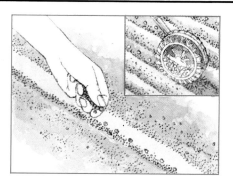

Empty some seeds from a packet into the palm of one hand, and distribute them between thumb and forefinger to sow sparingly along the drill. Patent sowing aids (inset) are simply pushed along a pre-formed drill. Check their accuracy on a plain surface first, such as a path or floor.

After sowing, use an inverted rake head, or your hands, to draw some soil back gently into the drill. Firm the replaced soil, either by tapping with the rake head or by gentle pressure from your foot. Mark one end of the row with a stick, and the other with a label, before removing the line.

PROTECTION

Seedbeds are a sure attraction for birds and cats. If your experience suggests extreme caution, cover the rows with wire or plastic netting stretched over canes. Otherwise, criss-cross black cotton over the rows between short sticks. A proprietary tape that vibrates and hums in the wind is most effective for the short time needed before the seeds come up.

THINNING

With one or two exceptions, such as spring onions and sparsely-sown radishes, all vegetable crops need thinning to prevent overcrowding. This applies to plants raised in seedbeds as well as to those sown in the open ground. Failure to thin inevitably leads to weak, spindly growth, as plants compete with each other for food, moisture and light.

Plants that were sown too thickly suffer unduly for being overcrowded at the seedling stage. Thinning out very overcrowded seedlings can also disturb the roots of those that are left.

Start to thin as soon as the plants are large enough to handle, but leave a surplus at the early stage in case of losses from pests or disease. Make one or two further thinnings later. For example, you might thin first so that the seedlings are 2.5cm (1in) apart, then later to 5cm (2in) apart, and finally to the distance recommended for that vegetable. On a seedbed, however, thin only once before transplanting to their permanent position.

Try not to disturb the plants that are left: thin when the soil is damp to reduce the risk of damage to their roots, and firm the soil around them if it is loose after thinning.

Tender crops, such as cucumbers and aubergines, need a warm start in life, and should be sown under glass. Some of them, indeed, need the continuing protection of a greenhouse throughout their lives, but others can be planted outdoors once all danger of frost is past. With some crops it is a matter of variety. There are types of cucumber and melon, for instance, that must be grown in a greenhouse. But others, with a hardier constitution, will grow outdoors during the summer. All marrows, squashes and pumpkins fall into this category.

Indoor sowing is also valuable for giving an earlier start to crops normally sown outdoors, such as beans and sweet corn. You can stagger the harvesting of some of your crops by sowing a proportion of their seeds under glass, a few weeks earlier than the rest, which you sow outdoors.

If you do not have a greenhouse, a garden frame with soil-warming cables provides good conditions for germination and growth (see p.18), as does an electric propagator. If you are using a soil-warmed bed, press the seed trays or pans well into the sand. Pack moist peat around them to help conserve the warmth.

PROVIDING WARMTH
During late winter and early spring, it is a good idea to use soil-warming cables or a propagator even for seeds raised in a greenhouse. (Install the cable exactly as you would in a frame.) Either method will cost less than heating the whole greenhouse to the relatively high temperature needed for germination. After germination, a soil-warmed bed will keep the seedlings growing, but some form of air heating will be needed for plants moved from a propagator fairly early in the season.

The need for artificial heat lessens as the season advances. Sowings delayed until mid-spring need only gentle warmth by night and perhaps none by day. Later still, seeds will germinate and seedlings will prosper in an unheated greenhouse.

The precise time of sowing depends partly on the amount of heat available, and partly on where the plants are to grow. For instance, if you are prepared to maintain a minimum temperature of 16°C (61°F), even on chilly nights, you can sow greenhouse cucumbers in a propagator during late winter. It is better to wait until spring, however, if you prefer to economize on fuel. A mid-spring sowing is quite early enough for plants, such as courgettes, which will be moved outside in late spring. If they are sown earlier than this, they may outgrow their pots before it is warm enough to move them outdoors, and they will not transplant successfully.

Seeds may be sown in an electrically-heated propagator and the seedlings grown on in a greenhouse or indoors on a sunny windowsill. The one-sided light on a windowsill makes for rather lanky growth, so the sooner seedlings can be moved outdoors the better.

CONTAINERS FOR PLANT-RAISING
Small seeds, such as lettuces, are sown by being sprinkled on a pan or tray of compost; the seedlings are then moved individually (pricked out) soon after germination. Larger seeds, such as those of marrows or sweet corn, are sown in small pots where they will remain until planting time.

Plastic seed trays are often used for seed-sowing, but shallow seed pans, which require less compost than a pot, are even better. Seedlings can also be grown on in a plastic seed tray and left in this rectangular container until they are ready for planting out. A pot measuring about 8cm (3in) across is big enough for planting individual larger seeds.

You can also use washed-out plastic margarine tubs for sowing small seeds, or yogurt pots for individual seeds, but rectangular trays and pans are most economical of space on greenhouse staging.

Pans and pots may be made of plastic or clay, and both are satisfactory. The plastic ones have the advantage, however, since they are cheaper, lighter-weight and easier to clean; they also need watering less often. It is worth soaking clay pots in water before using them for plant-raising, otherwise they absorb too much moisture from the compost. Cover drainage holes with pieces of broken pot first, to stop compost being washed through.

There are also compressed peat pots and peat blocks, in which large, marrow-type seeds may be sown, or seedlings pricked out individually. At planting time the whole pot or block, complete with its plant, is set in the soil. The compressed peat disintegrates and the plant roots grow through. Peat pots must be damp when planted, otherwise the peat will form a hard case.

SEED AND POTTING COMPOSTS
Ordinary garden soil is unsuitable for raising seeds. Used in pots and seed pans, it becomes muddy or hard, both of which discourage root growth. It also contains weed seeds and disease organisms.

Purpose-made seed and potting composts are the ideal growing medium for seeds, since they are sterilized and specially formulated to meet the needs of young plants. They are, of course, quite distinct from garden compost, which is made from decomposed vegetation. Seed and potting composts are either peat-based, with added plant foods, or are made from a mixture of sterilized loam (high-grade soil), sand, peat and fertilizers.

Soil-based composts, usually mixed to the John Innes formula, are sold in various grades, each containing a different quantity of fertilizer. In addition to a seed-sowing mix, there are three potting grades: No. 1 for seedlings, No. 2 for plants of intermediate size and No. 3 for growing large, vigorous plants, such as tomatoes, to maturity.

Peat-based composts are more likely to be of universal grade – that is, they suit plants of all ages, provided that additional fertilizer is given within six weeks or so of the plants being potted. Plants in loam compost will also need feeding eventually, but not as soon as those in peat.

SOWING THE SEEDS

Fill the container with moist compost and remove any surplus with a short batten or board. Firm the compost with the base of another pot or seed pan. Distribute the seeds evenly over the compost. After sowing, sprinkle just enough compost over the seeds to cover them. Use a sieve, or rub the compost gently between your hands, over the tray, so that it crumbles finely.

When sowing in pots, press two large seeds 1.3cm (½in) deep into the compost; place them slightly apart. Remove the weaker seedling if both germinate. Cover the pots with glass and paper.

Check the trays, pans or pots daily after the first few days for signs of germination. Remove the glass and paper or, if you are using a propagator, remove the tray, at the first sign of the seedlings coming through. Most seeds germinate in one to two weeks.

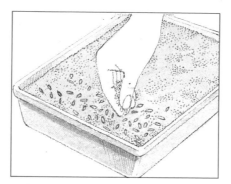

With your finger and thumb, sprinkle small seeds thinly and evenly over the surface of the compost. Leave larger spacings between seeds of intermediate size, such as tomatoes, or set them in equally spaced rows, about 1.3cm (½in) apart. Leave about 1.3cm (½in) between pelleted seeds.

Water the compost lightly with a fine-rosed can, then cover the container, first with glass to prevent drying out, then with folded newspaper to exclude light. Label the tray with the name of the seeds and the date of sowing. Turn the glass daily to remove condensation.

PRICKING OUT

Seedlings raised from scattered seeds need spacing out to prevent overcrowding. Prick them out as soon as they are large enough to handle, before they become tall, spindly and intertwined. Space lettuces, celeriac and other small plants about 4cm (1½in) apart in a tray. Allow 5cm (2in) for celery. Transplant tomatoes individually into 8cm (3in) pots.

Water the seedlings in with a fine rose and try to keep a constant temperature while they form new roots. They are best kept out of direct sunlight for the first day or two after being pricked out.

Peat-based composts need regular and careful watering since, once they dry out, it is difficult for them to absorb water again.

Pricking out consists of transplanting very small seedlings to another container in order to give them more space. Lift each seedling by one of its leaves to avoid damaging its stem. Use a pencil, a plant label or a miniature dibber to help ease it out of the compost.

Use the same dibber to make the new planting holes, and cover the seedlings with compost to just below their first 'seed' leaves. Firm the compost back in place around their roots. Water the seedlings in with a fine-rosed can and place them in a well-lit position.

HARDENING OFF

Acclimatize greenhouse-raised plants gradually before planting them outdoors, otherwise they might suffer a check in their development. If possible, stand them in a garden frame for up to two weeks, and gradually increase the ventilation. Cloches can be used instead, provided the weather is not too cold.

Alternatively, stand the plants outside in a sheltered spot by day, and move them back indoors or into the greenhouse at night, for at least the first week or ten days.

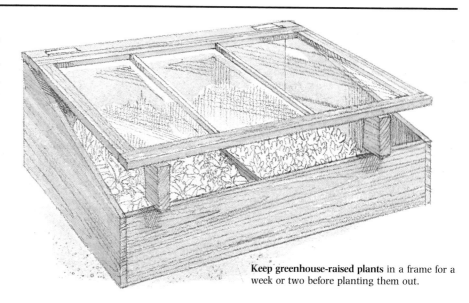

Keep greenhouse-raised plants in a frame for a week or two before planting them out.

USING A GREENHOUSE, pages 12–13
CLOCHES, pages 16–17

FRAMES, page 18
SOWING SEEDS OUTDOORS, pages 36–37

Water is crucial to the life of your crops: not only do plants need moisture but their foods have to be dissolved in water so that they can be taken up by the plant roots. A parched soil means that plants are starved of both water and food, since their roots cannot assimilate nutrients in dry form. Regular and adequate watering is essential during dry weather, especially during summer, when lower rainfall is likely to coincide with a high evaporation rate.

Soils vary in the amount of water they can hold; clay soils retain far more than sandy soils. The more any soil is cultivated and nourished, however, the greater becomes its capacity to store water. The need for artificial watering is therefore greatest on soils low in organic matter, especially those with a light, sandy structure.

Certain crops are particularly thirsty and therefore especially vulnerable to lack of water; these include tomatoes, cucumbers, marrows, squashes, pumpkins and beans. Melons need a lot of watering in the early stages. Leafy vegetables, such as broccoli and spinach, also need ample moisture if they are to crop consistently well.

There are a few crops, however, which are at risk from excessive moisture on or around maturity. Too much water may split ripening melons, or induce the growth of moulds on onions nearly ready for lifting.

WHEN TO WATER

As soil dries out, plants find it increasingly hard to draw up water, and they will eventually reach wilting point. Aim to water all your plants *before* they show signs of distress. Although it may be possible to revive them, wilting causes a check in their growth, and slows development. In some cases they will run to seed, or 'bolt'.

The appearance of the surface soil is not a good guide to its moisture content, except while plants are still small and have short roots. During that period the top layer must never be allowed to dry out. As the plants grow, you need to use a trowel to check the state of the soil further down – 23–25cm (9–10in) for well-developed plants.

Thorough applications of water, spaced well apart, are the most beneficial to plants. A policy of 'little and often' can do more harm than good, since you may be giving insufficient water to reach the plant roots. It is better to give enough water to soak right through the topsoil, which means applying about 23 litres per sq m (5 gallons per sq yd) if the soil shows signs of drying out. Water during the evening in summer.

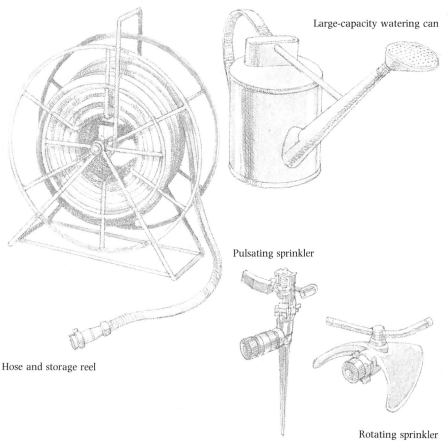

Large-capacity watering can

Hose and storage reel

Basic watering equipment consists of a hosepipe – preferably the reinforced type that will not kink and is unlikely to split – and a long-spouted can. A reel for storing the hose can also be considered a necessity. There are various forms of sprinklers; the choice is dictated partly by cost and partly by the size of the area to be irrigated.

Pulsating sprinkler

Rotating sprinkler

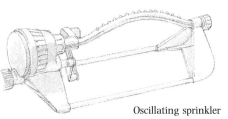

Oscillating sprinkler

Since they cover a rectangular area, perforated hoses are particularly useful for watering rows of vegetables or soft fruits. The water is ejected as a mist-like spray on either side.

Pulsating sprinklers have a long throw, which makes them a good choice for the larger vegetable plot. Some are mounted on stands to cover an even greater area, regardless of the height of nearby crops.

MULCHING

Mulching consists simply of spreading organic matter over the surface around plants, including soft fruit bushes as well as vegetables. Suitable materials include well-rotted manure, garden compost, peat, grass cuttings, leaves and bark chippings.

The object of mulching is to reduce the amount of evaporation from the soil and to suppress weeds. Mulching is also, in the longer term, an aid to soil fertility, since the material will eventually be dug into the soil and break down into humus.

A suitable depth of mulch is about 5cm (2in) for most materials, though less than this for grass cuttings. Leave a space around the trunks of grafted fruit trees: if the mulch comes into contact with the union between rootstock and scion (see p.89), there is a danger that roots will try to form from it.

Black polythene is an even more effective way of conserving moisture and smothering weeds, though it does nothing for soil fertility. It is especially useful for strawberry plants and bush tomatoes, since it prevents the fruits touching the soil. If you use it, sprinkle slug pellets on the soil first. Cut slits in the material for well-spaced plants, such as brassicas; lay it along each side of closely-spaced plants, such as root crops.

Wait until the soil has warmed up before spreading the first spring mulch, otherwise it will act as an insulant, keeping the ground cold and blocking out the sun. During dry weather, water the ground well before mulching.

WATERING AIDS

Hand watering with water drawn from a tap is too slow for most of the food garden, apart from containers. The least you can do is rig up a hose to save having to walk between the tap and the plants.

The quantity is easily judged when you are watering with a can. If you are using a hose, check first how long it takes to fill a can of known size, then relate this to the area being watered, keeping the tap on at a constant pressure.

Once you have a hose, it is a logical step to buy a sprinkler attachment for it, or some other automatic dispenser. The cost is low but the time saved is considerable.

The most basic of sprinkler attachments, with no moving parts, dispense a circular curtain of water around them. Those that are a little more sophisticated are adjustable to allow a square spray pattern. This helps to prevent gaps and overlaps.

Rotating sprinklers, which have a wider throw, sometimes have adjustable nozzles for varying the size of the spray droplets.

Pulsating sprinklers work with a circular action too. They emit the spray in fine bursts and cover a substantially greater area than the ordinary rotating kinds.

Oscillating sprinklers move from side to side instead of in a circle, and can be adjusted to cover square or rectangular patterns. The area watered is about the same as with the larger rotating sprinklers. The droplet size is rather heavy for seedlings and for very small plants.

Irrigation hoses are one of the most labour-saving forms of automatic dispenser. They consist of polythene tubing with multiple perforations, laid along plant rows. A steady trickle of water along the length of the tube saturates the soil.

Sprinkler hoses are flat in section, and release the water as a mistlike spray over the crops on either side of them. They are excellent for watering vegetable crops at all stages of growth, and also soft fruits. The spray is gentle enough not to damage young plants.

GREENHOUSE WATERING

A piped water supply to the greenhouse is a great time-saver. A good alternative is a water butt which can be replenished from a hose and/or from the greenhouse guttering. If it can be placed inside the greenhouse, the temperature of the water will be closer to that of the soil and compost in which plants are growing. However, lack of space in a small greenhouse may prevent this.

A long-spouted watering can is the most common watering aid, provided it has a fine rose for use with seedlings. A 4.5-litre (1 gallon) can is large enough for bench watering, but one twice this size is needed for tomatoes and cucumbers grown in greenhouse borders.

A capillary bench (see p.15) provides a simple means of semi-automatic watering for seedlings and other plants growing on staging. Plants growing in the border or in pots can be supplied by one of the drip nozzle systems, as described under Watering Containers, below.

WATERING CONTAINERS

Salad crops, tomatoes and herbs grown in containers need frequent watering – often twice daily during a warm, dry spell. Do not allow peat-based compost, in particular, to dry out, since it can be difficult to saturate again. Reduce the evaporation from gro-bags by cutting only small holes for the plant stems.

Limit the heavy moisture loss from absorbent containers, such as wooden plant tubs and clay pots, by lining them with polythene before planting. Be sure to leave the drainage hole uncovered.

As an alternative to hand watering, consider one of the proprietary systems that make use of drip nozzles; the flow can be regulated to keep the compost consistently moist. Such a system is especially useful at holiday times.

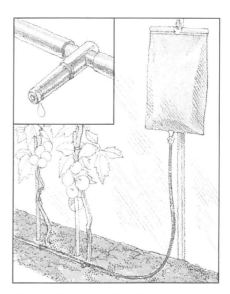

Drip watering systems, fed either from the mains or, as here, from a reservoir bag, supply water to individual containers and plants. Fertilizer can be added if required.

Apart from the numerous pests and diseases that attack specific plants, your crops also need protecting against the birds and animals that roam gardens looking for sources of food. The nature of the problem will vary according to where you live. Sparrows and cats are the bane of many town gardeners, while rabbits and pigeons may be more of a nuisance in the country.

Whatever the particular hazard, your aim is to protect your crops and deter the pests without harming the wild creatures and pets with which you share your garden.

BIRDS Large and small birds are an obvious source of damage, although they also help to control insect pests. Soft and tree fruits are particularly at risk from birds, which will spoil ripening fruits in summer and damage fruit buds in winter. Squirrels are also attracted to strawberries and some other soft fruits. You must either protect your crops with cotton or netting, or else deter the birds by unsettling them.

Deterrence has to be a fairly short-term policy, since bird scarers lose their effectiveness once they become familiar objects. For this reason it is a good idea to ring the changes at frequent intervals. However, only a formidable deterrent will keep pigeons off brassicas in winter or blackbirds off strawberries in summer.

The alternative is to net crops securely, preferably using a purpose-made cage which gives easy access and comfortable headroom. You may not have space in your garden for a permanent cage, however, or may not consider that you grow enough soft fruits to make one worthwhile. Protect individual plants by draping light nylon or plastic netting over them.

Large fruit trees are more of a problem; one partial solution is to secure individual fruits inside muslin or perforated polythene bags or sleeves. Black cotton thread wound between branches will deter birds but it is a time-consuming task to put it there if the tree is large.

CATS Seedbeds are irresistible to cats for use as lavatories, but little harm is done after this stage. You need only protect the bed for a few weeks until the crops have become established. Wire netting is one of the most effective solutions if you lay it flat on the ground, immediately after sowing. Seedlings will find their way through the mesh.

RABBITS Some cats will control rabbits but others cannot be relied on. Fencing is the answer if rabbits become a nuisance in your garden; use 3cm- (1¼in-) mesh rabbit netting.

Black cotton criss-crossed between short pegs or sticks, 5-8cm (2-3in) above the soil, will protect a seedbed or young seedlings from sparrows and other small birds. Though they could pass through the spaces between the strands, contact with the almost invisible threads alarms them.

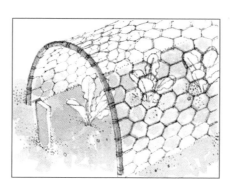

'Cloches', formed by bending a length of fine-gauge wire netting, are self-supporting. Alternatively, support plastic netting on wire hoops.

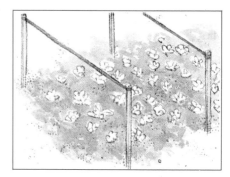

A humming line, a plastic tape that vibrates and hums even in a light wind, is an effective bird scarer for a short time. Fix the tape at intervals, stretching it between sticks.

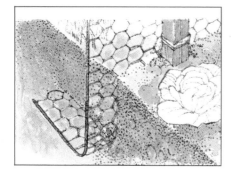

Wire netting will keep rabbits from the plot if the bottom edge is buried in the ground and the final 15cm (6in) turned outward to prevent their burrowing beneath. To allow for this concealed edge, buy the netting in a roll not less than 1.2m (4ft) wide.

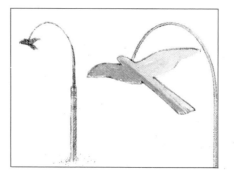

Cut-out hawks, bought or home-made, act as short-term deterrents. Almost any suspended object that swings in the breeze will serve the same purpose.

FURTHER PRECAUTIONS
- Growing seedlings in a greenhouse, a frame or under cloches will offer a reasonable degree of protection against larger pests.
- Never put plate scrapings or any animal matter on a compost heap; they will attract rats. Always keep the compost heap covered.
- Scatter slug pellets over a seedbed immediately after sowing if slugs or snails are a hazard.
- Grow fruit bushes close to the house where practicable; the presence of people deters birds.
- There are chemical deterrents for discouraging animals of all sorts, as well as birds. These are applied with a spray or a watering can.

All weeds are a threat to your crops, since they compete with the plants for water and nutrients and may also harbour pests and diseases. They therefore need to be effectively controlled.

The annual species of weeds can be destroyed relatively easily, by severing their stems with a hoe at any stage of growth. Perennial weeds are more of a problem; they have to be removed from the ground, complete with their roots, or treated with a weedkiller. Otherwise, many will grow again from even small pieces left in the soil.

IDENTIFYING THE WEEDS

It is important to be able to differentiate between the different kinds of weed so that you can adopt the best treatment to destroy them. The illustrations below show some of the most common annual weeds to invade fruit and vegetable gardens. Common perennial weeds are illustrated overleaf.

Apart from identification, there are other clues to help you distinguish one type of weed from another. Their growing habits differ, for a start. Annual weeds tend to grow densely in cultivated soil – in a vegetable plot, for instance – and often in large patches of a single species. There may be some perennial weeds mixed with them.

Annual weeds will also be found in untilled soil, but perennial species, such as couch grass, are more likely to dominate there. When establishing a food garden, it is essential to clear such weeds from the site first (see p.27).

PREVENTING WEEDS

Provided the site was thoroughly cleared at the outset, weed control should not present too much of a problem. Many gardeners find that a combination of regular hoeing and annual digging prior to planting, removing all perennial weeds at the same time, is sufficient to keep the weeds at bay. However, you may wish to adopt other means of checking annual weed growth.

Mulching (see p.43) is one of the main preventive steps. This inhibits the germination and growth of annual weeds, of which millions of seeds are always present in the soil. Dig out any perennial weeds and hoe off existing annual weeds before spreading a mulch. A 5cm (2in) layer of organic material is an effective weed-suppressant.

Close planting provides another method of controlling weed growth. This is practical if you adopt the bed system of vegetable growing (see p.132). You will need to hoe in the early stages, but once the crop is well established, reduced light and competition for moisture combine to deter the weeds.

Chemical weedkillers (see p.46) Annual weeds may be treated with a contact weedkiller, as used for perennial weeds. Residual weedkillers will kill newly-germinating seedlings and can be used to control weeds around soft fruits and some vegetables without harming the crops.

DEALING WITH ANNUAL WEEDS

Some gardeners take pleasure in weeding by hand but, unless you have time to spare, it is sensible to limit hand-weeding to the area immediately around the tender stems of young plants, as in a seedbed. Elsewhere, a sharpened hoe is a fast, accurate and deadly means of eradicating annual weeds.

Is is essential to hoe frequently, and as soon as possible after the weed seeds have germinated; if they are left until they are well grown, their removal will disturb other plant roots. The other requirement is to wait for a dry day, so that the weeds can be left to shrivel on the soil. If the hoed weeds are left in damp soil, perhaps partially covered, some of them may grow again. In showery weather, you will need to rake up the weeds and put them on the compost heap.

The best tool for the job is a Dutch hoe (see p.33) or else a hoe with a push-pull action. A short-handled onion hoe is useful for working close to plant stems.

Shepherd's purse
A common annual weed.

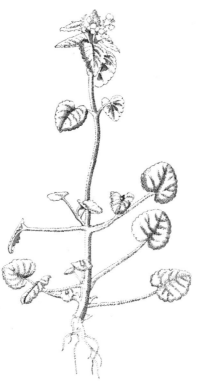

Red deadnettle
Easily controlled by hoeing.

Knot grass
A ground-hugging annual weed.

GROWING PLANTS NATURALLY, pages 20–21
TOOLS FOR THE VEGETABLE GARDEN, pages 32–33

MULCHING, page 43
PERENNIAL WEEDS: USING WEEDKILLERS, pages 46–47

SPACE-SAVING METHODS, pages 132–133

Because seeds are carried by birds or on the wind, no garden will ever be free of perennial weeds. To keep perennial weed problems to a minimum, it is vital to clear the plot effectively before you plant it with vegetables.

A chemical weedkiller provides the easiest means of killing persistent weeds that have established themselves in a neglected garden. The hardest types to get rid of are those that are multiplied by creeping rhizomes. These root-like structures spread underground from the parent plant and throw up vigorous shoots that form new plants. Rhizomatous weeds, which include bindweed and couch grass, are actually multiplied by digging. Forking the pieces out is another possible approach, but it is almost impossible to remove every piece from heavily infested land.

A mass clearance of persistent weeds will save endless work and frustration in the long term. After that the chief means of control is to dig out individual perennial weeds as they occur. If they are removed before they get established, there is no risk of a build-up of roots in the soil. Even couch grass and ground elder, two of the most persistent species, will not have a chance to form an extensive underground network.

Winter digging provides one of the best opportunities for the removal of perennial weeds. Though it interferes with the rhythmic digging action, always stop to pick out perennial stems and roots rather than turning them under. Either burn them or leave them to shrivel and die before you add them to the compost heap.

Take particular care not to let perennial weeds encroach on the plot from uncultivated ground alongside your land. Cut a definite edge if one does not exist, and maintain this either with boards or bricks let into the soil, or by applying a band of weedkiller to form a sterile barrier.

TYPES OF WEEDKILLER

You can, if you wish, use weedkillers to kill isolated perennial weeds, as well as for the mass clearance of an uncultivated site. Before you adopt this approach, however, bear in mind that forking weeds out is just as easy. Also, it costs nothing and does not expose your crops to unwanted chemicals.

If you decide to use a weedkiller, be sure to choose the right sort. There are three basic kinds, and each works in a different way. Before use, check the ingredients, which should be listed on the label, since a product that is excellent for one purpose may be useless for another.

Contact weedkillers These kill the foliage to which they are applied but have little or no effect on the plant roots. One application will kill annual weeds successfully, but several may be needed for perennials.

Most contact weedkillers become harmless once they touch the soil, and only local damage will be done if a few drops touch a cultivated plant by accident.

Paraquat and *diquat* are two widely-used contact weedkillers which destroy all green vegetation. There are also selective types for use on lawns.

Translocated weedkillers These move to all parts of the plant, from leaves to roots or the other way around. This makes them a valuable weapon against deep-rooted perennial weeds.

Glyphosate is a most effective translocated weedkiller that will destroy weeds and grasses of all types. It is inactivated on contact with the soil. *Aminotriazole* kills perennial grasses and a number of other weeds. *Alloxydium sodium* is a selective killer of couch and other perennial grasses. *Dalapon* controls perennial grasses but will also kill many other plants. It needs careful application. These four are often sold in formulations that contain other chemicals to give a wider measure of control.

Residual weedkillers These are applied to the soil and kill newly-germinated weed seedlings; they will keep the ground weed-free for an extended period by inhibiting the germination of new seedlings. The most useful version for the vegetable and fruit garden is *propachlor*, which prevents annual weeds appearing for up to eight weeks, and therefore gives new food plants a better start. It is suitable for strawberries and a number of vegetables, including onions, leeks, brassicas, turnips and swedes.

Simazine gives even longer control – up to a year; it kills existing small weeds, too. It is useful for pathways but, since it remains in suspension in the top layer of soil, in the food garden it should be used only around deep-rooted vegetables, such as asparagus and sweet corn, or between deeper-rooted fruit bushes.

Sodium chlorate is a very different kind of residual weedkiller. This formidable chemical kills all existing plant life, even trees, and prevents fresh growth from appearing for a considerable time. Its best use is to clear a site of weeds well before planting time. Sodium chlorate may linger in the soil for up to a year; in the meantime it may be washed laterally by rain to kill plants outside the treated area.

Another non-selective weedkiller for uncropped ground is *ammonium sulphamate*. This persists for two or three months and, like sodium chlorate, is a good choice for the initial clearance of a plot, but never for weed control between plants.

APPLYING WEEDKILLERS

Spraying is the easiest and most efficient means of wetting foliage, but with it comes the risk that spray drifts may harm other plants. Even small amounts of a translocated weedkiller can do much damage. As a precautionary measure, only spray during still weather and when it is not too hot. Early morning or evening are the best times. Fit a cone to the sprayer lance to help direct the droplets (see p.27) and keep the nozzle low.

A safer means is to use a dribble-bar attached to the watering can. This is recommended particularly when you are working between, or close to, plants. Various widths are available to suit different crop spacings.

Use an ordinary watering can, fitted with a rose, to apply a chemical such as sodium chlorate to a large area of uncropped ground.

To achieve even distribution of a residual weedkiller, which is usually in granular form, divide the area into metre or yard squares and sprinkle a measured amount over each.

USING WEEDKILLERS SAFELY

- Read and follow manufacturers' instructions, which relate to safety as well as results.
- Stick to the recommended concentration. Adding 'a little extra' is a waste of money and seldom helps. Do not mix with other chemicals unless you are advised to do so.
- Store weedkillers out of the reach of children and pets.
- Wash utensils and sprayers before and after use. Some chemicals leave a residue in spite of washing, so use a separate sprayer for each of these weedkillers.
- Do not store diluted weedkiller in bottles. Ideally, keep a separate sprayer or watering can, clearly marked, for use with weedkillers.

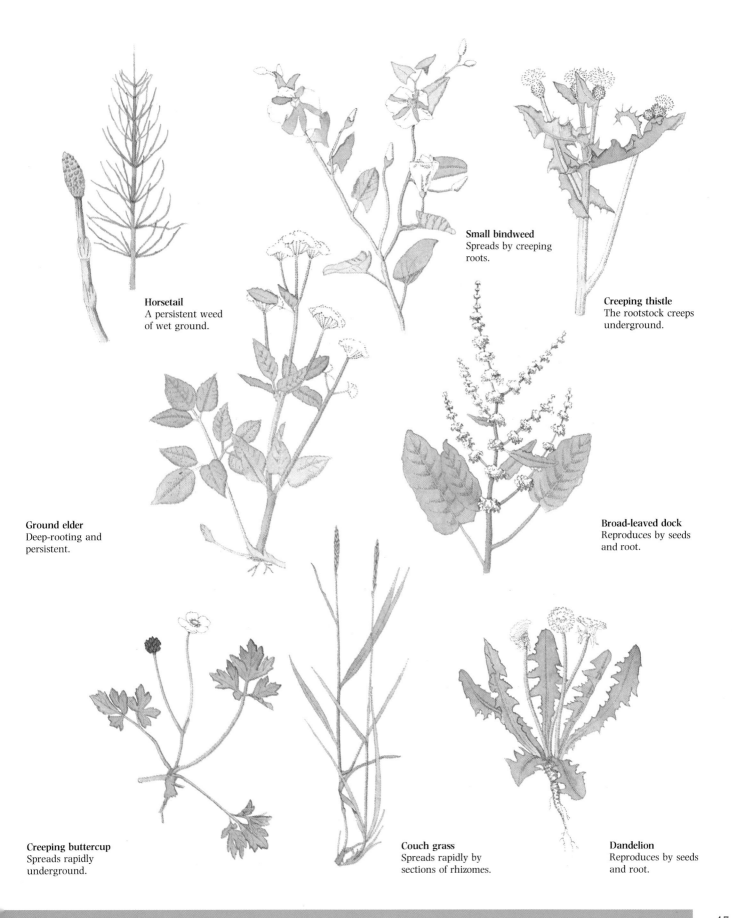

Horsetail
A persistent weed
of wet ground.

Small bindweed
Spreads by creeping
roots.

Creeping thistle
The rootstock creeps
underground.

Ground elder
Deep-rooting and
persistent.

Broad-leaved dock
Reproduces by seeds
and root.

Creeping buttercup
Spreads rapidly
underground.

Couch grass
Spreads rapidly by
sections of rhizomes.

Dandelion
Reproduces by seeds
and root.

The
FRUIT COLOUR CATALOGUE

The colour plates that follow show the wide range of soft and tree fruits suitable for growing in the food garden. While they cannot claim to be totally comprehensive, their aim is to suggest the scope available to home growers, many of the varieties shown being ignored by commercial fruit producers. A specialist nursery may offer fifty or more types of apple alone, each to be considered for its vigour, frost tolerance and season, as well as its use, flavour, appearance, keeping qualities and disease resistance.

The separate fruit entries, on pages 68–107, give specific details about individual cultivation requirements, as well as recommending varieties additional to those selected for illustration.

STRAWBERRIES Selected varieties

STRAWBERRY
'Ostara'

ALPINE STRAWBERRY
'Alexandria'
'Baron Solemacher'
'Delicious'

STRAWBERRY
'Red Gauntlet'
'Cambridge Vigour'

STRAWBERRY
'Sequoia'
'Cambridge Favourite'

STRAWBERRY
'Royal Sovereign'

SOFT FRUITS/BERRIES Selected varieties

SUMMER-FRUITING RASPBERRY
'Delight'
'Glen Cova'
'Glen Moy'
'Glen Prosen'
'Leo'
'Malling Jewel'

AUTUMN-FRUITING RASPBERRY
'Zeva'
'September'
'Heritage'

AUTUMN-FRUITING RASPBERRY
'Fallgold'

BLACK RASPBERRY
'Munger'

THORNLESS BLACKBERRY
'Oregon Thornless'

BLACKBERRY
'Himalaya Giant'
'Bedford Giant'
'Ashton Cross'

CULTIVATED BERRY
Dewberry

HYBRID BERRY
Boysenberry

HYBRID BERRY
Marionberry

HYBRID BERRY
Loganberry

CULTIVATED BERRY
Japanese Wineberry

HYBRID BERRY
Tayberry

CULTIVATION DETAILS SEE PAGES 70–74

CURRANTS AND BERRIES Selected varieties

CRANBERRY

HIGHBUSH BLUEBERRY
'Berkeley'
'Bluecrop'
'Coville'
'Earliblue'
'Herbert'

WHITE CURRANT
'White Dutch'
'White Versailles'

BLACKCURRANT
'Ben Lomond'
'Ben More'
'Boskoop Giant'
'Jet'
'Laxton Giant'

CHINESE GOOSEBERRY

RED CURRANT
'Jonkheer van Tets'
'Laxton No.1'
'Red Lake'
'Rondom'

GOOSEBERRY
'Whinham's Industry'

GOOSEBERRY
'Leveller'

GOOSEBERRY
'Captivator'

GOOSEBERRY
'Careless'
'Keepsake'
'Howard Lancer'

HYBRID BERRY
Worcesterberry

CULTIVATION DETAILS SEE PAGES 74–80

MELONS Selected varieties

NETTED (MUSK) MELON
'Blenheim Orange'

WINTER (CASABA) MELON
'Honeydew'
'Hero of Lockinge'

OGEN (CANTALOUPE) MELON
'Ogen'
'Early Sweet'

CANTALOUPE MELON
'Charentais'
'Sweetheart'

WATERMELON
'Sugar Jade'

NETTED MELON
'Galia'
'Emerald Gem'

CULTIVATION DETAILS SEE PAGES 82–83

55

GRAPES AND KIWI FRUIT Selected varieties

OUTDOOR GRAPE
'Pirovano 14'

GREENHOUSE GRAPE
'Alicante'
'Black Hamburg'

GREENHOUSE GRAPE
'Seyval Blanc'

KIWI FRUIT
'Hayward'

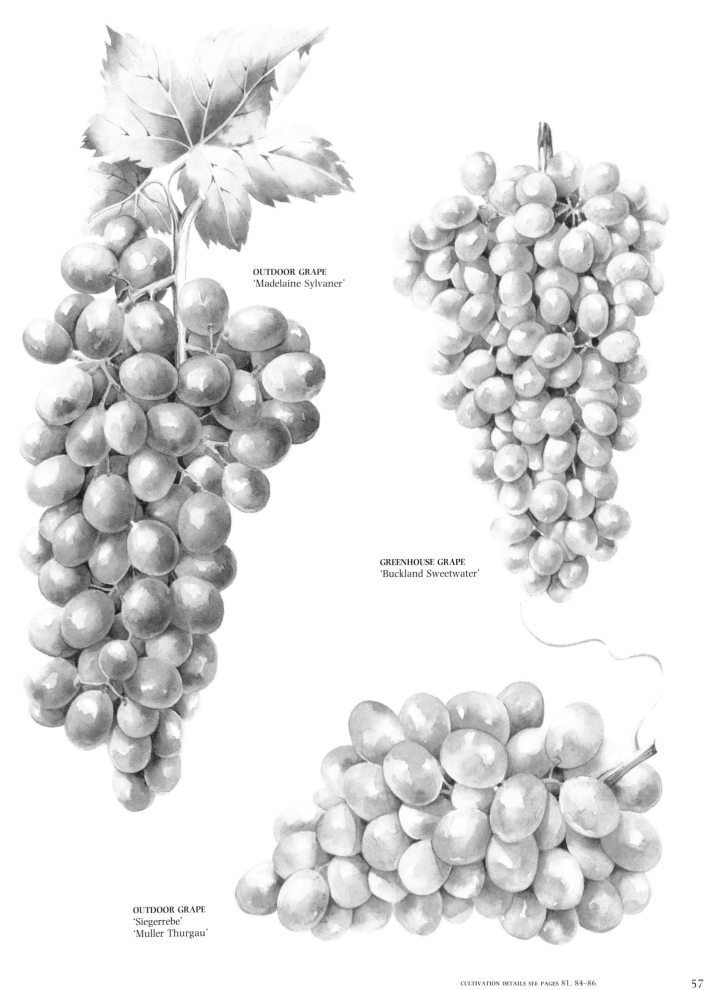

OUTDOOR GRAPE
'Madelaine Sylvaner'

GREENHOUSE GRAPE
'Buckland Sweetwater'

OUTDOOR GRAPE
'Siegerrebe'
'Muller Thurgau'

CULTIVATION DETAILS SEE PAGES 81, 84–86

APPLES Selected varieties

DESSERT APPLE
'Golden Delicious'
'Irish Peach'

DESSERT APPLE
'Cox's Orange Pippin'
'Kidd's Orange Red'
'Sunset'

COOKING APPLE
'Grenadier'

COOKING APPLE
'Bramley's Seedling'

DESSERT APPLE
'St. Edmund's Russet'
'Egremont Russet'

DESSERT APPLE
'Spartan'

CRAB APPLE

DESSERT APPLE
'Discovery'
'Worcester Pearmain'

DESSERT APPLE
'Starking'

DESSERT APPLE
'George Cave'
'Laxton's Superb'

DESSERT APPLE
'Laxton's Fortune'
'Ellison's Orange'
'Merton Knave'

CULTIVATION DETAILS SEE PAGES 90–95

PEARS, FIGS AND OTHER TREE FRUITS Selected varieties

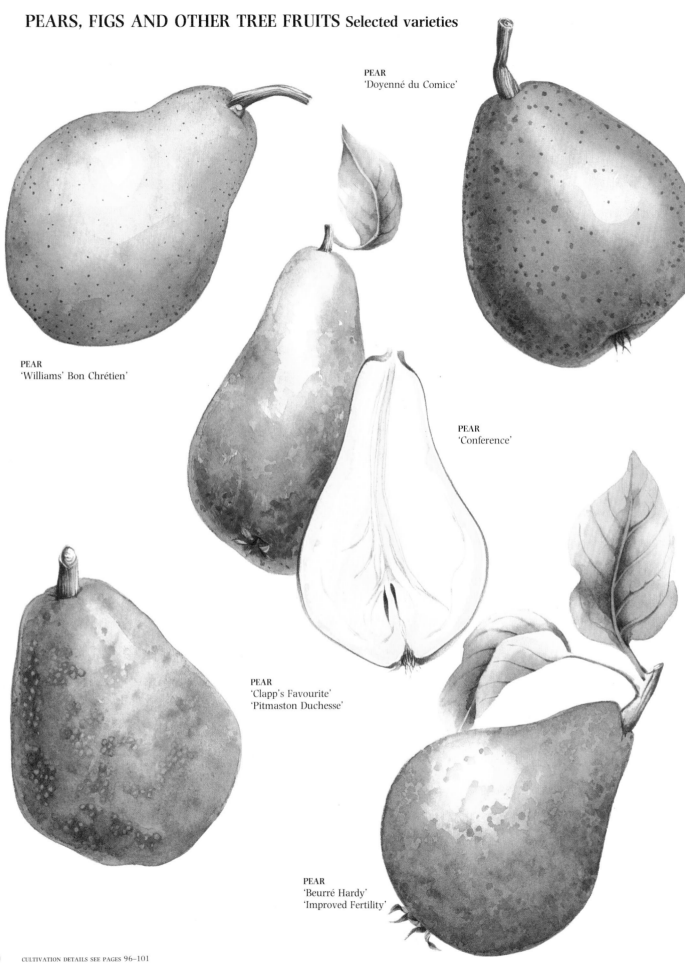

PEAR
'Doyenné du Comice'

PEAR
'Williams' Bon Chrétien'

PEAR
'Conference'

PEAR
'Clapp's Favourite'
'Pitmaston Duchesse'

PEAR
'Beurré Hardy'
'Improved Fertility'

CULTIVATION DETAILS SEE PAGES 96–101

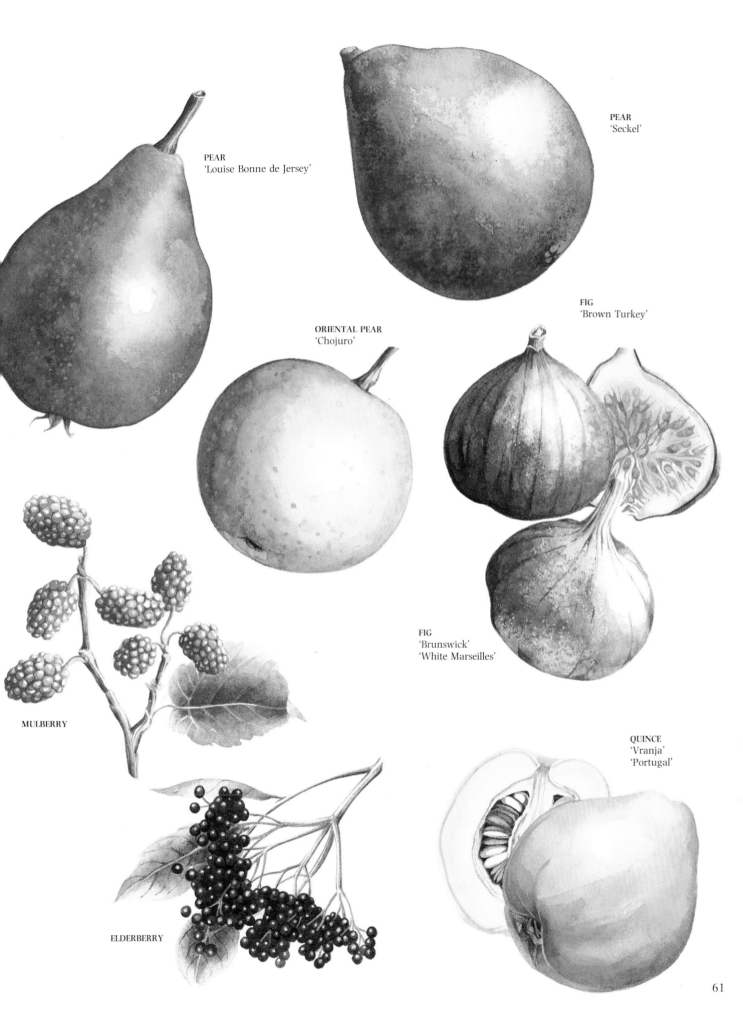

PEAR
'Seckel'

PEAR
'Louise Bonne de Jersey'

FIG
'Brown Turkey'

ORIENTAL PEAR
'Chojuro'

FIG
'Brunswick'
'White Marseilles'

MULBERRY

QUINCE
'Vranja'
'Portugal'

ELDERBERRY

STONE FRUITS Selected varieties

PLUM
'Victoria'

PLUM
'Warwickshire Drooper'
'Early Laxton'

PLUM
'Kirke's Blue'

PLUM
'Marjorie's Seedling'

DAMSON
'Merryweather'
'Shropshire Damson'

PLUM
'Czar'

PLUM
'Cherry Plum'

APRICOT
'New Large Early'
'Moorpark'
'Alfred'

PLUM (GAGE)
'Oullin's Gage'
'Cambridge Gage'

PLUM (GAGE)
'Greengage'

PEACH
'Rochester'
'Red Haven'

NECTARINE
'John Rivers'
'Lord Napier'

PEACH
'Duke of York'
'Royal George'

PEACH
'Amsden June'

CULTIVATION DETAILS SEE PAGES 102–106

CHERRIES Selected varieties

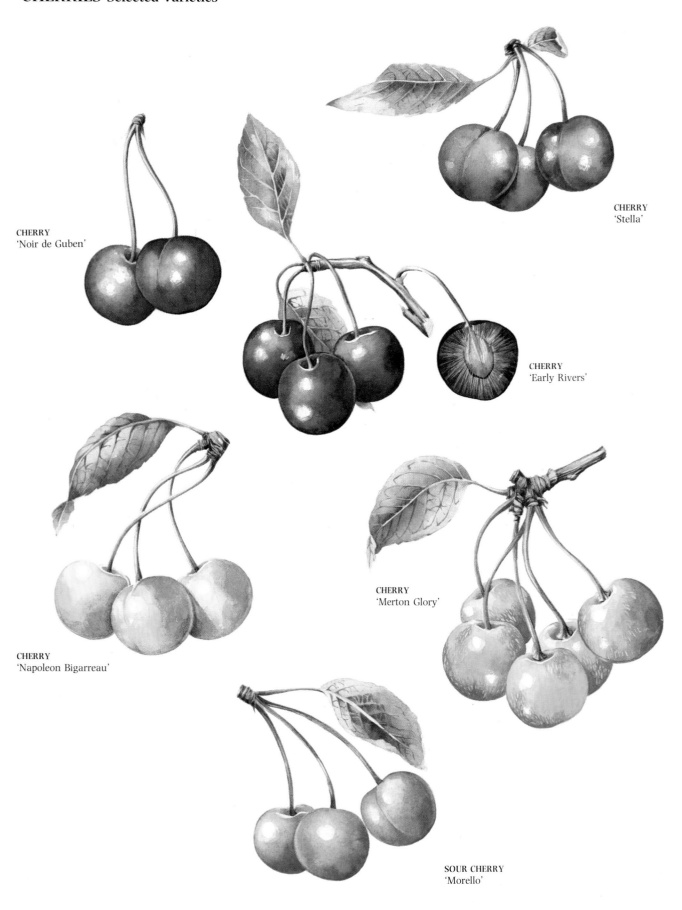

CHERRY
'Stella'

CHERRY
'Noir de Guben'

CHERRY
'Early Rivers'

CHERRY
'Merton Glory'

CHERRY
'Napoleon Bigarreau'

SOUR CHERRY
'Morello'

The
FRUIT GARDEN

One of gardening's greatest pleasures is to pick and eat home-grown, sun-ripened fruit. Apart from the satisfaction successful cultivation brings, the taste of garden-grown fruit is vastly superior to that on offer from any commercial producers. Certainly it should be sufficient to convince you that it is worth making room for fruit in your garden, however limited your space.

If you study the pages that follow you will be able to choose a selection of fruits to suit your palate and your size and style of garden. The modern trend toward growing fruit trees such as apples, pears and peaches on small or dwarfing rootstocks, which restricts their growth but not their fruitfulness, makes them eminently suitable for smaller gardens. And by training fruits into neat and conveniently-shaped cordons you can maximize your use of garden space.

Some of the newest types of fruit trees are small and tolerant enough to be suitable for container cultivation. Other good candidates for containers are strawberries, which do well in tubs, pots or barrels on balconies or patios. Both strawberries and melons will also thrive in gro-bags. The latter may need the protection of a greenhouse, however, particularly in colder areas.

A place can be found in any ornamental garden for fruit trees or bushes. Apart from their show of spring blossoms, they have appealing shapes and foliage that can be used to great effect in a landscaped area. Many, notably figs, blueberries, grapes and some varieties of apples, pears and cherries, also add to the autumn colours of the garden.

Any fruit-bearing plant that has a natural inclination to climb, or which can be trained upward or sideways, has great potential in garden design. You could try making a low hedge of gooseberries or blueberries, for example, or planting a grape vine or kiwi fruit so that it can be trained over a pergola. Instead of an ordinary, non-fruiting, flowering cherry, why not plant a *real* cherry? Or you might consider adding to your collection a fruit tree such as a mulberry, which your children and grandchildren can enjoy in years to come.

For the gardener who is already familiar with the basics of fruit gardening, this section offers some suggestions for novel or more adventurous projects. The new types of hybrid berries, such as boysenberries or tayberries, would be an interesting choice of less well-known fruit; or you could try autumn-fruiting raspberries, cranberries, alpine strawberries or oriental pears.

Finally, do not forget the potential offered by the walls of your house when planning your fruit garden. They not only provide a means of support for training fruit trees, but also give valuable shelter to more tender fruits such as peaches, apricots and nectarines.

Soft fruits are produced either on canes, such as raspberries, blackberries and other hybrid fruits, or on bushes, such as currants, gooseberries and blueberries; strawberries are produced on low-growing individual plants.

On average, soft fruits provide rather better value for space than tree fruits. They bear a worthwhile crop more quickly after planting and there is a better chance of consistently good yields. Soft fruits are also easy to grow and their pruning is more straightforward than for some tree fruits. These broad generalizations, to which there are inevitably a few exceptions, suggest that soft fruits are well able to earn their keep in a small garden.

Compared with tree fruits, soft fruits do need more protection, however. Some soft fruit crops – notably strawberries and raspberries – may be devastated by birds unless they are covered by netting.

WHERE TO GROW SOFT FRUITS

A sunny, sheltered site is best for soft fruits. Avoid planting them under trees or in a frost pocket. If planted alongside vegetables, position fruit bushes and canes where they will not shade low-growing crops. Raspberries, in particular, cast considerable shade during late winter and spring. If possible, plant the rows to run north and south, so that the fruits on each side receive an equal amount of sun. If you are planting on a slope, plant them in line with it – that is, up and down the slope, not across it.

Shelter is a considerable advantage, both for the growth of the plants and to assist pollinating insects. A hedge or a purpose-made plastic windbreak is best; both of these filter the wind without causing eddies or backdraughts.

Any well-drained, averagely fertile soil is suitable. Most soft fruits need a pH of about 6–6.5, the exceptions being blueberries and cranberries. These require a moisture-holding, acid soil with a pH as low as 4.5.

WHAT TO GROW?

Provided you have a freezer, there is every incentive to grow more of your favourite soft fruits than can be eaten fresh. Many freeze extremely well, though some are better than others; one major exception is strawberries, which become mushy when thawed, though they are excellent frozen as a purée.

It makes sense to grow the fruits you most enjoy eating, and which give a good return for the space if that is at a premium. Gooseberries and all three kinds of currant are among the most prolific soft fruits, with yields of 3.5–4.5kg (8–10lb) per bush. A successful blackberry may double these amounts, but it occupies rather a lot of space and needs training.

If you want to grow something more unusual, most hybrid berries give good returns, with perhaps 5kg (12lb) per bush; examples include loganberries, tayberries and boysenberries. Maincrop raspberries should yield up to 1kg (2lb) per plant. With 50cm (1½ft) between plants, a couple of 3.5m (12ft) rows will yield over 17kg (30lb) of delicious fruits.

When planting your soft fruit plot, study the spacings advised for each type and also consider how large an area you are prepared to cover with a fruit cage or netting. Raspberries and strawberries are the most vulnerable to bird damage. The former need a full-height cage, with standing headroom, but a structure just clearing the tops of strawberries will suffice.

Total losses from birds appear to remain the same whether few or many bushes are grown. Some gardeners prefer to take account of this by planting a few extra canes or bushes for the neighbouring blackbirds. This might be a rather extreme measure for strawberries, however.

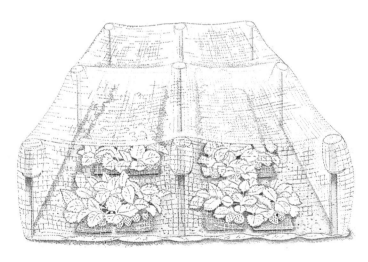

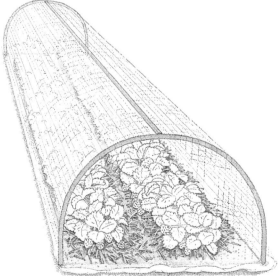

To protect strawberries, low-level support is easily provided by hammering in short stakes at intervals, their tops about 45cm (1½ft) clear of the soil. Place an inverted jam jar over each, then cover with small-mesh plastic netting. Draw the netting clear from one side before picking; replace it afterwards and secure it to the ground with bricks.

As an alternative (right), support for the netting can take the form of wire hoops.

BUYING CANES AND BUSHES

It is most important to ensure that the canes and bushes you buy are not infected with any of the virus diseases associated with soft fruits. These are widespread, incurable and have a serious effect on both growth and cropping.

Infected canes and bushes are therfore simply not worth growing. If you are buying new plants, deal only with well-established nurseries and, if such a scheme exists for the particular fruit you are buying, insist on stock officially certified as healthy and true to type. Such plants should crop satisfactorily for a number of years before they gradually succumb to virus infections. Raspberry canes, for example, can be expected to last in good health for about eight to nine years.

For this reason it is unwise to accept gifts of soft fruit plants or cuttings from friends or neighbours, as they may well be virus-infected. The same applies to old, neglected bushes and canes in your own garden. Dig them out, buy new stock and plant in fresh ground.

Soft fruits can be purchased as bare-rooted or container-grown plants. The main advantage of the latter, which are more expensive, is that they can be planted at any time of year, provided the soil is neither frozen nor waterlogged.

SOIL PREPARATION

Overall, check that there is an adequate depth of soil, and remember that the root systems of most soft fruit are more extensive that those of vegetables. In particular, make sure that there is not a layer of stone or compressed soil beneath the topsoil. Double dig the ground if there is, removing any pieces of rock.

Dig or cultivate the site well in advance of planting, adding a dressing of well-rotted organic material. Other, more particular needs are outlined with the growing instructions for each type of fruit, starting on the following page.

PLANTING

Late autumn or early winter are the best times to plant bare-rooted canes and bushes, though mild weather and suitable soil conditions may make this possible throughout the winter. Plant container-grown bushes at any time when the soil is neither frozen nor waterlogged.

Plant bare-rooted bushes in a hole broad enough to take the spread-out roots and of a depth that brings the soil mark on the stem level with the surrounding ground. Cut back any damaged roots, then cover the remainder with a mixture of soil and either peat or a proprietary planting mixture. Shake the stem to settle the mixture around the roots, firm the covering gently with your feet, then replace the remaining soil mix and firm again.

Plant container-grown bushes by taking out a hole a little larger than the rootball and filling in the space with a blend of soil and planting mixture.

AFTER-CARE

Make sure that the soil around summer-planted bushes and strawberry runners remains moist. Water thoroughly if a check made a short way below ground level suggests that the soil is drying out. Mature bushes also require watering during prolonged dry spells, especially on light soil. Hoe regularly to prevent weeds becoming established. Avoid deep hoeing around shallow-rooted plants, such as raspberries.

Keep a watchful eye for pests and diseases so that appropriate action can be taken in good time, before the trouble becomes too firmly established.

A full-height fruit cage provides the most effective form of protection for soft fruits. To avoid damage to the structure from a heavy fall of snow, replace the small-mesh roof netting with 10cm (4in) mesh for the winter.

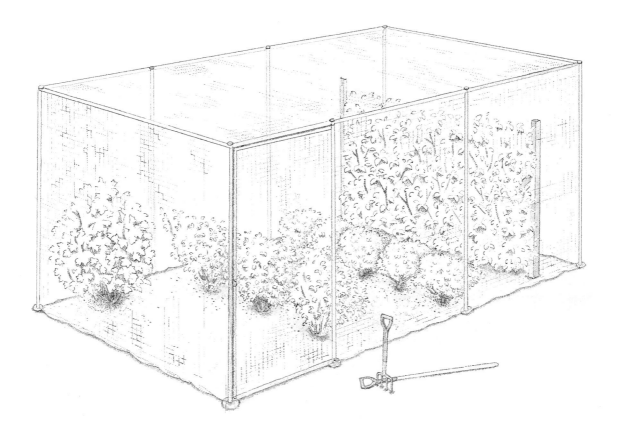

FREEZING FRUITS, pages 234–235

Rapid returns and delectable flavour are two sound reasons for growing strawberries (*Fragaria* sp.). Planted in high summer, the first crop will be ready less than a year later. They are also easy to grow, in beds or containers, while the berries are suitable for preserves as well as for eating fresh.

There are three types. The first two are grown from purchased plants which can remain in place for several years. The third is grown from seed.

Single crop strawberries produce their fruits over a two- to three-week period during early or midsummer. There are many varieties, the main difference being in size, flavour and precise time of ripening.

Perpetual varieties bear successive flushes of smaller fruit over a longer period between summer and autumn. Their flavour may not be quite up to the best of the single croppers and they are less hardy.

Alpine strawberries (*Fragaria vesca*), with tiny berries, are both delicious and decorative; they have a unique fragrance and taste. Raised annually from seed, they crop during the second half of summer. Their compact growth makes them particularly suitable for growing in containers or as an edging to flower borders. The small size of the fruits, produced in modest quantities over an extended period, means that at least 25 plants are needed to ensure a worthwhile picking at any one time.

Plant ordinary strawberries in well-drained but moisture-retentive soil, in an open position. They do best in slightly acid ground containing plenty of organic matter.

If you have a low-lying garden which is subject to late spring frosts, be prepared to cover the plants to protect the blossom. The other essential precaution, wherever you live, is to buy plants that are certified free from virus disease. These will give good results for four or five years; then you should buy new plants and grow them on a fresh site.

ALPINE STRAWBERRIES
Either buy the plants in spring, or sow the seeds under glass in autumn, over-wintering the pricked-out seedlings in an unheated greenhouse or frame. Plant out in a rich soil in a semi-shaded position in spring, spacing them about 30cm (1ft) apart in each direction.

Fruiting is from midsummer until late autumn. Pick regularly and keep the soil moist, to encourage continued cropping.

MAKING A START
Plant single-crop varieties between the middle of summer and the first days of autumn. Being slightly less hardy, perpetual varieties need to be planted by late summer to help them become well established before winter. Spring planting is possible, too, but in the case of single croppers you should nip off the flowers rather than try to harvest a crop during the first season, to ensure strong plants. Perpetual varieties planted in spring will crop the following autumn; remove the first flowers.

Dig the new strawberry bed well before planting so that it has time to settle, mixing in a dressing of rotted manure or compost. Scatter and rake in general fertilizer at 70g per sq m (2oz per sq yd) just before planting.

Plants can be bought either in pots or bare-rooted. Both are satisfactory, but both require that the soil be kept damp while new roots form. Set the plants 40cm (15in) apart in rows 75cm (2½ft) apart. For bare-rooted runners use a trowel to form a hole a little deeper than the roots, with a mound in the centre.

For pot-grown strawberries scoop out a hole large enough to take the soilball without breaking it or disturbing the roots. Water the plants in.

CARE OF THE CROP
For an early crop cover established or autumn-planted strawberries with cloches from later winter onward, spacing or partially opening the covers once pollinating insects are flying.

Keep the soil moistened around recently-planted strawberries. During dry weather watering may also be needed from about the time the fruits start to swell. Well-developed fruits are also a signal to tuck straw under the plants to support the berries clear of the soil.

You will have to decide whether to maintain the plants as individuals, removing all runners except any needed for propagation, or to develop a 'matted row' by allowing runners to root between plants. The latter yields a heavier crop but the berries will be smaller.

PROTECTING AND HARVESTING
Unless you are growing them in a permanent fruit cage, protect strawberries from birds soon after strawing the plants. Netting laid directly over the plants is better than nothing but the birds will peck through it and you will lose some fruits. Netting is more effective, and is easier to lift for picking, if it is supported clear of the plants.

As an alternative to a metal or wooden frame, lay the netting over inverted jam jars supported by short stakes. Pin one side of the netting to the ground with metal or wooden pegs, pulling the other side taut and holding it down with stones or bricks.

Given warm weather, strawberries ripen rapidly once the fruits have grown to full size. Watch carefully for the first signs of colour, subsequently checking the plants at least daily. Remove the fruit by pinching the stalk between forefinger and thumbnail. Avoid handling the berries as far as possible, since they bruise easily.

As soon as the last berries have been picked, use a pair of shears to cut off all the mature foliage close to the crown of single crop plants. Remove the old leaves from perpetual strawberries, leaving the new ones. Add the foliage and the straw to the compost heap. Hoe between the plants and rows, first digging out any perennial weeds, and cut off any surplus runners.

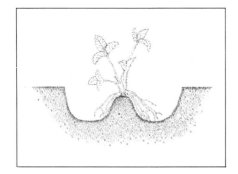

For bare-rooted strawberry plants, dig a hole wide enough for the roots to be spread out, with a mound in the centre to raise the crown level with the surrounding soil. Place the crown of the plant on the mound, level with the surface, with the roots spread outward and downward. Replace the soil and firm carefully.

Lay straw, black plastic sheeting or purpose-made strawberry mats under the plants when the fruits are quite well developed, to prevent them coming into contact with the soil. Sprinkle slug pellets under the plants first.

PROPAGATION

Use only vigorous, healthy-looking plants, since any virus infection present will be passed on. The runners used for the purpose are the wiry shoots (stolons), each bearing plantlets, that grow from the parent plant.

During early summer, select up to four strong runners on each plant. Bury an 8cm (3in) compost-filled pot in the soil beneath each tuft of young growth, securing this to the compost with a wire pin.

Nip off the far side of each runner but leave the plantlets attached to the parent for between one and two months; keep the compost moist.

It is a good idea to propagate some strawberry plants annually, replacing your oldest stock each time. The maximum age of strawberry plants is three to four years.

PESTS AND DISEASES

The pests most likely to occur are aphids, glasshouse red spider mite, strawberry beetle, strawberry mite, slugs, snails and birds.

Common disorders include grey mould, powdery mildew and virus diseases.

RECOMMENDED VARIETIES

Perpetual varieties
'Aromel' Noted for its fine flavour.
'Ostara' High-yielding, but subject to mildew.

Single-crop varieties
'Cambridge Favourite' One of the most reliable and heavy-cropping varieties.
'Cambridge Vigour' Especially well-flavoured during its first two years.
'Gorella' Early but prone to mildew.

'Jamil' Reliable cropper. Large, juicy fruits.
'Pantagruella' Very early; ideal for cloches. Compact habit allows close planting.
'Red Gauntlet' May have second crop. Average flavour. Resists mould and mildew.
'Royal Sovereign' Excellent flavour. Moderate cropper. Prone to virus.
'Tantallon' Vigorous and heavy-yielding. Good flavour. Disease-resistant.
'Totem' Possibly the best for freezing.

Alpine varieties
'Alexandria' Bushy plants with no runners. Sweet and juicy.
'Baron Solemacher' Vigorous growth. Crimson, aromatic fruits.
'Delicious' Runnerless; richly-flavoured.
'Yellow Wonder' Runnerless, with large yellow berries.

PROPAGATING

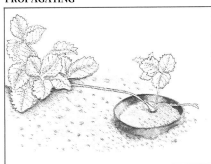

1 Sink pots of compost into the soil close to mature plants. Use bent wires to secure the first embryo plant on each runner to the compost. Cut off the continuation of the runner, but leave intact the piece joining the new plant to the parent plant. Keep the compost moist while roots form.

2 Between four and eight weeks later, when roots will have formed, sever the runner joining new and mature plants. Plant out the new strawberry in its permanent position after a few more days.

STRAWBERRIES IN CONTAINERS

Practical as well as decorative reasons give strawberries a distinct advantage as container plants. Supported clear of the ground, the fruit keeps clean and is at little risk from slugs. Picking is simple, as is protecting the berries from birds by draping netting over the top.

Barrels and earthenware strawberry pots, both with planting holes in their sides, are widely used for growing strawberries on patios or where space is restricted. If converting your own barrel, make the holes about 5cm (2in) in diameter and allow about 22cm (9in) between holes.

Other suitable containers include hanging baskets, large pots and troughs, and the tower-like plastic containers that provide a succession of planting pockets. Apart from more frequent hand watering and the absence of a need for strawing, after-care is much the same as for strawberries grown in the ground.

SOWING SEEDS, pages 36–39
STRAWBERRIES, page 49

GROWING SOFT FRUITS, pages 66–67
PESTS AND DISEASES, pages 108–111

Cultivated blackberries (*Rubus fruticosus*) bear larger, plumper, sweeter fruits than those gathered from the hedgerows. When successfully grown, a yield of 4.5–9kg (10–20lb) per plant can be expected and may even be exceeded.

Blackberries can be grown in all areas, though in exposed districts, subject to early frost in autumn, it makes sense to avoid the later-fruiting varieties. There are several types that ripen not long after midsummer. One or two varieties are available as certified virus-free stock and these are the best choice if they are suitable in other respects. Chief among these are 'Ashton Cross' and 'Bedford Giant'.

Strong, well-strained wires are needed for training blackberries since they are vigorous plants which grow on long, trailing canes. Many have vicious thorns, although there are also some thornless varieties. Blackberries can be trained against a wall or fence as well as in the open; thornless varieties lend themselves to training over an arch. Summer protection from birds will ensure that a heavier crop is harvested, although birds are less attracted to blackberries and loganberries than to raspberries. There may be no need to net if you are prepared to lose a few fruits.

From autumn onward the plants are sold bare-rooted or, at most times of year, in plastic containers. There is little to choose between these two forms, except that container-grown plants generally cost more.

MAKING A START
Plant bare-rooted plants in autumn or early winter, if possible, but otherwise plants can be put in at any time until spring when soil and weather conditions allow. Container-grown plants may go in at any time, subject to the weather.

Really taut wires are required to restrain and secure the sturdy stems of blackberries. If planting in the open, this means rigid end posts, so place a brick at the foot of each bracing strut to prevent the post being drawn into the ground. For the posts, use timber 8cm (3in) square, sunk 60cm (2ft) into the ground. If more than one plant is to be grown, hammer in 5cm (2in) stakes every 3m (10ft).

Strain four 10-gauge supporting wires between the braced posts, setting them 90cm (3ft), 1.2m (4ft), 1.5m (5ft) and 1.8m

TRAINING
There are several ways of arranging the stems of blackberries, including the fan, roping and weaving methods, with the fan method giving the heaviest yields.

In conventional fan training the fruiting canes are trained left and right along the wires, leaving the centre open for the new canes, which should be loosely bunched together and tied to the wires as they grow. Once the old canes are cut down (see Pruning, below), the new canes are securely tied, fanwise, to the wires, again leaving the centre empty.

A variation on this method, which makes for easier pruning and fruit picking, is to secure the new growths to the wires on one side of the plant only, keeping them separate from the year-old shoots that are bearing fruit. The plant thus fruits on either side of the rootstock alternately. Apart from making for easier handling, this method of training reduces the risk of infection spreading from the older shoots to the young ones.

To obtain the heaviest yields, train the shoots to the wires in the pattern of half a fan, securing them with soft string at each crossing point. Retain enough canes to allow a space of about 10cm (4in) between them at the point where they are fastened to the top wire.

The alternative method, called roping, is to train three or four canes up and then horizontally along each wire. This also allows for easy pruning and harvesting, but the yields will be lighter.

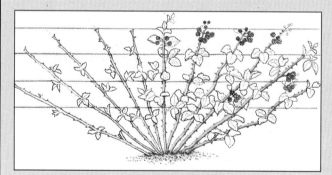

Fan training of blackberries, loganberries and other hybrid berries requires a lot of tying-in but gives a heavy crop of fruit. For easier pruning and management, the canes that grow in consecutive years are best trained to alternate sides.

Here, the new canes have been tied in on the left; the year-old, fruited canes are on the right. The canes are tied with soft string to the tightly-strained wires at each point where they cross.

In roping, an alternative method of training, three or four canes are tied horizontally to each wire. This is simple and fairly quick to do but yields are somewhat lower. As with fan training, the easiest means of separating year-old canes from new ones is to train them to alternate sides each year. Once the fruited canes have been cut out, that side will remain empty until the following spring.

(6ft) above the ground. If you are attaching the wires to vine eyes on a wall or fence, keep to the same spacings.

Dig in plenty of organic matter around each planting position; take care that no perennial weeds are left, especially those with creeping roots. Space the plants of most varieties about 3.7m (12ft) apart. One exception is 'Oregon Thornless', for which 1.8m (6ft) is sufficient; at the other extreme, the very vigorous 'Himalaya Giant' needs 4.5m (15ft) between plants.

Cut back bare-rooted plants to a bud 25–30cm (9–12in) from the base. Dig a hole large enough to take the spread-out roots, adding some peat or a proprietary planting mixture to the soil when replacing it. The soil should just cover the roots of the plant. Leave the stems of container-grown plants untrimmed, but add similar material round the rootball, digging a hole large enough to allow for this.

CARE OF THE CROP
During the first spring rake in a handful of general fertilizer around each plant; increase the area in subsequent years and distribute about 70g per sq m (2oz per sq yd).

As the weather warms up, water generously if the soil start to dry out, especially as the fruits start to develop but before they ripen.

PRUNING
Cut out the old canes immediately after fruiting, leaving the wires on this side of the plant bare. You will need to wear leather gloves for the thorned varieties of blackberry. Burn the old canes; do not try to compost them.

Keep as many healthy new canes as possible, in case the frost damages some unripe new canes. You can always remove any surplus canes once the winter is over, if they are all unscathed. Any dead cane tips can be cut back to the first live bud at the end of winter.

HARVESTING
Pick when the berries are black in colour and ripe; pick carefully to avoid squashing the ripest ones, and if possible only when the weather is dry. The core usually comes away with the fruit.

Blackberries can generally be picked over a period of several weeks.

PROPAGATION
Soon after midsummer, peg the tips of healthy shoots to the ground. The following spring, when they will have rooted, cut them free just above a bud, and replant into their permanent positions.

PROPAGATING
1 Before attempting tip-layering, satisfy yourself that the plant is healthy. The first step, shown here, is to bury the tip of a shoot about 15cm (6in) deep. replace the soil and firm it with your foot. If the shoot is springy, secure it to the ground with a length of wire bent to the shape of a hair-pin.

2 By the following spring the tip will have rooted. Sever the original stem about 30cm (1ft) from the ground and either move the new plant to its permanent site or else grow it on in a nursery bed before planting out a year later. If preferred, tips may be layered into pots of compost sunk into the ground.

PESTS AND DISEASES
Raspberry beetles are the chief pest. Cane spot, crown gall, grey mould and rust are possible troubles.

RECOMMENDED VARIETIES
'Ashton Cross' Vigorous, thorny plants bearing heavy crops of rather acid, medium-sized berries.
'Bedford Giant' Early, vigorous, prickly with clusters of large, sweet berries.
'Himalaya Giant' Extremely vigorous and thorny. Good crops of rather acid fruit.
'Merton Thornless' Compact habit, large fruits, good flavour. Thornless stems.
'Oregon Thornless' Unusual, parsley-like foliage. Sweet berries, crops well, fairly late.

It is said that fruit growers have to thank Judge J.H. Logan of Santa Cruz, California, for spotting this chance blackberry/raspberry cross in his garden more than a century ago. Truth or myth, loganberries are a distinctive fruit in their own right, being less rampant than blackberries and having larger fruits than either parent.

The flavour of loganberries is on the acid side and perhaps not to everyone's taste when eaten fresh. They freeze and cook well, however.

There are both thorny and thornless strains, but even the former lack the blackberry's lethal spikes. The fruits ripen during the second half of summer on stems that developed during the previous season.

Wire supports are needed, placed either in the open or attached with vine eyes to a wall. A thornless loganberry may also be trained over an archway.

Loganberries need a slightly acid (pH 6), moisture-retentive soil; medium to heavy loams are ideal. On light, sandy ground it is essential to add plenty of organic matter.

Virus-free stocks are generally available but may have to be sought after. These are sold under the code letters LY 59 (thorny) and LY 654 (thornless); the latter bears a lighter crop.

MAKING A START
Planting, together with the system of supporting wires, is the same as for blackberries (opposite), except for the spacing. Being somewhat less vigorous, loganberries do not need as much growing room as blackberries. The plants should be spaced about 2.5–3m (8–10ft) apart.

CARE OF THE CROP
Feeding and watering are the same as for blackberries, opposite.

TRAINING AND PRUNING
The method is the same as for blackberries. That is, train young shoots of the current year to one side only, keeping them separate from the year-old canes that are bearing fruit.

PROPAGATION
See blackberries, opposite.

PESTS AND DISEASES
Aphids and raspberry beetles may prove troublesome.

Possible ailments include cane spot, crown gall, grey mould and spur blight.

A number of hybrid berries have been brought into cultivation as a result of crossing various *Rubus* species, notably the raspberry (*Rubus idaeus*) and blackberry (*Rubus fruticosus*). Loganberries (see p.73) are the best-known and the most widely-grown of these, chiefly because they have been around for longer. But home food-growers are in a unique position to try the comparatively new fruits, such as the tayberry and marionberry. These berries are seldom found in the shops, since market growers prefer to concentrate on familiar fruits for which there is a known demand.

It would be unwise to grow hybrid berries in abundance, at the expense of their parent blackberries and raspberries, until you have tried them. But, out of personal interest, and the chance to enjoy an intriguing change of flavour, it is well worth growing one or two, if space permits.

Certain hybrid berries, such as the tayberry, are now reasonably well known and established. But others have failed to catch on, despite the enthusiastic claims of nurserymen. You might experience local difficulty in obtaining some of those described.

Though most hybrid berries owe part of their parentage to the raspberry, their cultivation and training are generally as for blackberries (see p.72). Nearly all are less vigorous than blackberries, however, and need closer planting, but this does make them more suitable for the small garden.

Other, rarer berries, such as the Japanese wineberry and the dewberry, are in fact cultivated forms of true species of *Rubus* in themselves. They are included here since there is an increasing interest in their domestic cultivation.

TAYBERRY

The tayberry is probably the best hybrid resulting from a blackberry/raspberry cross. The fruits are larger than loganberries and a deeper purple colour. They are firm and juicy, with a delicious sweet flavour. They freeze well and are produced in abundance.

Tayberries are moderately prickly and of medium vigour. Leave a space of 2.4m (8ft) between plants, otherwise treat them just like blackberries or loganberries. Certified virus-free stock is available from specialist fruit nurseries.

BOYSENBERRY

There are both thorny and thornless forms of this hybrid (*Rubus ursinus* 'Boysen'), which carries distinctively flavoured fruits shaped like raspberries but longer. The berries are dark red ripening to purplish-black and may have a dusty bloom. A yield of up to 4.5kg (10lb) can be expected from each plant.

A particular feature of the boysenberry is its resistance to drought, so it could be a good choice for light soils. It is moderately vigorous, and needs a planting distance of 2.4m (8ft).

MARIONBERRY

Though they look like blackberries, the large, juicy fruits of this relatively new hybrid resemble succulent loganberries in flavour. They are produced over an exceptionally long period – two months or more – from midsummer onward.

The plants are vigorous and thorny and need a spacing of about 3.6m (12ft) between them.

SUNBERRY

With its vigorous habit and spiny shoots, this hybrid has some drawbacks. But its great asset is the excellent flavour of the dark red loganberrylike fruits. It crops during the second half of summer, and requires a generous planting distance of 4.5m (15ft).

TUMMELBERRY

In many ways similar to the tayberry, which is one of its parents, this hybrid is somewhat hardier and therefore better suited to cold districts. The canes are long and covered in hairs, and it is a reasonably heavy cropper; the fruits are sharply flavoured.

Allow 2.4m (8ft) between plants.

JAPANESE WINEBERRY

The Japanese wineberry (*Rubus phoenicolasius*) is one of the most decorative and unusual plants for the food garden. Its fruits are an attractive golden-yellow ripening to light red, and the long, arching stems are covered with soft, striking red bristles, making quite a display in winter. It can be grown as an ornamental climber on a fence or trellis with little trouble.

The berries are small and seedy, but they are sweet, juicy and refreshing, with a mild flavour resembling that of grapes. The aromatic fruits all ripen at once; they make successful, delicate-flavoured jams and jellies.

Since it is not especially vigorous, a 1.8m (6ft) planting distance is sufficient.

DEWBERRY

Rather like a slender-growing blackberry, the dewberry (*Rubus caesius*) has well-flavoured fruits. The small berries are not shiny but have a white bloom over them.

Though the dewberry produces only a modest crop, the fruits ripen ahead of those of the blackberry. The stems trail over the ground, providing a form of ground cover, if the plant is not trained on wires.

WORCESTERBERRIES

The Worcesterberry (*Ribes divaricatum*) resembles a vigorous gooseberry, with smaller, purple fruits. It might appear to be a cross between a gooseberry and a blackcurrant, but it is in fact a species of currant. The shoots are thorny, the purple berries are well-flavoured and used mainly for cooking and jam-making. Planting and care are the same as for gooseberries (see pp.75–6), though with a more generous spacing of 2.4m (8ft) between plants.

The Worcesterberry's great virtue is its immunity to American gooseberry mildew. It is also a hardy and prolific cropper. However, its size tends to rule it out for very small gardens.

SOFT FRUITS/BERRIES, pages 50–51
BLACKBERRIES, page 72
PESTS AND DISEASES, pages 108–111
FREEZING FRUITS, pages 234–235

Gooseberries (*Ribes grossularia uva-crispa*) deserve to be more popular than they are, for they are among the easiest of fruits to grow. Though widely used for cooked dishes and jam-making, some varieties, such as 'Leveller' and 'Whinham's Industry', make tasty dessert fruits when fully ripened, seldom available in shops.

Gooseberries are long-lived plants, lasting for 20 years or more, and are not generally troubled by virus infections. Even so, certified virus-free stock is available for one or two varieties.

The immature berries of all gooseberry varieties are green but they ripen to an assortment of shades. Some remain green while others turn red, yellow or greenish-white; colour is an indication of ripeness. The fruits ripen, depending on the variety, between late spring and the second half of summer. A mature bush, if well cared for, may give a harvest of up to 4.5kg (10lb).

Any well-drained, fertile soil is suitable for growing gooseberries. If your soil is sandy, be sure to dig in ample moisture-holding organic material. The site can be in full sun or open shade, though it should not be under an overhanging tree. The chief precaution is to avoid a frost pocket, where the early spring flowers could be damaged.

GOOSEBERRY FORMS
The gooseberry plants may be grown as bushes, with a number of branches emerging above a short stem, or as upright cordons with one, two or three stems. The chief advantage of cordons is the extra large size of the berries they produce, and the limited amount of space they take up in the food garden. Pruning is reasonably straightforward in each case.

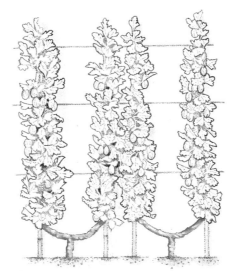

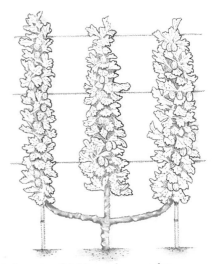

Gooseberry cordons with two stems.

A three-stem (triple) gooseberry cordon.

MAKING A START
Plant bare-rooted gooseberries during autumn or winter, and container-grown specimens at any season, when soil and weather conditions allow.

Prepare the soil well in advance by digging in bulky organic material. In addition, rake in a dressing of organic fertilizer at 70g per sq m (2oz per sq yd) around each position at planting time.

Space bushes 1.5m (5ft) apart; for cordons, see below.

Most gooseberries are sold when two years old. Form the planting hole with a spade, and mix peat, rotted compost or a proprietary planting mixture with the soil, then replace it and firm it with your feet. Plant bushes so that the soil comes to the same level as it did in the nursery, or just above; the original soil mark should be clearly visible.

After planting a bush, cut back the new growth on each shoot to a bud about half way along its length. Your eventual aim is to create a goblet-shaped bush with an open centre, so choose buds (from which fresh shoots will develop) that are well placed to make this possible. This means that they will be on the upper surface of drooping branches or on the outside of upright growths.

A total of about eight branches will be needed to form the mature bush; cut out other shoots just above their lowest bud.

TRAINING CORDONS
Cordons may be grown in the open, with the wires tightly strained between posts (see p.70), or fastened with vine eyes to a fence (see p.84). Allow 45cm (1½ft) between singles. 60cm (2ft) between doubles, 90cm (3ft) between triples.

After planting, select the number of shoots needed to form the stems (one, two or three), then cut away any others that are lower than 10–13cm (4–5in).

Once they begin to grow, support each stem of a cordon with a bamboo cane; secure these to wires 60cm (2ft) and 1.2m (4ft) above the ground. Fasten the canes for a double cordon 15cm (6in) on either side of the main stem. For a triple cordon, secure one cane in line with the main stem, the others 30cm (1ft) away.

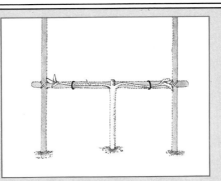

1 To form a double cordon (two stems), prune the stem at planting time to 20cm (8in) above the ground. Allow a bud to develop near the top on each side of the stem, rubbing out those beneath, and train the resultant shoots to the horizontal cane on each side.

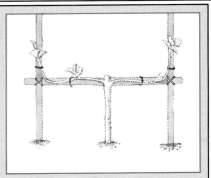

2 When the shoots reach the upright canes, fastened 15cm (6in) on each side of the main stem, train them vertically. A triple cordon is formed by retaining three buds on the main stem, then training the shoot that grows from the top bud to a cane fastened centrally.

CARE OF THE CROP

Because they are shallow-rooted, goose-berries may be harmed by careless hoeing. A better means of controlling weeds is to keep the soil mulched throughout the year, especially from spring onward.

Before mulching in the spring, scatter a balanced general fertilizer over the surface at 70g per sq m (2oz per sq yd), with an added 15–20g (½oz) of sulphate of potash. Water liberally if a dry spell concides with development of the berries.

Pull off any suckers that emerge from the soil near the bushes. In winter, firm in with your foot any plants loosened by frost.

Protection from birds is needed, but less so at harvest time than during the winter, when finches may strip off the fruit buds. Use netting or cotton threads if you are not growing your gooseberries in a fruit cage.

HARVESTING

Start picking the berries before they are fully developed, taking them at intervals from along the branches. These smaller berries are suitable for cooking or freezing, and the extended picking period allows those that are left to develop more fully.

Continue to pick for cooking until relatively few, well-spaced berries remain. Leave these until they become soft and coloured, ready for eating as dessert fruits, if they are of suitable varieties.

PRUNING

Continue to prune bushes both winter and summer, with an eye to the eventual shape needed. Early spring is the best time for winter pruning. Cut back by about half the new growth of branch leaders, and reduce the new growths of laterals to about 8cm (3in). Toward mid-summer, cut back all laterals to about the fifth leaf from the base.

In later years, the current season's laterals can be cut back to a bud within 2cm (1in) of the main branch, and strong new growths from the base can be allowed to replace congested, ageing branches from the centre of the bush.

Cordons are pruned a little differently, but their pruning must be done regularly each year, summer and winter, to keep their trained shape. Remove about a third of the new growth from the leading shoot and cut back laterals to three buds in early spring. Toward midsummer, cut back all new laterals to five leaves, as for bushes. Do not summer-prune the leaders until they are as tall as you want them to be: single cordons are usually grown to 1.5cm (5ft) high, double and triple to 1–1.2m (3–4ft) high.

An established gooseberry bush after it has been pruned in winter. Your major aim should be to avoid overcrowding in the centre.

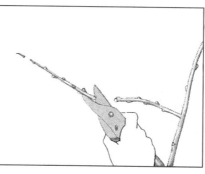

Winter pruning Cut back the leaders of main branches by about half the growth that was made during the previous year; cut just above an undamaged bud. At the same time, shorten laterals (side-growths) by up to 8cm (3in).

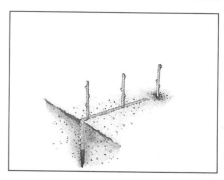

Summer pruning Between early summer and midsummer, cut back laterals – but not main shoots – to about the fifth leaf from the base. This reduces the risk of mildew and other fungus diseases.

PROPAGATION

New plants are easily raised from hardwood cuttings, taken during autumn. These will root in open ground, without protection, and be ready for planting out a year later.

Choose shoots that have grown during the current year. They should be reasonably straight, about 30cm (1ft) long, and with the wood firm and well-ripened.

Use a spade to form a broad slit about 20cm (8in) deep, placing some sharp sand in the base. Position the cuttings 15cm (6in) apart, with three buds above the soil. Press the soil back with the spade, then firm with your feet.

PESTS AND DISEASES

The most troublesome pests are capsid bugs and gooseberry sawflies.

Diseases may include American goose-berry mildew, grey mould and leaf spot.

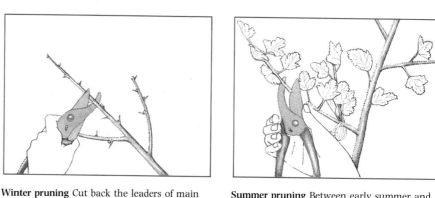

1 Remove straight, well-ripened shoots, each about 30cm (1ft) long, during the autumn. Cut off the soft tip and trim the base to just beneath a bud.

2 Form a slit and place some sharp sand in the base. Position the cuttings 15cm (6in) apart, each with three buds above the ground.

RECOMMENDED VARIETIES
'Captivator' Vigorous, almost thornless. Small red berries.
'Careless' Heavy crops of green-white fruits. An excellent all-rounder.
'Howard Lancer' Vigorous and a heavy cropper. Green fruits. Prone to mildew.
'Invicta' Very heavy crops of white fruits. Excellent culinary variety.
'Keepsake' Heavy and early crops of well-flavoured green fruits. Prone to mildew.
'Leveller' Large yellow fruits, excellent for dessert. Needs good soil.
'Whinham's Industry' A good all-rounder, with red fruits, but prone to mildew.

CAPE GOOSEBERRIES
This tender plant (*Physalis peruviana edulis*) is a decorative addition to the fruit garden. Its cherrylike fruits are enclosed in an orange-yellow, lantern-like calyx or husk. The fruits are ready to harvest when the calyces have turned papery and golden brown; the berries inside have a distinctive sweet taste, and may be eaten raw or used for making preserves. Each plant will produce up to a kilo (1–2lb) of fruit.

Cape gooseberries can be grown outdoors in a singularly warm and sheltered position, but you are more likely to obtain a satisfactory crop in a greenhouse. The plants must be raised under glass from a sowing made in gentle heat during early spring. The Cape gooseberry is grown as an annual, since it crops less heavily after the first year.

The plants respond to much the same care routines as greenhouse tomatoes (see p.168), to which they are related. Plant them 75cm (2½ft) apart outdoors or in the greenhouse border. Alternatively, plant individually in gro-bags or in 20cm (8in) pots.

Cape gooseberries will reach about 2m (6ft) and are well-branched, so you need to provide canes and netting for support. If the plants have not produced flowers by the time they are 30cm (1ft) high, pinch out their growing tips to induce branching.

Keep the plants moist while they are growing, but regulate their watering carefully later on, otherwise they will produce growth at the expense of fruit. Apply liquid fertilizer sparingly.

Red currants (*Ribes sativum*) are used principally for cooking or for making jelly. They are sometimes eaten as dessert fruits, but white currants are the favourites for this purpose. Both these fruits, which are closely related, need the same general care and pruning as gooseberries (see pp. 75–6), which is *not* the same as for blackcurrants.

Red and white currants produce their fruit buds in clusters at the base of one-year-old shoots and on short spurs on the older wood. A permanent framework of branches is therefore needed, as for gooseberries. This means that they may be grown as open, goblet-shaped bushes on a short stem, or as cordons with one, two or three stems.

Well-drained soil is essential. The bushes are hardy and may be planted in sun or partial shade, but always avoiding any frost pockets. Cordons can successfully be grown in the open or against a fence or wall. Protection from birds is needed, so use netting unless you are growing them in a fruit cage.

MAKING A START
A dressing of compost will help, though red and white currants are less 'hungry' than blackcurrants. They need potash, however, so in spring dress the site with sulphate of potash at 15g per sq m (½oz per sq yd), together with twice this amount of balanced fertilizer.

Plant bare-rooted bushes between autumn and spring – during autumn if possible – and container-grown plants at any time when soil conditions and weather allow. Leave 1.5m (5ft) between bushes. If the plants are to be grown as single-stemmed cordons space them about 40cm (15in) apart. Leave a minimum of 60cm (2ft) between double cordons and 90cm (3ft) between triples. Support the cordons with wires and canes, as for gooseberries.

CARE OF THE CROP
In late winter or spring check to see whether frost has loosened the soil and/or lifted plants. If it has, firm the earth back gently with your feet.

Each winter apply a dressing of potash in the same quantities as given at planting time. During the spring, sprinkle sulphate of ammonia over the root area at 35g per sq m (1oz per sq yd) and spread a mulch of well-rotted compost or peat over the soil surface.

Pull off any suckers that appear, but avoid regular hoeing in case you damage the roots. Water generously during prolonged dry weather.

HARVESTING
Pick the fruits in midsummer as soon as they are ripe, removing the stalks as well. Eat or freeze them as soon as possible.

PESTS AND DISEASES
Aphids, blackcurrant gall mites and capsid bugs are the most likely pests. Diseases include coral spot, grey mould and leaf spot.

RECOMMENDED VARIETIES
'Jonkheer van Tets' Early, heavy cropper. Rather vigorous.
'Laxton No. 1' Early, with good crop of large red berries. Good all-round choice.
'Red Lake' Heavy cropper. Fairly vigorous.
'Rondom' Produces good crops (red); late.
'White Dutch' Mid-season golden fruits.
'White Versailles' Early, well-flavoured sweet berries.

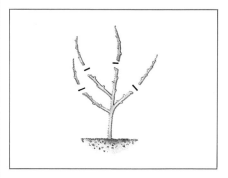

PRUNING
Prune red and white currant bushes immediately after planting. This one-year-old plant has each of its shoots cut back to four buds. New shoots will break at this point.

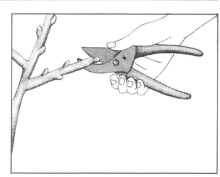

Prune exactly as for gooseberries: trim the shoots back to outward-facing buds that are well-placed to promote an open, goblet-shaped bush.

For cordons and two-year-old bushes, also follow the winter and summer pruning methods advised for gooseberries, opposite.

77

Blackcurrants (*Ribes nigrum*) are valued for their high Vitamin C content and are used almost exclusively for cooking and for flavouring. The main harvest is during the second half of summer, though some varieties, such as 'Boskoop Giant', crop a little earlier.

Blackcurrants are quite an easy crop to grow; their chief need is well-manured soil. Subject to this, a yield of up to 4.5kg (10lb) or more can be expected from each mature bush. The life expectancy of a blackcurrant bush is 15 years or more, especially for certified virus-free stock.

Choose either an open or a lightly shaded position for planting, but take care to avoid a site subject to late spring frosts.

MAKING A START
Dig plenty of manure or garden compost into the site before planting, and spread on a dressing of general fertilizer, at 70g per sq m (2oz per sq yd), at planting time. Distribute this around each planting position, setting the bushes 1.5m (5ft) apart.

Plant bare-rooted bushes between autumn and late winter (the earlier the better). Take out generous planting holes that will allow the bushes to sit a little deeper in the soil than they were in the nursery, so that the new shoots will grow direct from the soil. Immediately after planting, cut back each stem to the second bud above soil level, to encourage the production of several strong new shoots from the base. This should ensure heavy cropping in future years although it means sacrificing a crop the first summer.

Plant container-grown bushes at any time. Cut them back immediately after planting as for bare-rooted plants.

Spread a deep mulch around the plants in early spring and renew it each year once the soil has warmed up. Use peat, garden compost, leafmould or well-rotted manure.

CARE OF THE CROP
Sprinke sulphate of potash over the root area in mid-winter, at 35g per sq m (1oz per sq yd). At the end of winter, before mulching, give a dressing of sulphate of ammonia in similar quantities.

Soak the ground if there is a dry spell from late spring onward. Avoid hoeing, if possible, in case the shallow roots are damaged. Hand weeding is safer, but in any case the mulch should keep the weeds down.

HARVESTING AND PROTECTION
Make sure the fruits are fully ripe before you pick them: they turn black a week or two before they are quite ready. There are two methods of picking blackcurrants: one is to strip the berries from the stalks, so that they come off singly; the other is to remove them with the stalks intact. The latter is better if the fruit have to be kept for a while, and does not involve much extra work in the long run.

The spring flowers are vulnerable to frost, and the ripening fruits to damage by birds. Drape the bushes with hessian or several layers of netting if a night frost is likely, then remove it during the day. Net the bushes against birds when the first fruits begin to colour.

PRUNING
Blackcurrants fruit on the previous season's young wood, so the aim of pruning is to encourage new growth to develop. During the first autumn, cut out any weak shoots to a bud a little above the ground. Do the same a year later, purposely removing a few of the weaker growths to stimulate new ones from ground level.

Once the bushes are mature, remove about a quarter of the older, darker growths each autumn, even though this means losing the younger shoots that some of them bear. Cut out badly placed or damaged wood first. Then remove old branches which have no new shoots on them, and finally cut back fruited branches to a strong shoot. This will prevent overcrowding and encourage new, fruit-bearing growth.

PROPAGATION
As for gooseberries (see p.76).

PESTS AND DISEASES
Two particular pests are blackcurrant gall mite and leaf midges.

American gooseberry mildew, leaf spot and reversion are possible ailments.

RECOMMENDED VARIETIES
'Ben Lomond' Large berries in mid-season. A good all-rounder.
'Ben More' Neat habit, heavy crops, frost-resistant.
'Boskoop Giant' Earliest variety, so vulnerable to frost. Large sweet fruits.
'Jet' Late, very vigorous. Moderate crops of small berries.
'Laxton Giant' An early variety with large berries. Vulnerable to frost.

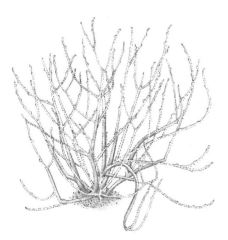

Before pruning

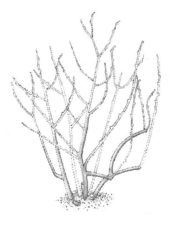

After pruning

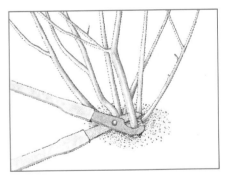

The object in pruning blackcurrants is to promote a continuing supply of young, fruit-bearing growths. This is done by cutting out up to a third of the older wood each year (above), though retaining some of the branches bearing year-old shoots. The older wood is darker and thicker.

The highbush blueberry (*Vaccinium corymbosum*) is the ideal fruit for a garden with really acid soil. While soil with a pH level just on the acid side of neutral suits the great majority of fruit and vegetables, blueberries need a pH of about 4.5, to match the peaty moorland from which the plants derive.

In most gardens this means creating special planting stations, in which acid peat is the main ingredient. An acidifying chemical may also be needed. The alternative is to grow the plants in containers, using an ericaceous compost, which is lime-free.

The highbush blueberry has a height and spread of around 1.5m (5ft), and makes a striking spectacle in autumn, when the leaves turn a glowing red. Because they are so decorative, blueberries could be grown in a shrub border with other acid-soil plants such as rhododendrons.

The dark blue berries, which ripen in late summer, are covered with an attractive greyish bloom. They have a distinctive flavour, at its best in the pies and tarts for which blueberries are famed.

MAKING A START
Blueberries are unlikely to succeed in soil with a pH of 5.5 or higher. If your soil is less acid than this, take out individual planting stations 60cm (2ft) sq and 30cm (1ft) deep. Break up the subsoil a little but do not remove any of it with the topsoil. Allow 1.5m (5ft) between stations.

Mix dampened sphagnum moss peat, or an ericaceous compost, in equal quantities with the soil removed, and add some sharp sand. The heavier the soil, the more sand is needed, up to a maximum of 25 per cent.

Return the mixture to the planting hole – the job should be completed a few weeks before you buy the plants. This may be between autumn and spring, if the plants are bare-rooted, or at any time of the year if they are container-grown.

Soils on the borderline of being too alkaline can be further acidified by simply adding flowers of sulphur at 130–250g per sq m (4–8oz per sq yd) – the heavier the soil, the more you will need.

Water the roots or soilball before planting if there is any hint of dryness. Plant the bushes in their individual stations at the same level as previously grown, and firm the soil/peat mixture thoroughly around their roots. Spread a mulch of peat or an acid leafmould (such as oak leaves), or sawdust, over the surface afterward.

GROWING IN CONTAINERS
Growing blueberries in tubs or pots is a good idea if your soil is alkaline. The containers need to be substantial, however, since blueberries have extensive root systems: the minimum suitable size is approximately 40cm (15in) square and deep. Each tub or pot must have a drainage hole, with a layer of crocks or stones laid over its base. Fill it with an ericaceous compost or a peat-based compost with no added lime.

Pay close attention to the watering needs of container-grown bushes, and use rainwater if you mains supply is hard. A drip-feed system can be recommended for convenience.

Unless the soil is naturally acid (ideally pH 4.5 or slightly higher), you should prepare special planting stations for blueberries. Mix sphagnum moss peat or an ericaceous compost with the soil in equal parts, and add sharp sand unless the soil is naturally light. Allow time for the mixture to settle before planting.

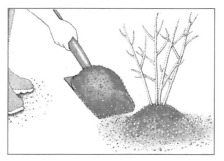

A mulch of peat or ericaceous compost added after planting will help to maintain the acid conditions, and prevent the soil and roots from drying out. Renew this mulch each spring after the plants have been fed and when the soil has had a chance to warm up. If applied too early, it prevents heat reaching the soil.

CARE OF THE CROP
Do not prune the stems after planting, but prevent fruiting during the first year by rubbing off the plump fruit buds with your thumb, leaving only the smaller buds that will form leaves.

It is vital not to let the roots dry out at any stage; even in spring there is an occasional risk of this. Collect rainwater for this purpose if you live in a hard-water area, and water plants thoroughly at the first hint of dryness. Continue watering throughout the summer as necessary. A drip feed system of watering could save you some time, and is particularly useful for plants grown in containers (see p.42).

Give an annual feed of a balanced general fertilizer at 70g per sq m (2oz per sq yd) in early spring, followed about a month later with a dressing of sulphate of ammonia at half this rate. Fork or rake this gently into the existing mulch, then add a fresh layer of peat. Manure is unsuitable for a blueberry bed.

Apply a high-potash liquid feed (as sold for tomatoes) while the berries are forming and ripening.

Hoeing is inadvisable, since the bushes have a network of roots near the surface. Any weeds that appear, despite the mulch, are best removed by hand.

GOOSEBERRIES, CURRANTS AND OTHER BERRIES, pages 52–53
WATERING AND MULCHING, pages 42–43

PESTS AND DISEASES, pages 108–111
FREEZING FRUITS, pages 134–135

HARVESTING AND PROTECTION

Wait until the berries are fully ripe before you pick them. Berries picked prematurely lack flavour. When ripe they are soft, blue-black with a waxy bloom and part easily from their stalks. Eat the blueberries fresh, or use them for cooking, within a couple of days; otherwise freeze them.

Protection from birds is essential. If the bushes are not grown in a fruit cage, drape netting over them from midsummer.

Blueberries are irresistible to birds. If you do not have a fruit cage, drape netting or muslin over the bushes for reasonable protection.

PRUNING

After the first three years, some pruning is needed annually in early spring. Cut back a few (one to four) of the oldest stems; either remove them altogether if there are plenty of young basal shoots, or trim them back to strong young shoots. The aim is to stimulate growths that will bear fruit a couple of years hence; blueberries fruit on the tips of the previous season's growth. It is also necessary to thin out established bushes that are becoming too dense.

Remove dead or weak branches, and those spreading close to the ground, at the same time.

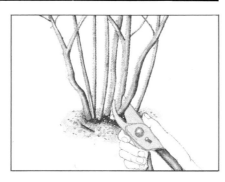

Prune blueberries in late winter or early spring by cutting back up to four of the oldest stems. This will encourage the plants to produce new fruit-bearing shoots.

PROPAGATION

Blueberries can be propagated either by layering in the autumn or by taking semi-hard cuttings in midsummer. In the autumn, select one or two long shoots and cut a nick in each so that it can be bent to touch the ground. Peg each shoot down with a pin of bent wire. After one or two years, sever the new plant from the parent.

Alternatively, take a semi-ripe shoot in midsummer by cutting cleanly just above a bud. Dip the heel in rooting powder and plant it in equal parts of peat and sand in a cold frame or unheated greenhouse. Spray the cutting with water until it has rooted.

PESTS AND DISEASES

Aphids may be troublesome occasionally.
Blueberry plants are rarely affected by disease.

RECOMMENDED VARIETIES

Though the plants are self-fertile, they will fruit better if at least two plants, each of a different variety, are grown.

'Berkeley' Vigorous and spreading. Good crops of large berries.

'Bluecrop' A vigorous, early, heavy-cropping cultivar.

'Coville' Heavy yields but late to ripen. Large berries, good flavour.

'Earliblue' Earliest to ripen but only moderate yields. Large, tasty berries.

'Herbert' Mid-season. Heavy crop of reputedly the best-flavoured berries.

The cranberry (*Vaccinium Macrocarpon*) is a close relative of the blueberry and needs much the same growing conditions – acid, free-draining soil – but even more moisture. It has a prostrate, creeping habit, however, so is unsuitable for containers. The foliage is evergreen and the plant slow-growing.

The oval red berries, from which cranberry sauce is made, ripen during late summer and early autumn.

GROWING AND HARVESTING

It is not practicable to form individual stations, as is done for blueberries, since cranberries are planted only 30cm (1ft) apart in each direction. Instead, prepare a bed by mixing equal parts of soil and acid peat, with added sharp sand, to a depth of about 20cm (8in). Lower the pH level, if necessary, by adding some flowers of sulphur to the soil.

Plant cranberries during the winter, subject to soil conditions and weather, preferably in a sunny position, and from then on make sure that the bed is constantly moist. A covering of sharp sand will reduce evaporation and suppress weeds.

Picking may be left until all the berries are ripe. Pruning, in early spring, consists of trimming to prevent any overcrowding and to remove untidy, wispy stems.

PESTS AND DISEASES

There are unlikely to be any troubles, except, perhaps, for aphids.

RECOMMENDED VARIETIES

Named cultivars are not in plentiful supply in Britain. In one official trial, 'CN' and 'Franklin' proved the most promising.

WATERING AND MULCHING, pages 42–43
GOOSEBERRIES, CURRANTS AND OTHER BERRIES, pages 52–53
FREEZING FRUITS, pages 234–235

The large, rough-skinned kiwi fruits (*Actinidia chinensis*) are also called Chinese gooseberries. They are indeed of Chinese origin but commercial production is concentrated in New Zealand – hence the more commonly used name. The fruits are refreshing, with a mild but delicious flavour. They are eaten raw, in both sweet and savoury dishes, or in salads.

Kiwi fruit are produced on a vine. The plant is a vigorous climber, entwining around any support. It has large, heart-shaped leaves and the female flowers are creamy white. The vines do not usually produce a harvest for three years or more if they are grown outdoors, and the fruits are generally smaller than the imported varieties sold in the shops.

The kiwi vine is a tender plant, winter-hardy only in mild districts. Even then, it is best grown in a sheltered spot, preferably against a south-facing wall. Avoid known frost pockets at all costs.

Low winter temperatures and spring frosts, which are the two potential dangers for kiwi fruits, can both be countered by planting the vine in a large, unheated greenhouse. If it is grown against an outside wall, a temporary shelter, in the form of a sheet of polythene, will reduce the risk of damage to the vine.

Any average, well-drained soil will do, provided some organic matter is dug in to help retain moisture.

MAKING A START
As well as a female, fruit-producing plant, a male is needed for pollination. Actinidias are rampant vines, so unless you have unlimited space, the best plan is to plant the two together, training the male one way and the female the other. Their potential spread is at least 4.5m (15ft), so the growth of plants raised in greenhouses may have to be restricted.

The best method of support is much the same as for blackberries (see p.73), though the wires should be fixed a little farther apart. Strain the wires between posts if plants are grown in the open, or attach them to vine eyes set in a wall or to screw eyes in a greenhouse.

Plant the kiwi fruits in spring. Before you do so, prepare the planting position by mixing peat or well-rotted compost in with the soil, together with 15g (½oz) of a general fertilizer. Alternatively, use a proprietary planting mixture. Set the two plants side by side and firm the mixture around the rootballs.

If you have the space, and want to grow more than one female kiwi fruit, space the plants 4.5–6m (10–15ft) apart. One male plant will pollinate up to six females.

CARE OF THE CROP
Feed annually, in spring, with a general fertilizer at 70g per sq m (2oz per sq yd), scattering this over a broad area around the stems. Spread a deep mulch of manure or compost over the same area.

Water generously during dry weather, at least until about midsummer, and especially if the plants are growing against a wall, where the soil dries out rapidly.

PRUNING AND TRAINING
Grow the male and female plants as espaliers – that is, each with one upright main stem, and with the shoots growing from this trained along the wires in one direction only.

To start the training process, cut each stem level with the bottom wire immediately after planting. Allow two shoots to develop; leave one to grow upright and train the other shoot horizontally along the first wire.

Tie a string to the wires as an additional support for the main, upright shoot. Repeat the cutting back procedure at each wire, to encourage the development of more shoots that can be trained horizontally. Rub off any unwanted buds that appear on the stem between wires.

During the summer, remove the tip of each horizontal branch, together with those of the side-shoots that will then form from behind the pinched-back shoots. The purpose of this is to encourage the formation of fruiting spurs.

In later years, thin out any congested growth during winter. Cut the three-year-old fruited laterals back to a dormant bud near the main cane to renew the fruiting laterals.

PESTS AND DISEASES
Aphids and capsid bugs may prove minor problems. Diseases seldom occur.

RECOMMENDED VARIETY
'Hayward' Late-flowering, and with large, well-flavoured fruits. This is the best of the limited choice available.

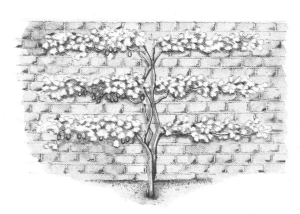

A male and a female kiwi fruit are planted together. The shoots from each have been trained in a single direction to form a conventional espalier shape.

In extremely mild and sheltered districts it is possible to grow kiwi fruits as freestanding plants on a pergola. Elsewhere, some form of protection is necessary.

The sweet, luscious flavour of melons (*Cucumis melo*) is particularly rewarding to the gardener when these tropical fruits are grown in a temperate climate. Yet melons are by no means a difficult crop: their cultivation demands close attention rather than great skill.

Melons are tender plants, and seed cannot successfully be sown outdoors except in the warmest of climates. For reliable results, sow the seeds in warmth – in a greenhouse, a soil-warmed frame or in an airing cupboard indoors. Any of the melon varieties may be grown in a greenhouse, while some relatively hardier varieties will produce good results in a frame or under cloches. These often thrive with no protection at all during warm summer weather.

The best-flavoured melons are cantaloupes and these are equally suitable for frames and cloches as for greenhouses. The fruits are small, however, so greenhouse owners may prefer to try one of the larger-fruited casaba or winter varieties, such as 'Emerald Gem', which are unsuitable for growing outside.

MAKING A START
Sowing time depends on where the melons are to grow. A mid-spring sowing will provide plants that can be moved outdoors in late spring, after the last frosts. But you can sow seeds in early spring if the young plants are to remain in a warm greenhouse. Slightly staggered sowing times will ensure that the melons do not ripen all at once.

A temperature of 18°C (65°F) is needed for germination, and it should then be kept within a degree or two of this as the seedlings develop. A propagator (see p.38) is ideal for maintaining the fairly high germination temperature, especially if this stage is carried out on a windowsill indoors.

Sow each seed singly in an 8cm (3in) pot of seed-sowing compost or in a peat pot. Press it edgeways into the middle of the pot, then water the compost and cover the pots, first with glass and then with paper.

Remove the paper and glass as soon as the seeds germinate. Stand the pots in a light but warm place and keep the compost reasonably moist.

Prepare the soil for planting, indoors or out, by forking in a dressing of well-rotted garden compost. Peat may be used instead, in which case add a handful of general fertilizer to each square metre. Do not use manure, which would produce too much foliage at the expense of fruit. Melons can also be planted in gro-bags, provided that some additional feeding is given from a fairly early stage.

Have cloches in position, or the lights of frames closed, two weeks before planting.

CARE OF THE CROP OUTDOORS
Wait until the risk of frost is completely over before planting out under cloches or in a frame. By this stage, the plants should have at least two or three true leaves. Water the melons in their pots first so that the rootballs are not disturbed. Set the plants 90cm (3ft) apart under cloches, or place each one in the middle of a frame. Draw the soil into a slight mound first, then make a hole wide and deep enough to take the rootball. The mound will help to keep the stem dry, since melons are susceptible to collar rot.

Pinch out the growing point of each plant as soon as five rough-edged leaves have developed. Side-shoots will then form, on which the fruits will be borne. Select the four strongest side-shoots and cut off the remainder with a sharp knife.

If you are growing melons in a frame, direct each shoot toward a corner. Arrange shoots under cloches in well-spaced pairs, in opposite directions. Once the flowers appear, open cloches or leave frame lights open, weather permitting, to allow insects in to pollinate. If the weather is cold, you may have to hand-pollinate the flowers, as for greenhouse-grown melons.

Leave frame lights open, and open cloches (or space them a little apart) whenever the weather is warm. Remove cloches altogether during prolonged sunny weather. The alternative, with both cloches and frame lights, is to leave them in place in hot weather. Ventilate them but apply a shading liquid to help keep plants cool.

When the fruits develop, remove the tips of the shoots two leaves beyond them, aiming to have one, equal-sized fruit on each shoot. Take off any others.

Keep the soil moist, especially as the fruits develop. At this stage feed plants every week or two with a high-potash liquid fertilizer. When the fruits are the size of apples, support them clear of the ground on an upturned plant pot or something similar, to prevent any possibility of rotting in contact with damp soil.

CARE OF THE CROP IN A GREENHOUSE
Plant the young melons in the prepared border or in gro-bags when they have five rough-edged leaves. Set them 75cm (2½ft) apart, first forming a shallow mound as advised for outdoor plants.

The object is to grow the plants as twin-stemmed cordons, first up to the eaves and then along the underside of the roof. For support, push two canes into the soil 15cm (6in) on each side of the plant. Tie the tops of the canes to a horizontal wire at eave level, then fasten further wires at 30cm (1ft) intervals up the side wall, behind the plants, and on the underside of the roof. Use vine eyes to secure the wires to the glazing bars of the greenhouse. An overall width of 90cm (3ft) is about right for a single melon plant.

Pinch out the tip of the plant when it is 15cm (6in) high. Remove all but two of the shoots that will develop, and secure each of these to a cane, using soft string. Continue to tie them at intervals until they are about 1.8m (6ft) long, then pinch out their growing points.

The effect of stopping the main shoots will be to encourage the production of side-shoots, or laterals. Tie these to the wires,

Sow the seeds on edge, pressing them into the compost. If you sow them singly, prepare one or two spare pots in case of failures. Otherwise, sow two per pot and remove one seedling if they both germinate.

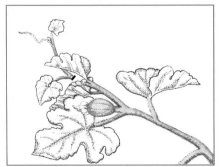

Swelling of the fruits is a signal to pinch out the ends of shoots two leaves beyond them. Do this when the fruits are marble-sized, allowing only one fruit per shoot.

POLLINATION

Insects cannot be relied on for pollination when you are growing melons under glass, so this will have to be done by hand. Pollinate the female flowers, each of which will have an embryo fruit beneath the petals, by brushing the pollen from a male flower on to its centre. Do this when four female flowers are open at the same time on different shoots of the same plant, and repeat the procedure on the following day. Try to pollinate in the middle of the day, if possible, when the atmosphere in the greenhouse is at its warmest. Remove any flowers that grow on the main stem.

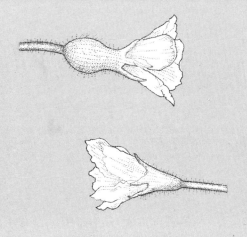

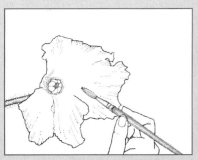

Female flowers (upper left) are easily distinguished by the embryo fruit behind the petals. To pollinate greenhouse melons, use cotton wool or a brush to transfer pollen from the male to the female flowers.

and remove the tip of each lateral once it has developed five leaves. Flower-bearing shoots will start to grow from the laterals.

Provide temporary shade in the greenhouse on hot, sunny days by means of blinds or liquid shading.

When the fruits start to develop, pinch out the tips of the shoots two leaves beyond them. Remove the largest and the smallest fruit, and any others, to leave two equal-sized melons on each stem. Any large melon left on would continue to grow at the expense of the others. Only allow one melon to remain on a side-shoot.

Feed with a high-potash liquid fertilizer every week or so, from the time that the fruits start to swell. Support the weight of the fruits by placing them in nets secured to the wires. Nets for this purpose are sold in large garden centres. If any melons are lying on the ground, support them on an upturned flower pot or similar, to keep them clear of the soil.

Melons need ample watering throughout the growing period; water daily as a rule, but do not saturate the soil. In particular, be careful not to wet the soil immediately around the stem.

HARVESTING

A softening of the outer end of the melon, opposite the stalk, is a sure sign of ripening. By then the characteristic scent will be obvious. Cut the fruits carefully from the stalks. Eat without too much delay, preferably chilled.

PESTS AND DISEASES

Glasshouse red spider mites can be troublesome if you are growing the melons in a greenhouse. Collar rot and cucumber mosaic virus are possible ailments.

Above Fruit-bearing laterals will develop on a twin-stemmed cordon when the tip of each stem is pinched out.

Right Use netting slings to take the weight of greenhouse melons.

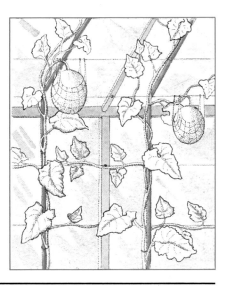

RECOMMENDED VARIETIES
For greenhouse only:
'Blenheim Orange' Attractive netted skin. Fruits of medium size with scarlet flesh.
'Emerald Gem' Green flesh and good flavour.
'Galia' Small melon with green netted skin and light green flesh; good taste and aroma.
'Hero of Lockinge' A white-fleshed variety with a rich flavour.
'Honeydew' Yellow or cream skin and light green flesh with an excellent flavour.
'Sugar Jade' Water melon with dark green skin and deep pink flesh; little aroma but very thirst-quenching.

For outdoors and greenhouse:
'Charentais' Delicious small fruits with orange-scarlet flesh.
'Early Sweet' The sweet, rounded fruits have netted skins and salmon-coloured flesh.
'Ogen' Popular small fruits with yellow-green flesh. Excellent flavour.
'Sweetheart' Fast-maturing grey-green fruits with sweet orange flesh.

GREENHOUSE EQUIPMENT, pages 14–15
FRAMES AND CLOCHES, pages 16–18

SOWING UNDER GLASS, pages 38–39
MELONS, pages 54–55

PESTS AND DISEASES, pages 108–111

Grape growing, or viticulture, has a long and illustrious history; the grapes are grown for making into wine and for drying as raisins as well as for eating as a dessert fruit. Only the table grapes are being considered here, for domestic cultivation.

The grapevine (*Vitis vinifera*) is a perennial deciduous climber that clings to its supports by means of tendrils. Though you cannot expect to harvest any fruit for at least three years, the vine, once established, is a long-lived plant and will last for between 20 and 40 years, so its cultivation could be a life-long commitment. You can expect an established wall-trained grapevine to yield up to 10kg (20lb) of fruit in a good year.

The grapes, produced in bunches, are generally described as being black or white, but in fact the white grapes may be any shade between green and amber-yellow, while the black varieties are from red to deep blue-black in colour.

The key question facing would-be grape growers is whether to grow the grapes indoors or out. Though there are varieties to suit either situation, there is no doubt that the best dessert fruits are harvested under glass.

Outdoors, grapes need a sheltered place in the sun if they are to ripen properly. Success is more likely in a mild area, and especially if you grow the vine against a sunny, south-facing wall or fence. Such protection is easily provided in many gardens. A wall is preferable since it serves as an overnight 'storage heater'. Be sure to choose a variety suitable for outdoor growing (see p.86).

Grapevines may also be grown in open ground, as they usually are commercially, but only in the most favoured districts. This method of growing also requires a more complicated system of training and pruning than the one covered here.

The type of soil is not critical, except for its drainage, which must be impeccable. Grapevines evolved in fairly arid conditions and the roots will not stand any suggestion of waterlogging. A gritty, sandy soil is ideal since it ensures free drainage. Heavy, soggy ground is unsuitable unless it can be improved by artificial drainage.

GROWING GRAPES UNDER GLASS
- Results are generally likely to be more consistent in an environment, such as a greenhouse or conservatory, which is under the gardener's close control.
- In terms of appearance, grapes grown under glass have a waxy bloom on their skin, whereas outdoor grapes have usually lost this due to the effects of wind and rain.
- Though heating is an asset for some grape varieties, many do well in a cold greenhouse.
- A greenhouse vine requires a lot of space, and your greenhouse needs to be about 3.5m (12ft) long if you wish to grow a couple of vines and still have space for other crops.

MAKING A START OUTDOORS

Use long vine eyes to secure a series of horizontal wires 13cm (5in) away from the wall at 30cm (1ft) intervals. Set the bottom wire 45cm (1½ft) above the ground.

Take steps to improve the soil's drainage, if necessary (see p.26), bearing in mind that a layer of stones or rubble will do little good unless there is an outlet for the water.

Toward the end of winter, dig plenty of manure or compost into the topsoil around each planting position. Space these 1.5m (5ft) apart if more than one vine is to be grown. Leave the soil to settle for a month or two, then rake a handful of general fertilizer into the surface a few days before planting.

Spring is the best time to plant both bare-rooted and container-grown vines. Firm the soil around the plants at the same level as they were in the nursery, with bare roots spread out evenly, but make sure that rootballs are undisturbed.

After planting, shorten the leading shoot (which will form the main stem, or 'rod') to about 60cm (2ft) and cut the others to a single bud. Tie a cane vertically to the wires; you can use this subsequently as a support for the main stem.

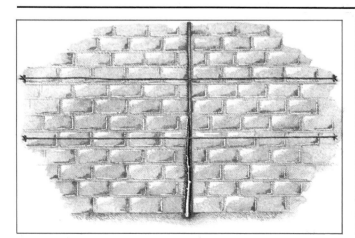

Outdoor vines growing against a wall. The horizontal support wires are 30cm (1ft) apart and secured by long vine eyes. The grapevine's leading shoots have been shortened to 60cm (2ft) immediately after planting.

In a greenhouse, the rods of the grapevine are secured to vertical canes and the laterals are trained to alternate wires on each side. As well as supporting the vine, this method of training ensures that the sun reaches all parts of the vine.

PRUNING AND TRAINING OUTDOORS

The method of training is basically the same as for a greenhouse vine (see below). Your object should be to secure a single rod from which horizontal stems are trained left and right on alternate wires. Training will keep the fast-growing vine under control, will ensure that all parts of the vine are exposed to the sun and will make care and harvesting easier.

The pruning system is also the one recommended for a greenhouse vine. The purpose of pruning is to maintain the vine's vigorous growth, encourage the development of new shoots for the next year, and limit the number of fruit-producing buds so that the vine does not produce too many small or inferior bunches of grapes. Pruning should be done in late spring or early summer, once all danger of frost is over.

There should be a small harvest of two or three bunches of grapes when the vine is three years old.

CARE OF THE CROP OUTDOORS

Water an outdoor vine regularly, especially during dry spells and if it is against a wall. A spring mulch of manure or compost is beneficial, and should be spread after scattering some general fertilizer (70g per sq m/ 2oz per sq yd) and scuffling this into the surface soil or into the remains of the previous year's mulch.

If wasps are a nuisance when the fruit are ripening, leave a jar containing some diluted honey, or a sugar solution, by the vine in order to attract, and drown, them.

MAKING A START IN A GREENHOUSE

Make sure that the soil in the greenhouse border is free-draining. If necessary, mix in grit or crushed rubble to give a more open texture. Dig in a generous dressing of manure or compost, then water it well and leave it for a few weeks to settle. Rake in a general fertilizer at 70g per sq m (2oz per sq yd) just before planting.

Fasten horizontal wires every 30cm (1ft) to the walls and roof, using vine eyes about 23cm (9in) long. Screw these to the glazing bars of a wooden greenhouse, or buy patent fixtures for an aluminium one, some of which slide into the grooves on the metal glazing bars. The purpose is to ensure air circulation between glass and foliage.

Set the plants about 23cm (9in) from the wall of the greenhouse, allowing 1.5m (5ft) between vines if more than one is to be grown. Plant them as described for outdoor vines. Immediately after planting, cut back the leading shoot to a bud 60cm (2ft) above the ground and the other shoots to a single bud. Tie a cane to the wires to support the main stem, or rod, as shown in the illustration on the facing page.

PRUNING AND TRAINING IN A GREENHOUSE

When a new shoot grows from the top of the rod, keep this tied to the cane. Train the side-shoots to the wires on alternate sides, and pinch out any that are not needed.

Pruning during the first and second years is particularly critical, since this will affect the quality of the fruits the vine is allowed to produce from the third year onward. Follow the summer and autumn pruning procedures outlined below and on p.86.

FIRST YEAR PRUNING

During the summer cut off the tips of the side-shoots beyond the fifth leaf. Pick off any flower trusses, too, since growth will suffer if the vines are allowed to bear fruit during their first two years.

In the autumn cut back the leading shoot – that is, the new growth at the top of the rod – by about half, cutting just above a bud. The purpose is to remove soft, unripened wood. At the same time, cut back each of the horizontal growths to leave stubs with just two buds each.

This pruning may seem drastic, but remember that the fruiting growths will be taken from these spurs each year, throughout the life of the vine.

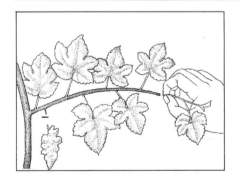

During the first summer, cut off the ends of laterals just beyond the fifth leaf. Remove flowers before fruits can develop.

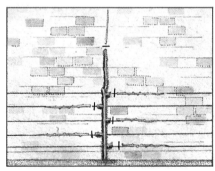

In the autumn, reduce the leading shoot by half. Cut back laterals to form stubs which each have only two buds.

GREENHOUSE EQUIPMENT, pages 14–15
IMPROVING DRAINAGE, page 26

SECOND AND THIRD YEAR PRUNING

During the autumn of the second year, repeat the same pattern of pruning and flower removal. Also, pinch back to a single leaf any smaller growths that develop on the main horizontal shoots.

In spite of being pruned back each autumn, the main stem will extend upward year by year. Keep it tied to the cane, fixing a second one under the roof when necessary. When the stem reaches the top wire, stop it at an adjacent bud.

Allow one shoot to grow from each stub, or spur, during the third year. Pinch out the unwanted weaker shoots once you can see which is the strongest. Leave the flowers on three of the shoots to form fruits, then prune the ends of these shoots three leaves beyond each cluster. Tip the other shoots at five leaves, as previously. Tie the laterals onto the supporting wires where necessary.

Pruning during the second summer is much the same as during the first. As well as trimming shoots and removing flowers, reduce sub-laterals to a single leaf.

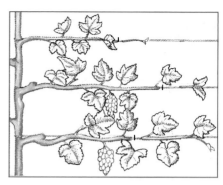

In the third year, allow up to three bunches of fruits to form on each vine. Prune the shoots concerned just beyond the second leaf after the bunch. Allow another bunch or two to develop each subsequent year, continuing until two or three bunches are left on each lateral.

CARE OF THE CROP IN A GREENHOUSE

Leave the greenhouse unheated during the winter, but make sure there is a little ventilation. Once the vine is established, untie the rods from the wires during the winter, lower them to the ground and scrub them gently but firmly with a clean, dry brush to remove the loose bark under which pests and their eggs are likely to be overwintering. Afterwards, apply a winter wash of tar-oil, having first diluted it according to the manufacturer's instructions. While the rods are down, clean the glass in the greenhouse thoroughly, with a mixture of water and disinfectant. Retie the rods to the wires.

Fork a dressing of manure or compost into the soil at about the same time. At the end of winter, just before starting the vines into growth, apply a general fertilizer at 70g per sq m (2oz per sq yd).

For an early harvest, start heating the greenhouse toward the end of the winter. Aim for a minimum temperature of about 10°C (50°F). Water the soil thoroughly and syringe the rods each morning with clear water. Damping the path will also help to create the required moist atmosphere.

Without artificial heating, the sun's warmth will start greenhouse vines into growth from mid-spring onward. Assist the process by closing the ventilators, watering the soil and syringing the rods daily. In colder areas, a little extra warmth is valuable on frosty nights.

Stop syringing and damping down when the vines start to flower. A daytime temperature of around 21°C (70°F) is ideal for a grapevine at this time.

For a good set of fruit, assist pollination either by tapping the flowering stems each day or by passing a soft brush over the flowers. The middle of the day is the best time. Though hardly necessary outdoors, this does help in the still atmosphere of a greenhouse, where insects are less plentiful.

Start damping down again, and syringing the foliage, once the flowers have set. Aim for a daytime temperature of about 21°C (70°F). Keep the vents shut at night to retain as much warmth as possible. Apply a liquid fertilizer every week or so and water regularly to prevent the soil drying out.

HARVESTING

The first signs of colour on the berries are a signal to stop feeding and gradually to reduce the amount of watering. Retain daytime warmth in a greenhouse by closing the ventilators at night.

Ripening is a fairly lengthy business, and takes several weeks from the first change of colour. When the grapes are ready (taste them if necessary), cut through the stem on each side of the stalk with secateurs. Handle them as little as possible; eat the grapes immediately or keep them in a cool, dark place for several weeks.

PESTS AND DISEASES

Chief among the several pests that may affect vines are glasshouse red spider mite, mealy bugs and scale insects.

Diseases and disorders include grey mould, honey fungus, powdery mildew, scald, shanking and splitting.

RECOMMENDED VARIETIES

Outdoor:
'**Brant**' Sweet, purple grapes. Strong-growing, with good yields.
'**Léon Millet**' A vigorous vine bearing good crops of very dark fruits.

Thinning
Thinning ensures that individual grapes are a good size. As soon as the grapes start to swell, using scissors with long-pointed blades, gradually, over a week or more, remove the smaller fruits from the centre of over-crowded bunches.

'**Madelaine Sylvaner**' An early, hardy variety. White grapes.
'**Müller Thurgau**' Fairly early, with good-quality golden fruits.
'**Pirovano 14**' Red-black grapes with excellent flavour. Ripens very early.
'**Siegerrebe**' Muscat-flavoured golden grapes, ripening mid-season.

Greenhouse:
'**Alicante**' Well-flavoured black fruits borne in large bunches.
'**Black Hamburg**' Unbeaten for quantity and quality of fruit.
'**Buckland Sweetwater**' Early crop of sweet white fruits. Another favourite variety.
'**Foster's Seedling**' White grapes with good flavour. Heavy cropper.
'**Seyval Blanc**' Reliable producer of golden dessert grapes.

GRAPES AND KIWI FRUIT, pages 56–57
PESTS AND DISEASES, pages 108–111

Many gardeners who will happily grow a row or two of soft fruits will hesitate at the thought of apples or apricots. But tree fruits need not be any harder to grow than soft fruits, and even space need not be a problem either, if you choose one of the restricted forms. However, growing tree fruits is a long-term project. Most fruit trees reach their full fruiting capacity only after several years but, with care, they will continue to produce fruit for a lifetime. And the rewards can be considerable. A pair of bush apples are capable of yielding 90g (200lb) of fruit, or a single, fan-trained apricot 9kg (20lb).

FRUIT TREE FORMS

There are two basic forms of fruit tree – restricted and unrestricted. Restricted forms, grown on wire supports, include cordons, espaliers and fans, any of which are a suitable choice for a small garden.

A fan-trained tree is generally grown against a sunny wall or fence; it is the best form for apricots, peaches and nectarines. Cordons, which have a main stem with short, fruiting spurs, are usually grown at an oblique angle against a wall, or trained on wires in the open; the yield per tree is relatively small but a row of cordons can be very productive for the ground space occupied. Espaliers have a main stem and carry their fruit on a number of horizontal branches. They can be grown against a wall or fence but, like cordons, they make good screens and dividers within the garden when grown in the open.

Restricted forms are created by pruning and training. Only certain kinds of fruits lend themselves to this treatment; these are detailed in the individual descriptions.

Unrestricted forms are freestanding and they naturally occupy more space; bush trees and dwarf pyramids are the main forms as far as gardens are concerned. Depending on their rootstock (see below), at least 3m (10ft) is needed between a pair of bush apple trees, and 1.2–1.8m (4–6ft) between dwarf pyramids.

ROOTSTOCKS

Many fruit trees, notably apples and pears, are not grown on their own roots. This is because they would not come true to type from their own pips or stones. Instead, the nurseryman grafts a shoot (called the scion) from the desired variety onto the roots of a different species, called the rootstock.

The significance of rootstocks is that the strength of their growth – their vigour – is known with some precision. This is important, for it plays a major part in determining the eventual size of the tree. Apple rootstocks are particularly well classified, and each is identified by a numbered prefix.

When you buy a fruit tree, make sure that its rootstock is suitable for the available space and the type of soil. In practical terms, this means that trees on a dwarfing rootstock are the best choice for a small garden. The more dwarfing the effect, however, the better the soil needs to be to ensure satisfactory growth. The influence of a dwarfing rootstock will help to counteract that of a vigorous variety of fruit tree (the scion), and vice versa.

This is, in reality, less complicated than it sounds. You need to choose a rootstock principally with apples, and even then there are only about four that need concern the home gardener. Remember that the same variety of apple – for example, 'Worcester Pearmain' – may be available on two or three different rootstocks. As a result, a bush tree might grow to as little as 1.2m (4ft) in height or as tall as 5.5m (18ft).

BUYING FRUIT TREES

It makes sense to grow the more unusual, and often more flavoursome, dessert varieties of fruit which are not always produced commercially. Plant two or three different varieties, if possible, and choose them carefully so that you can enjoy the fruits over an extended period. This is more practicable with restricted forms, such as cordons and espaliers, than with larger fruit trees.

Two- or three-year-old trees are the best buy, since they will bear fruit sooner than maidens (one-year-olds), and in the case of restricted forms, you will not have to do the initial training.

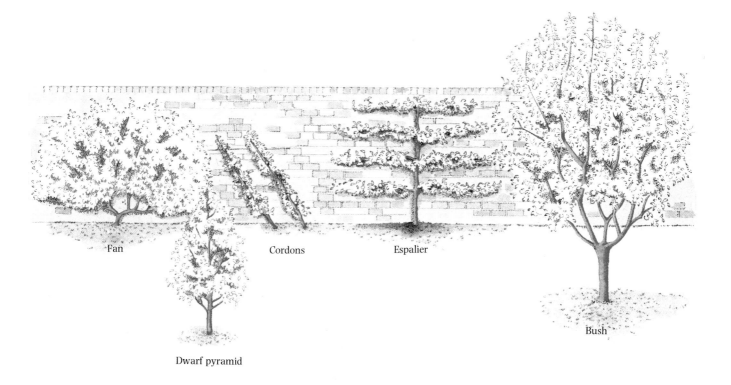

Fan

Cordons

Espalier

Bush

Dwarf pyramid

SITE AND SOIL

Spring frosts, rather than cold winters, are the chief hazard to fruit trees, since it is the blossom that is most vulnerable. Avoid planting tree fruits where cold air is liable to be trapped. For a dubious site, choose one of the late-flowering varieties.

Some fruits – notably peaches, figs and apricots – need warm, sheltered positions if they are to succeed. They are therefore unsuitable for cold, northerly gardens. A wall facing between south-east and south-west is ideal. A Morello cherry is one fruit tree that likes a north-facing wall.

As long as they have good drainage, most fruits will grow in a wide range of soils. Any exceptions are explained in the individual descriptions. It is important to prepare the planting positions well, and to dig in plenty of organic matter to give trees a good start.

SUPPORTS

All fruit trees, even bush forms, need staking, at least during their early years. The restricted forms of tree fruit require a permanent system of support wires.

Bush trees and dwarf pyramids Drive a stake some 45cm (1½ft) into the ground. Secure the stem to it with a plastic tree-tie. Alternatively, wrap sacking around the trunk to prevent chafing; tie with string.

Cordons and espaliers Ideally, buy pressure-treated end posts, or fix the posts in metal sockets driven into the ground.

For cordons, strain three galvanized wires between the posts at 75cm (2½ft), 1.5m (4½ft) and 2m (6½ft) above the ground. For espaliers, fasten the wires at the same levels as the horizontal branches.

Fans Fasten supporting wires every 15cm (6in), the first 45cm (1½ft) above ground.

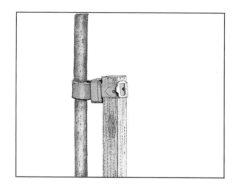

Support a bush tree or a dwarf pyramid with a stake, 5–8cm (2–3in) in diameter. Trees on vigorous rootstocks can dispense with such support after a few years, but those on dwarfing stock need lifelong support. This proprietary tree-tie has an anti-friction buffer. Erect the stake before the tree is planted.

To strain the wires used to support espaliers and cordons, fasten one end to an eyebolt passed through a hole in the post. Fit a washer under the nut and tighten with a spanner.

Erect the support wires before the tree is planted. Additional wires can be fixed later if you choose to form extra tiers on an espalier.

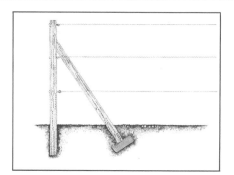

Provided the post has been pressure-treated against rot, it can be set straight in the soil, about 60cm (2ft) deep. Ram the soil back around it, then brace it with an angled strut mounted on a brick or slab.

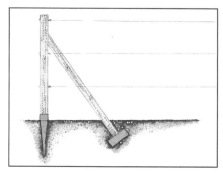

Instead of digging a hole, the post may be set in a metal post socket. This is hammered in and, by keeping the post out of the earth, avoids the need for pressure treatment.

PLANTING

There is a choice between bare-rooted trees, for planting between autumn and spring, and container-grown trees for planting at any time of year. In both cases, avoid planting in either frozen of very wet soil.

Prepare each planting position by taking out a spade-depth hole that is half as broad again as the area of the spread-out roots, or the width of the rootball in the case of container-grown trees.

Fork some well-rotted manure, compost, or a proprietary planting mixture, into the bottom of the hole and mix some compost with the soil that you have just removed.

If a supporting stake is needed – for a bush or dwarf pyramid – hammer this in a little off-centre. Shorten the long, thick roots and cut off any that are damaged or appear dead. Plant cordons with the stems leaning toward the north, if possible, so that they

will receive the maximum amount of light.

Check that the soil mark is level with the surrounding ground. Add or remove a little soil as necessary. Regardless of the soil mark, make sure that the bulge on the stem, where the upper and lower parts of the tree were grafted, is well above the surface.

Place some soil/compost mixture over the roots, and shake the stem up and down so that it settles in between the roots. Repeat the process until the hole is filled, then firm the soil with your foot. With a container-grown tree, simply firm the prepared soil mixture around the rootball.

POLLINATION

Some trees will bear fruits when fertilized by their own pollen. Peaches, apricots and some plums and gages come into this category and so can be grown singly. Others are wholly or partly self-sterile, and must be

cross-pollinated by another variety. This is true of most apples and pears, which means that at least two varieties have to be grown in order to ensure a good crop.

An obvious condition for cross-pollination is that the flowers of the two varieties should be open at the same time; check this point when deciding which to grow.

PROTECTION

Damage by birds is a problem for all fruit tree growers. Winter and spring are the critical times, for it is the blossom and the fruit buds that are most at risk.

Some restricted forms, such as cordons, can be grown in a fruit cage. Spray-on bird repellant, applied frequently, is one form of deterrent, or a patent humming line can be effective for a while. You may be able to net small trees, but this becomes more difficult once they are established.

TREE FRUITS, pages 58–64
THE FRUIT GARDEN, page 65

APPLES, pages 90–95

PRUNING

The initial training and subsequent pruning of tree fruits are essential to keep them in good shape and ensure that they are productive all their lives. Particular pruning needs are explained in the descriptions of individual fruits. It helps, however, to be aware of the basic aims and principles.

The initial purpose of pruning, during the first few years, is to train the tree to a particular shape, to create the framework on which crops will later be borne. Winter pruning, which stimulates growth, is the usual method for bush trees. Summer pruning, which retards growth, forms part of the programme for restricted trees.

Once the framework is established, after about four years – and as the tree matures – the emphasis changes to maintaining a balance between creating new, non-fruit-bearing replacement shoots and encouraging the older growths to bear fruit. Overcrowding has to be remedied, too, along with the removal of dead, diseased or badly-placed branches.

Pruning cuts are made just above a growth bud (not the larger fruit bud) that faces in the appropriate direction. The bud will develop into a shoot. The more severely a branch is pruned, the stronger the resultant growth. Strong growth is the aim during the early years of shaping the tree, since it creates non-fruit-bearing stems which form part of the tree's framework. Subsequently, lighter pruning will foster the production of fruit buds.

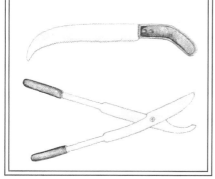

PRUNING TOOLS
A pruning saw is useful for cutting thick branches of fruit trees. Long-handled pruners will cut medium-size branches 2.5cm (1in) or more in diameter.

Make a pruning cut, slanted as here, just above a bud pointing in the direction in which you wish a shoot to grow.

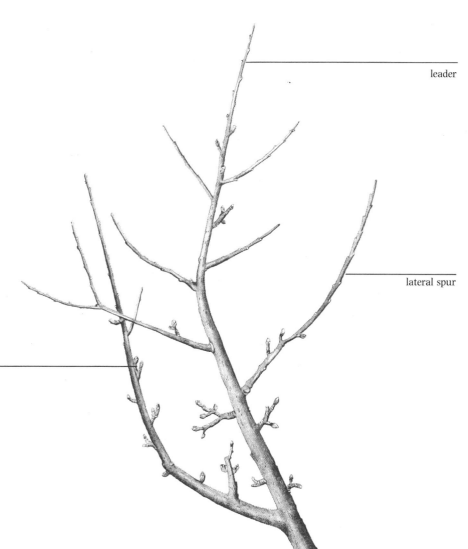

leader

lateral spur

Spurs are growths with multiple fruit buds. Some trees, in contrast, carry their fruits on the tips of shoots.

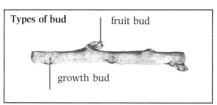

Types of bud fruit bud

growth bud

When pruning, it is necessary to distinguish between fruit buds and growth buds. Fruit buds are plump and rounded; growth buds, which develop into shoots, are small and flat by comparison.

Apples (*Malus domestica*) are one of the most worthwhile of tree fruits to grow. They are consistent croppers, provided the variety and form chosen are right for the site, and provided the trees have been carefully grown. They are also versatile trees, since they comprise an extensive range of dessert and cooking varieties and lend themselves to a number of trained forms. There are hundreds of apple varieties available, and many will keep well if correctly stored.

ROOTSTOCKS

Rootstocks have a considerable influence on the vigour and size of apple trees, as explained on p.87. As a rule, the more dwarfing the rootstock, the more fertile the soil needs to be. If your soil is less than fertile, you may need to choose trees grown on a more vigorous rootstock. The four most suitable rootstocks for garden apple trees are as follows:

M.27 This has the most dwarfing effect of all, even enabling fruit trees to be grown in containers. A bush in open ground grows about 1.2–1.5m (4–5ft) high and across.

This same effect helps to curb vigorous varieties but it is too discouraging an influence on weaker ones. Good soil is essential. The trees need staking throughout their lives.

M.9 Classed as 'very dwarfing', but less so than M.27. The average growth of a bush is from about 1.8m (6ft) high and 2.4m (8ft) across. Trees on this rootstock grow best on good soil, and should produce larger than usual fruits. It is a reasonable choice where space is restricted. The trees need permanent staking since their root system is rather brittle.

M.26 This has a moderately dwarfing effect, but the trees are stronger growing and will do well on most soils, including those that are light and inclined to be dry. It is a good all-round choice for average gardens, and makes a bush some 2.4m (8ft) high and 3.7m (12ft) across.

M.106 This, too, is semi-dwarfing, though less so than M.26. It does well on any normal soil and is suitable for most tree forms. It is a rootstock often used to give a little extra vigour to weaker varieties.

APPLE FORMS

Apple trees may be trained into any of the restricted forms, though fan-training is not often used. Alternatively, space permitting, they may be grown as bush trees or even as half-standards.

Bush trees can appear rather deceptively named since they have a spread (and planting distance) of from 1.2–4.5m (4–15ft), depending on rootstock. Even so, on M.27 and M.9 rootstocks they are a practi-

cal proposition for quite small gardens. Obviously, the more dwarf they are, the easier they are to prune and to harvest and they bear fruit relatively quickly; however, their cropping is less heavy than that of larger trees.

Half-standards, with a height and spread of over 4.5m (15ft) and a clear trunk 1.2m (4ft) high, are too large for the average-sized garden, though they make a striking spectacle in more spacious surroundings. Remember that a companion will be needed for pollination (this could be a restricted tree, however).

Cordons are thoroughly practical, offering the best means of planting several varieties in a restricted area. Allow 75–90cm (2$\frac{1}{2}$–3ft) between rows. Plant with the stem at 45°, and secure it to a cane tied to the horizontal wires.

Espaliers are elegant and surprisingly easy to prune. They make ideal trees for siting against a sunny wall or fence. Leave 3–4.5m (10–15ft) between trees planted in a single line against the same row of supporting wires.

Dwarf pyramids have a Christmas-tree shape, which explains their name. They are usually about 2m (7ft) high and are suitable for growing where space is somewhat restricted. Plant them 1.2–1.8m (4–6ft) apart in the open.

FAMILY TREES

Grafting three or more varieties onto a single rootstock enables one tree to produce several different kinds of apple. The varieties are selected for their simultaneous flowering, so there is no need for a second tree for pollination. Such a tree is generally grown as a bush.

A number of nurseries have family trees. They offer an ingenious means of saving space, but careful pruning is needed in order to achieve a balance and an evenly-fruiting head.

The **extreme dwarfing effect of M.27** makes it suitable only for the most vigorous varieties. Apples grown on this rootstock usually bear fruit at an early age.

Trees on M.9 rootstock, though still very dwarf, are somewhat larger than on M.27. Being less robust, dwarf trees need really good soil and the best of attention.

M.26, which has a less dwarfing effect, is a good all-round rootstock for apples grown in average soils. Even so, growth is still sufficiently restricted for the majority of gardens.

Dwarf pyramids are a good compromise: they take less space than a bush but need no supporting wires, as required by the trained forms of tree, such as cordons.

MAKING A START

Choose varieties of apple that are able to cross-pollinate one another (see p.95), and, since the blossom is vulnerable, give preference to late-flowering kinds if you live in a district where spring frost is likely.

Choose an open, sunny but sheltered site if possible. The ideal soil is moist and slightly acid, but most soils are suitable, provided they drain well and do not contain too much lime. Shelter is important, since strong winds could damage the blossom, and also for pollinating insects which fly in still conditions. If you live on the coast, or in an exposed situation, you may need to consider erecting a windbreak (see p.96).

Prepare the site with the addition of well-rotted organic matter, then plant the trees as described on p.89. The best time to plant is spring, or alternatively during winter, provided there is no frost. Make sure the union between rootstock and scion is at least 10cm (4in) above the soil.

After planting – or during the following spring if planted in winter – rake in a dressing of fertilizer (preferably organic) over the root area, at a rate of 90g per sq m (3oz per sq yd). Spread a mulch of rotted manure or garden compost around the trees to discourage weeds and conserve moisture, but do not let the mulch touch their stems since this may encourage them to put out roots at the union between scion and rootstock.

CARE OF THE CROP

Make certain that the soil does not dry out during the first season or two, while the root systems develop. Give it a thorough soaking in spring and repeat this a week or two later if necessary.

In subsequent years, apply sulphate of potash at 35g per sq m (1oz per sq yd) during the winter, followed by a similar dressing of sulphate of ammonia during the spring. Every two or three years give a spring dressing of superphosphate at 70g per sq m (2oz per sq yd). Treat an area just a little bigger than the spread of the branches, which corresponds roughly to the root area of the tree.

Renew the mulch annually, after the spring fertilizer dressing, at least during the first few years of a tree's life.

Trees on dwarfing rootstocks may flower and fruit precociously, whereas those on vigorous rootstocks may take several years. Discourage fruiting during the first year at least, by removing any flowers. Thereafter, allow an increasing number of fruits to set as the tree becomes established.

THINNING THE FRUITS

Mature trees benefit from having their fruits thinned if the crop is heavy. As well as reducing the strain on the tree itself, this will increase the average size of the fruits.

Wait until after the so-called 'June drop', when a number of small fruits are likely to fall. Then remove one or two apples from each overcrowded cluster, including the central 'king fruit', which is generally deformed. Leave only the two best fruits.

If, despite thinning, there is a risk of overloaded branches breaking, secure a stout pole to the tree's stem, with its top well above the upper branches. Tie nylon twine from it to any branches that are overladen, and adjust the strings to take the weight.

PICKING AND STORING

An apple that is ready for picking will part easily from the tree, with its stalk still attached, when it is gently lifted and simultaneously twisted. This test applies also to late varieties that mature in storage for eating at a later date.

An earlier sign of ripening may be a change of colour – the skin of dessert apples becomes a brighter colour – or the sight of windfalls. Not all apples on a tree ripen together, so do not strip them all as soon as the first fruits are ready.

Handle the apples with great care, for the slightest bruising impairs their keeping qualities. Store sound fruits of the keeping varieties (see p. 95) in a dark, cool, but frost-free place where there is some humidity, such as a garage or spare room.

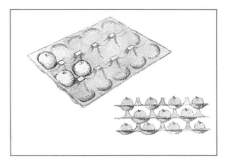

Depending on the variety, apples may keep for several months in a cool room. Purpose-made papier-mâché trays are inexpensive, reusable and allow easy sorting during storage. Wrapping is an advantage if humidity is low.

Thinning a heavy crop of apples reduces the strain on a tree and helps to ensure larger, better-quality fruits. It is less likely to be needed on trained trees. On bushes, leave about 13cm (5in) between dessert apples and half as much again between cookers.

Dwarf trees, especially, may need support to prevent a heavy crop breaking some of the branches. Tie strong twine to the top of a central pole during the weeks before picking.

The principles of pruning fruit trees are described on pages 88–89. The purpose of pruning is clearly demonstrated with apples; your aim is to create the framework and desired shape of the tree in the first few years, after which you must keep a balance between new growth and fruit production.

Depending on the form of apple tree you are growing, these aims are realized in different ways and at various times of year. It is important to follow carefully the pruning programme for a particular form of tree.

You can use either secateurs or a pruning knife for this formative pruning. A pruning saw and tree loppers, or long-armed secateurs, will be required only on a mature bush tree or for pruning a long-neglected apple tree that you have inherited.

PRUNING BUSH TREES

Two-year-old trees These will have several branches. The object during the first few years is to get these main branches, and the laterals that will grow from them, to form an open-centred, goblet-shaped tree. Three or four branches are needed initially, so remove any in excess of this number.

Since pruning stimulates growth, in the winter after planting a two-year-old tree, cut back each of the branches to just above an outward-facing bud. Shorten strong, vigorous branches by about half. Reduce weaker growths by two-thirds, since this more severe pruning will encourage stronger shoots to develop.

Leave container-grown trees, planted during the growing season, unpruned until the following winter.

Three-year-old trees Whether the tree has been growing in your own garden, or has just come from a nursery, lateral shoots will now have grown from the main branches. Retain about four of these in all, to help supplement the branch structure, and choose those best placed to fill gaps between the original shoots.

Cut back each selected lateral, and the leading shoots of the original branches. Reduce them by a third, if they are vigorous, and two-thirds if they are weak. Prune the other laterals, not needed to form the framework, to about four buds from their base, to form future fruiting spurs.

Fourth year onward Some further formative pruning will be needed, but from now on the purpose and pattern of the operation changes. While developing and maintaining the tree's shape, and preventing overcrowding, the chief object is now to encourage the formation of fruit buds.

The pruning of a mature bush takes one of two different forms, depending on the variety of the apple. Some bear their fruits on two-year-old shoots and on spurs (short

Prune a two-year-old bush tree with the aim of establishing a sturdy, open framework of branches. Reduce the stronger branches by half, the weaker ones by two-thirds. Hard pruning is a means of encouraging stronger growth.

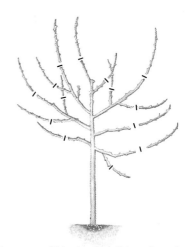

A three-year-old bush tree will have laterals growing from the branches that were pruned a year ago. Cut back both the main branches and laterals to buds that are well placed to extend the framework.

growths) growing from older wood, while others carry it mainly on the tips of shoots formed during the previous year. Some varieties combine both habits. The fruit-bearing characteristics of the recommended varieties are described on p.95.

Spur-bearing bush trees Until the tree is fully grown, continue to cut back the leading tips of branches by about a quarter, or a little more if growth is weak. Trim or cut out any laterals (year-old shoots) growing too close to the branch leaders.

On older trees, remove or shorten any branches that are too crowded or that cross or rub against each other. Keep the centre of the tree reasonably open.

To induce spur formation, prune, to about six buds each, the laterals that will have formed at a lower level – that is, away from the branch leaders. The following year, the sub-laterals that will grow from these (in addition to fruit buds) may themselves by spur-pruned or else removed altogether. Space is the deciding factor.

Tip-bearing bush trees Apart from keeping the centre open and removing crowded branches, as for spur-forming trees, comparatively little pruning is needed.

Cut back branch leaders by about a third, to a growth bud, even on mature trees, but leave all except the most vigorous laterals unpruned. Cut back by half any that are more than 25cm (10in) long.

Trees that bear some of their fruits on the tips of shoots, the rest on spurs, are best treated as spur-bearers.

Half-standards Prune as for bush trees.

Protect the cut with a wound sealant paint.

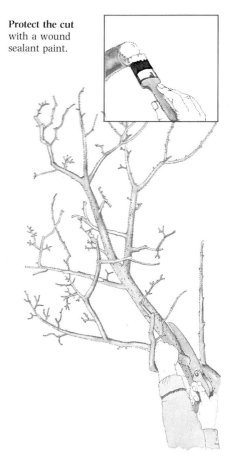

When removing a thick branch, make a small cut on the underside first, then complete the job by sawing through from above.

PRUNING AND TRAINING CORDONS

Only tip-bearing varieties need pruning after planting, by shortening the leader by about a quarter.

Mid- to late summer is pruning time, when laterals that have grown during the previous months are maturing. A typical mature shoot is at least 23cm (9in) long, with its base woody and firm. Cut back these laterals to just above the third leaf from the base, excluding the little group of leaves where lateral and main shoot meet. Reduce to a single leaf any mature side-shoots that are growing from existing spurs, but again exclude the basal cluster. Leave short or immature shoots until later. If, following early pruning, secondary growth occurs, cut this back to a basal bud in autumn.

When the main stem has grown to the top wire you can lower the cordon to a more acute angle, if you want to extend its length. In winter, untie the stem from its cane, lower it by a few degrees each year, taking care not to damage it, then retie it to the cane. Lowering the angle checks the growth of an overvigorous cordon by slowing down the movement of sap, but at the same time encourages fruit production. Lower it to no less than 35° from the horizontal.

Allow the tip to grow a little beyond the top wire each year, then cut it back in late spring to leave a thumbnail's length of year-old wood, terminating in a bud.

Summer pruning, which tends to inhibit growth, is the rule for cordons and other restricted tree forms.

Laterals are pruned to the third leaf above the basal cluster.

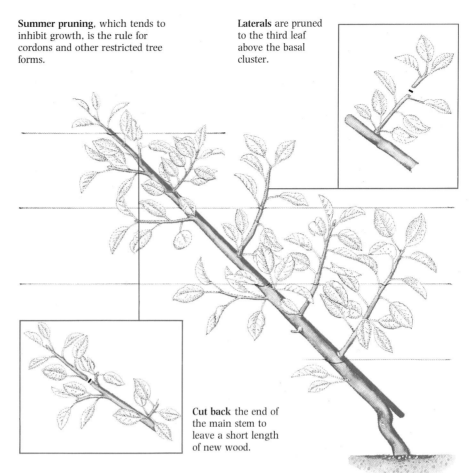

Cut back the end of the main stem to leave a short length of new wood.

PRUNING DWARF PYRAMIDS

Two-year-old trees After planting, cut back the previous year's growth of the central stem to about 23cm (9in). To keep the leader straight, cut to a bud on the opposite side to where a similar cut was made a year before, as shown by the kink in the stem. Prune the branch leaders slightly shorter than this; cut to buds on their undersides.

Three-year-old trees During the winter, reduce the central stem in the same way as you did a year ago; again, cut to a bud on the opposite side. This alternate cutting prevents the stem becoming lop-sided. If you are starting with a three-year-old tree, the nursery will have followed the same pruning procedure.

Do not prune branch leaders at this stage. From now on, until the tree is fully grown, prune them during the second half of summer; wait until the darkness and firmness of the wood shows that it is mature.

Summer pruning consists of cutting these branch leaders back to about five leaves, excluding the small cluster at the base, then reducing the length of the laterals. As with cordons, cut these back to three leaves above the basal cluster, or to a single leaf in the case of growths arising from existing side-shoots. Wait until autumn before cutting back to a single bud any secondary growths induced by the earlier pruning.

Continue with this winter–summer pruning routine, shortening the central stem in winter and other growths in summer, until the tree has attained full height. This will be between 1.8 and 2.5m (6–8ft), depending on the rootstock.

At this stage, prune the central leader by half its length in late spring and at the same time reduce the length of any growths that are tending to crowd the central stem. In subsequent years, cut the leader's new growth back to a 1.3cm ($\frac{1}{2}$in) stub, also in late spring.

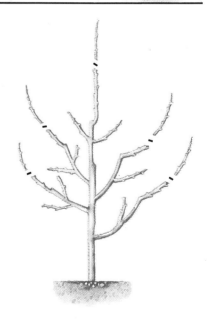

To prevent the main stem of a dwarf pyramid becoming lop-sided, winter-prune to a bud that is on the opposite side to the one chosen a year previously. Continue in this way until the tree is fully grown.

If you are a beginner at fruit growing, it is best to buy a partly-trained tree. You then have only to master the simple technique of creating additional tiers. The added advantage of buying a tree that already has two or more tiers of branches, trained by the nurseryman, is earlier fruiting. Alternatively, you could buy a maiden (one-year-old) tree, without any tiers, which will be less expensive but slightly more difficult to train.

Partly-trained espaliers Erect the wires against the wall after planting (see p.88), so that they correspond to the spacing between the existing tiers. At the same time, add a further wire or wires, the same distance away, if you wish to extend the tree. Tie the horizontal branches to the wires with soft string.

If you are content with a low tree and satisfied with the existing number of tiers, wait until late spring before cutting the previous year's growth of the main stem – the part above the upper tier – to 1.3cm ($\frac{1}{2}$in). Do the same in subsequent years.

However, since a taller tree takes no more ground space, most gardeners will wish to extend an espalier to at least four tiers. In this case, immediately after planting (or during the following winter in the case of a summer-planted, container-grown tree), cut the main stem to a bud 5cm (2in) above the next wire – that is, the third wire from the ground if you bought a two-tier espalier.

Fasten a vertical cane to the upper wires in line with the main stem; secure two others at 45°, forming a V with its base on the third wire, behind the top of the pruned main stem.

Allow only three shoots to grow near the top of the stem during the following spring. The uppermost will form a continuation of the main stem; two others, on opposite sides of the stem and in line with the wires, will form the next tier of horizontal growths. Rub out any other buds with your thumb to leave a clean stem.

As the shoots grow, keep the top one tied to the vertical cane, and tie the others to the angled canes. If the shoots at the sides develop unevenly, raise the weaker of the two to a less acute angle for a while. In the autumn, lower both side canes to nearer the horizontal wire. A year later, remove the canes altogether and tie the branches to the wires.

Repeat this procedure each year until the desired number of tiers is established. When you have formed the top tier, cut back the main stem to two side buds, leaving no third, upper bud.

If growth is sufficiently vigorous, leave the ends of the horizontal branches unpruned until they are long enough. If it is not, provide a boost by cutting back the previous year's growth by about a quarter.

This formative pruning and training is carried out in winter, but late spring is the time to cut the new growth on the main stem and branches back to 1.3cm ($\frac{1}{2}$in), once they are long enough. In addition, summer pruning is needed to encourage fruiting growths on the branches. The method is exactly the same as described for cordons on p.93.

Maiden espaliers The method of creating the first tier on a one-year-old tree is the same as for forming additional tiers on a partly-trained tree. Set up the wires, with the lowest about 40cm (15in) above the ground, then prune the newly-planted tree to a bud 5cm (2in) above this support.

Fasten a vertical cane and two angled canes as described; secure the shoots to them as they develop, from spring onward.

PESTS AND DISEASES

Among several troublesome pests are aphids, sawflies, capsid bugs, caterpillars, codling moths, fruit tree red spider mites, tortrix moths, winter moths and woolly aphids.

Potential diseases and disorders include fireblight, brown rot, canker, honey fungus, powdery mildew, scab and silver leaf.

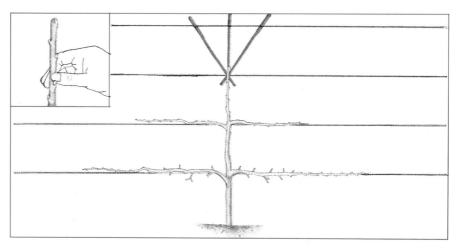

To form a new tier on an espalier, cut back the main stem to a bud 5cm (2in) above the next wire. Rub out all but three well-placed buds at the top. Tie canes to the wires as supports for the shoots that will develop.

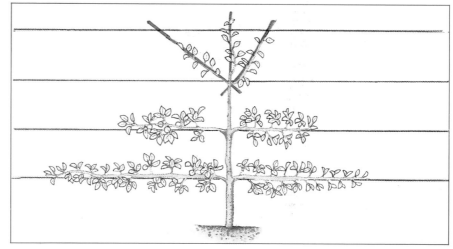

Shoots have grown from the three buds that were left, but one (on the right) is a little less robust than the other. To give it a boost, the cane and shoot have been raised to nearer the vertical. Lowering has the opposite effect.

RECOMMENDED VARIETIES

Pollination groups are listed A, B, C, D or E. At least two trees in the same group are needed for cross-pollination. Varieties marked * are poor pollinators, so two other trees must be grown in addition.

Average keeping times are given at the end of each entry, except where apples should be used within a few weeks of picking.

DESSERT APPLES (listed in their approximate order of picking)

'George Cave' Group B. Spur/tip bearer. Medium-sized yellow-green fruits with red markings. Juicy, crisp and sweet.

'Discovery' Group C. Spur bearer. Medium-sized bright red fruits with a little yellow. Juicy, good flavour and with some frost resistance.

'Irish Peach' Group B. Tip bearer. Excellent flavour and texture if eaten soon after picking. Bears rather erratically.

'Epicure' Group C. Spur bearer. The red-striped fruits are sweet, juicy and aromatic. A variety with few troubles.

'Merton Knave' Group C. Spur bearer. Red-flushed fruits with a sweet, rich flavour. Sound and reliable.

'James Grieve' Group C. Spur bearer. Green-red, rather soft apples with an excellent flavour. Good cropper but susceptible to canker.

'Worcester Pearmain' Group C. Tip bearer. Bright scarlet fruits that are juicy and full of flavour if allowed to ripen on the tree.

'Ellison's Orange' Group D. Spur bearer. Green-yellow fruits, red flushed, with a rich aroma and flavour. Prone to canker and may bear biennially.

'Laxton's Fortune' Group C. Spur bearer. Red-striped yellow fruits. Very sweet and juicy but trees are susceptible to canker and may bear biennially.

'St. Edmund's Russet' Group B. Spur/tip bearer. Pale yellow, turning to gold. Small fruits but densely textured and well flavoured.

'Egremont Russet' Group B. Spur bearer. Medium-sized yellow fruits, renowned for their crisp texture and distinctive taste. Keeps two or three months.

'Lord Lambourne' Group B. Spur/tip bearer. A reliable and heavy cropper, bearing crimson-flushed yellow fruits. Crisp, juicy and sweet. Keeps about two months.

'American Mother' Group E. Spur bearer. Golden fruits with a dark red flush. Sweet, juicy and well-flavoured. Keeps two or three months.

'Ribston Pippin' Group B*. Spur bearer. Yellow fruits with a red flush and slight russeting. Sweetly aromatic, with a firm texture. Keeps about two to three months.

'Sunset' Group C. Spur bearer. Similar to Cox's Orange Pippin, of which it is a seedling, but easier to grow and more disease-resistant. Keeps two to three months.

'Jonathan' Group C. Medium-sized fruits with bright red flush over waxy yellow skin. Tree fairly vigorous and spreading, with greyish foliage. Fruits keep well.

'Starking' Group D. A sport of 'Delicious', with medium to large red-striped fruits. Firm yellow flesh is sweet. Keeps well.

'Spartan' Group C. Spur bearer. Dark red, medium-sized fruits that will keep until Christmas. Firm, juicy and distinctively flavoured. Keeps up to four months.

'Kidd's Orange Red' Group C. Spur bearer. Like 'Sunset', the fruits are similar to Cox's but the tree is easier to grow and less disease-prone. Keeps about three months.

'Cox's Orange Pippin' Group C. Spur bearer. Famed for its superb flavour but needs first-class conditions and care and is unsuitable for colder areas. Disease-prone. Keeps two or three months.

'Orleans Reinette' Group D. Spur bearer. Prolific crops of golden-yellow, red-flushed fruits, but may bear biennially. Crisp; excellent flavour. Keeps two or three months.

'Ashmead's Kernel' Group D. Spur bearer. Pale green, russeted apples with a delightful aroma and flavour. Moderate growth and crops. Keeps three or four months.

'Golden Delicious' Group D. Spur bearer. Golden yellow, medium-sized fruits with crisp flesh and a pleasant, mild flavour. Easy to grow and moderately vigorous but requires favoured position to give a good skin texture. Keeps for three months.

'Tydeman's Late Orange' Group D. Spur bearer. Medium-sized yellow fruits with an orange flush. Similar to Cox's in flavour, though sharper. Keeps five or six months.

'Sturmer Pippin' Group C*. Late cultivar noted for its flavour. Greenish-yellow fruits, flushed with brown. Well-flavoured, crisp yellow flesh. Needs light soil and warm situation to develop its full flavour; leave on the tree as long as possible before picking. Compact growth and regular cropper. Keeps for six months.

'Crispin' Group C*. Spur bearer. The yellow-green, orange-flushed fruits are crisp and sweet. Heavy crops but may bear biennially. Keeps about four months.

'Idared' Group B. Spur bearer. Red-flushed green fruits. Crisp and juicy and may also be used for cooking. Keeps up to six months.

'Laxton's Superb' Group D*. Late apples, medium-sized with a yellow-green, red-streaked skin. Well-flavoured, firm and juicy flesh. Long season and frost-resistant flowers, so suitable for northerly gardens. Moderately vigorous. A tendency to biennial bearing. Keeps five or six months.

COOKING APPLES

'Grenadier' Group C. Spur bearer. A large apple, green turning yellow. Cooks well, with a fine flavour. Compact and usually trouble-free.

'George Neal' Group B. Spur bearer. Medium to large fruits which are juicy and well flavoured. Early flowers, so vulnerable to frost.

'Golden Noble' Group D. Spur bearer. One of the best cooking apples, reducing to a pulp and well-flavoured. Keeps about two months.

'Howgate Wonder' Group D. Spur bearer. Large, red-striped apples with a fine flavour. Flowers late, so worth considering for frosty sites. Keeps four or five months.

'Lane's Prince Albert' Group C. Spur bearer. Large, red-flecked green fruits that do not disintegrate when sliced and cooked. Heavy cropper. Keep up to five months.

'Bramley's Seedling' Group C*. Spur/tip bearer. Large, green-yellow fruits that cook well. Very vigorous, so a dwarfing rootstock is needed. Keeps about four months.

Pears (*Pyrus communis*) are a rewarding crop to grow. Unlike some commercially grown pears, which are tough-skinned to withstand bruising during travel, the best of garden-grown fruits virtually melt in the mouth. Provided they are planted in a suitable site, pears are not difficult to grow.

Pears come into flowering earlier than apples, so spring frosts are a hazard. Besides avoiding a frost pocket, you should thus choose a particularly sheltered spot in the garden if possible. There are fewer pollinating insects around when the flowers of pear trees are open, and you want to ensure that they will fly, and carry their pollen, even in windy weather. You may have to consider planting a hedge to serve as a windbreak.

Pears also benefit from warmth, and although they are not an obvious choice for exposed or northern gardens, you could always choose to grow cordons against a south-facing wall. Pears give the best results on well-manured, moisture-holding soil. Shallow, chalky soils are unsuitable.

Pears can be grown in any of the forms described for apples. Supports, training and pruning are essentially the same. Yields are lower as a rule, however.

ROOTSTOCKS

Quince rootstocks are used for pears and are effective in controlling vigour. Of those classified, Malling Quince A and Malling Quince C are the ones most widely used for garden trees. Quince A is slightly more vigorous, and a good choice where the soil is poor or dry. Quince C makes for more compact growth and earlier fruiting, but needs a good soil for satisfactory growth.

Pears are a little slower than apples to bear fruit, though on Quince C you can expect the first fruits about four years after planting. On Quince A they will take between four and eight years.

There are a few varieties of pear, including the popular 'William's', that are incompatible with quince. For these, a compatible variety is grafted on to the rootstock first, followed by the incompatible variety. The two unions of such a tree show as a double bulge near the foot of the stem.

POLLINATION

As with apples, most pears need another variety nearby to ensure cross-pollination. The varieties must flower at the same time (see Recommended Varieties, opposite).

With space-saving in mind, cordons offer an easy means of growing two or more varieties in even a small garden. If your neighbour has a pear, you may get away with planting only one, but you must first identify the variety and flowering group.

MAKING A START

Pears thrive in moist, organically-rich soil, so dig in plenty of manure or compost some weeks before planting. Immediately before planting, rake in a dressing of general fertilizer at 70g per sq m (2oz per sq yd).

Plant bare-rooted trees between autumn and early spring, and container-grown trees at any time – subject to soil and weather conditions. Follow the method of planting and support outlined on pp.88–9.

Planting distances are as follows; the first, closer spacing is for trees grown on Quince C rootstock:

Bush trees 3–4.5m (10–15ft)
Half standards 4.5–6m (15–20ft)
Cordons 75–90cm (2½–3ft)
Dwarf pyramids 1.2–1.5m (4–5ft)
Espaliers 3–4.5m (10–15ft)

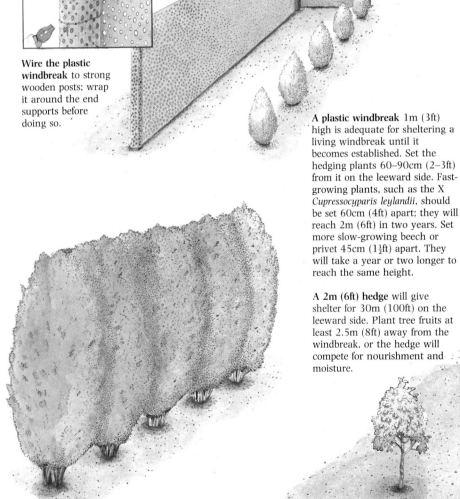

Wire the plastic windbreak to strong wooden posts; wrap it around the end supports before doing so.

A **plastic windbreak** 1m (3ft) high is adequate for sheltering a living windbreak until it becomes established. Set the hedging plants 60–90cm (2–3ft) from it on the leeward side. Fast-growing plants, such as the X *Cupressocyparis leylandii*, should be set 60cm (4ft) apart; they will reach 2m (6ft) in two years. Set more slow-growing beech or privet 45cm (1½ft) apart. They will take a year or two longer to reach the same height.

A **2m (6ft) hedge** will give shelter for 30m (100ft) on the leeward side. Plant tree fruits at least 2.5m (8ft) away from the windbreak, or the hedge will compete for nourishment and moisture.

Shelter pear trees from strong winds if the garden is very exposed. A living screen, protected by a plastic windbreak while it becomes established, is better than a wall or fence. A solid barrier would result in air turbulence.

CARE OF THE CROP

Feed the trees annually, in winter and spring, as for apples (see p.91). A moisture-retaining mulch is particularly valuable for pears, since they do not perform well in dry soil. Renew this each spring after applying the fertilizer.

Water the root area thoroughly during a dry spring or summer; pears are less able than apples to withstand drought. Repeat the watering after a week if there is still no rain. It is essential to soak the soil, not merely to wet the surface; allow about 18 litres per sq m (4 gallons per sq yd).

Thin a heavy crop of fruitlets after the 'June drop', as for apples, and support any overladen branches as the fruits develop.

PICKING AND STORING

Gather early varieties while they are still firm, and before they ripen. Their texture will suffer if they are left longer. Cut through the stalks if they do not part easily from the tree. Leave mid-season and late varieties until they are easy to remove by lifting and gently twisting.

Store the keeping varieties of pear in slatted trays. The atmosphere can be a little drier and warmer than for apples, so an unused room in the house would be suitable. Handle the fruits carefully, since they bruise easily. Any of the dessert varieties of pear may be cooked, provided they are still firm and not fully ripe.

PRUNING

Follow the same pruning procedures as for apples (see pp.92–4), although established bush pears will put up with somewhat heavier pruning when necessary.

With the exception of 'Jargonelle' and 'Joséphine de Malines', which are tip bearers, pears fruit on spurs growing from wood that is at least two years old. Shorten the new growth of leaders by about a third and cut back laterals to three or four buds. Shorten or remove spur systems that become crowded or overgrown. Also, cut back any main branches that cross each other or fill the centre of the tree.

Prune tip bearers lightly, by cutting back only the longest laterals to four buds.

Summer pruning of trained forms of pear tree is the same as for apples, except that it can be done a week or so earlier, when the summer growth matures.

PESTS AND DISEASES

Among potentially troublesome pests are aphids, codling moth, pear and cherry slugworm, pear leaf blister mites, pear midge, tortrix moth and winter moth.

Ailments that affect pears include canker, brown rot, fireblight and scab.

RECOMMENDED VARIETIES

Pollination groups are listed A, B, C or D. At least two trees in the same group are needed for cross-pollination. Varieties marked * are poor pollinators, so two additional trees must be grown. Except where indicated, all are dessert varieties and spur bearers (listed in approximate order of ripening).

'Jargonelle' Group C*. Tip bearer. Juicy and sweet with a musky aroma.
'William's Bon Chrétien' Group C. Large, well-flavoured yellow fruits. Prone to scab.
'Pitmaston Duchess' Group D*. A large, sweetly-flavoured dessert variety that also cooks well. Vigorous; susceptible to scab.
'Louise Bonne de Jersey' Group B. Red-flushed fruits with sweet, melting flesh.
'Conference' Group C. Yellow-green fruits with sweet, juicy flesh. Regular cropper.
'Improved Fertility' Group D. A dual-purpose dessert/cooking variety, with well-flavoured, medium-sized fruits. Crops well.
'Beurré Hardy' Group C. Heavy crops of delicately-flavoured fruits. Late to start.
'Doyenne du Comice' Group D. Large, golden-yellow fruits with an outstanding flavour. Needs warmth and shelter.
'Winter Nelis' Group D. Dark green, medium-sized fruits with a rich flavour. Pick in autumn for eating in winter.
'Joséphine de Malines' Group C. Tip bearer. Another variety to store for winter eating. Small fruits with tender, juicy flesh.
'Gorham' Group D. Large fruits, yellow with a light brown russet. Melting flesh, with a sweet, musky flavour. Vigorous.
'Seckel' Group B. Small, almost round with brownish-yellow skin which flushes red when ripe. Yellow flesh, well flavoured. Good cropper but late to start.
'Clapp's Favourite' Group D. Large, rectangular-shaped pear with scarlet blush. Excellent quality and flavour, but juicy flesh softens rapidly. Susceptible to fireblight.
'Chojuro' Oriental pear popular in the United States. Shaped like an apple, with a yellow skin. Flesh firm and crunchy.

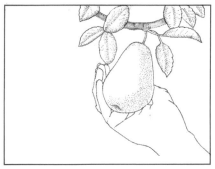

Pears must be picked before they are fully ripe, otherwise their texture will suffer. A lightening of skin colour is a good indication of readiness. The stalks of early varieties may have to be cut, but later kinds should part easily when gently twisted.

Though wrapping pears in paper may help to check the spread of rot, it makes it more difficult to detect when fruits are ripening. Frequent inspection is vital, as the fruits stay in top condition only briefly. Many growers prefer not to wrap.

Lay the pears in slatted trays, either singly or in tiers, and leave spaces between the fruits. For the final stages of ripening, place the fruits in a warm room for a day or two. Handle them with the greatest care to avoid bruising.

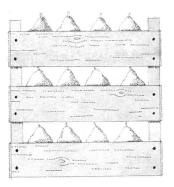

MULCHING, page 43
PEARS, FIGS AND OTHER TREE FRUITS, pages 60–61

GROWING TREE FRUITS, pages 88–89
APPLES, pages 90–95

PESTS AND DISEASES, pages 108–111
STORING FRUITS, page 226

97

The fig (*Ficus carica*) is a handsome tree, and well worth including in the food garden, provided it can be given a sunny position and induced to crop well. It will develop fruit without fertilization so a single tree can be grown. The fruits are sweet and aromatic and can be eaten with savoury foods or as a dessert. The skin colour varies from green to deep purple, depending on variety, and is edible. The fleshy inside contains masses of tiny edible pips.

Fig trees fruit best in warm climate zones; they need warmth to ripen the fruits and immunity from winter frosts to protect them. However, they can also be grown in cooler temperate districts, provided they are grown in the sunniest position the garden can offer, and protected in the winter. It is not practical to cultivate them under glass, since figs are rampant growers and need more space than a garden-sized greenhouse can provide.

The best way to grow a fig is by training it as a fan against a sunny south- or south-west-facing wall. An alternative, given a suitably sheltered spot, is to grow it as a freestanding bush. A possible solution in a cooler climate zone is to plant it in a container, such as a large tub or pot, which is sunk into the ground for most of the year but moved into a greenhouse or basement for the winter. Take special care to see that pot-grown figs never dry out.

Left to their natural devices, figs make masses of growth but produce few fruits. Restricting their roots and keeping the soil on the poor side are the means of redressing the balance. Good drainage and lime are the other main requirements of figs, if they are to fruit successfully.

Two crops of fruit are produced each year. The first, resulting from fruitlets formed during the previous season, ripens in late summer. The second crop grows on the current year's wood, and does not have time to ripen before winter, so it should be picked and discarded.

RESTRICTING THE ROOTS

A fig should be planted either in a container or into a planting hole lined with bricks or stone slabs, to prevent the tree forming strong tap roots.

A 30cm (1ft) pot is a suitable container. Place crocks or stones over the base first and then fill with John Innes potting compost No. 3. The container can either stand on a paved area or be buried up to its rim in soil.

For a permanent planting position for a bush or wall tree, dig a hole measuring 60cm (2ft) square and deep, then line the sides with bricks, paving slabs or concrete. Cover the base with crocks, followed by a layer of broken stones or brick rubble. Fill the remaining hole with soil; mix in about 225g (8oz) of bonemeal, too.

To restrict the roots, which is essential for a fig's prolific cropping, make a concrete- or brick-lined planting hole. Leave the base uncovered.

Place a deep layer of rubble or stones in the bottom of the hole, up to a depth of about 30cm (1ft). Fill the remainder with soil, with some mortar rubble added to it.

MAKING A START

Buy a two-year-old tree and specify whether you want a fan or a bush form. Once you have built a restricting planting box, or prepared your container, sprinkle lime over the surface of the soil, unless your soil is already alkaline.

Plant the fig in winter, about 15cm (6in) from the wall, and approximately 10cm (4in) deeper than it was in the nursery. Spread the roots out over the planting hole, then cover with soil and firm the ground with your foot. Ensure that the soil or compost is never allowed to dry out, at least while the root system is becoming established.

Fasten the horizontal wires for a fan-trained tree at 15cm (6in) intervals, with the lowest wire 45cm ($1\frac{1}{2}$ft) from the ground. Allow for a span about 3.5m (12ft) wide and 2.5m (8ft) high.

CARE OF THE CROP

Spread a mulch over and beyond the root area of a fig planted in the ground, and renew this each year in early winter. Water frequently during dry spells.

Apart from the mulch, do not feed the tree for the first two or three years. After this interval, dress the ground with a handful of bonemeal each spring, followed by an application of a high-potash liquid fertilizer as the fruits swell. Dress with lime every two or three years. Do not fertilize a mature fig, or water it heavily, during late summer, since this will force it into new growth which will be vulnerable to damage by winter frosts.

Replace the top layer of the compost for pot-grown figs a year after planting. Another year later, repot the tree in fresh compost: tease away a proportion of the old compost before repotting it. Repeat the top dressing and repot it in alternate years.

HARVESTING

During the second half of summer, hang netting over the trees to protect the ripening fruits from birds. The fruits are ripe and ready to pick when they become soft to the touch and hang downward from their stalks. The skins may start to split. Eat or preserve figs as soon as they are gathered.

WINTER PROTECTION

It is the young shoots and the fruits at their tips that are at risk. If possible, bring container-grown plants under cover.

For trees planted in the ground, cover the shoots and branches as best you can, by securing straw or bracken around them with strips of hessian. Cover the trees in late autumn, and leave the protection in place until the following mid-spring. Do not cover them with plastic sheeting, however, as this prevents a free movement of air.

PRUNING AND TRAINING

Prune bush and container-grown figs in the same way as bush apples (see p.92) during their first three years, in order to establish a framework of branches. By then they will be approaching the fruiting stage.

For a fan-trained tree, fasten canes to the wires at 45°. Train the first branches, which will already have been started in the nursery, onto these canes. Further canes will be needed in due course for the secondary branches that develop.

If the tree you have planted is two years old, cut back both branches in spring to a bud about 45cm (1½ft) from their base. During the summer allow four shoots to develop on each branch – two on the upper side, one on the underside and one at the end. Tie these to the wires or to additional canes with soft string. Remove all other growths by rubbing them out.

The following year, in late winter, prune each shoot to a bud that will continue the direction of growth; leave 60cm (2ft) of the previous year's wood. Summer-prune again to provide more shoots for adding to the fan structure. Continue, if necessary, during the following year until the whole space is occupied. Expect a fan-trained fig to take about three to four years to more or less cover the wall.

Once bush trees and fans have made their framework, trim all young growths back to five leaves in early summer – no later – to promote fruiting growths for the following year. Keep shoots tied to the wires during the summer. Do not overcrowd the framework of a fig tree, since both the new growth and the figs themselves need plenty of sunlight to be able to reach them.

In spring, remove any diseased branches or any damaged by frost. Also, cut off outward-pointing shoots and those growing toward the wall.

During late autumn, remove any partly-grown fruits that are too small to develop and ripen before the first frosts. This is the second crop, produced on growth made during the current season. If the growing season has not been long or hot enough, they will be small and still green by autumn.

Take care not to disturb the embryo fruits near the tips of the shoots. The fruits for harvesting develop at the apex of the previous summer's shoots, and remain throughout the winter as pea-sized embryo fruits.

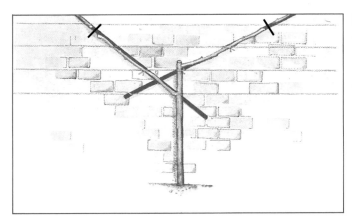

Secure two canes to the wires at fairly flat angles as supports for the two young shoots. Cut each of these back to a bud about 45cm (1½ft) from the main stem, then tie the remainder of each stem to one of the canes.

Allow just four shoots to develop on each of the two branches during the summer – one at the end, to form an extension, two on top and one on the underside. Fix canes on to the wires for support and tie the shoots to these. Rub out other buds.

A fan-trained fig may look like this after two or three years. Note the even spacing of the branches, which still have plenty of scope for growth along the canes.

PESTS AND DISEASES

Few, if any, pests appear to trouble figs. However, coral spot is a fairly common disease, and both canker and grey mould may occur.

RECOMMENDED VARIETIES

'Brown Turkey' This is the most widely grown variety. It produces brown-red fruits, with a blue bloom, which are large and sweet. It is perhaps the most reliable cropper.

'Brunswick' Slightly earlier to ripen than 'Brown Turkey', with large, sweet fruits. These are greenish, with a brown flush.

'White Marseilles' Early to mid-season, with a pale green skin and whitish flesh. Juicy and rich.

Plums grow in a wide range of colours, shapes and sizes; several of the forms are in fact known by different names. The plum family (*Prunus domestica*) comprises gages and damsons; each of these related fruits is grown in much the same way, although their needs do differ a little.

Dessert plums have a succulent flavour accentuated in home-grown fruits, but they require a sunnier, more sheltered position than cooking varieties. Cooking plums are generally hardier and will cope with a greater degree of exposure.

The greengage type is an elite form of plum with a distinctive and quite delicious flavour. It is less hardy and does best if grown against a south-facing wall, where the fruits will ripen to perfection.

Damsons, used principally for cooking and wine-making, are the toughest plums of all. They grow satisfactorily in cool, damp districts where neither plums nor gages would prosper. Damsons are self-fertile, so only a single tree need be grown. So are many plums and gages, in fact, although they may crop more heavily if another variety is planted nearby (see opposite).

All trees may be grown as a bush or a dwarf pyramid, or may be fan-trained against a wall. Wall-trained trees have the added advantage of being easier to protect against birds and spring frosts. Plums are not suited to other restricted forms, however, such as cordons or espaliers.

Plums and gages ripen between midsummer and early autumn, damsons from late summer. A fan-trained plum should yield up to 11kg (25lb) of fruit in a good year; a dwarf pyramid will produce perhaps twice this amount. All plums can be bottled or made into jam but only the dessert varieties are suitable for eating fresh.

ROOTSTOCKS
Plums were formerly considered too large for many gardens, but the introduction of a dwarfing rootstock has made them a practical proposition for even quite small gardens.

The most widely used rootstock is 'St. Julien A'. This has a semi-dwarfing effect, but bush trees will still have a spread of up to about 4.5m (15ft), and pyramids of about 3.5m (12ft).

A greater degree of dwarfing is given by the relatively new 'Pixy' rootstock. Good soil is needed for satisfactory growth, but its effect is to limit development considerably. Either of these rootstocks is suitable for fan-trained trees.

MAKING A START
Plums require a deep, moisture-retentive soil and a sheltered, frost-free site, if possible, since they flower early. Clear the ground of perennial weeds before planting.

Plant bare-rooted trees between autumn and spring, the earlier the better. Container-grown trees may be planted at any time, subject to soil and weather conditions (see pp.88–9 for details of planting).

Space bush trees and dwarf pyramids to suit the rootstock, from 3–4.5m (10–15ft) apart. Allow this space between fans if you are setting more than one against a wall.

Plant a fan-trained tree 23cm (9in) away from the wall. Fasten wires to the wall at 15cm (6in) intervals, with the lowest 45cm (1½ft) above the ground. Support bush trees and pyramids with a stake (see pp.88–9).

CARE OF THE CROP
Mulch the tree after planting and ensure that the soil does not dry out during the first season or two. Take care not to disturb the roots when weeding, otherwise the tree will throw up suckers. If suckers do appear, pull them up rather than cutting them off.

Except on the poorest soil, feeding is unnecessary until the tree has started to bear fruit. Thereafter, apply a late-winter dressing of sulphate of potash at 15g per sq m (½oz per sq yd), followed by a similar amount of sulphate of ammonia in the spring. Give a spring dressing of superphosphate at 70g per sq m (2oz per sq yd) every two or three years.

If you prefer, apply an annual spring dressing of a general fertilizer, at 70g per sq m (2oz per sq yd). This should keep the tree growing and cropping satisfactorily.

Cover wall-trained trees overnight if frost is expected while they are flowering. Fine-mesh plastic sheeting, sold for greenhouse shading, can be used as a roller blind. Support it just clear of the branches on wire 'runners'.

PRUNING AND TRAINING
Prune young plums during the spring and mature plums during the summer. Winter, which is the normal season for pruning many other fruits, brings a greater risk of infection by silver leaf disease, which can enter the pruning cuts.
Bush trees Leave newly-planted two- and three-year-old trees unpruned for a year – that is, until the second spring after planting. Then, if the tree was bought as a two-year-old, choose three or four of the best-placed shoots to form the main branches, and cut each back by half to an outward-facing bud. Remove any others.

The following year – or, if you buy a three-year-old tree, in the first spring after

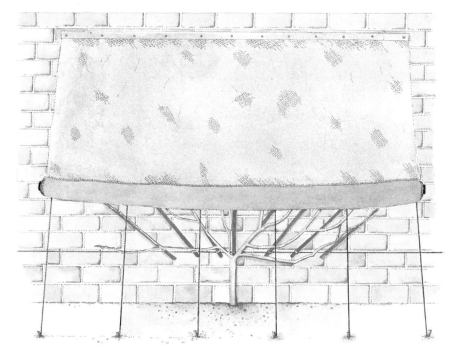

Protect a wall-trained tree from frost by means of a roll-down blind made from hessian or fine-mesh greenhouse shading. Support it on canes or wire runners. A similar device made of netting will keep birds off ripening fruit.

planting—cut back branch leaders by a third of the previous year's growth. This will include a number that have grown as laterals from the original shoots. From then on, prune only to remove or shorten misplaced or diseased branches, and to keep the centre of the tree open.

Dwarf pyramids During the spring after planting, prune the prevous year's growth on the main stem by two-thirds. Cut to a bud on the side opposite to the one chosen last year, in order to keep the stem in balance.

Each summer, shorten the current year's growth on branch leaders to 20cm (8in) and side-shoots to 15cm (6in). Once the tree has reached the required height, cut the main leader back almost to its base. Do this in spring and repeat each year.

Fans Build up the framework of branches as described for figs (see p.101). Once the tree is established, summer-prune it; shorten to about six leaves any shoots that are not needed to extend the fan structure. After harvesting, reduce these same shoots by half their length.

THINNING AND HARVESTING
Plum trees can carry remarkably heavy crops in good years. Since the branches of plum trees tend to be brittle, thinning the fruits is recommended to prevent branches breaking by being overladen. Thin when the fruits are the size of hazelnuts and once the stones have formed; repeat the thinning when fruits are about twice this size, to leave at least 5cm (2in) between fruits.

Later, if there still seems a risk of damage, support the trees with a central pole, as described for apples on p.91.

Hang netting over the trees, if possible, before the fruits start to ripen. Pick plums for cooking and preserving just before they are ripe, but leave dessert varieties to ripen fully on the tree. Pick plums with their stalks intact. Since plums do not ripen simultaneously, there is a good succession of fruits.

PESTS AND DISEASES
Plums suffer from aphids, caterpillars, fruit tree red spider mites and sawflies.

Among a number of possible diseases are brown rot, canker, rust and silver leaf.

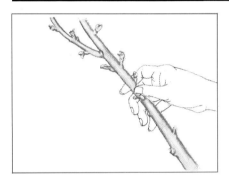
On a fan-trained plum, keep only the shoots that grow parallel with the wall. Rub out buds pointing outward or inward.

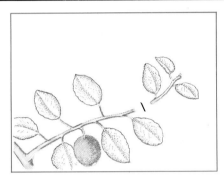
Summer-prune fan-trained trees by shortening to about six leaves those shoots not intended to extend the framework.

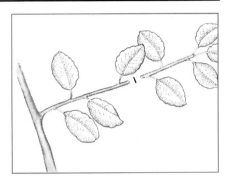
After the fruits have been gathered, cut back by half the shoots that were shortened earlier in the summer.

RECOMMENDED VARIETIES
Except where pollinators are suggested, the following varieties are self-fertile. In this case only one tree need be grown. Varieties are listed in approximate order of ripening.

'Czar' Cooking. The medium-sized purple fruits have a good flavour. The tree bears heavy crops and has some frost resistance.
'Cherry plum' Cooking. Small, heart-shaped scarlet fruit with yellow juicy flesh. A vigorous, round-headed tree with showy blossom.
'Early Laxton' Dessert and cooking. Red-flushed yellow fruits with pale blue bloom. Firm and juicy with good flavour. Pick early before fruits drop.
'Early Transparent Gage' Dessert. Small, round, yellow-green fruits, with sweet, rich flavour. A compact, heavy-cropping tree.

'Oullin's Gage' Dessert. Large, golden, sweet fruits which also freeze and bottle well. Vigorous, upright habit.
'Pershore Yellow' Cooking. Yellow skin and flesh, average flavour. A reliable cropper.
'Cambridge Gage' Dessert. An improved form of the original greengage. Yellowish fruits with a delicious flavour. Vigorous. Pollinate with 'Kirke's Blue' or 'Victoria'.
'Victoria' Dessert and cooking. Large, pale red fruits with excellent flavour. Moderate habit. Heavy and regular cropper.
'Warwickshire Drooper' Dessert and cooking. The tree has a somewhat weeping habit. Large yellow fruits that cook and freeze well.
'Greengage' Dessert. Small round plum with olive green skin, ripening to yellow-green. Greenish-yellow juicy flesh, sweet and well-flavoured. Grows vigorously, but

irregular cropping. Needs a warm climate.
'Kirke's Blue' Dessert. Medium/large fruits, dark purple with blue bloom. Sweet, juicy flesh. Moderately vigorous but needs sheltered situation for regular cropping. Pollinate with 'Cambridge Gage' or 'Victoria'.
'Marjorie's Seedling' Dessert and cooking. Large, blue-black fruits with yellow flesh. Late to flower, so often misses spring frosts.

Damsons
'Merryweather' Fairly vigorous. Large fruits with a good flavour.
'Shropshire Damson' Compact habit. Medium fruits and well-flavoured.

STONE FRUITS, pages 62–63
GROWING TREE FRUITS, pages 88–89
PESTS AND DISEASES, pages 108–111
BOTTLING, pages 228–229
FREEZING FRUITS, pages 234–235

Peaches and nectarines (*Prunus persica*) are closely related and their cultivation is broadly similar. Nectarines are smooth-skinned sports or mutations of the peach, which has a naturally downy or furry skin; they are generally smaller than peaches. Both fruits have juicy yellow flesh and an excellent flavour. They can be frozen, bottled or used in cooking but are at their best eaten fresh.

Of more practical importance, nectarines are less hardy than peaches and produce smaller crops. Even in quite mild climates, they are best grown against a sunny wall, and they are unsuitable for cold areas. Peaches are the safer choice for most food gardens, unless you prefer to grow nectarines for their singularly rich flavour.

Peaches are relatively hardy and will tolerate moderately cold winters, provided the summers are sufficiently warm and sunny to ripen the fruits. The chief hazard to peaches is spring frosts while they are in flower, since they are an early-flowering tree fruit. Peaches are also adversely affected by strong, cold winds, so a sheltered garden is needed if you live in an exposed district. The colder the garden, the more important it is to grow a variety that ripens early, before the end of summer.

Well-drained soil is essential, though it needs to contain plenty of moisture-holding organic matter. A pH fairly close to neutral is ideal, so lime dressings may be needed from time to time if the soil is markedly acid.

Provided there is shelter, peaches may be grown as bushes in the open, or else fan-trained against a wall. Either way, they need plenty of sunshine, so the wall for both peaches and nectarines needs to face in a direction between south-east and south-west. An average annual yield from a bush peach is around 20kg (40lb). A fan peach would produce half this amount and the crop from a fan nectarine would be substantially lighter.

Birds can be a hazard to the fruit buds in winter and the ripening fruits in summer. It is difficult to protect bush trees, which are too tall for a standard fruit cage, but it is fairly easy to devise a roll-up netting cover for wall-trained trees (see p.102); use 2cm (¾in) plastic netting for this.

Garden trees are nearly always supplied on 'St Julien A' rootstock, variously described as semi-dwarfing and semi-vigorous. This will result in a bush tree with a spread of 4.5m (15ft), or a fan extending to the same width. Peaches and nectarines are self-fertile, so only one tree need be grown.

MAKING A START
For a fan-trained peach, fasten horizontal wires to the wall with vine eyes; space them 15cm (6in) apart with the lowest about 45cm (1½ft) above the ground. Prepare the planting positions for all trees by digging in some well-rotted manure or garden compost. Improve the drainage first if necessary; a good layer of rubble just beneath spade depth may be sufficient.

Buy two-year-old or three-year-old trees from a nursery. Plant bare-rooted trees during the autumn or early winter; hammer in a supporting stake for bush trees first (see p.88). Dig a large hole so that the roots can be well spread out and plant the tree to the same depth as it was in the nursery.

Allow 4.5m (15ft) between trees if you are planting more than one. Plant fan trees at least 15cm (6in) from the wall, and 3.5–4.5m (12–15ft) apart if you are growing more than one. Incline the stem slightly toward the wall. For both kinds of tree spread a mulch of rotted manure or compost over and beyond the root area.

CARE OF THE CROP
Make sure that the site does not dry out during a dry spring or summer, especially for the first two years.

From the third year onward, give annual dressings of fertilizer. Apply a late-winter dressing of sulphate of potash at 15g per sq m (½oz per sq yd), followed by a similar amount of sulphate of ammonia in spring. Give a spring dressing of superphosphate at 70g per sq m (2oz per sq yd) every two or three years. If you prefer, apply an annual spring dressing of a general fertilizer, at 70g per sq m (2oz per sq yd), instead of the straight fertilizers. Renew the mulch afterward.

Since the flowers often open before many insects are flying about, it is worth trying to assist fertilization throughout the flowering period. It is important to try to give the flowers some protection if frost threatens.

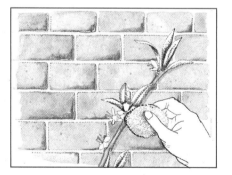

Hand-pollination helps to ensure a maximum crop. Make this a daily task while the flowers are open. Transfer the pollen by touching the flowers lightly with a tuft of cotton wool or a fine-haired brush. The best time for this is around midday and when the sun is shining.

THINNING AND HARVESTING
Thin the fruits from early summer onward if you are fortunate enough to get a heavy crop. Thin over a period, starting when the fruits are the size of large peas. Aim to leave 15–23cm (6–9in) between them.

Ripe peaches and nectarines part easily from the tree when lifted and gently twisted. Handle them very carefully and store them unwrapped in a cool place for a week or two if they cannot be eaten at once.

STONE FRUITS, pages 62–63
GROWING TREE FRUITS, pages 88–89
FIGS, pages 100–101
PLUMS, pages 102–103

  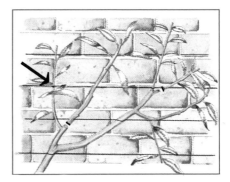

This year-old shoot will carry the coming season's fruits. In spring, leave a replacement shoot to develop at its base but reduce other growths to a single leaf.

The branch has been trained and tied in as an extension of the main framework. Shoots growing from it are thinned out in spring to a spacing of about 15cm (6in).

At the end of summer, after the fruits have been picked, prune the laterals that carried them back to the replacement shoots that were left at their base. Tie the replacement shoots in to the horizontal wires.

PRUNING AND TRAINING

Fans Build up the framework in the same way as described for figs (see pp.100–101); train the shoots to canes attached to the horizontal wires.

Once the tree is mature, fruits will be borne on shoots that developed during the previous season. The aim of pruning is therefore to stimulate the constant annual renewal of young shoots. To start the process, allow upward- or downward-pointing shoots to develop at about 15cm (6in) intervals along the branches. Rub out surplus shoots, including any growing outward or toward the wall. Tie in the chosen shoots to the wires and cut their tips off if they are more than 45cm (1½ft) long.

During each successive spring, pinch out inward- or outward-pointing buds as soon as they break. Allow a growth bud near the base of each year-old lateral to develop into a replacement growth, and reduce the others to a single leaf. Tie the replacement in as it grows, but tip it if it becomes longer than the year-old lateral that it will replace.

During the early summer repeat the thinning and tying-in of shoots that develop along the branches. Shorten the fruit-bearing laterals to six leaves, and their replacements to ten leaves. In late summer, after picking, prune back the fruited laterals.

Bush trees Establish the branch framework by pruning in late spring in the same way as for bush plums (see p.103). Cut back to 10cm (4in) shoots that are not required to form secondary branches. Remove all blossom during the first spring after planting, and most of it during the second year.

Once the tree is mature, prune in spring to remove badly-placed branches and to encourage new growth. Do this by cutting off a proportion of older, unproductive wood. Apply a wound-sealing paint, since peaches are susceptible to bacterial canker.

PESTS AND DISEASES

Aphids, glasshouse red spider mites and scale insects are the most likely pests.

Brown rot, canker, powdery mildew, peach leaf curl and silver leaf are fairly common ailments.

RECOMMENDED VARIETIES

The following varieties are listed in their approximate order of ripening.

Peaches

'Amsden June' Ripens in midsummer. Good flavour, average crops. Whitish flesh.

'Duke of York' Large, crimson fruits. A good choice for a wall.

'Peregrine' Large, firm, highly-coloured fruits with an excellent flavour. A favourite variety.

'Rochester' Large fruits with yellow flesh and good flavour. Flowers a little later than 'Peregrine'.

'Red Haven' Bears heavy crops of medium-sized red fruits. Yellow flesh.

'Royal George' A good cropper, noted for its flavour. Ripens toward the end of summer.

Nectarines

'John Rivers' Ripens in midsummer; the yellow fruits have a rich flavour.

'Lord Napier' Large, crimson-flushed yellow fruits. The most widely-grown nectarine.

The following pages help you to identify and control the various pests and diseases that may affect fruits. Those most likely to blight particular fruits are listed in their individual descriptions, but if you are careful your fruits may be very little affected.

The best way to avoid attack by pests or infection by disease is to make sure that your soil is nourished and improved regularly and kept free from weeds, so that the plants you grow are strong and healthy. Always follow the correct cultivation and pruning procedures.

It is a matter of individual choice whether you make use of commercial pesticides or rely on more homely remedies and organic sprays. Both courses of action are suggested here, where alternatives exist.

The commercial chemicals mentioned (marked □) are a selection from the many options often available; they are described by their chemical names, not by brand names. You may need to check labels and packages carefully, or else study the leaflets and booklets provided by pesticide manufacturers, to be sure of what you are buying.

Commercial pesticides vary considerably in their toxicity. Pirimicarb, for example, is a most efficient killer of aphids but has no adverse effect on other insects, including beneficial predators. When using chemicals, always carry out the manufacturer's instructions to the letter, and follow the guidelines given on p.21, Care with Chemicals. Do not spray fruit trees when in flower because bees and other pollinating insects may be killed.

The organic remedies suggested (marked △), which are claimed to be safer, are those recommended by the Henry Doubleday Research Association (HDRA), leading advocates of organic gardening (see pp.20–21).

APHIDS
These small insects live in clusters on buds, leaves and shoot tips of fruit trees. They feed on the sap, causing distortion and stunted growth, and often spread disease.
□ Spray in midwinter with tar-oil emulsion. In spring and summer spray active colonies with permethrin, pirimicarb, malathion, fenitrothion or dimethoate.
△ Spray with rhubarb and elderleaf mixture, or quassia and soapy water.

WOOLLY APHIDS
These aphids are recognized by their tufts of waxy wool. Apples are particularly susceptible.
□ Spray trees with a winter-wash of tar-oil emulsion. During the active season, spray with dimethoate or brush with a spray-strength solution of permethrin, malathion, pirimicarb or pirimiphos-methyl.
△ Paint affected parts with methylated spirits as early in spring as possible.

BLACKCURRANT GALL MITES
Damaging pests that cause buds to swell, then cease to develop – hence the disorder's common name, 'big bud'. They also spread reversion diseases.
□ Pick off affected buds in late winter. Spray with benomyl when the flowers first open, and repeat every ten days.
△ Spray with diluted permanganate of potash (30g/1oz in 10 litres/2 gallons of water).

CAPSID BUGS
Apples, gooseberries and currants are vulnerable to these pests. They feed on sap and inject toxic saliva, causing ragged holes in the leaves, and deformed and scabbed fruits.
□ As a prevention, spray after petal-fall with permethrin, primiphos-methyl, malathion or dimethoate, or dust or spray with derris. Follow maker's instructions for repeat sprays.

CATERPILLARS
Caterpillars are the larvae of many moths and butterflies that feed on the leaves of bushes and trees at any time from spring onward. Particularly troublesome ones are listed separately below.
□ Pick them off by hand if numbers are small. Otherwise, spray with trichlorphon, malathion, permethrin or pirimiphos-methyl, or dust or spray with derris.
△ Spray with quassia or nicotine.

TORTRIX MOTHS
The caterpillars spin a silken web around the leaves and stems of apple and pear trees to provide themselves with cover.
□ Spray forcefully with permethrin, trichlorphon or pirimiphos-methyl.

WINTER MOTHS
The caterpillars attack buds and young leaves of fruit trees. In addition to evident damage, leaves may be spun together with silken threads.
□ Spray with fenitrothion, permethrin or pirimiphos-methyl as the buds open and leaves develop. Spray with tar-oil emulsion in winter.
△ Place grease bands around the tree trunks in autumn.

CODLING MOTHS
Their grubs are usually the maggots found in apples and pears.
□ Permethrin is effective if sprayed every two weeks during the first half of summer while fruits are developing.
△ Tie sacking around tree trunks and branches during midsummer to trap caterpillars seeking a place to hibernate after leaving the fruits.

PEAR AND CHERRY SLUGWORM
These dark, mucous-covered caterpillars consume the foliage of pear and cherry trees, sometimes reducing it to a skeleton.
□ Permethrin, fenitrothion and malathion are effective sprays. Alternatively, spray or dust with derris.
△ Spray with quassia.

FRUIT TREE RED SPIDER MITES

These tiny sap-sucking insects cause discoloured leaves and early leaf-fall on apples, plums and apricots.
□ Malathion and pirimiphos-methyl are effective sprays; also the systemic insecticide dimethoate.

GLASSHOUSE RED SPIDER MITES

A number of outdoor fruits, including peaches, strawberries and grapes, may be affected, as well as indoor crops of melons. Mottling and yellowing of the leaves are the early signs, followed by leaf fall. Fine, silky webbing may be seen.
□ Spray at 10-day intervals with dimethoate or malathion.
△ Maintain a humid atmosphere.

LEAFHOPPERS

These aptly-named insects cause the upper surface of many kinds of leaves to become mottled. Damage is slight but disease may be spread.
□ Malathion, permethrin and dimethoate are effective sprays.

LEAF MIDGES

Blackcurrants are at risk from these minute larvae that cluster on the tips of shoots, causing distortion and stunting.
□ Spray with dimethoate.

MEALY BUGS

The leaves of greenhouse vines become stunted, with patches of waxy threads covering colonies of grubs or clusters of yellow eggs. Damage can be serious if unchecked.
□ Spray with malathion, dimethoate or permethrin before the fruit swells. A winter-wash of tar-oil breaks the life cycle.

PEAR LEAF BLISTER MITES

The young leaves of pear trees become disfigured with yellow or red spots and blisters. Pustules may develop on fruits.
□ There is no effective spray. The only remedy is to pick off and burn damaged leaves.

PEAR MIDGE

Pale orange maggots infest the fruits themselves. Affected pears will become discoloured and fall early.
□ Collect and destroy fallen fruits. Spray with permethrin when the flowers are about to open.
△ Thin the fruits when they are about 2.5cm (1in) long, concentrating on the misshapen ones which are usually the ones that contain the larvae.

RASPBERRY BEETLES

The grubs feed on the ripening raspberries, blackberries and loganberries.
□ Spray plants with permethrin once every two weeks in the period between flowering and harvesting.
△ Spray bushes with pyrethrum or quassia.

STRAWBERRY BEETLE

These quite large, shiny black beetles, which are easily seen, remove the seeds from the fruits, causing them to shrivel.
□ Methiocarb slug pellets give some control. The beetles may also be trapped in jam jars buried up to their rims in the soil.

SAWFLIES

Different species attack apples, gooseberries and plums. The caterpillars of apple and plum sawflies burrow into the fruitlets, causing them to drop. Gooseberry sawflies strip foliage.
□ If there has been trouble previously, spray plants with permethrin, pirimiphos-methyl, fenitrothion or dimethoate after the petals fall.
△ Spray with derris, pyrethrum, nicotine or quassia.

SCALE INSECTS

The clusters of tiny scales sometimes found on the stems and the undersides of leaves of peaches, apricots and vines are, in fact, the females of this sap-sucking species of insect. The scales are yellow or brown, and flat or slightly rounded.
□ Winter spraying with tar-oil emulsion gives good control. Malathion, permethrin and dimethoate are suitable sprays in the growing season.

SLUGS AND SNAILS

Strawberries are most at risk; the fruits may suffer considerable damage during damp weather if no counter-action is taken.
□ Scatter metaldehyde or methiocarb pellets in small groupings before the straw is laid around the plants. Keep the surrounding area free from weeds.
△ Trap the pests by sinking a soup plate, containing dilute, sweetened beer, level with the soil. Several such traps may be needed.

AMERICAN GOOSEBERRY MILDEW

Leaves, shoot tips and fruits are covered with a white, powdery growth, which results in distortion. It also affects blackcurrants.
□ Spray with dinocap, thiophanate-methyl, benomyl or bupirimate with triforine. Follow makers' instructions.
△ Spray with a mixture of 90g (3oz) washing soda and 30g (1oz) soapflakes dissolved in 4.5 litres (1 gallon) of hot water. Allow to cool before use.

BROWN SPOT

A fungus that attacks ripe fruits, especially plums, including those in store. Spreads rapidly to other fruits by entering where the skin is damaged.
□ Difficult to treat by spraying. The main safeguard is to remove and burn infected fruits as soon as you see them. Wash your hands before touching other fruits.

CANE BLIGHT

A fungus disease that attacks the base of raspberry canes; it results in discoloration and brittleness. The leaves wither and die-back occurs.
□ Cut back damaged canes to beneath soil level and burn the wood removed. Spray new growth with cupric carbonate or Bordeaux mixture.
△ Spray with potassium permanganate.

CANE SPOT

This fungus disease principally affects raspberries, loganberries, blackberries and various hybrid berries. Purple-edged brown spots develop on the leaves and canes. Foliage and fruits may be distorted.
□ Spray with Bordeaux mixture, cupric carbonate, benomyl or thiophanate-methyl at 14-day intervals, after cutting out and burning the worst-affected canes.

CANKER

The fungal canker that afflicts apples and pears causes the bark on branches to shrink and expose the inner wood. The gummy canker that develops on peaches, plums and cherries causes the leaves to wither; it is bacterial in origin.
□ To treat apple canker, cut off badly affected spurs and small branches. Trim away damaged wood from larger branches and apply a fungicidal paint. Spray in winter with tar-oil emulsion.
△ Remove branches damaged or killed by bacterial canker; treat cuts with a fungicidal pruning paint. Spray with cupric carbonate or Bordeaux mixture.
△ Summer prune to remove damaged wood; winter spray with Burgundy mixture.

CORAL SPOT

A fungus that may attack trees and soft fruits. Spore masses appear on old or dead shoots and branches.
□ Cut off affected wood a little way beyond the spores. Treat cuts with a fungicidal sealing paint.
△ Cut back any branch that dies at the tip. Feed red and white currant bushes, which are particularly susceptible, only with low-nitrogen organic material and do not keep bushes for longer than 12 years.

CROWN GALL

A number of soft fruits, including blackberries and loganberries, may be affected by this bacterial disease. Rounded growths, or galls, develop on the roots, sometimes stunting growth.
□ Prevent by avoiding root damage, which allows the infection to enter. When replanting in the same area, first dip the plant roots in a copper fungicide.

CUCUMBER MOSAIC VIRUS

The leaves of infected melons become mottled and the plants stunted. Highly infectious, it is often spread by aphids.
□ As a precaution, prevent aphid colonies from becoming established. Burn infected plants as soon as you see them. Avoid carrying the spores on hands or tools.

COLLAR ROT

This soil-borne fungus causes the stems of greenhouse melons to rot close to soil level.
□ If spotted early, plants may be saved by first paring away damaged tissue, then dusting with a fungicidal powder, such as captan. Avoid overwatering to reduce the likelihood of attack.

DIE-BACK

The death of young shoots and larger branches may be due to severe weather or to a specific disease. Die-back is common on apricots, in this instance being due to a fungus.
□ Cut back to sound wood, then treat the cut with sealing paint. Try to improve growing conditions generally.

FIREBLIGHT

Both apples and pears may be attacked by this bacterial disease. It causes foliage to wither and shoots to die, with cankers forming at their base.
□ Suspected outbreaks must be reported to the Ministry of Agriculture, Fisheries and Food, who will advise you on what to do. For the local address, see under Agriculture in your telephone directory.

GREY MOULD

A widespread fungus disease, particularly troublesome on soft fruits. Berries with the soft grey covering invariably rot.
□ Because the infection starts at flowering time, spray preventively from the time flowers open with benomyl or thiophanate-methyl. Repeat every 14 days. It is worth spraying as soon as you see any symptoms if preventive action has not been taken.
△ Dust with flowers of sulphur.

HONEY FUNGUS

Named for the colour of the toadstools that emerge from the base of the infected trees and bushes, this is a particularly persistent and widespread organism which kills infected plants.
□ Remove and burn infected trees and bushes, and as many of their roots as possible. Treat the soil with a phenolic compound.

LEAF SPOT

Various fungus infections cause spotting and browning of the leaves, and early leaf fall. Weak plants are most likely to succumb.
□ Most fungicides, including those based on copper, benomyl and thiophanate-methyl, give good control. Remove badly-affected leaves and burn fallen leaves

in autumn.
△ Spray with Burgundy mixture and avoid dressings of nitrogen-rich manure.

PEACH LEAF CURL

A fungus specific to peaches, nectarines and other *Prunus* species. It causes leaves to blister, followed by their premature fall.
□ Spray in winter with mancozeb or a copper fungicide. Remove diseased leaves and burn them.

POWDERY MILDEW

The leaves, flowers and shoots of many trees and bushes may develop a powdery coating, which causes them to shrivel.
□ Spray every two weeks, from the time the buds burst, with benomyl, thiophanate-methyl or bupirimate with triforine.
△ Spray with Burgundy mixture in mid-winter.

REVERSION

This disease of blackcurrants, spread by mites, causes bushes to crop poorly. Other symptoms are that the leaves become smaller, with fewer segments, while flower buds are hairless and magenta-coloured.
□ There is no cure. Lift and burn diseased bushes.

RUST

A fungus infection that attacks a wide range of plants, including plums and blackberries. Symptoms are brown or yellowish masses of spores on the leaves.
□ Remove and burn badly affected foliage. Improve growing conditions. In severe or persistent outbreaks, spray with cupric carbonate,

mancozeb or bupirimate and triforine.

SCAB

The scabs form on the fruits of apples or pears and often result in cracks. The leaves of affected trees are blotched.
□ Spray weekly with cupric carbonate, mancozeb, benomyl or bupirimate and triforine, once the scales fall from the opening buds.
△ At pruning time, remove any spurs or

shoots with blisters or cracked areas. Sweep up leaves in autumn and burn them; spray the tree with Burgundy mixture.

SCALD

A condition caused by excessive heat, often in greenhouses, which shows as pale, wrinkled patches on fruits. This may result in rotting. Grapes are particularly vulnerable.
□ Cut off damaged fruits. Provide shade and extra ventilation and promote a more humid atmosphere.

SHANKING

A disorder of grapes resulting from a poor root system, lack of nourishment or over-heavy cropping. As a result, the berries do not ripen and eventually shrivel.
□ The remedy lies in better growing conditions. Feed and mulch the bed, and give plenty of water, to prevent the same trouble recurring next year. Limit the

number of branches and reduce the number of grapes on each bunch.

SILVER LEAF

This fungus disease affects plums, especially, but also apples, pears and some other fruit trees. The leaves become silvered and peel off easily, but a more serious symptom is that the branches die back by stages. To distinguish it from false silver leaf, which is caused by poor growing conditions,

check that affected branches show a dark stain when cut across. With false silver leaf there is no stain.
□ Cut back diseased branches well beyond the point at which staining can be seen. Treat cuts with a fungicidal wound-sealing paint. For false silver leaf, give greater attention to feeding and watering.

SPUR BLIGHT

A fungal disease causing purple patches to appear on raspberry and loganberry canes, and brown spots on their leaves. Spurs and axillary buds shrivel and die.
□ Cut out and burn affected canes after fruiting. In spring spray the emerging canes with Bordeaux mixture, benomyl or

thiophanate-methyl, Repeat every two weeks until plants cease flowering.

VIRUS DISEASES

Strawberries and raspberries are particularly vulnerable to virus infections, which cause distortion, wilting and oddly-coloured foliage and stems. They are spread principally by insects.
□ There is no cure. Lift and burn infected plants, and replace them with virus-free stock in fresh ground.

Keep insects, especially aphids, in check.

The

VEGETABLE COLOUR
CATALOGUE I

Much of the appeal of home-grown vegetables lies in their variety as well as their flavour and freshness. While the following colour plates cannot claim to be comprehensive, they suggest the scope available to food growers within certain categories of vegetable: legumes (peas and beans), stalks and shoots, tubers and root vegetables, and vegetable fruits such as tomatoes, cucumbers and marrows. (The colour plates for brassicas, salad vegetables and herbs are on pages 176–192.)

The separate vegetable entries, on pages 134–171, give specific details about sowing and individual cultivation requirements, as well as recommending varieties additional to those illustrated in the colour plates.

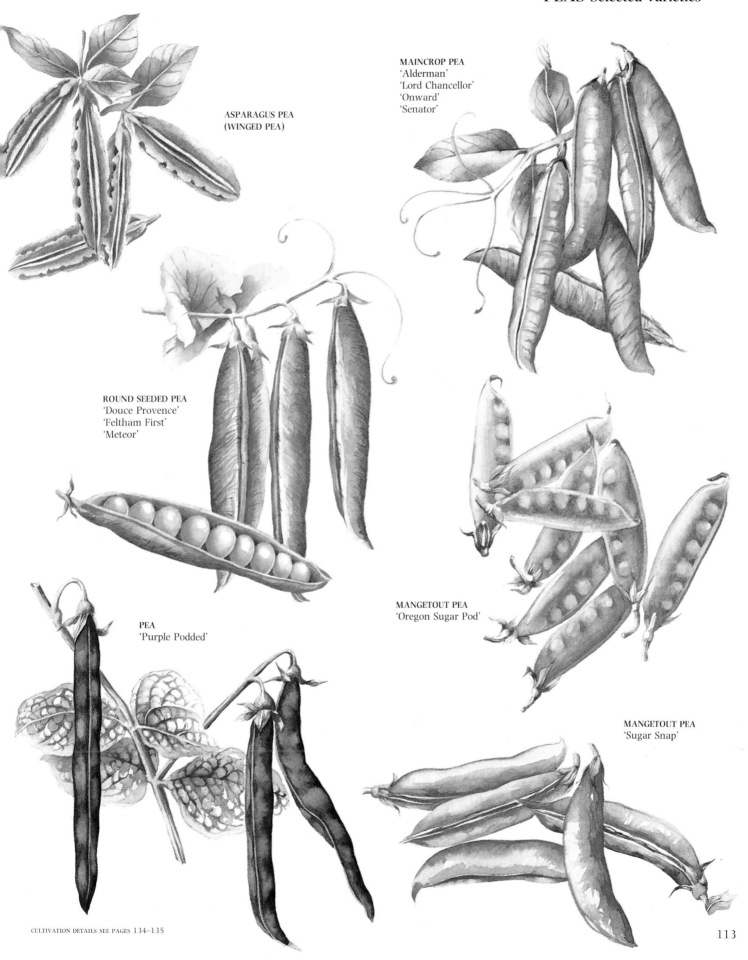

MAINCROP PEA
'Alderman'
'Lord Chancellor'
'Onward'
'Senator'

ASPARAGUS PEA
(WINGED PEA)

ROUND SEEDED PEA
'Douce Provence'
'Feltham First'
'Meteor'

PEA
'Purple Podded'

MANGETOUT PEA
'Oregon Sugar Pod'

MANGETOUT PEA
'Sugar Snap'

BEANS, SWEET CORN AND ARTICHOKES Selected varieties

FRENCH BEAN
'Masterpiece'
'The Prince'
'Hunter'

FRENCH BEAN
'Kinghorn Wax'
'Mont d'Or'

BROAD BEAN
'Aquadulce'
'Imperial Green Longpod'
'Imperial White Windsor'
'Jubilee Hysor'

FRENCH BEAN
'Royal Burgundy'

FRENCH BEAN (HARICOT)
'Chevrier Vert'

RUNNER BEAN
'Achievement'
'Butler'
'Enorma'
'Polestar'
'Scarlet Emperor'

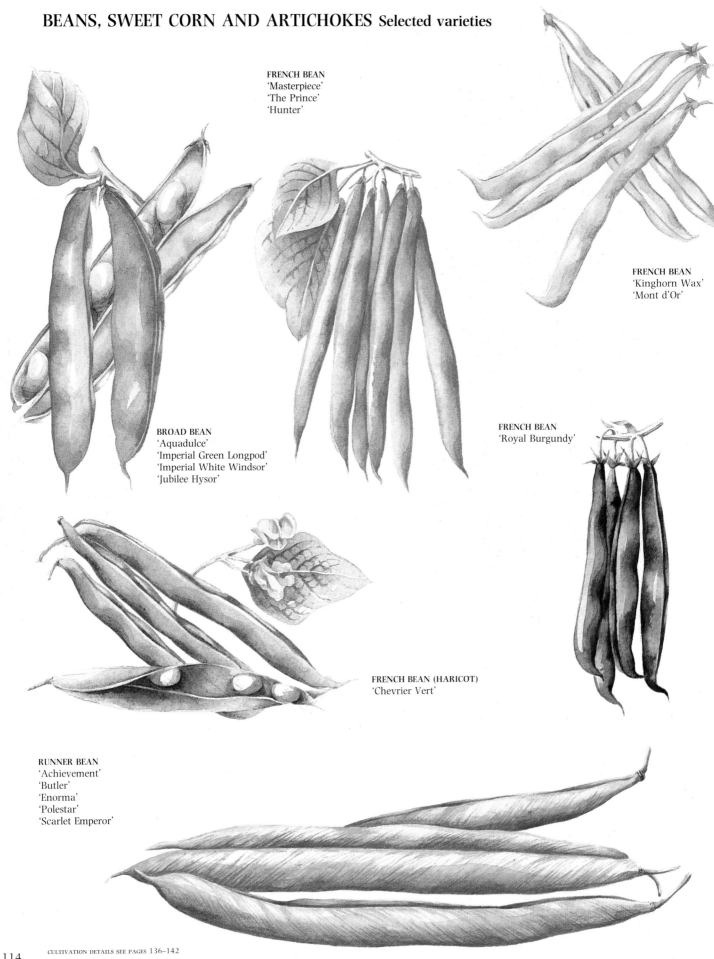

CULTIVATION DETAILS SEE PAGES 136–142

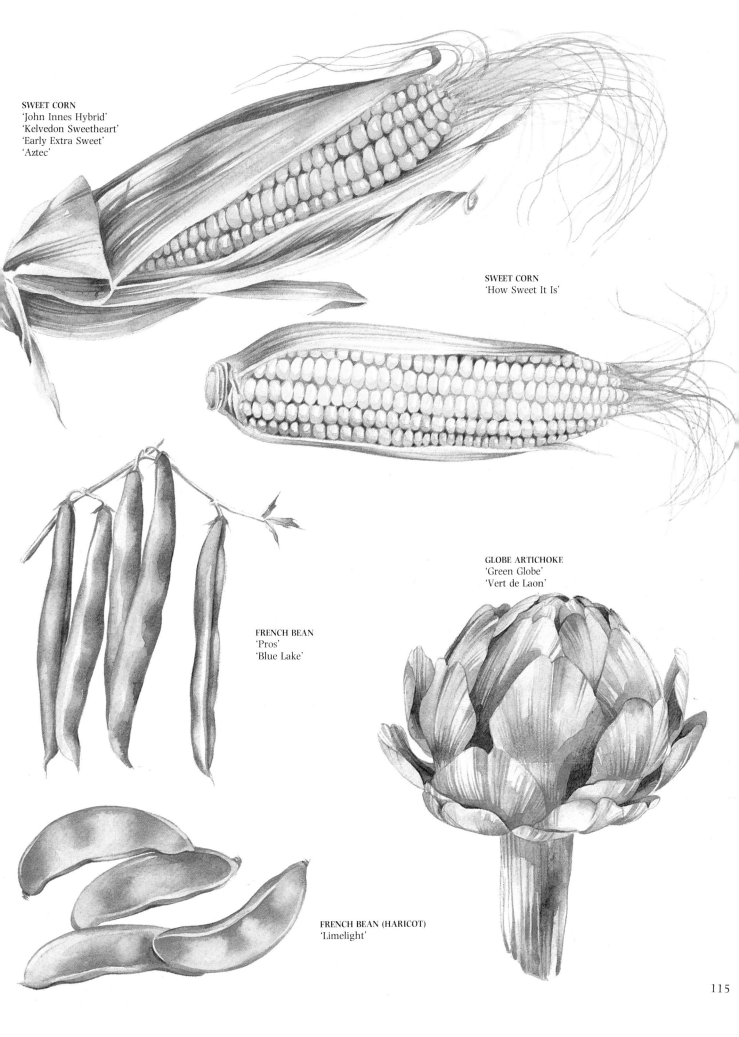

SWEET CORN
'John Innes Hybrid'
'Kelvedon Sweetheart'
'Early Extra Sweet'
'Aztec'

SWEET CORN
'How Sweet It Is'

GLOBE ARTICHOKE
'Green Globe'
'Vert de Laon'

FRENCH BEAN
'Pros'
'Blue Lake'

FRENCH BEAN (HARICOT)
'Limelight'

STALKS AND SHOOTS Selected varieties

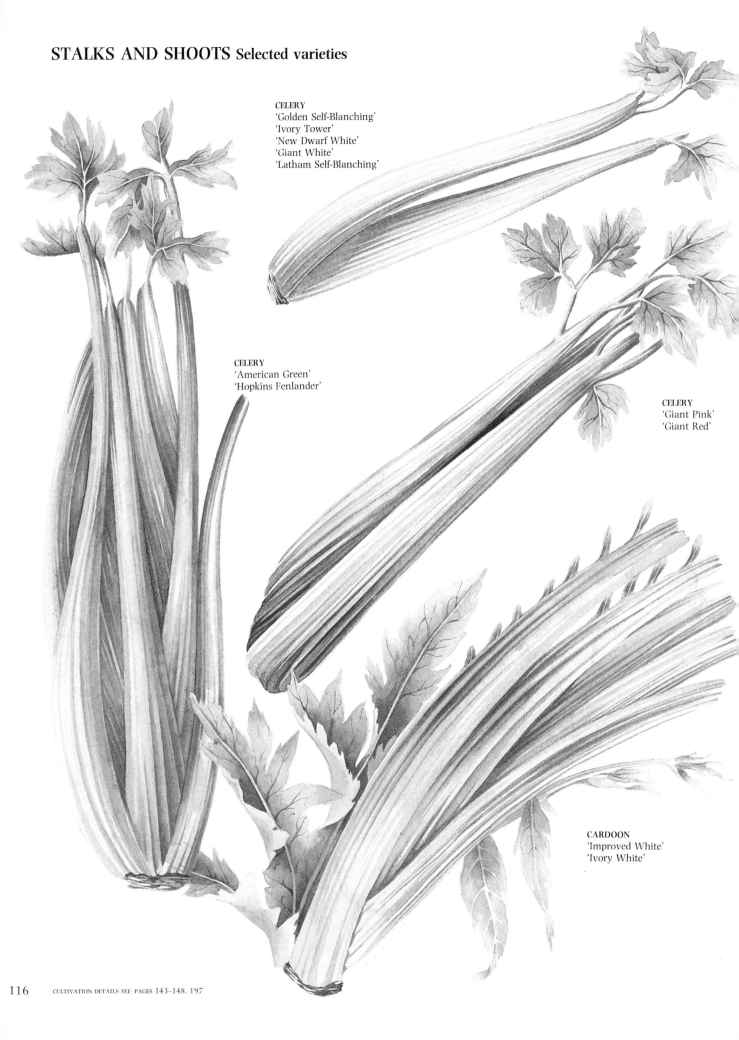

CELERY
'Golden Self-Blanching'
'Ivory Tower'
'New Dwarf White'
'Giant White'
'Latham Self-Blanching'

CELERY
'American Green'
'Hopkins Fenlander'

CELERY
'Giant Pink'
'Giant Red'

CARDOON
'Improved White'
'Ivory White'

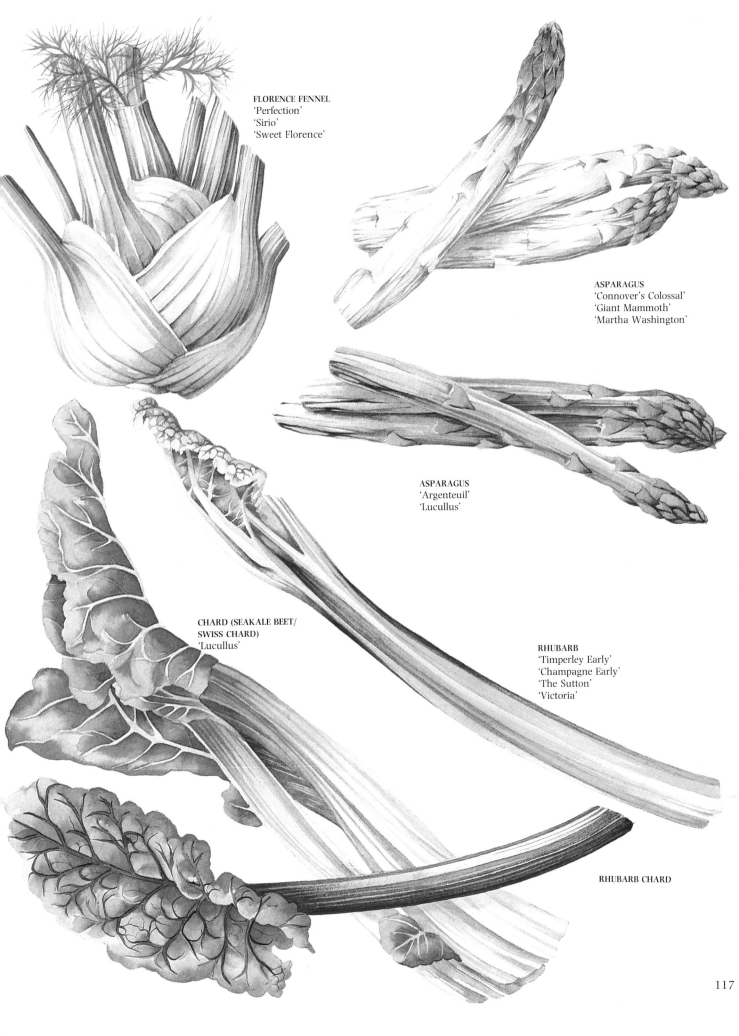

FLORENCE FENNEL
'Perfection'
'Sirio'
'Sweet Florence'

ASPARAGUS
'Connover's Colossal'
'Giant Mammoth'
'Martha Washington'

ASPARAGUS
'Argenteuil'
'Lucullus'

**CHARD (SEAKALE BEET/
SWISS CHARD)**
'Lucullus'

RHUBARB
'Timperley Early'
'Champagne Early'
'The Sutton'
'Victoria'

RHUBARB CHARD

POTATOES AND OTHER TUBERS
Selected varieties

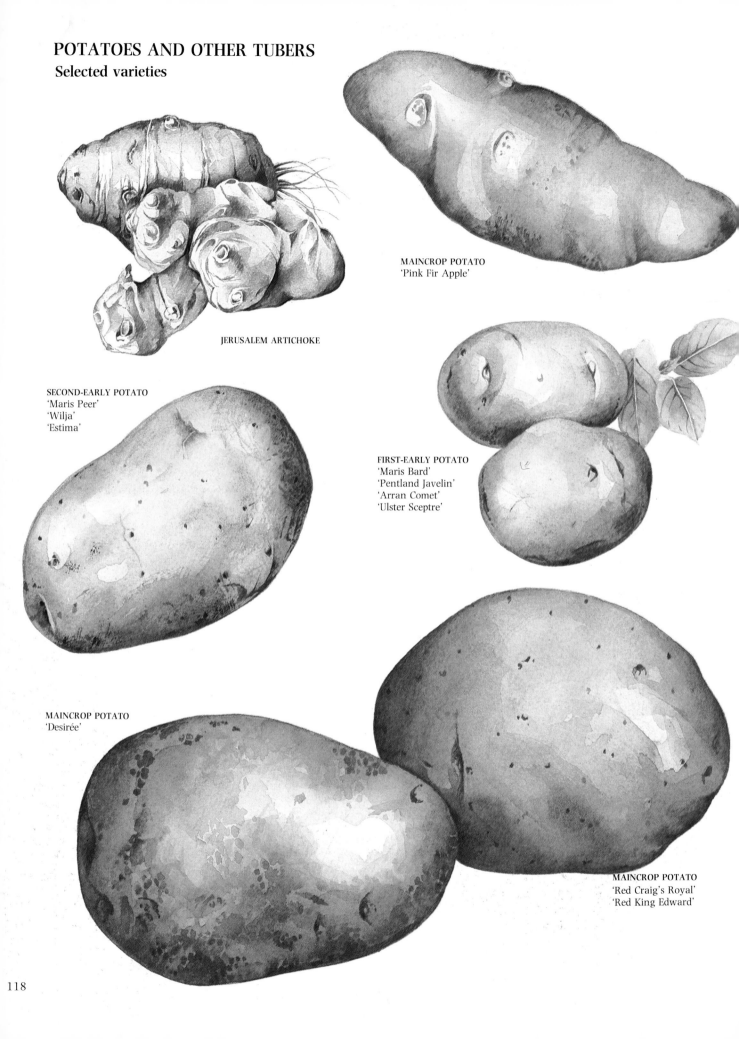

MAINCROP POTATO
'Pink Fir Apple'

JERUSALEM ARTICHOKE

SECOND-EARLY POTATO
'Maris Peer'
'Wilja'
'Estima'

FIRST-EARLY POTATO
'Maris Bard'
'Pentland Javelin'
'Arran Comet'
'Ulster Sceptre'

MAINCROP POTATO
'Desirée'

MAINCROP POTATO
'Red Craig's Royal'
'Red King Edward'

FIRST-EARLY POTATO
'Foremost'

MAINCROP POTATO
'King Edward'

MAINCROP POTATO
'Pentland Crown'

MAINCROP POTATO
'Majestic'
'Maris Piper'
'Pentland Dell'

NOVELTY POTATO
'Purple Congo'

CULTIVATION DETAILS SEE PAGES 150–151

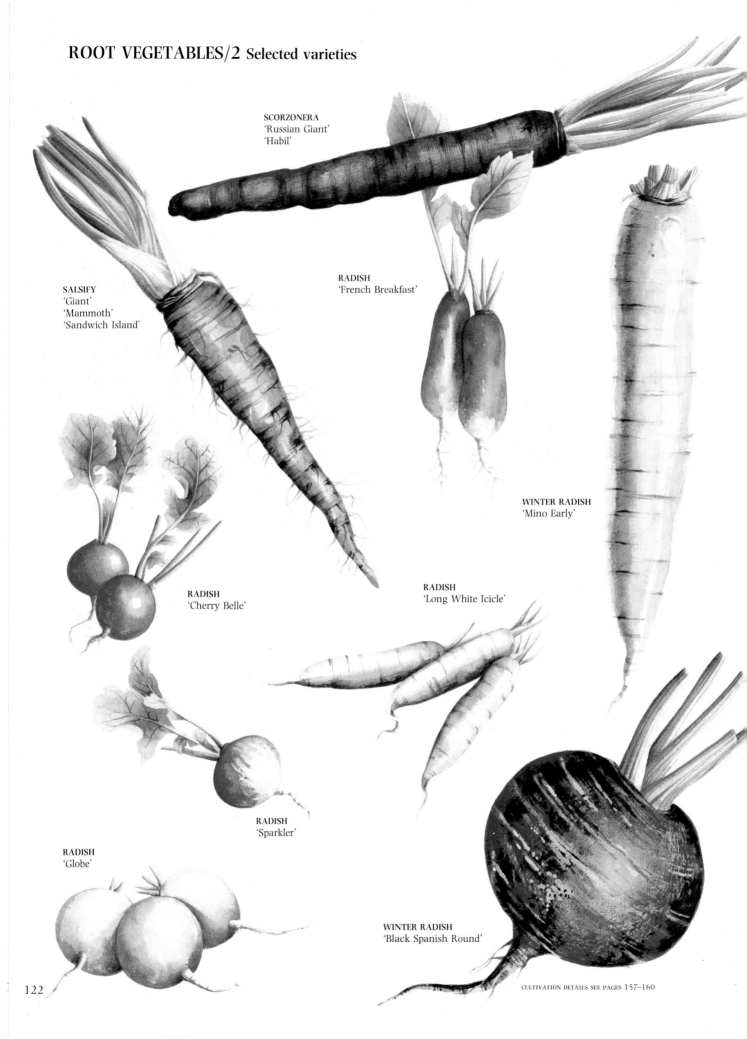

ROOT VEGETABLES/2 Selected varieties

SCORZONERA
'Russian Giant'
'Habil'

RADISH
'French Breakfast'

SALSIFY
'Giant'
'Mammoth'
'Sandwich Island'

WINTER RADISH
'Mino Early'

RADISH
'Cherry Belle'

RADISH
'Long White Icicle'

RADISH
'Sparkler'

RADISH
'Globe'

WINTER RADISH
'Black Spanish Round'

CULTIVATION DETAILS SEE PAGES 157–160

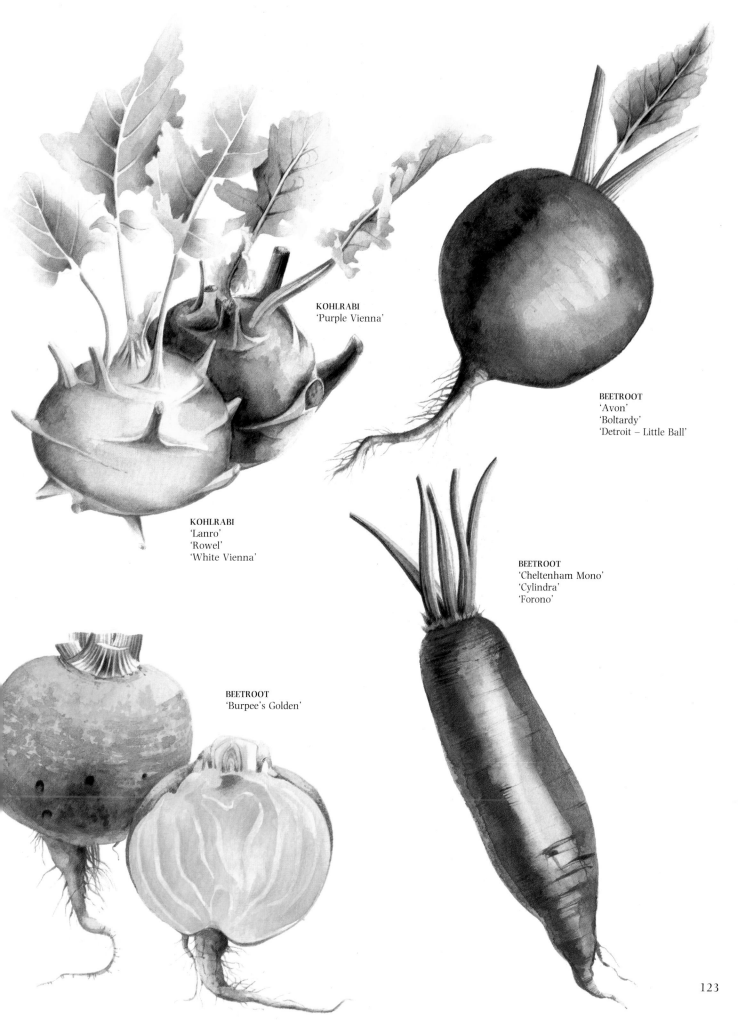

KOHLRABI
'Purple Vienna'

KOHLRABI
'Lanro'
'Rowel'
'White Vienna'

BEETROOT
'Avon'
'Boltardy'
'Detroit – Little Ball'

BEETROOT
'Cheltenham Mono'
'Cylindra'
'Forono'

BEETROOT
'Burpee's Golden'

123

SQUASHES AND PUMPKINS Selected varieties

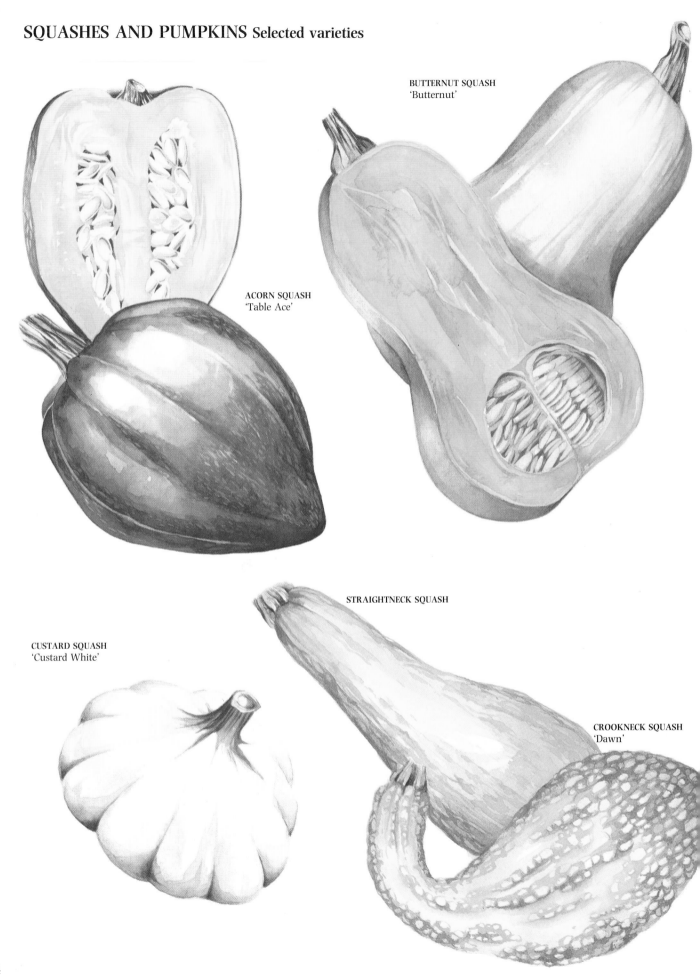

BUTTERNUT SQUASH
'Butternut'

ACORN SQUASH
'Table Ace'

STRAIGHTNECK SQUASH

CUSTARD SQUASH
'Custard White'

CROOKNECK SQUASH
'Dawn'

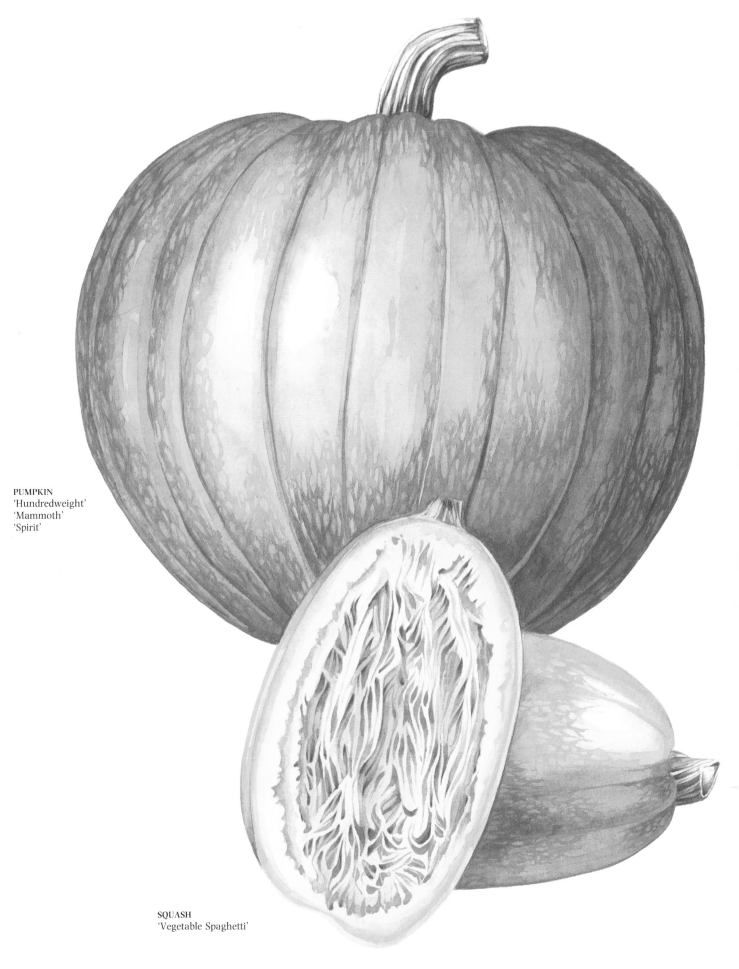

PUMPKIN
'Hundredweight'
'Mammoth'
'Spirit'

SQUASH
'Vegetable Spaghetti'

VEGETABLE FRUITS Selected varieties

MARROW
'Long Green Bush'
'Long Green Trailing'

RIDGE CUCUMBER
'Burpee Hybrid'
'Bush Crop'
'King of the Ridge'
'Patio Pik'
'Burpless Tasty Green'

GREENHOUSE CUCUMBER
'Butcher's Disease Resisting'
'Conqueror'
'Pepinex'
'Pepita'
'Telegraph'

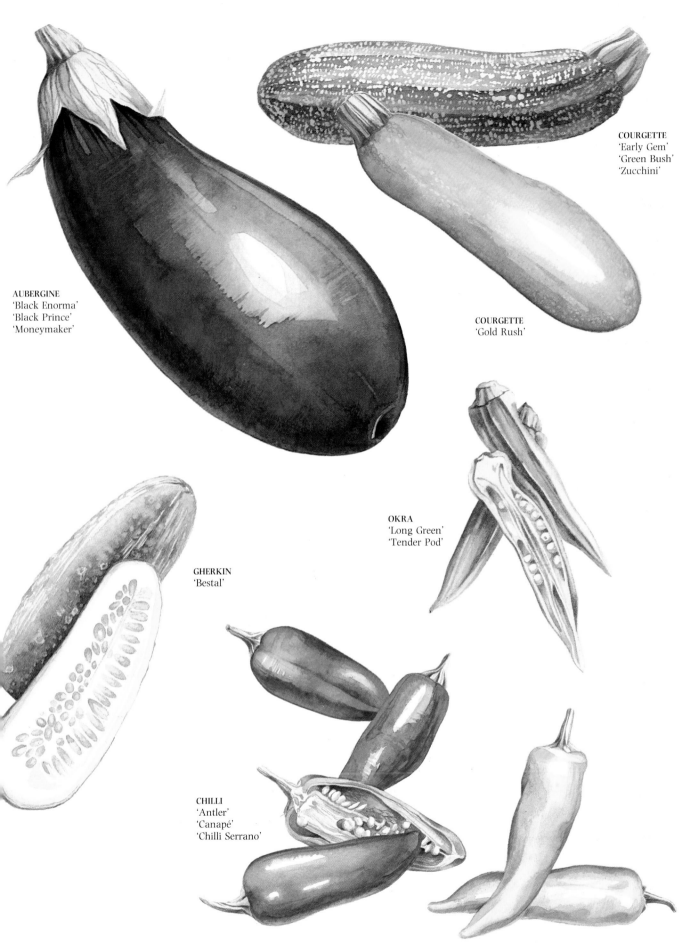

COURGETTE
'Early Gem'
'Green Bush'
'Zucchini'

AUBERGINE
'Black Enorma'
'Black Prince'
'Moneymaker'

COURGETTE
'Gold Rush'

OKRA
'Long Green'
'Tender Pod'

GHERKIN
'Bestal'

CHILLI
'Antler'
'Canapé'
'Chilli Serrano'

CULTIVATION DETAILS SEE PAGES 161–167

127

TOMATOES, PEPPERS AND MUSHROOMS Selected varieties

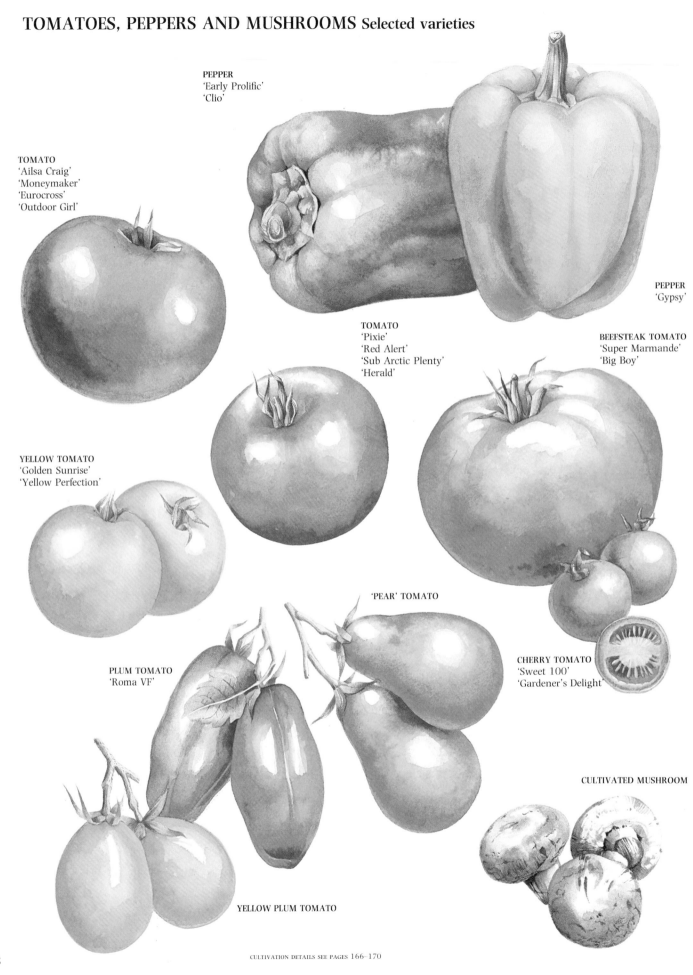

PEPPER
'Early Prolific'
'Clio'

TOMATO
'Ailsa Craig'
'Moneymaker'
'Eurocross'
'Outdoor Girl'

PEPPER
'Gypsy'

TOMATO
'Pixie'
'Red Alert'
'Sub Arctic Plenty'
'Herald'

BEEFSTEAK TOMATO
'Super Marmande'
'Big Boy'

YELLOW TOMATO
'Golden Sunrise'
'Yellow Perfection'

'PEAR' TOMATO

CHERRY TOMATO
'Sweet 100'
'Gardener's Delight'

PLUM TOMATO
'Roma VF'

CULTIVATED MUSHROOM

YELLOW PLUM TOMATO

128

CULTIVATION DETAILS SEE PAGES 166–170

VEGETABLE GARDEN I

Vegetable gardening is an intensely personal matter, not least because it offers you the opportunity of choosing to cultivate those vegetables you and your family most like to eat. By growing your own crops, you can enjoy them in the sure knowledge that they are not only full of flavour and goodness but also free from harmful chemicals and pesticides.

The selection of vegetable crops available to today's food gardener is huge – and increases every year as seed suppliers introduce new varieties. Yellow beetroot, courgettes and tomatoes; white radishes; pink celery; purple beans and onions; and miniature, globe-shaped carrots are just a few of the many new vegetables you can choose from.

The techniques of vegetable cultivation depend more on the group of plants to which each belongs than on the individual variety. Because plants with common characteristics share the same basic needs, the vegetables in the following section are grouped together according to those needs. The major groupings are: pods and seeds; stalks and shoots; root vegetables; vegetable fruits; brassicas and other leafy vegetables; the onion family; and herbs.

As well as heeding and following the best cultivation techniques detailed throughout the book, you also need to plan carefully to get the best out of your vegetable garden. Forethought is needed if, for example, you want to have fresh vegetables on your table every week – or even every day – of the year, if you want to harvest your favourite crops for the longest possible period, or if your aim is to grow as wide a range of vegetables as you possibly can.

When planning your vegetable garden you must take account of climate (and of the ways in which you can protect plants from the weather with cloches or by using a greenhouse), of the space you have available, and of the need to practise crop rotation. This last is essential to the health and welfare of the vegetable garden, since growing the same types of crop in the same place each year can lead to a damaging build-up of disease-causing organisms in the soil.

Unless your garden is very large, space is likely to be one of your greatest constraints. Again, planning can help you make the most of the area you have available for vegetables, particularly if you aim for some inter-cropping or catch-cropping (see pp.132–3). If space is at a premium, you should plan to set plants as close together as possible, without restricting their growth or depriving them of the light they need in order to thrive. Often, grouping vegetables in wide bands, rather than growing them in single rows is a good way to make the most of the space available.

Whatever vegetables you choose to grow, never forget that the key to success lies in the soil. Well-nourished soil is the ingredient vital to growing your own vegetables, and tending the soil is an ongoing task, since you must always return to the ground what has been taken out of it in the form of food crops.

Planning the vegetable plot means considering what kinds of crops to grow each year and where to grow them – as well as deciding on when to make a start. It does not mean drawing up a precise, row-by-row annual cropping plan; this would inevitably be disrupted by tricks of weather and by seasonal disparities.

CHOOSING YOUR CROPS

The most obvious choice is to grow what you most enjoy eating, but this needs qualifying. Among favoured crops, it makes sense to concentrate on kinds not always readily available in shops – some Chinese vegetables, for instance – or those that are best freshly gathered, such as early peas and sweet corn.

Choose vegetables suited to the conditions that you can provide. This means, for example, avoiding tomatoes and cucumbers if you live in a cold area, and celeriac if your soil is particularly sandy and dry. Do not plant vegetables that are expected to mature when you will be on holiday.

Likewise, choose crops to match the available space. There is not much point planting cabbages or maincrop potatoes in a garden where every bit of ground is precious. Crops should not be crammed together at less than the recommended spacings, though very close planting is acceptable in beds (see p.133).

You must decide, too, whether simply to aim for summer and early winter crops or to attempt year-round production. The first few months of the year are the most difficult to make productive; they call for careful selection of varieties and choice of sowing dates. Details are included, where appropriate, in individual vegetable descriptions.

CROP CATEGORIES

Some vegetables are sown in rows in the place where they are to grow; this applies, for example, to most root crops. After the seedlings have emerged, they are thinned out to allow them adequate space to develop. Peas are grown in this way, too, but the seeds are spaced at sowing time and no further thinning is needed.

Many other crops are sown in a separate seedbed, and the seedlings transferred to their final quarters when they are partly grown. Leeks and most brassicas are planted in this way. They need a lot of growing space, and the two-stage operation means that the ground is occupied for less time.

Tender plants, such as tomatoes or marrows, are also grown in two stages. They are raised under glass in spring, then moved outdoors when the soil has warmed up and the risk of night frosts is over. Between the two environments they must have a period

of acclimatization, termed 'hardening off', in a cold frame or, possibly, under cloches.

By sowing many vegetable seeds in a warm environment, then setting young plants outdoors or under cloches, you can get earlier crops of perfectly hardy vegetables, such as lettuces.

A few crops are planted as bulbs (shallots and, sometimes, onions) or tubers (potatoes, Jerusalem artichokes). These are placed in their final growing position.

A few perennial vegetables remain in the same position for a number of years. The chief crops of this type are asparagus, globe artichokes and rhubarb. Despite occupying their site all year round, each provides only a single harvest. Such crops therefore offer poor value for space in a small or average-sized garden, although you may still choose to grow them as a luxury vegetable – asparagus and globe artichokes are rarely inexpensive to buy.

HERBS

There is room for herbs in even the smallest garden (see p.41). If you are restricted to two or three pots on a patio, or a windowbox outside the kitchen, this still allows basic herbs, such as mint, chives,

Winter Only a few winter vegetables remain in the ground: most of the plot is left vacant for digging. Most gardeners try to complete this task by Christmas, especially if the soil is heavy, and leave the ground rough for the frost to crumble.

parsley and thyme, to be grown. If a small patch of garden can be set aside for growing a larger range, so much the better. Position them where they will not interfere with the annual rotation of crops, possibly even in the flower border.

Further suggestions as to what herbs to grow, and how to set about it, are given on pp.219–223.

WHEN TO START

Aim to have the plot cleared of perennial weeds, then manured and dug ready for the first spring sowings and plantings. On heavy, sticky soil this means completing the work by early winter, since it is likely to be too wet after that. This will also give time for frost to crumble the clods. Heavy soil dug in spring breaks down less readily for seed sowing.

To make a spring start on undug, heavy soil, wait until the surface is reasonably dry and then randomly turn over one or two patches with a fork. Once the lumps can be broken into a reasonably crumbly tilth – with neither sticky nor rock-hard clods – it is worth digging the whole area. Provided this stage has been reached, a motor cultivator will speed up the 'forcing' of a tilth.

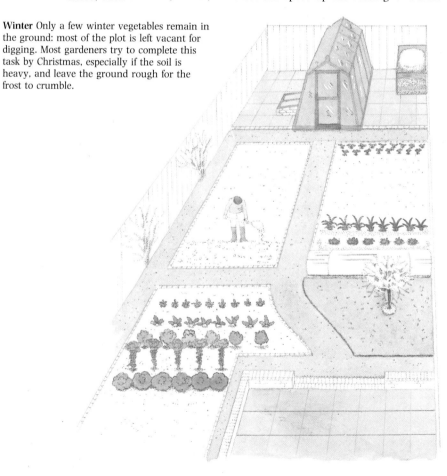

Such problems do not arise on light, quick-draining soil. When dug at any time of year the soil crumbles readily, so spring manuring and digging may be followed almost at once by sowing or planting. It is as well to allow a week or two for the soil to settle, however.

If a start has been made in summer for some reason, on soil of any type, it will be too late to sow slow-growing crops such as parsnips, Brussels sprouts, leeks or maincrop onions. Concentrate for this first season on such rapid growers as lettuces, radishes, spring onions, early peas, spinach, baby beetroots, early carrots and turnips. Remember, also, to sow spring cabbage seeds between mid- and late summer, for cutting the following year.

PLANNING THE VEGETABLE PLOT
Crop rotation and its manuring routine (see p.25) is a significant factor in how you allocate the space each year. If you practise crop rotation your vegetable plot will probably be divided into three, whatever its shape, with possibly some extra space allowed for permanent vegetables. The size of each section will depend on your favourites among vegetables.

Before planning out the plot in detail, make a note of how much space you need to allow between rows of particular crops. Plan out a section at a time, and remember to allow space for a seedbed. To make the best use of the space, aim to follow one crop with another immediately: this practice is known as 'successional cropping'.

WHERE TO GROW VEGETABLES
Most vegetables need all the light and warmth they can get, which means a site open to the sun for at least half the day. They simply will not grow in more or less permanent shade. The two exceptions, which do reasonably well in partial shade (although not under trees), are Jerusalem artichokes and spinach beet. A rapidly maturing crop of lettuce will grow in light shade during the warmest months.

Free drainage is another essential. Though celery, celeriac and leeks do best in moist soil, no vegetable will put up with waterlogging. Dry soil also checks growth, but this can be remedied by irrigation and by digging in plenty of organic material. Dry, light soils warm up quickly in spring and give the earliest crops.

Shelter is not essential, but growth is faster when crops are protected from strong winds – particularly those that blow from a cold quarter. If your whole garden is exposed, consider planting a hedge or erecting a fence or screen.

Try not to be put off growing food crops by a shortage of space. An area of only a little over 9 sq m (11 sq yd) should keep a family in summer salads. A 3m (10ft) double row of runners will yield up to 18kg (40lb) of beans, while nearly 3kg (6lb) is considered a good yield for a single greenhouse tomato plant. Forget the dream of total self-sufficiency and concentrate instead on a relatively small number of carefully chosen crops.

If there simply is not space, or conditions are unsuitable, consider growing at least a few vegetables in the flower border or in containers (see p.132). Suitably decorative crops for a border include globe artichokes, asparagus, beetroots, ornamental cabbages, sweet corn and tomatoes. For containers, which include pots, tubs and grobags, choose any of the salad crops (lettuces, radishes, spring onions), or carrots, French beans and semi-ornamental summer crops such as peppers, aubergines, courgettes and tomatoes.

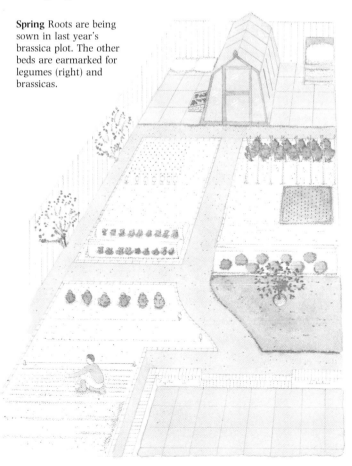

Spring Roots are being sown in last year's brassica plot. The other beds are earmarked for legumes (right) and brassicas.

Summer The plots are all full, and the sprinkler is in action to keep plants growing through the warm days.

If your food garden is smaller than you would like, there are several ways in which to make better use of the available space. If you follow any, or all, of these, a significantly greater output from a given area will result. All the intensive methods depend for success on a high level of soil fertility; if necessary, take steps to improve this (see p.25).

CATCH-CROPPING

The idea of catch-cropping is to make use of patches of ground left empty between harvesting one crop and planting another. For instance, if marrows or melons are to be planted out in late spring or early summer, on a part of the plot where parsnips or swedes were grown during the winter, there should be time to grow a crop of lettuces or spring onions after the last root vegetables have been harvested and before the soil is warm enough for the marrows or melons to go in. There may be even more time to spare before winter cabbages and broccoli are planted out.

The fast-growing vegetables most suitable for catch-cropping include – as well as lettuces and spring onions – short-rooted carrots, small beetroots, turnips, radishes, kohlrabi and spinach. In all cases choose quick-maturing, 'early' varieties.

Catch-cropping can also be practised at the other end of the season, using the same fast-growing vegetables to follow the harvesting of early potatoes, broad beans or spring cabbages. Unoccupied soil should be a rare sight between late spring and autumn, if the food garden is fully productive.

INTER-CROPPING

This space-saving method exploits the differences in growth rates between crops. Fast-growing crops of the types mentioned above are sown between those that mature more slowly. By the time the slow-growing vegetables are big enough to fill the space around them, the fast-growers will have been harvested. Both the spaces between rows, and the spaces between slow-growing plants within a row, can be used in this way.

Winter brassicas, in particular, lend themselves to this sort of treatment. Fast-maturing crops can be grown in between and alongside before they get too large.

The success of this intensive cropping depends to a large extent upon well-fed soil and plenty of moisture. Always remove the secondary crop before overcrowding can occur.

Inter-cropping makes use of the spaces between slow-growing plants, such as parsnips and some brassicas. Here, fast-maturing lettuces and radishes have been sown between Brussels sprouts. They will be harvested before the main crop needs the space.

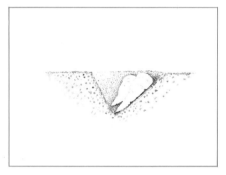

Overwintered crops, such as parsnips and leeks, may still be occupying valuable space at sowing time. A simple solution is to dig a shallow trench elsewhere, then to lift the remainder of the crop and place it in the trench with a covering of soil. This space-saving process is termed 'heeling in'.

GROWING IN CONTAINERS

Many vegetables can be grown in large containers sited on the patio, and save on precious room in the vegetable plot. They may even benefit by being given a sunnier position. Tomatoes, aubergines, peppers and cucumbers are all suitable for this method of growing. Pots, tubs and boxes need to be at least 23cm (9in) deep and wide; smaller containers may dry out in a matter of hours.

Garden soil is seldom suitable as a growing medium for container-grown crops, and the cost of bought compost can be high. Use garden soil in containers only if you have a crumbly, fertile loam; even then you will probably have to add sand and peat to achieve a good balance of moisture-retention and free drainage.

When buying compost, choose either a soil-based John Innes type or a peat-based product. The soil-based compost will tend to retain its nutrients longer, but in both cases supplementary liquid feeding will be needed as the crop develops. Tomatoes in particular need generous feeding. If you are using home-mixed compost, add some thoroughly rotted manure or garden compost during the preparation stage, together with a balanced fertilizer.

Ensure that there is a drainage outlet in the bottom of the container. Cover the hole or holes with curved crocks, then place a layer of similar pieces or small stones over the base. Stand containers on slats or bricks so that the drainage outlet is clear. All containers need frequent watering.

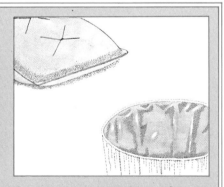

To minimize evaporation from gro-bags (top), cut only small holes, or slits, for the plants. You can simply lift a corner for watering. Never let the peaty compost dry out: apart from harming the plants, it may prove difficult to saturate again.

Evaporation from wooden containers can be reduced by lining them with polythene.

GROWING VEGETABLES IN BEDS

The bed system of growing vegetables, rather than growing them in long rows, is another means of saving space. The beds need to be narrow enough to allow planting, weeding and other cultivation tasks to be performed from the sides, without treading between the crops. This allows closer plant spacings and therefore a higher cropping rate.

Extra output is not the only advantage. On heavy ground, especially, walking between the plants on an ordinary plot compresses the soil and spoils its texture. The looser soil in beds drains better, warms up earlier in spring and is much easier to work into a tilth for seed-sowing. There is a marginal advantage, too, in that closely-spaced plants tend to suppress weeds. To some extent this is countered, however, by the difficulty of hoeing between them.

Though the paths may be left as bare earth – on light soil, anyway – it is a considerable advantage to provide a firmer surface that will suppress weeds and not be reduced to mud. Bricks or small concrete slabs are ideal.

For most gardeners a convenient bed width is 1.2m (4ft), making the maximum reach 60cm (2ft) from either side. If you use cloches, make at least some of the beds sufficiently wide to take a double row; a single row of cloches would waste space.

There is no limit to the length of a bed, though it might be convenient to divide a long plot by means of a central path. There would then be no need to walk the length of a bed in order to reach the other side. Make the paths about 45cm (1½ft) wide.

MAKING THE BEDS

In making the beds, double digging (see pp. 34–5) really does pay, at least for the initial preparation. Once you have formed the beds, it should only be necessary to double dig every few years. Double digging will also help to raise the level of the bed, thereby assisting drainage.

Mark out the bed shapes before you start to dig, and once you have given some thought to layout and spacing. Some gardeners like to leave a slightly broader path between each pair of beds to allow room for wheeling a barrow. This is certainly an advantage if space is not too restricted.

Remove the topsoil and loosen the subsoil; take care not to mix any of it with topsoil. Subject to the requirements of your crop rotation (see p.25), fork a good dressing of compost or manure into the upper layer, or apply a dressing of lime to the dug surface. Try to complete the digging and preparation well in advance of sowing or planting to give the beds time to settle.

PLANTING THE CROPS

When sowing and planting, remember that spacing between rows is the same as that left between plants within a row. This equidistant spacing should be the same as, or a little greater than, that usually allowed between plants in a row.

For instance, if you normally leave 30cm (1ft) between rows of beetroots and thin the plants to a spacing of 10cm (4in), allow about 13cm (5in) in each direction when growing them in a bed. As a general rule, the more space you allow, the larger the plants will grow, though size is also influenced by soil fertility. The ideal spacing will have been achieved if the leaves of fully mature plants just reach those of their neighbours.

MANAGING THE BEDS

Keep the beds weeded and hoed while the plants are small. As plants grow, they will tend to suppress further weed growth. A short-handled onion hoe is useful for working between closely-planted crops.

Carry out all cultivation from the paths, and never walk on the beds. Once a bed is established, it should be possible to turn the soil with a fork, mixing in manure or compost as you do so, instead of digging with a spade.

Staggered planting, with the vegetables in one row set opposite the spaces in adjoining rows, makes maximum use of bed space. By the time plants reach maturity, most of the ground should be covered with foliage. Because cultivation is carried out from the side, there is no need to walk between the plants.

It is easier to organize rotation of crops when vegetables are grown in beds. During a given year, set one bed aside for brassicas, another for root crops and a third for legumes. Earth paths may be left between beds on light soil; on heavier ground, especially where drainage is poor, it is an advantage to lay bricks, gravel or paving slabs.

WAYS TO BETTER SOIL, page 25

DIGGING THE PLOT, pages 34–35
DECIDING WHAT TO GROW, pages 130–131

Commercially frozen peas are the nation's most popular vegetable, yet their flavour cannot compare with that of home-grown peas. Their perfection lies in being harvested and cooked at the right stage.

Peas (*Pisum sativum*) are not an ideal crop for those with limited space, since they take up a lot of room for a relatively small yield. They also need supporting, and are prone to several pests and diseases, so they are not amongst the easiest of vegetables to cultivate. But the reward lies in their flavour.

The devoted gardener can harvest peas from late spring until late summer, and may even choose to dry some for the winter. This calls for a lot of space and careful planning, however, as well as judicious selection of varieties. Most gardeners are content with a row or two of 'earlies', with possibly one or two later sorts to follow.

TYPES OF PEA

Peas are classified principally according to season, which is based upon their speed of growth. The height of individual varieties ranges from 45cm (1½ft) to about 1.8m (6ft). Short varieties are easiest to support and need less space between rows than taller kinds, but they give a smaller crop.

First earlies Round-seeded varieties, which are the hardiest, may be sown in autumn and over-wintered under cloches, or else sown in spring. Types with wrinkled seeds (wrinkled when dried, that is) have heavier, tastier and sweeter crops. But, being less hardy, they are suitable for spring sowing only. Autumn sowings mature first.

Second earlies Wrinkle-seeded. A spring sowing gives a midsummer crop.

Maincrop Sown a week or two later than second earlies, harvest will be during the second half of summer. All are wrinkle-seeded; many are heavy yielding.

Mangetout (sugar or snow pea) Pods and their contents are cooked and eaten whole before the seeds fully develop.

Petit pois Varieties with tiny, sweet peas.

Asparagus pea (winged pea) The asparagus pea (*Lotus tetragonolobus*) is not a true pea, but has asparagus-flavoured pods. These are cooked and eaten whole.

All types of pea grow best in soil that holds moisture well but is free-draining. As this implies, it must contain plenty of organic matter, either dug in well ahead of sowing or mixed into the bottom of a trench, as for runner beans (see pp.138–9). Early or over-wintered crops do best in light soil.

MAKING A START: PROTECTED SOWINGS

For an early, over-wintered crop, sow a dwarf, round-seeded variety in late autumn and cover with cloches. To discourage mice, first wet the seeds with paraffin.

Use a draw hoe to form flat drills 20cm (8in) wide and 5cm (2in) deep; allow 60cm (2ft) between drills. Set the seeds in three rows, spacing them 5cm (2in) apart in each direction. Cover the seeds with the soil removed to form the drill. Set traps under the cloches if you need to as an added safeguard against mice.

Follow exactly the same sequence for a sowing in late winter or early spring, as soon as the soil is workable. Cover with cloches until later in the spring.

Place the cloches in position a week or two ahead of sowing to help warm and dry the soil. It is pointless to sow in cold, wet soil, since germination will be slow and the risk of disease greater; the seeds may even rot.

Peas may also be sown under glass in late winter for subsequent planting outdoors. This enables you to make a start while the soil outside is still too wet and cold. A good method is to sow the seeds individually in 6cm (2½in) peat pots, then cover them with glass and paper until they germinate. Gentle warmth – about 7°C/45°F – will help to get them started.

Aim to plant out the seedlings in mid-spring, complete with the pots, before they get too leggy. Harden them off in a cold frame for a week or two before you do so.

Leave just a little space between the pots when planting.

As an alternative to peat pots, sow the seeds in lengths of plastic guttering filled with seed compost. Sow in two rows, 5cm (2in) apart, and germinate in gentle warmth. When planting out in mid-spring, after hardening off, form a rounded drill to match the guttering and simply slide the row of plants into it.

UNPROTECTED SOWINGS

Either round-seeded varieties, or first-early wrinkled types, may be used for unprotected sowings during early to mid-spring, spaced as for autumn-sown peas. Allow the same distance between drills as the height of the chosen variety.

Without cloches, it is essential to protect the seedbed from birds. Effective methods of protection include cloche-shaped guards made from wire netting, humming line tape stretched over the rows, or black cotton criss-crossed between pegs on either side of each row (see p.44).

Peas need support as soon as they are 8cm (3in) tall, otherwise they will trail along the ground and be at risk from attack by slugs and snails. Insert twiggy sticks along the row or fix some form of netting, as shown in the illustrations. Traditional pea sticks, if obtainable, are still the best means of support for tall-growing varieties.

Sow wrinkled, maincrop varieties during the second half of spring for a mid- to late-summer crop. A final harvest, in early autumn, can be secured by sowing first-early wrinkled peas in early summer; choose a mildew-resistant variety.

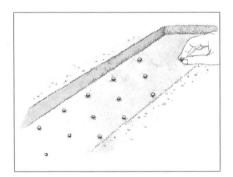

Make outdoor sowings of peas in wide, shallow trenches; space the seeds 5cm (2in) apart in each direction. A covering of cloches will protect early crops from birds and cats as well as from the weather.

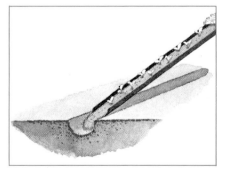

Germinating the seedlings in a length of fairly broad guttering allows them to be transferred from greenhouse to outdoor bed without root disturbance. Simply slide them out into a drill of matching shape.

CARE OF THE CROP

During dry weather, keep the rows well watered from the time the peas start to flower. A mulch of finely-shredded manure or compost will help to keep the soil moist.

For summer-flowering varieties, spray with derris, fenitrothion or permethrin, a week after the flowers appear, to prevent maggoty peas.

HARVESTING

Pick normal varieties when the peas are well developed but before they quite fill the pods. Picking every day or two, without ever letting the pods mature fully, ensures continuous cropping.

Pick mangetout varieties when they are about 5cm (2in) long and before the seeds start to swell.

Harvest asparagus peas daily: do not let them exceed 4cm (1½in) in length.

If peas are to be dried, leave them to ripen on the plants. To finish the process, lift the complete plants, and hang them upside down in an airy shed or shelter. When fully dry, shell the peas and store them in airtight tins or jars.

When all fresh peas are harvested, sever the main stem of each plant at ground level and put the plants on the compost heap. Leave the roots in the soil so that the beneficial nitrogen, stored in their nodules, can be released to aid soil fertility.

PESTS AND DISEASES

Among several pests which affect peas, the most troublesome are aphids, bean seed fly, pea moth, pea thrips, slugs, snails and mice.

The most likely ailments are damping off, foot rot and mildew.

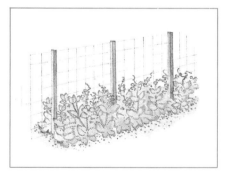

Twiggy sticks, sold in garden centres and shops during the spring, provide the best support for peas. Insert them along the row, and make sure that there is plenty of support fairly close to the ground to which the tendrils can cling.

A length of netting provides a good alternative form of support. Secure it to firm stakes and, if necessary, loop twine around the pea haulm (main stem) to ensure that it clings securely, even in wet or windy weather.

RECOMMENDED VARIETIES

First-early (* = round-seeded)
*'**Douce Provence**' 60cm (2ft). Hardy but sweet-flavoured.
*'**Feltham First**' 45cm (1½ft). Good crops of large pods.
'**Hurst Beagle**' 45cm (1½ft). Good flavour; well-filled pods.
'**Little Marvel**' 45cm (1½ft). Extra good flavour. Very popular.
*'**Meteor**' 45cm (1½ft). Extremely hardy. Prolific crops.
'**Progress No. 9**' 50cm (20in). Heavy yields of well-filled pods.

Second-early
'**Early Onward**' 60cm (2ft). Heavy crops of sweet-tasting peas.
'**Hurst Green Shaft**' 75cm (2½ft). Disease-resistant and fine flavour.
'**Kelvedon Wonder**' 45cm (1½ft). Mildew-resistant, so good for summer sowing.
'**Purple Podded**' 1.5m (5ft). Pods are purple. Peas are green and of good flavour; suitable for drying.
'**Show Perfection**' Up to 1.5m (5ft). Large, uniform pods and fine flavour.

Maincrop
'**Alderman**' Up to 1.8m (6ft). Heavy crops of large, well-filled pods.
'**Lord Chancellor**' Up to 1.2m (4ft). One of the latest to mature.
'**Onward**' 75cm (2½ft). Noted for heavy cropping and disease resistance.
'**Senator**' 90cm (3ft). Heavy yields and excellent flavour.

Mangetout
'**Oregon Sugar Pod**' 90cm (3ft). Large, fleshy pods on compact plants.
'**Sugar Snap**' Up to 1.8m (6ft). Can also be left for the peas to mature.

Petit pois
'**Cobri**' 60cm (2ft). Sweet flavour. Pick when very young.
'**Waverex**' 75cm (2½ft). Sweet and tender. Good for freezing.

SOWING UNDER GLASS, pages 38–39
PLANTING VEGETABLES, page 40
CROP PROTECTION, page 44
PEAS, page 113
PESTS AND DISEASES, pages 172–175
FREEZING VEGETABLES, pages 232–233

Broad beans (*Vicia faba*) are one of the first of the summer vegetables. They will grow on most soils and can generally be relied upon to crop well. The young beans can be cooked in their pods, while the larger ones are shelled before use. There are two main types: the longpods, which have kidney-shaped seeds in long pods, and the Windsors, which have round seeds in short, broad pods. Both types have white- and green-seeded varieties; the green-seeded varieties freeze better, as a rule. In addition to these, there are several dwarf varieties.

Depending on the climate zone in which you live (see p.10), you will have to decide when to sow broad beans and which variety to grow. In milder districts, an early crop can be harvested from late spring onward from an outdoor sowing made the previous autumn. Alternatively, the seeds may be sown in a cold frame or a greenhouse for planting out during the spring: this is recommended for colder areas. Maincrop sowings, suitable for all areas, are made outdoors from early spring onward.

For autumn or winter sowing, choose one of the longpod varieties, which are extremely hardy, or possibly a dwarf variety if cloches are available. For maincrop sowing you may prefer one of the Windsor varieties, which are shorter but have a sweeter flavour. Dwarf varieties are also suitable for maincrop sowings.

Most soils will suit broad beans, but avoid using the same part of the plot in successive years (see Crop rotation, p.25). Neutral or slightly acid ground is ideal. Choose a fairly sunny position, preferably a sheltered one for an autumn-sown crop. Dig in manure unless it was added for the previous crop.

MAKING A START

Autumn sowing Sow in late autumn in pairs of rows 23cm (9in) apart, with 60cm (2ft) between adjacent pairs. This spacing gives growing plants some wind resistance.

Using a dibber, sow the seeds 5cm (2in) deep and 23cm (9in) apart. Sow the second row of each pair opposite the spaces in the first row. Insert a few spare seeds near the ends of the rows, for possible gap-filling. Discard any seeds with holes in them: this is evidence of seed beetle grubs.

Scatter slug pellets over the ground after sowing. Cover the rows with cloches, if you have them, and remove these as soon as the plants outgrow them. In late winter, spread a dressing of general fertilizer at 90g per sq m (3oz per sq yd).

Sowing under glass Sow in mid-winter: place the seeds 5cm (2in) apart and 2.5cm (1in) deep in a box of seed compost. Cover with glass and paper until after germination, but do not give them any heat. Plant out in spring, at the spacing given above, after you have hardened the plants off and dressed the bed with general fertilizer.

Spring sowing Sow as soon as the soil is dry enough to crumble to a tilth, having first applied a dressing of general fertilizer. Covering the bed with a floating cloche (see p.17) will speed germination and growth.

CARE OF THE CROP

Hoe between the rows as the plants begin to grow. Pinch out the top 8cm (3in) of each stem when the beans are in full flower. Support taller varieties by inserting canes around the outside of paired rows; tie string between them and across the rows. Water the plants during dry spells.

HARVESTING

Pick some of the pods while they are only 8cm (3in) long, for cooking and eating whole. Use the bulk of the pods for shelling, but do not leave them on the plants too long, otherwise they become too large and tough. The tops of plants may be cooked and eaten like spinach. After harvesting, dig the plants up; put them on the compost heap.

PESTS AND DISEASES

Pests include bean seed fly, blackfly, pea and bean weevils, slugs, snails and mice.

Two fungus diseases are chocolate spot and foot rot.

RECOMMENDED VARIETIES
Longpods
These are the hardiest type, best for autumn sowing, and give the heaviest yields. They include green- and white-seeded varieties.
'Aquadulce' The favourite for autumn sowing. White.
'Hylon' Very long pods with white seeds.
'Imperial Green Longpod' Massive pods and heavy yields. Green-seeded.

Windsors
Less hardy but with a sweeter flavour. White- or green-seeded.
'Imperial White Windsor' Longer podded than some Windsors. White.
'Jubilee Hysor' Heavy cropper with a fine flavour. Green.

Dwarfs
'Bonny Lad' Makes a bushy plant, so sow in single rows 60cm (2ft) apart. White.
'The Sutton' Suitable for autumn sowing (under cloches) or spring sowing. White.

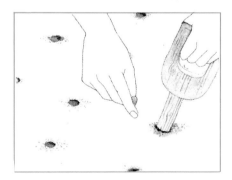

Sow broad beans in double rows, using a dibber or a trowel. Place the seeds in one row opposite the spaces in the other. Leave 23cm (9in) between pairs of rows and between the seeds in a row.

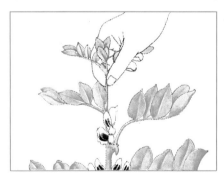

Pinch out the growing point of broad bean plants to deter blackfly. Do this when the first pods start to develop – or sooner if these pests appear. Pinching the tip also speeds the development of the crop.

Support all but the shortest varieties with canes and string. The best method is to insert pairs of canes on each side of the row, secure string between them around the outside and then pass it across between the plants.

French beans (*Phaseolus vulgaris*) have a distinctive flavour and texture, and summer meals are scarcely complete without them. They are ready at least two weeks earlier than runner beans. If you have enough space to grow both French and runner beans, you could have a supply of fresh beans all summer.

French beans come in several forms and may be yellow or purple as well as green. There are both flat-podded and pencil-podded types; the flat-podded beans tend to become stringy if allowed to grow large. Short-podded varieties of either type may be topped and tailed and cooked whole, while the ripe seeds of some varieties may be shelled and stored for use as haricots. Most French beans form dwarf, bushy plants but there are also climbing varieties.

All French beans need a sunny site and a light, well-drained but well-manured or composted soil. The soil may need the addition of lime, to bring it closer to a pH of 6.5. Choose a sheltered spot, otherwise the plants may be knocked over by the wind.

You can advance crops by sowing the seeds in a greenhouse and then planting seedlings out under cloches. You can also sow direct in the ground under cloches.

MAKING A START

Dig the site during the winter, and add plenty of manure or compost.

For direct sowing outdoors, wait until the soil is dry and has started to warm up, which usually means in late spring. French beans cannot withstand frost, while sowings in cold, wet soil invariably fail. Set cloches in place two weeks earlier.

Take out a drill, 5cm (2in) deep, and sow the seeds of bush varieties 8cm (3in) apart – much closer than the conventional spacing. Allow 45cm (1½ft) between rows.

If you are growing the beans in a bed, leave 15cm (6in) between plants in each direction. Make the holes with a trowel.

To raise plants in an unheated greenhouse, sow the seeds in mid-spring. Set them 5cm (2in) apart in trays of seed compost; cover them with glass and paper.

Dress the planting site with general fertilizer at 90g per sq m (3oz per sq yd). Harden the plants off in late spring, but wait until after the last frosts before planting them out if they are to be unprotected. If you are planting them under cloches, put these in place two weeks in advance. Allow 45cm (1½ft) between rows and 8–10cm (3–4in) between plants.

For climbing French beans, erect one of the forms of support advised for runner beans (see p.138); plant or sow at the foot of the uprights. If you are planting against netting, allow 15cm (6in) between plants.

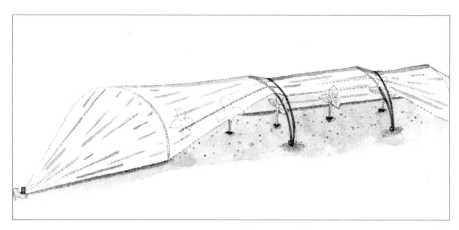

Sown or planted under cloches, French beans get off to a better start and produce an earlier crop. Cloches can be left in place until the plants are well-grown, but some ventilation may be needed during warm spring weather.

CARE OF THE CROP

A mulch around established plants will help to keep the weeds down and the soil's moisture in. Give plenty of water during dry spells and spray the plants with water on dry days when flowers begin to appear, to help them to set. If the plot is exposed, insert twiggy sticks at intervals for support.

HARVESTING

French beans will start to crop within eight weeks of sowing, and may produce pods for up to eight weeks after that. Start picking when the pods will snap in half and before the seeds cause them to bulge.

Leave haricot varieties until the pods turn yellow. Then lift the plants on a dry day, and hang them under cover, for example in a well-ventilated shed. Shell the pods when they are brittle, then store the beans in airtight tins when thoroughly dry.

PESTS AND DISEASES

French beans may be attacked by bean seed flies, blackfly, pea and bean weevils, and slugs and snails.

Potential diseases include anthracnose, foot rot, grey mould and halo blight.

RECOMMENDED VARIETIES
Dwarf bush
'**Bina**' Flat but stringless pods.
'**Kinghorn Wax**' Flattish yellow pods with green seeds. Good flavour.
'**Loch Ness**' Pencil-podded, with upright growth and little branching.
'**Masterpiece**' Quick-maturing, flat-podded type. Good for cooking whole.
'**Mont d'Or**' Yellow, waxy, rounded pods with fine flavour.
'**Pros**' Small to medium rounded pods; good for freezing and cooking whole.

The plants have relatively insecure roots and will benefit from the support of twiggy sticks. When picking, avoid loosening the roots by holding the plants with one hand while removing the beans with the other. Frequent picking ensures heavy yields.

'**Royal Burgundy**' Long, round, purple pods that turn green in boiling water. Crops heavily; succulent flavour.
'**Tendergreen**' Early pencil-podded variety.
'**The Prince**' Early, flat-podded, popular.

Climbing
'**Blue Lake**' Stringless, white-seeded pods. Suitable for haricots, too.
'**Hunter**' Flat but stringless pods produced over a long period.

For drying as haricots
'**Chevrier Vert**' Pods may be eaten green, or the seeds harvested either while still soft (termed flageolets) or as fully-ripe haricots.
'**Comtessa de Chambord**' Thin-shaped variety of haricot which needs less soaking before it is cooked.
'**Limelight**' Flat-podded and equally suitable for eating green.

SOWING SEEDS OUTDOORS, pages 36–37
SOWING UNDER GLASS, pages 38–39

BEANS, SWEET CORN AND ARTICHOKES, pages 114–115
PESTS AND DISEASES, pages 172–175

FREEZING VEGETABLES, pages 232–233

This vigorous, tall-growing crop might seem an odd choice for a small garden, yet in fact it is ideal. Limited ground area puts a premium on vertical space, which runner beans (*Phaseolus multiflorus*), also called stick or string beans, exploit to the full. On good soil they will grow to 2.5m (8ft) or more, and bear a prolific crop from close to ground level upward, though most gardeners are content with a more manageable height of 1.8m (6ft).

Runners are larger and coarser than French beans, with a more pronounced flavour. They are also a little less hardy than French beans, and respond best to a warm, sheltered spot in the garden. They grow most readily in milder districts, but wherever they are grown they need a well-manured, deep bed for maximum root development. In cold areas it is a great help to sow the seeds in a greenhouse and to plant the seedlings out under cloches. It also helps to choose a quick-maturing variety.

Because they are twining plants, runner beans need some form of support. This can be provided in a number of ways, as shown in the illustrations. Whatever system you use, it needs to be strong.

Tent-shaped or wigwam structures are suitable for the vegetable plot; trellis or netting may be erected beside a wall or fence or as a screen. Red-flowered varieties of runner bean present an especially brilliant spectacle when in full bloom.

One or two dwarf varieties of runner form low, bushy plants which have the advantage of not needing support structures. They will bush out of their own accord, without any pinching out, and are a good solution for windy areas. It is also possible to turn the normal, tall varieties such as 'Kelvedon Marvel' into dwarfs by pinching out the tip of the main stem at an early stage. This can create considerable work, since it also becomes necessary to pinch out the resultant side-shoots, which is approximately a weekly task.

Yields from all dwarf runners are much smaller than from plants grown up supports, but because they are fast-maturing, dwarf beans are useful for early and late crops and ideal for growing under cloches. Remove the cloches when the first flowers appear on the plants.

The runner bean harvest extends from summer into autumn, provided the pods are picked every two or three days and before seeds are formed. Never leave old pods on the plants because they are past their best; they will inhibit the development of new flowers and pods.

The sowing times suggested are the earliest that are safe for spring crops. The season can be considerably extended, though, by successional sowing until early summer.

Overall, the yields from runner beans reflect the amount of care put into the soil preparation. Though you can expect some sort of harvest even on poor soil, it will increase dramatically if a heavy dressing of organic matter is dug in during the previous winter. Additionally, lime may be needed, since the soil should not be too acid.

MAKING A START

First decide how you are going to support the beans, and where you will position the plants. Then mark out the planting site and dig a spade-depth trench, about 40cm (15in) wide. Place a thick layer of manure or compost on the bottom and fork this into the soil. Mark the position of the trench with pegs when you replace the topsoil.

Rake a general fertilizer into this planting site, at 90g per sq m (3oz per sq yd), during the spring before sowing or planting. Erect supports at the same time to avoid disturbing the young plants later on, unless you propose to use cloches.

For the earliest crop, or if you live in a cold area, sow the seeds in a greenhouse during mid-spring. Either place them 5cm (2in) apart in a box of seed compost or, for preference, use peat pots and sow two seeds in each pot.

Cover them with glass and paper until the

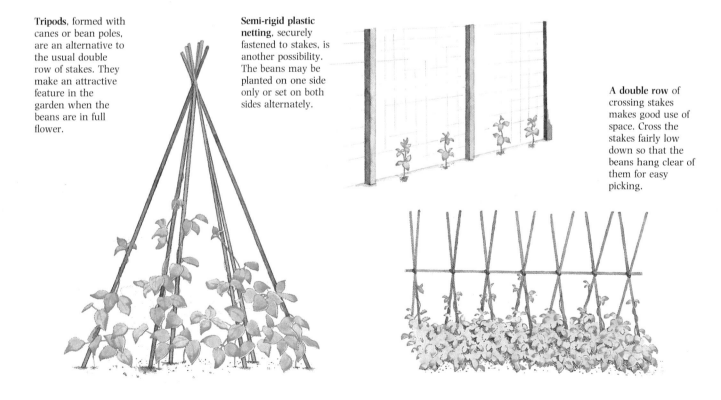

Tripods, formed with canes or bean poles, are an alternative to the usual double row of stakes. They make an attractive feature in the garden when the beans are in full flower.

Semi-rigid plastic netting, securely fastened to stakes, is another possibility. The beans may be planted on one side only or set on both sides alternately.

A double row of crossing stakes makes good use of space. Cross the stakes fairly low down so that the beans hang clear of them for easy picking.

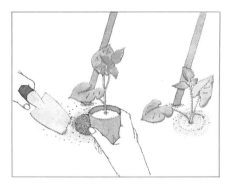

When planting greenhouse-raised runner beans, keep the rootball or peat pot intact. Set a plant beneath each supporting pole, and water them in if the soil is dry.

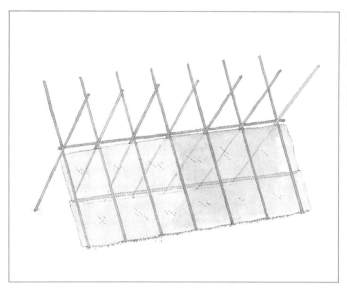

Polythene sheeting can be stapled or pinned to the lower part of the poles to form a giant cloche which will protect the plants until they are growing strongly. Draw soil around the base of the plastic.

seeds germinate. Remove the weaker of the seedlings if two appear.

Start to harden off the seedlings in late spring and plant them out 10–14 days later. If you are planting them against angled poles, set them on the underside, one to each support. In the case of peat pots, plant the whole container.

Either protect the seedlings with cloches or, if the supports are already in position, secure polythene sheeting to the poles with staples or drawing pins to form a kind of giant cloche (see above).

If you are planting against netting or trellis, allow 15cm (6in) between plants. When planting peat pots, especially, make sure that the ground does not dry out afterward, particularly in beds that are close to walls.

It is not safe to sow runner beans without protection until late spring, after the last frosts. The alternative is to sow under cloches. Again, polythene can be secured to the poles if these are already in position. Sow two seeds in each station, 5cm (2in) deep, and remove the weaker seedling if both germinate.

For dwarf varieties, space the seeds or plants 15cm (6in) apart. Allow 45cm (1½ft) between rows, and stagger the plants to provide maximum growing space. Pinch out any straggly side-shoots that subsequently develop.

To form a bush out of a tall-growing variety, pinch out the tip when the plant is about 30cm (1ft) high. Subsequently, pinch out the tips of the side-shoots regularly to maintain a compact, bushy form.

Slug pellets should be scattered around newly-planted beans or over the ground where seedlings are due to emerge.

CARE OF THE CROP

Remove cloches or polythene protection as soon as the plants are growing strongly. At this stage, with the soil well-warmed, spread a mulch of manure around the plants. If necessary, tie the stems to the supports or give the plants an initial turn or two around the support. Their inclination is to climb anti-clockwise, but sometimes they seem reluctant to start.

Take care that the soil does not dry out, especially when the plants extend up the supports and start to flower. Pinch the tip from each main stem when it reaches the top of its support.

HARVESTING

Start picking when the beans are about 15cm (6in) long. The secret of prolonged cropping is to pick every day or two, and always remove the pods before the seeds have time to swell. They are easily seen from the outside. The more frequently you pick, the heavier the harvest. Runner beans are at their best if cooked or frozen while still young and tender.

After the crop is harvested, cut down the stems but leave the roots in the ground, since they add nitrogen to the soil.

PESTS AND DISEASES

Though often trouble-free, plants may be attacked by bean seed fly and blackfly, as well as by slugs and snails.

Anthracnose, chocolate spot, foot rot, halo blight and virus diseases are liable to occur on runner beans.

RECOMMENDED VARIETIES

'Achievement' Long, high-quality pods produced in abundance.
'Butler' Medium-length, stringless pods. Long cropping period.
'Enorma' Heavy crops of long, slender, high-quality pods.
'Kelvedon Marvel' One of the earliest to crop. Short pods but prolific.
'Polestar' Early, extra-heavy crops of stringless beans.
'Scarlet Emperor' Heavy crops of long-podded beans. Early.

Dwarf varieties

'Gulliver' Heavy yields for a dwarf variety. About 38cm (15in) high.
'Hammond's Dwarf' The original dwarf runner bean. Up to 45cm (1½ft) high.
'Pickwick' Compact, bushy and fairly early. About 30cm (1ft) high.

SOWING OUTDOORS, pages 36–37
SOWING UNDER GLASS, pages 38–39

BEANS, SWEET CORN AND ARTICHOKES, pages 114–115
PESTS AND DISEASES, pages 172–175

FREEZING VEGETABLES, pages 232–233

The globe artichoke (*Cynara scolymus*) is a herbaceous perennial which is prized for the distinctive flavour of parts of its flower-heads. This thistle-like plant is equally at home in the flower border as in the vegetable plot: not only does it bear large flower-heads, but its silvery-grey, deeply-cut leaves also form a splendid backdrop for more colourful plants. This large vegetable demands a fair amount of space, right through the year, which is another reason why the rear of the herbaceous border may be a more suitable place for it than permanent occupation of the vegetable garden.

The globe artichoke is a native of North Africa; it is not especially difficult to grow, but does not easily tolerate northern winters. Except in the mildest districts, its rootbase must be protected during the colder months. With a good covering of leaves or straw, it should survive all but exceptionally severe winters. Losses are most likely on heavy soil.

The usual (and best) way to start is with offsets, or rooted suckers, which are obtainable from many nurseries and garden centres. The alternative is to raise the plants from seed. This saves money but gives variable results. If your seed-raised plants do not crop well, take offsets from your best plants and start again. You can expect about six flower-heads on each plant.

Fertile, well-drained soil, with good drainage, is needed if globe artichokes are to produce plenty of large flower-heads. Sticky clay is unsuitable until it has been improved with generous dressings of organic matter. A sunny, sheltered spot is the best position.

MAKING A START

Spring is planting time, but well before then decide where the plants are to grow so that the site can be dug and manured. The artichokes, which will grow up to 1.5m (5ft) tall, have a spread of up to 90cm (3ft), so allow this amount of space around each plant. They require an open position, well away from the shade of trees.

Work in plenty of rotted manure or compost, at least a bucketful to the square metre or yard, together with a good dressing of bonemeal. Up to 450g (1lb) per square metre or yard would not be excessive, bearing in mind that the plants will remain in the same site for three or four years. Their production invariably declines after this time.

Growing from offsets During spring, place the offsets 75–90cm (2½-3ft) apart in each direction, and at the same depth as they were previously. The soil mark is easily seen. Use a trowel to plant them, and afterwards firm the soil with your foot. Water the plants in and make sure that the soil remains damp while the offsets make fresh roots.

In dry weather, the plants may wilt and suffer a check. Reduce this risk by trimming off the outer quarter of each leaf immediately after planting to reduce moisture loss. Temporary shading with newspaper is a help, or an open-ended cloche can be placed over each plant and the glass sprayed with greenhouse-shading liquid.

In late spring, spread a mulch of rotted manure or compost around the plants to help conserve moisture.

Growing from seed Raise the plants in a seedbed by sowing the seeds 2.5cm (1in) deep, with 30cm (1ft) between drills. Thin the seedlings to 15cm (6in) apart. Grow these on for a year and then plant them out the following spring, as for offsets.

CARE OF THE CROP

Keep the plot hoed to prevent competition from weeds. Water during dry spells before the soil becomes parched and the plants suffer. From the second spring onward, rake in a dressing of general fertilizer around the plants at 70g per sq m (2oz per sq yd).

It is better to resist taking a crop the first summer. It would, in any case, be very small. Nipping off the flower buds as they appear will help to ensure more and better flower-heads during later years.

Harvesting starts during the second year. For the largest heads, restrict the number of stems to five or six, and cut off the others near ground level. Also, pinch out some of the smaller flowers that form on the side-shoots.

In late autumn, cut down the main stems close to the ground. If you live in a cold area, draw some soil over the crowns and then cover them with leaves, straw or bracken. A surround of wire netting will prevent the material being blown away. In warmer areas, the soil may not be essential, but it is nevertheless a good precaution.

Another precautionary measure, appropriate for cold, northerly gardens, is to remove some offsets at this time and grow them on in 15cm (6in) pots in a cold frame for the winter. They will serve as replacements if the older plants are lost.

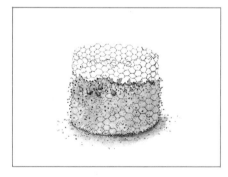

In cold areas, a covering of straw or leaves will protect the crowns during a hard winter. Encircle this with a netting surround to prevent the material being blown away or scattered by birds.

HARVESTING

Starting with the largest heads, which will be on the ends of the main stems, cut the flower-heads, together with the tops of the stems, while they are still green and before they start to open. The edible parts are the fleshy, curving segments at the base of the scales and the bottom of the flower, which is called the fond or heart; this is revealed by removing the hairy 'choke' from inside the flower-head.

After removing the head, cut back each stem to half its original length. Encourage a further crop of flowers by applying a liquid fertilizer every two weeks for a couple of months after the first flower-heads are cut.

Use secateurs to remove the flower-heads, starting with the largest one at the top of each main stem. Harvest when these heads are fully developed but before they change colour and start to open.

THE CROPPING PLAN
Year 1 Restrict flower buds as they appear in order to produce larger heads in the next two years.

Year 2 Restrict each plant to four to six stems and let flower-heads develop on these. Nip off any smaller buds from side-shoots. Harvest the flower-heads.

Year 3 Harvest four to six flower-heads per plant. Remove other buds.

Year 4 Globe artichokes are past their best by this stage. Take offsets from plants in spring or late autumn. Aim to replace a third of your stock in this way each year.

PROPAGATION

Take offsets in spring or late autumn. First scrape some soil away from the base of the plant, then cut downward, close to strong shoots. to remove them from the rootstock; make sure each shoot has a section of root attached. A large, sharp knife is the best tool. Once you have taken the offsets, discard the rest of the plant.

If offsets are taken in spring, plant them out immediately. If in late autumn, over-winter them in pots in a cold frame before planting them out the following spring. Since the plants of globe artichokes are past their best after three or four years, it is a good idea to replace up to a third of them annually.

To propagate globe artichokes, use a long, sharp knife to remove offsets from the main plant, each with a good section of root. Trim the leaves back to reduce moisture loss after they have been transplanted.

Offsets taken during the spring should be replanted at once. Those taken during late autumn will stand a better chance if potted in compost and overwintered in a cold frame.

PESTS AND DISEASES
Blackfly, together with slugs and snails, are the most likely pests.

The flower-heads may be affected by petal blight disease.

RECOMMENDED VARIETIES
'Green Globe' Readily available as seed. Moderately hardy.
'Purple Globe' Hardier than 'Green Globe' but less well-flavoured.
'Vert de Laon' Widely available as offsets. Excellent flavour. Fairly hardy.

CHARDS
Chards are blanched leaf shoots; they are obtained from three- or four-year-old plants that have borne their final crop of flower-heads and are not needed to supply offsets.

To produce chards, cut down the main stems after harvesting, to within 30cm (1ft) of the ground, and allow new shoots to grow. Mulch and water the plants frequently. When the shoots are about 60cm (2ft) high, tie them together, then tie black polythene around them to exclude the light. Earth them up like celery or cardoons to blanch them. The stems are cooked and eaten like cardoons, to which they are related (see p.143).

Sweet corn (*Zea mays*), also known as corn on the cob, maize or simply corn, is exceedingly tender and tasty, provided it can be gathered just before being cooked. The cobs sold in the shops are dry and bland by comparison, since sweet corn deteriorates rapidly once it is picked. So try to find room in the food garden for this easily-grown vegetable. If space is limited, you could grow a few plants in the flower border: their fine foliage and feathery flowers make them suitably decorative. Both white and yellow sweet corn are available, and some bicoloured, as well as yellow and purple multicoloured, varieties are being introduced from America, though these are as yet relatively unusual.

Sweet corn is best grown in a block rather than singly or in a row. This helps to ensure the pollination of the female flowers – the 'silks' at the ends of the embryo cobs – by the male flowers at the top of each plant.

Cropping is most reliable in fairly mild areas. However, a reasonable success rate can be expected in colder districts provided you grow a quick-maturing variety and give the plants an early start. Results depend on the season to a large extent.

In all districts it is an advantage to raise plants in a greenhouse or on a sunny windowsill indoors. This gives them an earlier start and more time to grow. Outdoor sowing can be successful, but the cobs will develop rather late if a dry summer slows their growth. A floating cloche (see p.17) will speed early development.

Sunshine, and a soil that retains moisture, are the main requirements of sweet corn. Dig the site during the previous winter, and add plenty of manure.

Tap the top of the plant just beneath the tassels to help pollinate the female flowers.

MAKING A START

Just before sowing or planting outdoors, rake a dressing of general fertilizer into the soil at 70g per sq m (2oz per sq yd). Repeat this dressing when the plants appear to be growing well.

Sweet corn plants do not like being disturbed by transplanting. If you are raising early plants under glass or indoors, sow the seeds in peat pots or other small pots – two per pot – in mid-spring. Germinate them at about 13°C (55°F), and keep them covered with glass and paper until the seedlings appear. Remove the weaker one if two develop. Harden the seedlings off in late spring and plant them out, complete with their peat pot or soilball, after the last frosts, either in the open or under cloches. Space the seedlings as for outdoor-sown plants.

For a protected sowing outdoors, first warm the site by using cloches. Then sow the seeds under cloches or under a floating cloche during the second half of spring. Place two seeds 1cm (½in) deep in each station: space them 40cm (15in) apart in rows 60cm (2ft) apart. Leave only the stronger seedling after germination.

If no protection is given, wait until late spring before sowing. The soil must be warm and the danger of night frosts over.

CARE OF THE CROP

Sweet corn grows rapidly, so remove a floating cloche before it starts to hamper growth and ordinary cloches as soon as the tallest plants reach the glass or plastic.

Avoid deep hoeing, since the plants are shallow-rooted. Mulching, once the soil is really warm, is a better way to check weeds. Make sure that the soil does not dry out. Support tall plants with canes if the garden is exposed. Remove any side-shoots that grow from the base, when they are about 15cm (6in) long.

HARVESTING

Start harvesting when the tassels of the sweet corn become brown and withered. The seeds, exposed by opening the outer sheath and pricked with a knife point or a fingernail, exude a watery fluid if unripe, and a 'milky' liquid when they are ripe. Pick them by twisting the ears off the plants. Cook or freeze them as soon as possible.

PESTS AND DISEASES

Frit fly is one of the few pests to trouble sweet corn.

Smut is an occasional fungus disease.

RECOMMENDED VARIETIES

The varieties are given in their approximate order of ripening; all are hybrids.

'John Innes Hybrid' Early, well-flavoured, medium-sized cobs.
'Kelvedon Sweetheart' Similar to the above variety.
'Early Extra Sweet' Very sweet, and remains so when frozen.
'Aztec' Large, well-filled cobs. Good flavour.
'How Sweet It Is' White, sweet-flavoured variety that keeps well.
'Earlyglow' Very sweet, and remains so longer than most after gathering.
'Kelvedon Glory' Heavy crops of well-flavoured cobs.

Draw soil around the base of developing plants to increase their stability and ensure that the roots are adequately covered. Additional support with canes may be needed on a site that is particularly exposed.

Browning of the silks, or female flowers, is a sign that the cobs may be ready for eating. Before picking, test by peeling back part of the sheath and piercing a seed with your thumbnail. The liquid exuded should be milky. If it is watery, the cob is not yet ready.

Cardoons (*Cynara cardunculus*) are tall plants, similar to globe artichokes in appearance. They are, indeed, handsome enough to take a place at the back of a flower border. Cardoons need similar soil and growing conditions to celery (see pp.146–7). Their blanched stems and leaf midribs are usually served cooked.

MAKING A START
Prepare the site during the winter by forking in a generous dressing of manure or compost. In late spring, after the last frosts, rake in a dressing of general fertilizer at 70g per sq m (2oz per sq yd), just before sowing.

Sow the seeds directly in the ground in groups of three or four, and set the groups 45–60cm (1½–2ft) apart in each direction. Subsequently, remove all but the strongest seedling from each group. Alternatively, sow the seeds singly in pots under glass in early spring and harden them off ready for planting out in late spring. You can put cloches over the seedlings for the first four weeks or so. Keep the plants well watered throughout the summer and give a weak liquid feed every week or two.

BLANCHING AND HARVESTING
In late summer, tie the leaves together with string, then tie black polythene around each plant, leaving only a little of the top uncovered. Blanching takes four or five weeks, after which the plants may be dug up; discard the tough outer leaves.

RECOMMENDED VARIETIES
'**Tours**' Has the best taste and longer stems, but the leaves are very prickly.
'**Improved White**' and '**Ivory White**' are hardier, non-prickly, but liable to bolt.

Florence fennel (*Foeniculum vulgare*), also known as sweet fennel or finocchio, belongs to the same species as the herb called fennel and has a similar aniseed flavour. But it is the bulbous base that is harvested for eating as a cooked vegetable; its crisp, celery-like texture also makes it suitable for eating raw in salads. Florence fennel needs a richer soil than the herb. Its feathery foliage, which grows to about 60cm (2ft), makes Florence fennel a plant attractive enough for the flower border.

Florence fennel grows best in light, well-drained soil that has been well dressed with manure or compost. It needs a sunny, sheltered position.

MAKING A START
One of the difficulties of growing Florence fennel is that it easily runs to seed. It may do this if the seeds are sown too early or if the plants suffer a check, perhaps due to dryness, during the growing season.

Dress the bed with general fertilizer at 70g per sq m (2oz per sq yd) just before sowing. Sow the seeds between mid-spring and midsummer; avoid early sowing for the varieties 'Sweet Florence' and 'Sirio'. Plants sown in midsummer will mature in autumn, whereas spring and early summer sowings give a late-summer harvest.

Sow the seeds sparingly in shallow drills; leave 45cm (1½ft) between rows. Thin the seedlings to about 20–30cm (8in–1ft). Water the bed at the first hint of drying out, in order to produce bulbous stems and to reduce the risk of plants running to seed.

BLANCHING AND HARVESTING
Swelling of the stem base is a signal to draw earth around and over this part of the plant.

Continue to keep the swollen base covered until it is about the size of a tennis ball, which will be about two or three weeks later. Then sever it from the roots with a sharp knife. Cut off the tops, too, which may be used in the same way as the herb fennel (see p.221).

PESTS AND DISEASES
Florence fennel is not subject to any particular troubles.

RECOMMENDED VARIETIES
'**Perfection**' Less subject to bolting, even when sown early.
'**Sirio**' Good flavour and quick maturing. Suitable for later sowings.
'**Sweet Florence**' Well-flavoured variety, better for late sowing.
'**Zefa Fino**' A recently-introduced variety less likely to bolt than the traditional varieties.

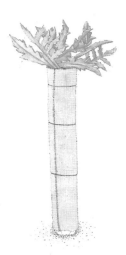

Secure black polythene around the stems during late summer to blanch the stalks of cardoons in preparation for eating.

Use a hoe to draw soil around the base of Florence fennel when the stem starts to swell. Repeat, if necessary, so that the bulb remains covered and becomes blanched.

Florence fennel may be harvested once the bulbs are fully formed. Use a sharp knife to cut close to the ground. If the stumps are left, secondary shoots will grow.

SOWING SEEDS OUTDOORS, pages 36–37
SOWING UNDER GLASS, pages 38–39

STALKS AND SHOOTS, pages 116–117
CELERY, pages 146–147

PESTS AND DISEASES, pages 172–175

143

ASPARAGUS

Asparagus (*Asparagus officinalis*) is often regarded as an aristocratic or even luxury vegetable, partly due to its short season, but mainly because of the delicate flavour of its young shoots, or spears. Asparagus is always expensive in the shops, not only on account of its limited season but because growing it is labour-intensive, since it has to be hand-picked.

Whether you choose to grow this perennial vegetable yourself depends on how highly you value its flavour, and whether you have enough room. Asparagus needs a considerable area of ground, which it occupies right through the year. Growing it also requires a lot of patience, since it takes two seasons to produce its first crop. However, once established, it will go on providing its annual six-week harvest for 10 to 20 years.

Asparagus needs good soil. The ideal soil is fertile, well-drained and neutral or just slightly acid. If your soil is on the damp side, it will help to grow asparagus in a raised bed (see p.133). Choose a sunny, fairly sheltered position, and avoid a frost pocket or a site that is very windy.

Asparagus can be raised from seed, but it then takes an extra year to produce spears for cutting. It is best to buy asparagus as one-year-old crowns which can usually be bought direct from a nursery, or otherwise purchased by mail order from a specialist grower.

If you buy crowns from a nursery, they will have been in soil, so take care that the roots do not become dry before they are planted. Crowns sent by mail order are purposely despatched dry, and not in moist

wrappings, to survive the post. It is important that air is allowed to circulate around these roots, before they are planted, to prevent the development of moulds or fungi. If immediate planting is not possible on receipt of the parcel, spread the crowns out in a frost-free, dry place for a few days until you are ready to use them.

MAKING A START
It is worth preparing an asparagus bed with some care, bearing in mind how long the crop will be growing in the same site, and in view of the plant's extensive root system. The first step is to dig the site during the autumn; remove every trace of perennial weeds as you do so. Work in a good dressing of rotted compost or manure; allow a bucketful to the square metre or yard.

You will need a planting trench 30cm (1ft) wide, with 90cm (3ft) left between trenches if you plan to grow more than one row. The distance between plants in the trench should be 45cm (1½ft). If you are growing 12 plants, which will give a good yield for a family, you will need two trenches each 2.7m (9ft) long.

In mid-spring, dig out the trench to a depth of 20cm (8in). Mix some sharp sand with the soil removed, then replace sufficient to form a ridge along the base of the trench about 8cm (3in) high.

Set the plants or one-year-old crowns on the ridge in the trench, and spread out the roots. Cover them with 8cm (3in) of soil.

GROWING ASPARAGUS FROM SEED
Soak the seeds for several hours in tepid water before sowing them. Sow them outdoors in spring, in drills 1cm (½in) deep and 30cm (1ft) apart. When the seedlings are at least 15cm (6in) high, thin them out to 15cm (6in) apart; water frequently during dry spells. Set the plants out in their permanent site the following spring.

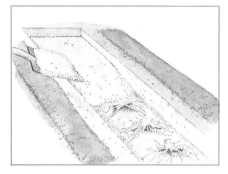

Place the crowns, with roots spread out, on a shallow ridge of free-draining soil laid in the trench. Cover them at once with soil. Leave surplus soil on the surface alongside the trench for the time being.

CARE OF THE CROP
Replace the remainder of the soil, little by little, during the first summer, by gently drawing soil from the sides of the trench while hoeing. By the time autumn comes, the trench should be filled.

Do not cut any shoots during the first spring after planting. A year later, cut just a few of the thicker ones, taking one or two from each plant.

Hand-weed between the plants, or hoe very carefully once shoots have ceased to emerge. A hoe must be used with great care between asparagus plants, since there is a risk of causing root damage.

Make sure the bed never dries out. Each spring, apply a general fertilizer at 70g per sq m (2oz per sq yd): mix this gently into the surface. Spread a 5cm (2in) mulch of well-rotted manure or garden compost over the soil surface afterwards. This will help to

control weeds, but should weeds still prove troublesome you will have to remove them carefully by hand.

Aparagus can be 'earthed up', like potatoes; this process will produce longer, blanched spears. To make ridges, draw up some soil from the surrounding area to a depth of about 13cm (5in). Do this just before the asparagus is ready to be cut, and spread it out again in the autumn. If you prefer, you can grow asparagus on the flat, in which case the spears will be shorter, but ready for cutting earlier. The annual process of manuring gradually builds up ridges along the rows to a certain extent.

Pick berries from the ferns before they can fall, otherwise your trench will be invaded by unwanted seedlings. Support the ferns with string and canes if they are exposed to wind. If the plants are allowed to rock, there is risk of their roots being

loosened in the soil and rot developing.

Cut the stems down to within 2.5cm (1in) of the soil once the growth turns yellow in autumn, then spread a mulch of well-rotted manure or compost over the asparagus bed.

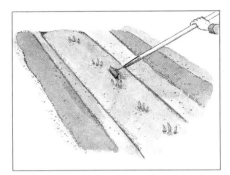

Draw more soil around the plants when the shoots emerge, pulling in the remainder from the sides during the summer to fill the trench flush with the surrounding soil. Weed the bed often, and take special care that no perennial weeds are allowed to become established.

Cut the stems down almost to ground level during the autumn once the foliage has changed colour. Collect and burn the stems, and remove the supporting canes if any were used. Spread a mulch of compost or well-rotted manure over the bed afterward.

ASPARAGUS: THE FIVE YEAR-PLAN

Year 1 Plant out young roots grown from seed the year before or purchased as one-year-old crowns.

Year 2 Do not cut any shoots.

Year 3 Cut only one or two of the thicker stems from each plant.

Year 4 Cut all spears when 10cm (4in) high. Cut for five weeks only.

Year 5 Cut all spears, for up to seven weeks. Continue harvesting all spears annually for 15 to 20 years.

HARVESTING

Two years after planting, cut the emerging spears when they are 10cm (4in) high; sever them 8cm (3in) below the surface. Do this with a sharp, serrated knife, since the base of the stalk is tough. Stop cutting after five weeks and leave any shoots that emerge later to grow into ferns. This will build up the crowns for the next season's crop. Cut over a period of approximately six or seven weeks in subsequent years.

Rather than let the spears grow longer than 10cm (4in), cut a few each day, as they reach this size, until there are enough for a meal. Stand them in iced water for a while, then cover and refrigerate them to keep them fresh until you have sufficient spears to make a dish.

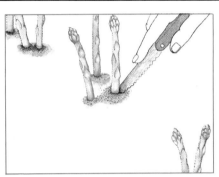

A sharp, serrated knife is best for cutting asparagus, preferably a purpose-made asparagus knife. Wait until each shoot, or 'spear', is about 10cm (4in) above the ground and make the cut well below the surface. Cut for five weeks during the first year of cropping.

PESTS AND DISEASES

Asparagus beetles, slugs and snails are the chief pests.

Damage may also be caused by fungus diseases, rust and violet root rot.

RECOMMENDED VARIETIES

'Connover's Colossal' A much-favoured early variety, with long fat spears. Best on sandy soil.
'Giant Mammoth' Has a slightly more open bud and is a good choice for heavier soils.
'Limbras' An early F1 hybrid variety, which gives high yields.
'Lucullus' Seedless and heavy-yielding, with long, straight spears.
'Larac' Early, heavy crops of thick, succulent stems.
'Martha Washington' Heavy crops of long, purple-tinged spears.

SOWING SEEDS OUTDOORS, pages 36–37
STALKS AND SHOOTS, pages 116–117
DECIDING WHAT TO GROW, pages 130–131
PESTS AND DISEASES, pages 172–175

Celery (*Apium graveolens*) is a most valuable crop, both for eating as a cooked vegetable and as flavouring for soups and many cooked dishes. Its crisp texture and distinctive flavour also makes it ideal for eating raw in salads. The leaves of celery, too, are strongly-flavoured and are used for seasoning and garnishing. There are three types of trench-grown celery; they have white, pink or red stems. Self-blanching celery is either green or pale yellow.

When grown in the conventional way, by using a trench, celery is one of the more demanding vegetables. The stems must be blanched for at least a couple of months, a process necessary to improve their flavour and texture and to increase the length of stems. Blanching is effected by growing the plants in trenches and drawing soil around

them. Trench-grown celery is excellently flavoured and, being hardy, is useful as a winter vegetable: it can remain in the ground for lifting as needed until well into the new year.

Should you wish to save yourself the effort, however, you will choose the self-blanching kind. Self-blanching celery yields smaller stems, with a milder flavour and, since the plants are less hardy, they must be harvested before the first autumn frosts.

The plants of self-blanching celery are grown closely spaced in a block, so that the dense foliage excludes most of the light from the stems. Plants on the outside of the block are shielded from light by a banking of straw or a boarded edge.

Both types of celery need rich, moisture-retentive soil in an open situation; a heavy

soil is suitable. The key to moisture-holding lies in ample supplies of bulky organic matter, such as rotted manure or garden compost. The best results are obtained in ground that is neutral or only slightly acid.

TRENCH CELERY: MAKING A START

Prepare the ground during the winter by removing the soil from a trench 40cm (15in) wide and 30cm (1ft) deep. This is the width for a single row. If you prefer to plant a double row, make the trench 60cm (2ft) wide. Single rows are better for small quantities; although a double row is space-saving, it makes earthing up more difficult.

Spread a thick layer of manure or compost over the bottom of the trench – it should be at least 5cm (2in) deep – and work it into the earth with a fork. Then replace most of the soil that you have dug out, to leave the trench just 10cm (4in) deep. Leave the remainder of the soil along the sides of the trench.

Sow the seeds in early to mid-spring if you have a greenhouse for raising the plants.

They require a temperature of about 10–16°C (50–60°F), so an electric propagator will be useful if the greenhouse is not heated to this temperature. Indoors, choose a warm but light place for germination and avoid too early a start.

Sow the tiny seeds in a small pot or a shallow pan, and cover it with glass only. Celery seed germinates better in light, but it takes at least two weeks for seedlings to emerge. Prick out the seedlings 6cm (2in) apart in a seed tray when they are large enough to handle. Grow them on in gentle warmth; do not allow the temperature to fall too low at night. Throughout their entire growing period it is important to avoid checks to their development caused by a sudden change in growing conditions.

If you are raising the seedlings indoors,

place them close to a well-lit window to reduce the risk of their becoming spindly.

Harden the plants off in late spring by moving them to a cold frame for 10–14 days. If possible, wait for some mild weather before you do this. Prepare the trench and rake in a dressing of general fertilizer at 90g per sq m (3oz per sq yd). Add a further 70g per sq m (2oz per sq yd) when earthing up the plants.

When the plants are fully hardened, set them 23cm (9in) apart in the trench. If you are planting a double row, leave 40cm (15in) between the rows and 25cm (10in) between the plants. Set them in pairs and water them thoroughly after planting. Scatter slug pellets between the young plants.

Make sure that the soil does not dry out during the summer by watering generously.

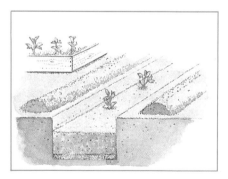

To **allow for** subsequent earthing up, plant celery in a prepared trench some 10cm (4in) deeper than the surrounding ground. Leave the surplus soil in a low ridge along each side.

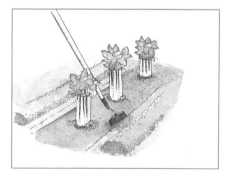

Before earthing up, tie the stems loosely together, below the leaves. Take care that no soil falls between the stalks of the celery when earthing up. Wrapping thick brown paper or corrugated card around the stems before tying them will help to prevent this.

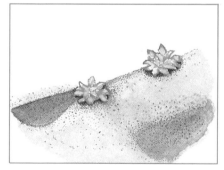

Draw earth around the plants, a little at a time, on at least three occasions, until only the leaves remain visible. Blanching will be complete from about two weeks after the final earthing up.

TRENCH CELERY: EARTHING UP

Earthing up is done in three stages, the first when the plants have grown 30cm (1ft) high. Water the trench and remove any side-shoots from the base of the plants, then tie the stems together loosely just beneath the leaves, allowing room for the hearts to develop. Draw a little soil from the sides of the trench to cover the lower part of the stems. Scatter slug pellets over the soil.

Repeat the earthing up three weeks later, and bring the soil nearer to the leaves. Scatter on more slug pellets. Give the celery a final earthing after another three weeks, this time encasing the stems right up to the base of the leaves. Slope the sides sharply, to ensure that the rain runs away from the plants and into the ground. Some additional soil may be needed.

TRENCH CELERY: HARVESTING

Start lifting celery with a fork during the autumn, about two weeks after the final earthing. Open the ridge from one end and, after lifting the plants, earth it up again as a protection against frost. If you have grown both white and coloured varieties, lift the white ones first since they are least hardy. Use pink varieties next, then the red ones.

A touch of frost improves the crispness and flavour of celery, but late crops may rot if they are frozen in the ground. In severe weather, it is worth protecting the plants by putting down a layer of straw or bracken on top of the ridge.

Lift the celery with a fork; take care to insert it beneath the plant and not through the stems. Use white varieties first, followed by those with pink and red stems.

SELF-BLANCHING CELERY: MAKING A START

Self-blanching celery is best grown in a square block, not in rows. Work out the size required according to the number of plants you intend to grow: they should be spaced 23cm (9in) apart in each direction. Dig the ground during the winter, and work in a thick dressing of rotted manure or compost – allow at least a bucketful to the square metre or yard.

Sow the seeds in early to mid-spring, as for trench celery. Prick out the seedlings as soon as they can be handled. Harden the plants in a cold frame during late spring and scatter a general fertilizer over the planting site at 90g per sq m (3oz per sq yd). Give another dressing at 70g per sq m (2oz per sq yd) a few weeks later. Plant out once all danger of frost is past, when the seedlings have five or six leaves. The plants have a tendency to bolt if they are subjected to cold or dry conditions, so do not plant them out too early in the season.

Set the plants 23cm (9in) apart in each direction, with their crowns flush with the soil, to form a square block. Water them well, and keep the plants watered as necessary throughout the growing season to prevent the soil from drying out. Scatter slug pellets between the young plants. Remove side-shoots from the base as soon as they start to appear.

In midsummer, when the plants are well-developed, place a layer of straw around the edge of the block to exclude light from the outside of the plants. Alternatively, use planks placed on edge to form a light-excluding box around the plants. However, straw will still be needed to cover plants that are exposed when lifting starts.

SELF-BLANCHING CELERY: HARVESTING

Start lifting in the second half of summer, using a fork. Aim to finish lifting by the first autumn frosts. Tuck straw up against the plants that are exposed when others are removed. If there is a surplus, the stems may be frozen for subsequent cooking, though not for eating raw since the texture of celery is adversely affected during freezing.

PESTS AND DISEASES

Slugs and snails are a menace to all types of celery, especially on heavier soils. Celery fly (or leaf miner) and carrot fly can also be troublesome on this crop.

The principal ailments are due to boron deficiency, cucumber mosaic virus, celery heart rot and celery leaf spot.

Pack straw around a block of self-blanching celery to cover the outer plants. The plants' own dense foliage will exclude light from those that are on the inside.

RECOMMENDED VARIETIES

Trench-grown celery
'Giant Pink' One of the hardier varieties, with long, pale pink stems.
'Giant Red' Withstands the cold well, and lasts until nearly the end of winter. Shell-pink stems.
'Giant White' Excellent flavour, with solid, crisp stems.
'Hopkin's Fenlander' Bulky white stems. Slightly hardier than some white celeries.
'New Dwarf White' Early to mid-season variety, with compact stems that are a little easier to blanch than taller sorts.

Self-blanching celery
'American Green' Long, high-quality stems that remain pale green.
'Celebrity' The long stems are crisp and early, and the plant is resistant to bolting (running to seed).
'Golden Self-Blanching' An early variety with compact growth. May bolt if it is sown too early.
'Lathom Self-Blanching' High-yielding and resistant to bolting. Fine flavour.
'Ivory Tower' Matures from late summer. Tall, with substantial white stems.

SOWING UNDER GLASS, pages 38–39
PLANTING VEGETABLES, page 40

STALKS AND SHOOTS, pages 116–117
PESTS AND DISEASES, pages 172–175

FREEZING VEGETABLES, pages 232–233

Although it grows like a vegetable, rhubarb (*Rheum rhaponticum*) is invariably eaten as a form of dessert fruit. There are few more accommodating food plants, for it tolerates most well-drained soils and goes on producing its spring harvest for five years or many more if you lift and divide it regularly. Furthermore, its large leaves smother weeds and reduce the need for hoeing. Rhubarb can also be 'forced' in order to provide an early crop of slender, delicately-flavoured stems; any maincrop surplus is easily frozen.

Like most vegetables, rhubarb needs a sunny spot. And, although it will produce some sort of crop even on poorish soil, the reward for generous feeding and summer watering is a much greater yield of thick, succulent stems.

Rhubarb may be grown from the 'crowns' (root divisions) which are widely available at nurseries and garden centres, or from seed. Though they save a little money, seed-grown plants give more variable results and must be left for an extra year before the first harvest is taken.

MAKING A START

From crowns Plant crowns at any time during the winter or early spring when soil and weather conditions allow. Each crown will need up to a square metre or yard of growing space. Prepare the planting stations a few weeks in advance by digging out holes 45cm (1½ft) square, 30cm (1ft) deep.

Place a thick layer of rotted manure or compost in the base and fork this into the lower soil. Mix some more manure with the topsoil before replacing it. Mark each position with a peg and make sure that no perennial weeds are left in the area. A week before planting, work in a dressing of general fertilizer at the rate of 170g per sq m (5oz per sq yd).

Plant with the buds just on the surface, and firm the soil around each crown.

From seeds Sow in a seedbed in spring: set the seeds about 2.5cm (1in) deep, and thin seedlings to 23cm (9in). Set the plants out in prepared stations, as for crowns, the following autumn.

CARE OF THE CROP

Keep the plants watered during dry summer weather. Give crowns and older plants a spring dressing of general fertilizer at 170g per sq m (5oz per sq yd), and repeat this after a few weeks. Hoe the dressing in carefully so that the crowns are not damaged. Spread a mulch of rotted manure or compost around them and top this up in autumn.

Cut off any flowering stems as they appear, since their development weakens the plants.

HARVESTING AND FORCING

Unforced stems are ready for gathering from spring until early summer. Take a few stems from each crown a year after planting, but wait another year for rhubarb grown from seedlings. Even on mature plants, always leave a few stems behind at any one picking. To gather them, grasp the stem near the base and pull from the roots with a slight twisting action. Cut off the leaves and put them on the compost heap.

Wait until the plants are at least three years old before attempting to force them. For a really early crop, lift one or two roots in autumn, when the leaves die back, and leave them on the surface to become frosted. This gives the plants the impression that it is winter, and they become dormant. Early in the winter, place them right way up in boxes, with moist peat packed around them, and stand the boxes in a shed, basement, spare room or greenhouse where the temperature is approximately 7–10°C (45–50°F).

If necessary, cover the crowns with black polythene to exclude the light. The stalks will be ready in five to six weeks. After harvesting, replant the crowns but do not force them again for several years.

To advance the main harvest by two or three weeks, cover some of the outdoor crowns with boxes or an upturned bucket, and pack straw or compost around and over them. Do not force these roots again for a couple of years.

PROPAGATION

When new plants are needed – and, in any case, every five years or so – lift the roots in early spring and divide them into several segments, each with a growth bud.

PESTS AND DISEASES

Stem and bulb eelworms are among the pests to trouble rhubarb.

Crown rot and honey fungus are the most likely ailments.

RECOMMENDED VARIETIES

'Timperley Early' One of the best for early crops and forcing. Thin stems.

'Champagne Early' Sweet, scarlet stalks. Good for outdoor forcing.

'The Sutton' A maincrop variety with long stalks. Slow to run to seed.

'Victoria' Red stalks with good flavour. A late variety.

Divide mature rhubarb crowns with a spade; they can be split into four or five segments. Those around the outside of the clump are best. Each must have a bud and part of the root.

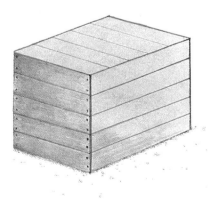

An upturned box, a bucket or a large pot are equally suitable for 'forcing' an early crop of rhubarb outdoors. Do this in winter, after covering the crowns with straw. Forcing weakens the plant, so do not repeat it the following year.

JERUSALEM ARTICHOKES

Jerusalem artichokes (*Helianthus tuberosus*) are unrelated to globe artichokes. Their tubers have a distinctive yet delicate sweet flavour and are a good winter standby. The plants are hardy members of the sunflower family, and will grow as tall as 3m (10ft), although by removing the upper, flowering part of the stem in midsummer you can keep them to about half this height. This helps reduce the risk of wind damage and assists the production of artichoke tubers.

Jerusalem artichokes are not unlike knobbly potatoes in appearance, though some smoother-skinned varieties are now available. They are recommended for soups or sauces, or for roasting. Scrubbing is the easiest way to clean them. They can be cooked in their skins then peeled afterward if you wish.

Treat Jerusalem artichokes as an annual crop, even though any tubers left in the ground will survive the winter and send up fresh shoots the following spring. Remember that unless the site is cleared each year, it will soon turn into a jungle of stems and undersized tubers.

The plants are not fussy about soil, provided it is reasonably well-drained, and they will also tolerate light shade. This makes them ideal for planting in odd corners and patches within the garden – perhaps beside the compost heap, or in another part where little else can be usefully grown.

They are also a good first crop to plant when breaking new ground, including heavy soil. Their fibrous roots help to improve the soil structure and there is plenty of space to hoe between plants. In addition, a row of Jerusalem artichokes can make a screen or an effective windbreak in the summer when plants are fully clad with foliage.

MAKING A START

Dig the site in late autumn or early winter, and remove any perennial weeds, together with their roots, as you do so. Add a dressing of manure or compost to improve the yield of tubers on poor soil, but remember that this could result in an excessive amount of foliage on more fertile ground.

Plant the tubers at the end of winter or during spring. The plants are quite hardy and a reasonably early start provides an extended growing season.

Tubers can be bought at the greengrocers if none are available at the local garden centres. Although named varieties exist, they can be hard to find. Tubers should be firm and about the size of a hen's egg. Any that are much larger may be cut in half, but make sure that there is a bud on each piece.

Plant the tubers 10–13cm (4–5in) deep and about 40cm (15in) apart, using a trowel. Leave 90cm (3ft) between rows.

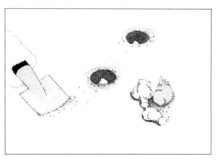

Use a trowel to plant the tubers at 40cm (15in) spacings in averagely fertile soil. If the site is exposed, draw soil around the stems and support the plants with canes.

CARE OF THE CROP

Draw some soil around the stems when they are 30cm (1ft) high to help keep plants more stable. If the garden is exposed or subject to wind eddies, insert a stout bamboo cane alongside each plant so that the developing stem can be tied to it. Even if unsupported plants are not flattened by the wind, constant rocking disturbs their roots and checks development.

Another way to reduce wind-rock is by cutting the tops off during the summer, to leave about 1.5–1.8m (5–6ft) of stem. During the autumn, after the leaves have withered, cut the stems down to within 15cm (6in) of the ground.

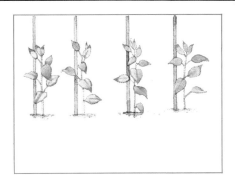

In exposed areas, support artichoke plants by tying them to bamboo stakes with soft string. Choose stakes at least 2m (6ft) tall. Such support will prevent root movement, which hinders tuber development.

HARVESTING

Tubers may be lifted as needed from autumn onward, once the leaves have withered. Dig each root with a fork and take great care that no tubers, however small, are left behind.

Tubers may be stored in the same way as potatoes, but they retain more flavour if left in the soil throughout the winter and used when desired. Remember to keep some of the smaller, healthy-looking tubers for planting out the following spring.

PESTS AND DISEASES

Cutworms and root aphids may sometimes prove troublesome. Disease is seldom a problem.

Potatoes (*Solanum tuberosum*) are the most widely grown and most commonly eaten vegetable in the western world. Though they are always readily available in the shops, the main advantage of growing your own is that you can choose from among dozens of interesting varieties, most of them far superior in flavour and texture to the heavy-cropping types grown commercially.

Although average potato yields are quite impressive – up to 35kg (80lb) for maincrops, for instance, from a plot 3m (10ft) square – whether you grow them or not depends on how much ground can be spared.

If your garden is small, you could perhaps consider growing a few 'earlies'. If harvested in early summer, when their skins are still not set, they have a wonderful flavour.

After the potatoes are harvested, the ground can then be used for later crops such as brassicas or leeks. If you cannot spare any space in the vegetable plot, a few earlies can even be grown in pots in a heated or unheated greenhouse.

All potatoes are half-hardy, which means that they will grow outdoors provided they are not subjected to frost; they need an unshaded position. Most soils are suitable, though somewhat acid conditions are best since potatoes dislike chalky soils: a pH of 6–6.5 is ideal. For early potatoes, choose a sheltered position and avoid frost pockets. Heavy yields depend on plenty of manure or compost being dug into the soil during the autumn or early winter before planting.

Potatoes are an excellent first crop for ground just cleared of weeds.

TYPES OF POTATO

First-earlies are quick-maturing; plant a little before mid-spring and harvest in early summer.

Second-earlies are planted a week or two later and lifted from midsummer.

Maincrop varieties are planted in late spring and mature in late summer or early autumn; store for winter use.

Within each of these groups there are individual varieties that differ in texture, shape, colour, size, yield and cooking qualities. Some are fussy about soil; others show varying degrees of disease resistance.

The flavour of a variety can also vary depending on the type of soil and on the kind of organic dressings that have been added to it.

MAKING A START

The tubers supplied for planting are called 'seed potatoes'. Try to buy 'certified seed', which means that it is free from virus disease, and look for tubers that are, on average, about the size of a hen's egg. If many are significantly larger than this, you will get fewer potatoes for your money without a corresponding increase in the numbers harvested from each plant.

Earlies and second-earlies may be given a prompt start, well before the last of the spring frosts, by encouraging them to form shoots before they are planted. This is termed sprouting, or 'chitting'. Maincrop potatoes may be treated in the same way, although the advantage is less marked.

Buy early and second-early seed potatoes during late winter, ready for immediate

sprouting. Buy maincrop varieties at the same time, or a few weeks later.

Stand potatoes that are to be sprouted in a shallow box or tray: place them so that their 'eyes' (embryo shoots) are uppermost. Put the box in a cool but frost-free room or shed where there is a reasonable amount of light, but never in direct sunlight.

Shoots will develop over a period of four to six weeks. They should be short and stubby (about 1–2cm/½–1in), rather than long, thin and straggling.

First-earlies

Plant the sprouted tubers during the period up to mid-spring, but wait until the ground is dry enough to be worked easily. Just before planting, rake in a dressing of general fertilizer at 170g per sq m (5oz per sq yd).

Set up a line to mark the first row, then

use a trowel to make the holes. Place the bottom of each tuber about 10cm (4in) deep, with the sprouts uppermost. Allow 30cm (1ft) between potatoes in the row and 45cm (1½ft) between rows. As each row is planted, and before moving the line, draw a little soil from each side of the row to form a shallow ridge.

Second-earlies

Plant these about mid-spring in the same way as earlies, but space the tubers 40cm (15in) apart and with 60cm (2ft) between rows. They may have to stay in the soil for a few weeks longer than the first-earlies.

Maincrop

Plant during the second half of spring, whether or not the tubers have been sprouted. Place them 40cm (15in) apart, with 75cm (2½ft) between rows.

CARE OF THE CROP

Look out for the emerging shoots, which will first show as a slight disturbance of the soil. For earlies, especially, it is important to draw or earth up some extra soil over these first growths as protection against frost. Use a draw hoe to do this, and take care not to cut through shoots just beneath the soil. If frost threatens when growth is well advanced, cover the shoots overnight with straw, bracken or newspaper.

Earthing up must continue throughout the growing period. Earth up the plants when they are about 25cm (10in) high, and then every two weeks or so until the foliage meets between rows. If they are left unearthed, some of the tubers will develop close to the surface, where they will turn green and become inedible, even poisonous.

Early potatoes, especially, are accelerated by setting the tubers to sprout before planting. If they are placed in the light and protected from frost, strong, stubby shoots will develop. Lack of light or too much warmth will result in long, thin, pale shoots.

Planting with a trowel is the easiest method for potatoes; make the holes 10cm (4in) deep. The alternative is to form a furrow of the same depth with a draw hoe. Plant the tubers with sprouts uppermost. The spacing will depend on whether they are earlies, second-earlies or maincrop.

Another purpose of earthing up is to bury the roots more deeply; the extra moisture farther down will aid root and tuber development. Earthing up also suppresses weeds, though these will in any case tend to decrease as the foliage meets over the rows.

All potatoes, but especially earlies, need generous watering during dry weather to maintain high yields. With maincrop plantings, the longer growing period may help to balance out the effect of wet and dry spells.

To safeguard against potato blight, which cannot be cured once it becomes established, spray in early summer with dithane, maneb, zineb or Bordeaux mixture. Continue to spray every two weeks throughout the summer months. The disease is especially troublesome during warm, wet summers.

Earthing up, using a draw hoe, ensures that the new tubers forming on the roots will be covered with soil. Left uncovered and therefore exposed to the light, they would turn green and become inedible.

Preventive spraying, starting early in summer, is the only practical way to combat potato blight. Use a pressure sprayer, and direct the fungicide onto both the upper and lower surfaces of the foliage.

HARVESTING AND STORING

Early varieties should be ready from the time that the plants are in full flower, which will be about 12 weeks after planting. For the first gathering, before the crop as a whole is ready, scrape a little soil from the ridge and remove any egg-sized tubers that can be seen; replace the soil afterward. These first potatoes are at their best when the skin rubs off easily with your thumb.

Lift second-earlies, as needed, to follow the first-earlies. Some can remain undug until the end of summer.

Maincrop potatoes take about 20 weeks to come to full maturity. They can be dug up for storing once the foliage has withered, but you can dig a few earlier than this for immediate eating. Make sure, before lifting

them, that the skins are fully set – that they cannot be rubbed off with your thumb.

Lift maincrop potatoes on a sunny day, and leave them on the soil surface for an hour or two to dry. Lift all tubers, however small, otherwise they will help to perpetuate any disease in the soil and will grow again as weeds or 'volunteers' the next year. Use up any damaged potatoes immediately. Burn any that are diseased.

Store maincrop potatoes in a dry, frost-free room or shed, either in a heap on the floor or else in a box, tea chest or a thick paper or hessian sack. They must be covered in order to exclude light, otherwise they turn green and are dangerous to eat. Check the stored potatoes regularly and throw out any that are rotting.

When lifting whole roots, push the fork in well to the side of the plant, otherwise some of the tubers may be speared. Use a broad-tined potato fork to lift the crop, if you have one. Dig up only as many early potatoes as you can eat for one or two meals; the longer they are out of the ground, the harder they are to scrape.

PESTS AND DISEASES

The pests most likely to give trouble are cutworms, potato cyst eelworms, slugs, snails and wireworms.

Potato diseases include gangrene, leaf roll virus, mosaic virus, potato blight, scab and spraing.

RECOMMENDED VARIETIES
First-early
'Arran Comet' Early and heavy-yielding. Best on light soil. Prone to virus diseases.
'Foremost' Cooks well, with good flavour. Stores well, provided skins are set.
'Maris Bard' Very early, with heavy crop. Resists virus diseases but prone to scab.
'Pentland Javelin' High quality, but a little later than some. Resists mosaic virus and eelworms.
'Ulster Sceptre' Very early and with good yields. Seed susceptible to gangrene.

Second-early
'Estima' Excellent yields. Resists blight but susceptible to mosaic virus and scab.
'Maris Peer' Yields well, provided the soil does not dry out. Resists blight and scab.
'Wilja' Good yields, consistent cropper and cooks well. Prone to mosaic virus but resists fungus diseases.

Maincrop
'Desirée' Heavy crops of pink-skinned, well-flavoured tubers. Cooks well but susceptible to scab.
'King Edward' A good cropper that cooks superbly. Drought and mosaic virus are potential problems.
'Majestic' Good crop of white, oval tubers of uniform shape. A good keeper.
'Maris Piper' Good crops of well-flavoured tubers, but may be affected by dry conditions. Although prone to slug and scab

damage, they are resistant to eelworms.
'Pentland Crown' Noted for quantity rather than quality. Resistant to leaf-roll virus and mosaic virus.
'Pentland Dell' Heavy cropper, but avoid planting early in cold soil. Susceptible to blight and spraing.
'Pink Fir Apple' A long-established variety that retains its new-potato flavour even when stored. Fairly light crops.
'Red King Edward' Red-skinned variation of 'King Edward VII'. Cooks well.
'Romano' Quite heavy crops of uniform tubers that cook well. Resists many diseases but susceptible to drought.
'Purple Congo' Purple- or blue-fleshed variety available from specialist suppliers. Grown mainly for their novelty value, but reasonably flavoured.

POTATOES AND TUBERS, pages 118–119
PESTS AND DISEASES, pages 172–175

STORING VEGETABLES, page 227

The carrot (*Daucus carota*) is a surprisingly varied vegetable – in flavour, shape and rate of growth. The earliest kinds, given good conditions, can be on the dinner table a mere 10–12 weeks after sowing. Others, with larger roots, will take twice as long as this to mature.

The delicate taste and texture of the fastest-growing carrots is typical of the early summer vegetables. Those of intermediate size, which mature a little later, are almost as delicious when pulled young or they may be grated for salads. Larger, maincrop varieties are an invaluable ingredient of soups, casseroles and many other winter dishes, as well as for eating raw.

To enjoy home-grown carrots for most of the year, it is a great help to have cloches or a cold frame. Either will enable a really early crop to be grown, for harvesting from early summer onward, as well as a crop of tender young roots in early winter when there are usually only large roots available for storing. The carrots most suitable for these first and last sowings are the short-rooted kinds – either finger-shaped, such as 'Amsterdam Forcing', or resembling a golf-ball, like 'Early French Frame'.

At other times you will do better with one of the intermediate types – intermediate, that is, between the small-rooted early carrots and some of the very long varieties, which need deep soil to fulfil their potential. Among the intermediate types of carrot are stump-rooted, cylindrical varieties or tapering varieties.

All carrots thrive on light, free-draining soil in a sunny position. Intermediate and maincrop varieties will in fact tolerate partial shade. The ideal pH is 6–6.5; apply lime if necessary.

Choose a stump-rooted variety if your soil is heavy or stony, and never sow carrots in ground that has been recently manured, or the roots will fork in all directions. Choose a sheltered spot for early crops, if possible.

MAKING A START

Dig the site during autumn or early winter and leave the surface rough. In the spring, break down any remaining lumps with a pronged cultivator and scatter a dressing of general fertilizer at about 35g per sq m (1oz per sq yd). Rake the surface to a fine tilth.

Sowing under cloches

Prepare the soil in late winter or early spring, as soon as it is dry enough to crumble. Place cloches in position two weeks before sowing, since the seeds will not germinate in cold soil. Light ground is an advantage for these early sowings.

Either scatter the seeds very thinly, then rake them lightly into the surface, or else form shallow drills 5–8cm (2–3in) apart and sow the seeds thinly in these. There is room for several parallel drills under an average-sized cloche. After the seeds have germinated, thin the seedlings to about 5cm (2in) apart.

Sowing in the open

From early spring onward, once the soil has begun to warm up, sow early and intermediate types for harvesting in summer. On open ground leave 15cm (6in) between rows and thin to about 5cm (2in) apart. In beds, space them about 8cm (3in) apart, each way.

Make the last sowings of maincrop varieties, which may be stored for the winter, by early summer. A late-summer sowing of short-rooted carrots, cloched from early autumn onward, will provide tender young roots for early winter.

THINNING

The characteristic aroma given off when carrot seedlings are thinned attracts carrot flies; these are damaging pests that lay their eggs against the roots of those remaining. Minimize the need for the thinning operation by sowing sparsely. This is easier if the seeds are first mixed with dry sand or fine soil, or if pelleted seeds are used.

The best time for thinning is on dull or damp evenings; water around the plants both before and after thinning them out. Thin them to 4–5cm (1½–2in) apart, depending on the size of root needed: the larger the root, the more space required. Bury the thinnings under other material in the compost heap.

Among a variety of precautions against carrot flies, the Henry Doubleday Research Association suggests planting garlic or onions in alternate rows with the carrots; spreading lawn-mowings between the rows; or hanging strips of paraffin-soaked blanket over them. The theory, in each case, is that the smell of the carrots will be smothered or disguised.

Some gardeners grow sage or scorzonera alongside or among the carrots with the same object in view. Others erect barriers against the incoming flies. Chemical treatment of the seedbed can be helpful, too; bromophos and diazinon are among the substances recommended.

Sow carrot seeds thinly to reduce the need for further thinning, with its attendant risk of carrot fly. To make this easier, mix the seeds as evenly as possible with some dry, sharp sand before sowing them.

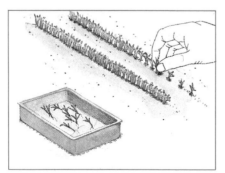

When thinning, preferably during damp weather and in the evening, place the carrots that you remove into a tray or pot. If they are left on the ground, their smell is liable to attract carrot flies to the crop.

CARE OF THE CROP

Remove cloches or frame lights after mid-spring, depending on the growth of the plants and the weather. Do this in stages, leaving gaps between individual cloches or partly raising the skirt of a tunnel cloche, and gradually opening a frame light, to prevent a sudden shock to the young plants.

The need for hoeing will be kept to a minimum if the plants are closely spaced. The best means of keeping weeds in check initially, before the foliage spreads, is by hand-weeding or by using a short-handled hoe.

Water frequently during dry weather and keep the soil moist at all times. Once the soil has been allowed to dry out, there is a danger that rain or sudden watering may cause the roots to split.

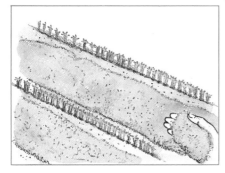

A scattering of lawn-mowings between rows of young carrots, especially after thinning, is helpful in preventing the attention of carrot flies. Attacks are most likely to occur if the soil is dry.

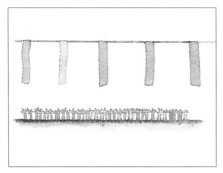

Another way to confuse carrot flies, which are attracted in the first instance by the smell of the crop, is to hang strips of absorbent material soaked in paraffin over the rows of seedlings.

HARVESTING

Pull early carrots from late spring onward: they have a sweet flavour and are very tender. Treat this as a final thinning: the extra space left between the remaining carrots will speed their growth. Water the rows before pulling them.

Continue lifting later sowings throughout the summer, as needed. In the autumn lift the remaining carrots: ease them out of the ground with a fork before the first frosts occur. Either use or discard any that are damaged, and store the rest. Trim the leaves to within 1cm ($\frac{1}{2}$in) of the crown and place the roots in layers of dry peat in a box. Examine them for rotting regularly throughout the winter.

It is also possible to leave carrots, like parsnips, in the ground during the winter, provided the soil is free-draining and the roots are healthy and undamaged. A covering of leaves or straw is helpful during mid-winter to prevent frost damage.

PESTS AND DISEASES

Carrot flies are the chief problem. Cutworms may also cause damage.

The principal diseases are sclerotinia and violet root rot.

RECOMMENDED VARIETIES
Short-rooted
'Amsterdam Forcing' Slender, stump-rooted and cylindrical carrots. Suitable for early crops, either with protection or in the open.
'Chantenay Red Cored' Stump-rooted carrots maturing during mid-season but also suitable for winter storage.
'Early French Frame' Quick-growing round roots for protected or early sowings.
'Nantes Express' A medium-sized, stump-rooted, cylindrical type, suitable for successional sowings.

Intermediate and maincrop
'Autumn King' Large, tapering roots. Widely grown for storing.
'Berlicum Berjo' Large, blunt-tipped, cylindrical roots. A good choice for storing.
'Cardinal' Long, cylindrical roots for summer or autumn use.
'James's Scarlet Intermediate' A conical maincrop variety.
'St. Valery' High-yielding, with long, tapering roots. Needs deep soil.

Hamburg parsley (*Petroselinum crispum*), sometimes known as turnip-rooted parsley, is a dual-purpose vegetable with edible roots and leaves that deserves to be more widely grown. The plant belongs to the same species as the 'ordinary' parsley grown as a herb and has the same distinctively-flavoured leaves, but, because it is a good deal hardier, the leaves stay green and edible throughout the winter. Despite a relatively coarse texture, they are valuable for flavouring and garnishing. The roots of Hamburg parsley resemble small parsnips and are cooked in a similar way; their flavour is rather like a cross between celeriac and turnip.

The roots mature during the autumn and may be dug as needed during the winter; in this, as in their growth cycle, they have more in common with both parsnips and salsify than with parsley. Hamburg parsley will also thrive in much the same conditions as parsnips, though it will tolerate a little shade. A fertile, moisture-retaining soil is best, preferably one that has been manured for a previous crop. Dig it during the autumn or early winter before sowing.

MAKING A START

Sow seeds in mid-spring; apply a dressing of general fertilizer two weeks before planting, at 70g per sq m (2oz per sq yd). Leave 25cm (10in) between the drills and thin the seedlings to 15cm (6in) spacings.

CARE OF THE CROP

Hoe regularly to prevent competition from weeds. Water during dry spells to ensure that these rather slow-growing plants continue to make steady progress.

HARVESTING

Start lifting the roots from autumn onward, when they are about 15–18cm (6–7in) long. Unlike most vegetables, the largest roots taste best. Either leave the crop in the ground to use as needed during the winter, or lift and store the roots in peat before the turn of the year. This is generally the best course in very cold areas or on heavy soil.

PESTS AND DISEASES

Pests are seldom a problem. The roots may be affected by parsnip canker.

CLOCHES AND FRAMES, pages 16–18
ROOT VEGETABLES, pages 120–121

PESTS AND DISEASES pages 172–175
STORING VEGETABLES, page 227

Parsnips (*Peucedanum sativum*) are one of the slowest-growing root vegetables: they occupy their section of the garden for nearly 12 months on end. However, they are an undemanding vegetable and extremely hardy. Unlike most other root vegetables, they are sufficiently hardy to be left in the ground until they are needed. Their sweet flavour makes a welcome change during the winter, which is their main season of use. Parsnips can also be made into wine.

Their extended growing period may seem to make parsnips a doubtful proposition for small gardens, but remember that it is possible to take a quick crop of lettuces or radishes from the same strip of ground. These should be sown in the same drills as the parsnips and harvested before the principal crop needs its full quota of space.

Some varieties of parsnip have much longer roots than others. These need deep, well-worked soil with few stones, otherwise they will become stunted or distorted, with forked roots. Choose a shorter-rooted variety if you have shallow soil, or else prepare individual stations with a mixture of sifted soil and peat.

Like most vegetables, parsnips grow best in a sunny position. They like a fertile, well-drained soil, but the ground must not be freshly manured, otherwise the roots will fork. Instead, parsnips should be grown on a part of the plot that has received a heavy organic dressing from an earlier crop. Dig it during the autumn or early winter, before sowing the seeds, and dress the surface with lime if it is on the acid side (that is, with a pH of 6 or lower).

MAKING A START

Be sure to use fresh seed. Parsnip seeds left over from one year may not geminate successfully the next.

Because parsnips develop slowly and need a long growing period, sowing in early spring is often advised, but unless you have a light soil, which warms up rapidly in spring, it is better, as a rule, to wait for a few weeks. Later sowings usually catch up, with fewer losses, and the plants are also less likely to suffer from canker.

Around mid-spring, apply a dressing of general fertilizer at 90g per sq m (3oz per sq yd) and rake the soil to a fine tilth. Draw the drills 25–30cm (10–12in) apart, depending on the size of the variety, and 1cm ($\frac{1}{2}$in) deep.

Sow the seeds in groups of three or four;

leave from 10-20cm (4–8in) between adjacent groups, depending partly on the size of the variety but also on how large you wish the roots to grow. On very shallow or stony soil, form planting stations with a crowbar.

If you wish to inter-crop with radishes or small lettuces (such as 'Tom Thumb'), choose the larger spacings and sow the catch-crop seeds thinly between the groups of parsnips. They will mature before the main crop extends very far. Since parsnip seeds take a long time to germinate, sowing radishes or lettuces will also mark the rows before the seedlings appear, enabling you to hoe around carefully.

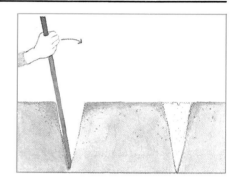

Use a crowbar to form individual stations for parsnips on stony ground. Drive it in as deep as possible, and rotate it at a slight angle. Fill the hole with peat or sifted soil, then sow the seeds on top.

CARE OF THE CROP

Apart from removing the surplus seedlings to leave the strongest one in each group, and thinning any other crop growing between them, the chief summer task is hoeing. A mulch of rotted compost would be beneficial, if you have plenty available.

Keep the soil moist by watering occasionally during prolonged dry weather, otherwise there is a danger that a sudden downpour will cause the roots to split.

HARVESTING

Roots may be eaten from autumn onward, as soon as the plant leaves die back. However, their flavour is improved if they are left until after the first frosts. Cover the plants with straw or leaves, to ease lifting and to mark the rows.

Start lifting parsnips with a fork after the first frosts. The foliage will soon die away, but a covering of straw will mark the position of the roots and help to prevent the soil freezing hard.

PESTS AND DISEASES

Carrot fly and celery fly are potential pests.

Parsnip canker is easily the most troublesome disease.

RECOMMENDED VARIETIES

'Avonresister' Small, bulbous and very sweet. Canker-resistant.

'Cobham Improved Marrow' Medium-length roots; canker-resistant.

'Hollow Crown Improved' Long-rooted and with a good flavour.

'Intermediate' Small, early-maturing roots. Good for shallow soils.

'Tender and True' Long, smooth-skinned roots with good canker resistance.

'White Gem' Medium-sized, bulbous roots. Canker-resistant.

PLANTING VEGETABLES, page 40
CARROTS AND OTHER ROOT VEGETABLES, pages 120–121
PESTS AND DISEASES, pages 172–175

Swedes (*Brassica campestris* 'Rutabaga') were once widely grown on farms as cattle feed, and still seem to do best in open, airy situations. Their name derives from 'Swedish turnip', since they are a close relative of the turnip. Swedes are extremely hardy, well able to survive wintery weather if left unharvested, and have a surprisingly delicate flavour; they are milder and sweeter than the turnip. The flesh is yellow, as a rule, but in some cases it is white. The 'purple top' cultivars are considered the best varieties for most gardens.

From a gardener's viewpoint, swedes are an undemanding crop but they do need a fairly long growing season. A sowing in late spring will provide roots for harvesting from autumn onward, and that should last through the winter.

Any fertile, well-drained soil is suitable, provided it is not acid. The ideal pH is 6–6.5, so be preared to apply lime if a soil test gives a lower reading.

The soil must also be moisture-retentive if the plants are to maintain steady growth throughout the summer. This means that it must contain plenty of organic matter, but this should have been applied for an earlier crop. Do not sow swedes in freshly-manured ground.

Swedes are members of the brassica family and, as such, are prone to some of the same ailments, including club root. For this reason, it is better not to include them in the 'root' section of the three-year rotation of vegetables, which normally follows brassicas. Instead, include them in the brassica plot so that there is a two-year interval before crops in this group are grown in the same spot again.

Dig the ground during the previous autumn or winter, and give a dressing of lime if needed. Leave this on the surface for the rain to wash in.

MAKING A START
Sow between mid-spring and early summer. The earlier sowing is advisable in cold districts, where a slightly longer growing season is needed. Apply a general fertilizer, at 70g per sq m (2oz per sq yd), a week or two before sowing.

Draw the drills 40cm (15in) apart and about 1cm (½in) deep. Sow the seeds thinly, and later reduce the seedlings to leave about 25cm (10in) between plants.

Some gardeners also make a midsummer sowing of swedes to provide a crop of tops or 'greens' for the following spring. For this purpose the rows may be set closer together (about 15cm/6in apart), or the seeds broadcast in a small patch. The plants can be left practically unthinned and harvested as required.

Swedes, although certainly a root crop, are also brassicas and, therefore, subject to such soil-borne ailments as club root. With this in mind, include them with cabbages, cauliflowers and other brassicas in the crop rotation scheme.

CARE OF THE CROP
Dust the rows with derris as soon as the seedlings emerge, as a precaution against flea beetles. The damage they inflict can be severe, especially during dry weather. Thin the seedlings as soon as they are large enough to handle.

Water the rows, as needed, to prevent the soil from drying out. As well as discouraging splitting in the event of heavy rain, this will help the plants to grow steadily instead of becoming stunted and woody. Watering whenever necessary will also improve the size and quantity of the roots, though it may make their flavour less pronounced. Hoe regularly to prevent competition from weeds.

Growth is checked and roots become woody if the ground in which swedes are grown becomes too dry during the summer. Start watering before this can happen; a sprinkler hose is ideal for row crops.

HARVESTING
Immature swedes have a mild flavour; they can be pulled in late summer. Otherwise, the roots are ready from autumn onward: lift them with a fork. They may be left in the soil for use as needed during the winter, or else lifted *en masse* in early winter. Twist their tops off, and store them in peat (see p.227).

Swedes are less likely to become woody if they are stored, and harvesting them all at once avoids the need to lift them from wet or frozen ground later in the winter.

PESTS AND DISEASES
A number of pests may prove troublesome, including cabbage root flies, cutworms, flea beetles, turnip gall weevils and wireworms.

The diseases and ailments most likely to affect swedes are boron deficiency, club root and mildew.

RECOMMENDED VARIETIES
'Best of All' Purple-skinned and very hardy.
'Marian' Excellent quality; resistant to club root and mildew. A widely-grown variety.
'Western Perfection' Quick-growing, so good for colder areas.

CROP ROTATION, page 25
SOWING SEEDS OUTDOORS, pages 36–37

CARROTS AND OTHER ROOT VEGETABLES, pages 120–121
PESTS AND DISEASES, PAGES 172–175

STORING VEGETABLES, page 227

Celeriac (*Apium graveolens*) is a turnip-rooted form of celery, grown for its swollen base. From a cultivation point of view, it offers a less troublesome alternative to celery since there is no blanching involved and the plants seldom run to seed; pests and diseases are also less of a problem. Celeriac makes a good substitute for celery when used as a flavouring in soups, stews and other cooked dishes; the celery-flavoured root can also be cooked as a separate vegetable in its own right, or grated and used raw in salads.

The roots should be allowed to swell to a good size, unlike comparable vegetables such as kohlrabi, and this means a long growing season is needed. Although celeriac is a hardy plant, it has to be raised under glass from an early spring sowing in order to give it an adequate length of time to grow. After hardening off, the seedlings are planted in their final, outdoor bed during late spring. Choose a position that gets the sun for preference, though celeriac will also tolerate light shade.

Celeriac demands plenty of moisture and can be grown in damper parts of the garden. On dry, light soil, lacking organic matter, the roots will swell little if at all. On soils of all types, they need frequent watering throughout the summer if the weather is dry. The surest way to provide favourable conditions is by digging in a heavy dressing of rotted manure or compost – at least a bucketful to the square metre or yard – during the previous autumn or winter. A mulch is also beneficial.

MAKING A START
Sow in early spring, sprinkling the tiny seeds thinly over a pan of seed compost and just covering them. After watering lightly, place glass and paper over the pan and germinate in a temperature of not less than 10°C (50°F). Uncover as soon as the seedlings emerge.

Seeds may also be germinated in a warm place indoors, and the seedlings raised on a sunny windowsill, but in this case sow a week or two later to reduce the risk of seedlings becoming spindly and drawn.

Prick the seedlings out 5cm (2in) apart into a tray of potting compost as soon as they are large enough to handle. Grow them on steadily, with sufficient heat to prevent too much of a temperature drop at night-time.

Toward late spring, move the tray to a cold frame to allow the plants to harden off. Give the bed where they will be planted a dressing of general fertilizer at 70g per sq m (2oz per sq yd). Ten to fourteen days later, depending on the weather, plant them out 30cm (1ft) apart in each direction, with the bottom of each stem just level with the soil surface. Water the plants in gently.

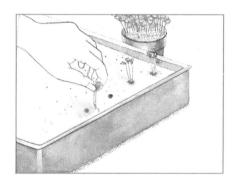

Celeriac plants must be raised under glass to give them the long growing season that they need. Prick out the seedlings, grown from a sowing in early spring, into a seed tray at 5cm (2in) spacings. Provide some warmth, especially at night, to encourage steady growth.

In common with other plants raised indoors, celeriac needs a hardening-off period before being planted outdoors. Place young plants in a cold frame for 10–14 days, and gradually increase the amount of ventilation in order to acclimatize them to colder conditions.

CARE OF THE CROP
Keep the soil moist throughout the summer; water the plants immediately a dry spell occurs. Spread a mulch of peat or rotted compost around the plants once they are established. From this stage onward, give the plants a liquid feed every two weeks.

Cut off any side-shoots that appear, since they will otherwise spoil the shape of the root or affect its growth. During mid- or late summer, remove the lower, older leaves from each plant, exposing the crown. Draw a little soil around the swollen roots to help keep them white.

HARVESTING
Lift the roots from autumn onward, once they have attained maximum size. They do not deteriorate if left in the soil, so you can use them as needed.

If you give them a good covering of straw,

secured with netting (see p.159), they may remain in the ground throughout the winter. However, in particularly cold areas, or on heavy soil, they are better lifted before the end of the year and stored in peat in a box (see p.127).

PESTS AND DISEASES
Carrot flies, celery flies and slugs and snails are the principal pests.

Possible diseases of celeriac include boron deficiency and leaf spot.

RECOMMENDED VARIETIES
'Marble Ball' Large, globe-shaped roots. Disease-resistant.
'Tellus' Fast-growing, round roots. Does not discolour when cooked.

Remove some of the older, outside leaves at some time after midsummer, to expose more of the crown, or root. It is vital to keep the soil moist throughout the growing period, otherwise the plants may produce only leaves. This can be difficult on sandy soil.

SOWING UNDER GLASS, pages 38–39
CARROTS AND OTHER ROOT VEGETABLES, pages 120–121
PESTS AND DISEASES, pages 172–175
STORING VEGETABLES, page 227

Of all vegetables, radishes (*Raphanus sativus*) are probably the easiest and most accommodating. Their germination is reliable and their speed of growth phenomenal. It is not unusual to start pulling the roots of summer radishes a mere three weeks after sowing the seeds.

Radishes are also hardy plants, which means the first sowing under a cloche or frame can be made in late winter. Cloches may also be used at the tail end of the year to protect sowings made until the end of autumn. If you make early and late sowings, it is therefore possible to enjoy summer radishes during most months of the year; these are eaten young, when fresh and crisp, as a raw salad vegetable. The white types of summer radish are longer-rooted than most red ones.

In addition, you could also try the much larger winter radishes, with roots weighing up to as much as half a kilo (1lb). They are suitable for storing during winter, just like carrots or beetroot. They are somewhat coarser and stronger tasting than the summer types and may need to be cooked first, rather than being used for eating raw in salads.

Summer radishes are shallow-rooted and need a crumbly, rich, moisture-retaining soil structure. They do not need a deeply dug soil since they are not in the ground for more than a few weeks. The essential factor is rapid growth: they need to grow fast in order to be crisp and mild-flavoured. Slow-grown radishes are soft or woody in texture and too hot to the palate.

Winter radishes do best in light, well-drained ground to which organic matter was added for the previous crop. A dressing of peat will help if the ground is on the heavy side. Sow them in ground that was dug the previous autumn or winter.

A sunny spot will aid the rapid growth of summer radishes, though in high summer they will need to be given a position in light shade in order to check their tendency to run to seed.

Summer radishes are ideal for catch-cropping and inter-cropping (see p.132). By growing them on ground temporarily vacant between crops, or else between plants that develop more slowly, there should be no need to allocate a special space for them. Even so, treat radishes as part of the crop rotation, and avoid growing them on the same ground in successive years.

MAKING A START

For an early sowing of summer radishes, put cloches in position, or close frame lights, soon after mid-winter. At the same time, apply a dressing of general fertilizer at 35g per sq m (1oz per sq yd) to the ground where the radishes are to grow.

Allow two or three weeks for the soil to become a little drier and warmer, then sow the seeds in shallow drills 1cm (½in) deep and 15cm (6in) apart. If the seeds are spaced about 2.5cm (1in) apart, little or no thinning will be needed and the plants should grow rapidly.

Make unprotected sowings in the same way, from spring onward. Sow little and often so that there is a continuous supply of tender roots. During dry weather, water the drill thoroughly before sowing the seeds.

Sow winter radishes around midsummer in drills 1cm (½in) deep and 25cm (10in) apart; thin the seedlings to 13cm (5in) spacings. Water the drills first during dry weather. Chinese and Spanish varieties may run to seed if they are sown too early.

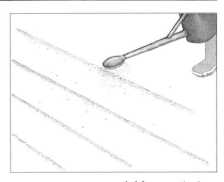

Frequent sowings are needed for a continuing supply of radishes, but germination may prove slower in summer than in spring. One solution is to water the drills in advance of sowing, using a fine rose on the watering can so as not to disturb the soil.

CARE OF THE CROP

If flea beetles prove troublesome, dust the rows with derris as soon as the seedlings emerge. You may also need to net the crop against birds.

Water frequently during dry weather to maintain rapid growth, and hoe to prevent competition from weeds.

HARVESTING

Pull summer radishes as needed while they are still young and tender – that is, before they are fully grown.

Winter radishes should be ready to eat about two to three months after sowing. Lift them during autumn, then remove the leafy tops and store them in dry peat in a box.

PESTS AND DISEASES

Flea beetles are the chief pest. Slugs may also cause damage, but disease is unlikely.

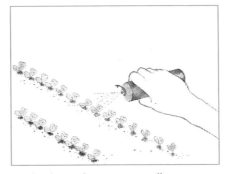

Flea beetle attacks on young seedlings are very common, especially during dry weather. The simple answer is to dust the rows with derris, using a proprietary puffer pack. A single application is often sufficient, but you may need to give a second one.

RECOMMENDED VARIETIES
Summer
'Cherry Belle' Fast-growing, scarlet globe.
'French Breakfast' Cylindrical, with a mild flavour.
'Globe' A round white radish, crisp and well-flavoured.
'Long White Icicle' Tapering, with white skin and a mild flavour.
'Prinz Rotin' Globe-shaped. Stays in good condition even if not harvested promptly.
'Sparkler' Medium-sized round, red root, tipped with white.

Winter
'Black Spanish Round' Black skin, white flesh and very hardy.
'China Rose' Cylindrical, rose-pink skin.
'Mino Early' A mild-flavoured Japanese variety; slender roots over 30cm (1ft) long.

SOWING SEEDS OUTDOORS, pages 36–37
RADISHES AND OTHER ROOT VEGETABLES, pages 122–123
SPACE-SAVING METHODS, pages 132–133
PESTS AND DISEASES, pages 172–175
STORING VEGETABLES, page 227

The sweet, richly-coloured roots of *Beta vulgaris* form an essential part of summer salads when cold and are also delicious served as a hot vegetable or made into soups such as bortsch; young roots are good raw, too. The globe-shaped varieties are the ones to grow for salads and should be chosen for early sowings. Beetroot may also be stored for the winter, and the more usual choice for this is one of the slower-growing, long-rooted kinds.

A beetroot 'seed' normally produces a cluster of plants, which makes thinning a fiddly and time-consuming task. This can be avoided by sowing a monogerm variety, which produces single seedlings instead of clusters. Another consideration to bear in mind when buying seeds is that the earliest sowings are liable to run to seed or 'bolt'. This can be avoided by choosing a bolt-resistant variety.

Beetroot are quite easy to grow, especially if you have light but fertile soil that is either neutral or only slightly acid (which may mean adding lime to raise the pH level). Never sow beetroot on freshly-manured ground, or the roots will become forked. Good crops can also be grown on heavier soils once the structure has been improved with organic matter.

Prepare the soil by digging during late autumn or winter; spread lime on the surface afterward if it is too acid.

MAKING A START

Spread a general fertilizer over the ground, at 90g per sq m (3oz per sq yd), a week or two before sowing. Give a further 170g (5oz) while the crop is growing. Put cloches in position for an early crop.

Provided the soil is dry enough, sow seed under cloches or in a cold frame in late winter or early spring; soak the seeds first for an hour in slightly warm water. Sow thinly in drills 1cm ($\frac{1}{2}$in) deep and 20cm (8in) apart; thin to 8cm (3in) spacings.

Follow a few weeks later with an outdoor sowing at the same spacings; soak the seeds first. Protect the seedlings from birds with black cotton, netting or a humming line.

For maincrop sowings, made in late spring or early summer, leave 30cm (1ft) between the rows and 8–10cm (3–4in) between plants.

Soaking beetroot seeds for an hour or two before sowing helps to soften their outer coat and ensure prompt germination. This is less important when sowing in damp ground but still reduces possible delay.

CARE OF THE CROP

Thin the seedlings as soon as they are large enough to handle. A well-sharpened, short-handled hoe can be a help. Subsequently, keep the ground weed-free until the beetroot foliage meets over the rows.

Keep the soil moist during dry weather, otherwise sudden wetting may cause the roots to split.

Remove cloches from mid-spring onward so that the plants gradually become accustomed to cooler conditions.

Late thinnings of half-grown roots make excellent eating, while the extra growing space gives a boost to those that remain.

Beetroots are hungry feeders. In addition to the base dressing applied before sowing the seeds, give a further, heavier dressing of general fertilizer once the plants have started to grow strongly.

HARVESTING

Lift the globe-shaped roots by hand before they become too big and woody, since the smaller ones taste sweetest.

Dig maincrop roots for storing in early autumn; use a garden fork to loosen the soil around them. Twist off the tops to leave the bottom 5cm (2in) of stalk still attached. The roots will 'bleed' if the tops are cut off too close to them.

Store the roots in boxes of dry peat in a frost-free room or shed (see p.227).

PESTS AND DISEASES

Blackfly and mangold fly can be troublesome.

Diseases and ailments include boron and magnesium deficiencies, damping off, leaf spot and heart rot.

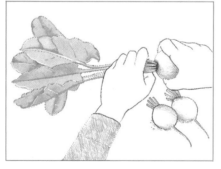

After lifting beetroots from the ground, whether for eating at once or for storage, twist the leafy tops off rather than cutting them with a knife. This reduces 'bleeding' from the root. Leave a 5cm (2in) tuft of stalks.

RECOMMENDED VARIETIES
Globe
'Avon – Early' The roots are well-coloured and have good resistance to bolting.
'Boltardy' A favourite for early sowing, being bolt-resistant and of high quality.
'Burpee's Golden' Golden-yellow roots with a fine flavour. Leaves may be cooked like spinach.
'Detroit – Little Ball' Small, fast-growing roots with some resistance to bolting.
'Monodet' A monogerm variety that also resists bolting. Good-quality roots.

Long-rooted
'Cheltenham Mono' A monogerm variety. Good for storing.
'Cylindra' Long and cylinder-shaped, giving even-sized slices. Stores well.
'Forono' Another cylinder-shaped beet. Slow to become woody.

SOWING SEEDS OUTDOORS, pages 36–37
CROP PROTECTION, page 44

RADISHES AND OTHER ROOT VEGETABLES, pages 122–123
PESTS AND DISEASES, pages 172–175

STORING VEGETABLES, page 227

This relatively uncommon vegetable (*Tragopogon porrifolius*) is also known as oyster plant, or vegetable oyster. The name derives from its taste – a delicate, elusive flavour reminiscent of oysters.

Salsify is grown principally for its roots, which are long, off-white and slender, not unlike immature parsnips. There is a second, quite different crop, known as 'chards', harvested from the same plants in spring.

The best conditions for salsify are a deep, well-worked soil, preferably fairly light and without too many stones. It should have had a good dressing of manure or compost within the last year or two, but do not add any more the autumn or winter before sowing in case it causes the roots to fork.

Choose a sunny, well-drained site and double-dig the proposed strip.

Double digging provides the deeply worked soil in which salsify thrives. It will assist development of the long roots and ensure that there is not a hard pan to impede growth. Fork over the lower layer before replacing the topsoil, and sprinkle lime over the surface if the soil is on the acid side (below pH6).

This plant (*Scorzonera hispanica*) closely resembles salsify and is often known as 'black salsify'. Its long, tapering roots have a similar flavour and they need exactly the same growing conditions.

The chief difference is in the colour of the skin: scorzonera has a dark, purplish-brown skin, quite unlike the creamy colour of salsify. The flesh, however, is white and has a more pronounced flavour than that of salsify. Scorzonera is also a perennial, whereas salsify is a biennial.

Choose and prepare the site as described for salsify. Double digging is a valuable aid to root development; avoid fresh manure or compost.

The sowing and after-care are as for salsify, but remember that scorzonera tends to run to seed if sown too early.

MAKING A START
Salsify is a slow-growing plant and needs a long season to develop. You therefore need to sow seeds in mid-spring to provide this. A week or two beforehand, prepare the site by spreading a general fertilizer over the ground at 90g per sq m (3oz per sq yd). Scuffle this into the surface with a pronged cultivator or a rake, but leave the final raking and firming until the period just before you sow.

It is worth noting that salsify seed does not last for very long – two years at the most. Rather than risk disappointment, it is better to buy fresh seed each spring.

Draw the drills 25–30cm (10–12in) apart and about 1cm ($\frac{1}{2}$in) deep. The seeds may be sown in clusters of three or four at 15cm (6in) spacings, or else distributed evenly and then thinned to this spacing.

CARE OF THE CROP
Thin the seedlings, or reduce clusters to single plants, as soon as they are large enough to handle. At the same time, hand-weed around the plants to reduce the risk of competition.

Subsequently, keep the crop watered during dry weather, and hoe as necessary to keep the ground weed-free. A mulch of peat or rotted compost will help to provide the right conditions for steady growth.

HARVESTING
The roots are ready for eating from mid-autumn onward. When digging them up, bear their length in mind and try not to break off the lower part. You may find it easier to use a spade rather than a fork: thrust this in on each side of the plant as deeply as possible in order to loosen the soil before attempting to pull the root free.

The roots are extremely hardy, and may be left in the ground throughout the winter. Alternatively, to avoid having to dig them out of muddy or frozen ground, lift them in early winter and store them in a box of peat. If you do leave them in the ground, a covering of straw or leaves, secured with netting, will reduce the risk of the soil freezing around them.

PESTS AND DISEASES
Pest problems are rare with salsify.

A fungus disease called white blister may affect their leaves.

RECOMMENDED VARIETIES
There is little to choose between the three varieties generally available: **'Giant'**, **'Mammoth'** and **'Sandwich Island'**. All are creamy-white, with tapering roots and a delicate flavour.

HARVESTING SALSIFY CHARDS
For a harvest of blanched shoots, leave some of the roots undug. Cover them with a deep layer of straw or leaves, up to 15cm (6in) thick, when they first show signs of growth in the spring. A wire netting surround, supported by short stakes, will prevent the covering from blowing away.

Gather the blanched shoots when they are about 15cm (6in) long and use them raw in salads or cooked like asparagus. If you prefer to leave the shoots unblanched, harvest them as a green vegetable and cook like spinach.

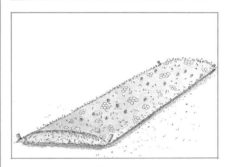

A winter covering of straw not only helps to protect the crop but also keeps the ground itself from becoming frozen. Peg netting over the top to stop it being blown away or disturbed by birds.

HARVESTING
The roots may be left in the ground or lifted and stored, as for salsify. Any that are unused by spring may be left to continue growing during the new season. The roots will have expanded by the following autumn and winter, but will not have become coarse.

PESTS AND DISEASES
As for salsify.

RECOMMENDED VARIETIES
'Russian Giant' and **'Habil'** are the varieties most often available.

SOWING SEEDS OUTDOORS, pages 36–37
RADISHES AND OTHER ROOT VEGETABLES, pages 122–123

PESTS AND DISEASES, pages 172–175
STORING VEGETABLES, page 227

Home-grown turnips (*Brassica campestris*) have little in common with the tired, hard roots that find their way into the shops. If they are grown early and quickly, ready to be eaten within a couple of months of sowing, their flavour is as delicate as their texture. There are also maincrop varieties of turnip, which have a firmer texture and store well for the winter. But good growing conditions will ensure that even their flavour is mild and their texture far from coarse. Turnips are flat, round or long in shape.

The early, quick-growing varieties of turnip are ideal for catch-cropping and inter-cropping (see p.132). Protect the earliest crops with cloches or a cold frame.

A late-summer sowing of turnips will supply an abundant crop of tender turnip-top leaves, which make a good alternative to ordinary spring greens (immature spring cabbages).

Turnips belong to the brassica family and are subject to the same problems and ailments. For this reason, include them with other brassicas in your rotation plan.

Turnips tolerate all types of soil, but grow best on a light, fertile one. Choose an open, sunny situation where the soil was manured for a previous crop. After digging during the previous autumn or winter, apply lime if the soil is below pH6.

The above-ground 'root' of this strange-looking vegetable is actually its swollen stem. Kohlrabi (*Brassica oleracea*) has a turnip-like flavour and, as with the early varieties of turnip, is best eaten while still young and tender. It also needs the same soil and similar growing conditions as the turnip and can be grown as a catch-crop or for inter-cropping.

The main difference between the two vegetables is that kohlrabi can be grown where summers are hot and dry, and where turnips would probably fail. Kohlrabi can stand conditions of drought and heat without losing its flavour. A fellow member of the brassica family, kohlrabi should be grouped with other brassicas in the rotation scheme.

Pests and diseases are as for turnips.

MAKING A START
Sow seed from late winter onward if you are using cloches or a frame, or from early spring without protection. In both cases, the soil must be sufficiently dry and crumbly. Spread a dressing of general fertilizer at 70g per sq m (2oz per sq yd) two weeks before sowing. At the same time, place cloches in position.

Sow the early varieties in drills 23cm (9in) apart and 1cm ($\frac{1}{2}$in) deep; firm the seedbed well. Thin the seedlings to 13cm (5in). Make a couple more sowings until the end of spring for a succession of crops.

Sow maincrop varieties in midsummer. Draw the drills 30cm (1ft) apart and thin the seedlings to 23cm (9in). For 'spring greens', sow a maincrop variety in late summer in rows 8–10cm (3–4in) apart. Sow thinly and do no further thinning.

CARE OF THE CROP
Thin turnips as soon as seedlings are large enough to grasp between finger and thumb. Dust the plants with derris to deter flea beetles. Keep the soil moist during dry weather, or the plants will stop growing.

HARVESTING
Pull spring and summer crops when they reach the size of golf-balls. Harvest maincrop roots from autumn onward; either leave them in the soil until needed (if in a mild area), or store them in peat in a large box (see p.227). Twist off the leafy tops first.

PESTS AND DISEASES
The main pests are cabbage root fly, flea beetle, cutworms and turnip gall weevil.

Ailments include boron deficiency, club root and turnip mosaic virus.

Instead of being grown for their roots, turnips may be sown for a spring harvest of tops. Broadcast a small area of seeds in autumn or early spring, and cut the tops with shears 2.5cm (1in) above the ground when they are 15cm (6in) high.

RECOMMENDED VARIETIES
Early
'Jersey Navet' Cylindrical turnip with white flesh.
'Milan White' One of the earliest, with a flattened shape and ivory-white flesh.
'Purple Top Milan' Very early. The flattened white root has a purple top.
'Snowball' A popular, globe-shaped variety with white flesh.
'Veitch's Red Globe' Round, medium-sized roots with purple-red tops.

Maincrop
'Golden Ball' Yellow flesh, good flavour, keeps well.
'Manchester Market' Large, white and globe-shaped. Keeps well.

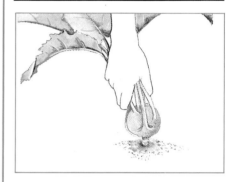

Harvest kohlrabi by pulling the entire plant from the ground. If lifted before the 'roots' (swollen stems) become tough, the leaves may be cooked in the same way as turnip tops. Though winter storage is possible, the crop is better eaten straight from the ground.

Sow kohlrabi from late winter onward (under cloches for the earliest sowings), with the same spacings and after-care as for turnips. Take particular care not to damage the roots when hoeing.

Lift when the bulbous stems are the size of a tennis ball. Pull the whole plant from the ground by the leaves. The later roots may be left in the ground or else lifted and stored, though they shrivel more than most other roots in storage.

RECOMMENDED VARIETIES
'Lanro' White skin and flesh, with a delicate flavour. A high yielder.
'Purple Vienna' Purple skin, with white flesh.
'Rowel' White, crisp flesh. Slow to become woody.
'White Vienna' Compact variety, which is slow to bolt.

Marrows and courgettes, squashes and pumpkins, are all curcubits, or members of the cucumber family and all grow on annual vines with large, lobed leaves and yellow flowers. Although their cultivation requirements are broadly similar, there are significant differences between these vegetable fruits, not only in shape, size and colour, but also in flavour and texture.

Squashes have always been very popular in America and are becoming increasingly available in Europe too. They come in many forms but fall into two basic groups – summer and winter types.

Summer squashes (*Curcubita moschata*) have soft skin and pale, soft, fine-grained flesh. They are eaten fresh, as soon as they are gathered, which is usually at an immature stage. This group includes straightneck and crookneck squashes, and those with scalloped rims. Though there is little variety in the flavour of the different summer squashes, the texture of the cooked flesh varies considerably.

Winter squashes, on the other hand, have a tough, shell-like skin that allows them to be stored. Winter squashes (*Curcubita maxima*) are less watery than marrows; the fibrous, orange flesh has a more solid texture and contains more nourishment. However, they need several months of sunshine to mature, so they are best suited to southern districts which have

reasonably long summers. The winter squash group includes small acorn squashes and the larger Hubbard, butternut and banana squashes. In a class of its own is the unusual 'Vegetable Spaghetti' squash: after cooking it whole, the inside comes away in spaghetti-like strands.

Pumpkins are the largest of the winter squashes and take up a lot of room; they are not a good choice for those with limited space in the food garden. They have orange, yellow or blue-grey skin and coarse, strongly-flavoured flesh. When grown for show, pumpkins may reach weights of over 150kg (300lb).

Much smaller fruits than this can be grown and have several culinary uses, as well as forming excellent Hallowe'en lanterns when hollowed out. The miniature kinds weigh only half a kilo or a kilo (1–2lb) and may be cooked with a savoury filling, served as a vegetable or, of course, used as the basis for the traditional American dessert, pumpkin pie.

Marrows (*Curcubita pepo*) were once grown with size in mind, too, but the bland taste of the fully-grown fruits is declining in popularity compared with the flavour of the smaller young fruits. Courgettes, also known by their Italian name, *zucchini*, are simply small, immature marrows, cut when 10–13cm (4–5in) long. Any marrow plant will produce them but the best choice is one

of the F1 hybrid varieties, specially bred to produce numerous small fruits.

Both marrow and squash plants are obtainable in bush and trailing types. Bush varieties need less space and are earlier cropping; they do not form a true 'bush' but they have a reasonably compact habit, which is more practical for most gardens.

The trailing varieties throw out long shoots, which extend over the ground for a considerable distance. Large plants, such as pumpkins, can be trained into a circular form by pinning down the main shoots with wire pins or wooden pegs. Alternatively, trailing plants can be trained up tripods made of stout canes or over strong trelliswork of some kind. Growing the plants up a trellis also enables the fruits to get more sun and to ripen faster. It makes harvesting the crop easier, too.

Most pumpkins have a trailing habit and need a great deal of space. The fruits that can grow to an enormous size are of interest mainly on the show bench, but smaller, better-flavoured pumpkins can be harvested earlier from suitable varieties.

If space is at a premium, trailing marrows or squashes may be trained over a trellis or similar structure. Heavy fruits may need supporting individually in nets or slings.

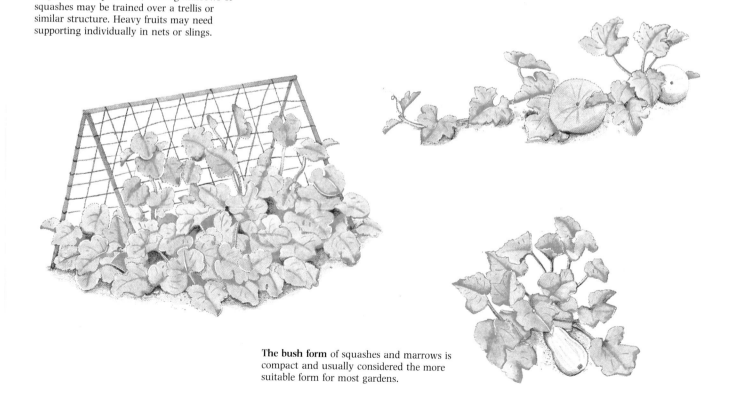

The bush form of squashes and marrows is compact and usually considered the more suitable form for most gardens.

The cucumber (*Cucumis sativus*) is available in two quite different forms. The long, smooth-skinned, evenly-shaped 'frame cucumbers' sold by greengrocers have to be grown under glass. You need a warm greenhouse to enjoy them from early summer onward; if you grow them in an unheated greenhouse or frame, they will mature a couple of months later.

The other type, termed 'ridge cucumbers', may be grown outdoors from seeds raised either in a greenhouse or indoors. They are generally smaller than greenhouse varieties and have more knobbly skins but they are no longer the oddly-shaped, prickly-skinned, bitter-tasting vegetable of gardens past. The new, improved varieties of ridge cucumber are longer and more evenly formed, with smoother skins, and a milder flavour.

Modern ridge cucumbers include those with a bush habit and some much-improved F1 hybrids. There are also Japanese varieties, which are longer and smooth-skinned; all-female varieties (see below); ball-shaped 'apple' cucumbers; and gherkins. All are sown and grown in much the same way, except that the Japanese varieties are best trained up netting.

Some varieties of both frame and ridge cucumbers are termed 'all-female'. They have the advantages of being seedless, and of producing few, if any, male flowers. In the case of greenhouse plants, these flowers must be picked off to prevent them pollinating the female flowers and causing the fruits to become bitter. Male flowers should not be removed from ridge cucumbers.

RIDGE CUCUMBERS

Ridge cucumbers, so-called because they were formerly grown on ridges, are both easier to grow, and considerably more hardy, than frame cucumbers, although they are unable to tolerate frost. They are ready from midsummer onward.

Ridge cucumbers can even be grown in pots and tubs on a patio provided they are planted in rich compost and kept moist.

MAKING A START

Prepare planting sites in advance, in a sunny, sheltered spot. Dig out holes 30cm (1ft) square and deep, mix in half a bucketful of well-rotted compost or manure with the soil, and then replace it. Allow 75cm (2½ft) between ordinary varieties and 45cm (1½ft) between Japanese types that will be supported. Gherkins, best sown where they are to grow, need to be 60cm (2ft) apart.

In mid-spring, sow seeds in peat pots indoors, as described for greenhouse plants, opposite, and harden off the seedlings for a couple of weeks before planting them out. Two weeks before planting, rake about two dessertspoons of general fertilizer into each planting site. Set the young plants out very carefully, preferably under cloches.

Alternatively, wait until late spring and then sow the seeds direct, after warming the site with cloches. Sow two seeds in each position, and remove the weaker seedling if both germinate. Take precautions against slugs. Remove the cloches once the plants are growing strongly.

GROWING GHERKINS

Gherkins are small ridge cucumbers used for pickling. They are usually grown on flat ground, but it is also possible to plant them in a pot of organically-rich compost standing on a sunny patio. Train the stems to a cane and the laterals to wires or similar supports.

CARE OF THE CROP

Erect a netting or trellis support, 1.5m (5ft) high, for Japanese varieties. Train the stems to this, tying them as necessary, and pinch out the tips when they reach the tops of the supports.

Remove the tips of ordinary varieties after six true leaves have appeared. Fruit-bearing side-shoots should then form, but if any prove barren pinch them out after the seventh leaf. Do not remove male flowers, since it is important that the females are pollinated.

Water frequently and generously, and never let the soil dry out. A mulch of straw will reduce evaporation, suppress weeds and keep the fruits clean. Feed every 10–14 days with a high-potash liquid fertilizer once the fruits start to form. As the fruits start to swell, put a piece of tile or slate under them to keep them off the soil.

Pinch out the tips of ridge cucumber shoots after the sixth leaf. This will encourage the formation of fruiting side-shoots. In contrast to greenhouse cucumbers, the male flowers should be left on the plants of ridge varieties.

HARVESTING

Cut the fruits as soon as they are large enough to use, without waiting for them to attain maximum size. As a rule, the harder you pick, the more fruits the plants will produce. Pick gherkins when they are only 5–8cm (2–3in) long.

PESTS AND DISEASES

Cucumber pests include aphids, glasshouse whitefly, red spider mites, slugs and snails.

Diseases and ailments are cucumber mosaic virus, foot rot, grey mould and powdery mildew.

GREENHOUSE OR FRAME CUCUMBERS

Consider first whether the greenhouse can be made warm enough for an early crop. Following an early sowing, a temperature of at least 16°C (60°F) will have to be maintained at a time of year when the weather is unreliable. All-female varieties need 21°C (70°F).

MAKING A START IN HEAT

For an early crop, sow in late winter or early spring. Place two seeds edgeways in 8cm (3in) pots filled with seed compost. Peat pots are ideal, since cucumbers resent root disturbance at planting time. Cover the pots with glass and paper and germinate the seeds at a temperature of 24°C (75°F).

Uncover the pots after germination, remove the weaker seedling, and grow the plants on in a minimum temperature of 16°C (60°F), or 21°C (70°F) for all-female varieties, for at least the first month. Fasten horizontal supporting wires at 15cm (6in) intervals, preferably across the end of the greenhouse, and about 30cm (1ft) away from the glass.

When the seedlings have two true leaves (in addition to the smooth, elliptical seed leaves), plant them out into 25cm (10in) pots of potting compost, one per pot, or into gro-bags, two per bag. Water them in and stand the containers under the wires. Allow 75–90cm (2½–3ft) between individual plants. Fasten a cane behind each plant for supporting the stem.

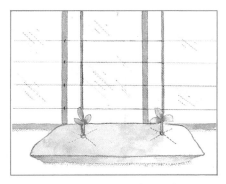

When planting indoor cucumbers, either in the greenhouse border or in gro-bags, secure a cane to the wires behind each plant. This will support the main stem, while the wires take the weight of the fruit-bearing laterals.

TRAINING AND AFTER-CARE

Pinch out the tip of each main shoot when it reaches the roof. Side-shoots, or laterals, will then form, and it is these that will bear the fruits. Tie the laterals to the wires.

Pinch out the tips of laterals two leaves beyond where fruits form. If a lateral shows no sign of fruiting, stop it at 60cm (2ft) in any case. Remove all male flowers – the ones without the swelling of an embryo fruit – including any that chance to appear on all-female plants.

Cucumbers do best in warm, humid conditions, with the growing medium kept moist at all times. Watering or spraying the floor of the greenhouse will increase humidity, but whether you are able to do this regularly must depend on what other plants are being grown in the greenhouse. Continuously humid conditions would be disastrous for tomatoes, for instance. Shade the plants from strong sunshine and apply a high-potash liquid fertilizer every 10–14 days when the fruits start to develop.

HARVESTING

Cut the cucumbers as soon as they have reached the size typical for the variety. Picked too small, they are bitter; left too long, the plant will stop producing.

PESTS AND DISEASES

As for ridge cucumbers, opposite.

Once tiny cucumbers appear and start to grow on the laterals of greenhouse plants, pinch out the shoots just beyond two leaves after the fruit. Feed the plants at least every two weeks from this stage on.

UNHEATED GREENHOUSES

A later cucumber crop can be grown in an unheated greenhouse or a cold frame. Sow the seeds in heat in midspring. Plant and train a greenhouse cucumber as outlined above.

Set one plant per frame in a raised mound of compost at the highest part of the frame. Pinch out the growing point once the plant has six true leaves. Shade the glass with liquid shading and open the light 5cm (2in) on sunny days. Water and spray frequently.

Peg down the four best laterals, and direct each one to a corner of the frame. Remove others. Pinch out their growing tips when they near the corners, or two leaves beyond the first fruit when it develops. Remove male flowers.

RECOMMENDED VARIETIES
Greenhouse
'Butcher's Disease Resisting' Heavy crops of slightly ribbed fruits.
'Conqueror' Long, smooth-skinned fruits, good for an unheated greenhouse or frame.
'Pepinex' An all-female variety bearing long, dark green fruits.
'Petita' All-female variety, bearing heavy crops of smallish fruits. Good for cool conditions.
'Telegraph' Long, smooth-skinned fruits. A reliable favourite.

Ordinary ridge
'Burpee Hybrid' F1 hybrid. Dark green fruits. Very reliable.
'King of the Ridge' Noted for its reliability and flavour.

Bush
'Bush Crop' F1 hybrid. Compact and high-yielding.
'Patio-Pik' F1 hybrid. Very compact, early and prolific.

Japanese
'Burpless Tasty Green' Fruits as smooth and uniform as greenhouse varieties.
'Chinese Long Green' Smooth-skinned and exceptionally long.

Apple
'Crystal Apple' Masses of egg-sized, pale-skinned fruits.

Gherkin
'Bestal' F1 hybrid. Early, uniform fruits.

USING A GREENHOUSE, pages 12–13
SOWING UNDER GLASS, pages 38–39
WATERING AND MULCHING, pages 42–43
VEGETABLE FRUITS, pages 126–127
PESTS AND DISEASES, pages 172–175
BOTTLING, pages 228–229
165

The aubergine (*Solanum melongena*) is of tropical origin. While in cold areas it is essentially a greenhouse crop, elsewhere it may succeed outdoors in a reasonably sheltered position.

These fruits are now an everyday sight in greengrocers, yet the plants remain unfamiliar to many gardeners. They have a height and spread of about 60cm (2ft), prickly leaves and stems and attractive purple flowers. Most varieties have black or purple fruits but there are also white and speckled varieties. Their size and shape vary, too, but it is from the common oval shape that the aubergine gets its other name, 'eggplant'.

If you live in a mild district and have a sunny wall or fence, it is well worth trying to grow aubergines outdoors. In a good summer they should succeed, though the harvest may not be as good as it would be under glass.

Be prepared for failure during an indifferent season, however. Aubergines, being tropical plants, are accustomed to warm days and nights and plenty of sunshine. Cool, damp conditions do not suit them.

The most foolproof solution is to grow them in a greenhouse. Apart from the warmth needed to raise the plants, an unheated house is perfectly adequate. The greenhouse conditions that suit summer tomato crops are also ideal for aubergines.

Without a greenhouse, the chances of success outdoors will be improved if the plants, raised in warmth, are given the protection of a frame or cloches. Unless you use the tallest of barn cloches, they will eventually outgrow this covering, but not until the warmest weeks of the year.

Aubergines may also be grown in pots or gro-bags on a sunny patio. Fill pots with a John Innes No. 3 compost. When planted in the ground, whether indoors or out, the soil must be free-draining and well-manured. The best plan is to prepare a station for each plant, allowing 45cm (1½ft) between plants. Dig out a hole 30cm (1ft) square and mix at least half a bucketful of rotted manure with the soil before replacing it.

MAKING A START

Whether you plan to grow the plants outdoors or in a greenhouse, sow the seeds in early spring in a temperature of about 18°C (65°F). Set the seeds singly in 8cm (3in) pots, and prepare one or two extra in case any fail to germinate. Cover the pots with glass and paper until the seedlings appear.

Grow the seedlings on in a temperature of around 16°C (60°F). Too much warmth will make them weak and spindly, but if they have too little warmth they will stop growing.

Planting outdoors

Harden the plants off during late spring by placing them in a cold frame. Gradually increase the amount of ventilation over a two-week period before planting them out. After setting the plants in the frame, scatter a dressing of general fertilizer over the prepared stations in the ground: a dessertspoonful to each one. Cover them with cloches if these are available.

Outdoor plants may also be grown in 20cm (8in) pots or in gro-bags. Unless they are protected by cloches, wait until the risk of frost is over before planting. Stand pots 45cm (1½ft) apart. Plant three aubergines in a standard-sized gro-bag.

Planting in a greenhouse

Prepare the soil as for outdoor plants, or use gro-bags or 20cm (8in) pots.

Plant in mid-spring if the greenhouse has heating. Wait for a week or two longer if the house is unheated, but meanwhile keep the plants in a warmed area of staging. Much depends on the weather, of course, and on prevailing night-time temperatures.

CARE OF THE CROP

Water the plants in, and subsequently ensure that the soil does not dry out.

Pinch out the tops of the plants when they are 30cm (1ft) high, which will encourage fruit-bearing shoots to form. Support the plants with canes and string if they make a lot of soft growth.

Outdoors, allow only one fruit to develop on each shoot, with a maximum of four per plant. Remove other flowers and any side-shoots that form on the laterals. Pinch out the tips of the shoots a few leaves beyond where the fruits have formed. Indoors, a few extra fruits may be left on plants that are growing strongly – up to three per branch.

Apply a liquid high-potash fertilizer every two weeks once the first fruits start to swell. Syringing the plants with clear water, once or twice daily, will help to suppress red spider mites.

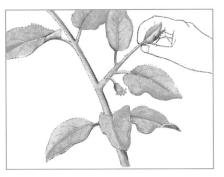

To **assist the fruits** to grow and ripen, allow only one to develop on each shoot. Remove other flowers and pinch out the tips of shoots at two or three leaves beyond the fruit that is left on the plants.

HARVESTING

Cut the fruits from midsummer onward, or somewhat later outdoors, once they have an even colour overall and while they are still glossy. Once they lose their shine they start to become tough and the seeds turn bitter. Cut the stems with scissors or secateurs, and handle the fruits carefully. Aubergines will keep for up to two weeks.

PESTS AND DISEASES

Aphids, red spider mites and whitefly may give trouble, especially in a greenhouse.

RECOMMENDED VARIETIES

'Black Enorma' Large, black, plentiful fruits.
'Black Prince' F1 hybrid. An early crop of long, slim fruits.
'Easter Egg' Oval fruits are white-skinned.
'Moneymaker' F1 hybrid. Early and productive, with quite large fruits.

These two plants are species of *Capsicum*, the generic name by which peppers, or sweet peppers, are also known. There are red and yellow peppers, the green peppers being simply the unripe fruits of both types. There are also white and purplish-black varieties of pepper, though these are rarer. Chillis are a variation of the same species (*Capsicum annuum*); they have a slender, bean-pod shape and a much hotter flavour. They are used in pickles and spicy dishes.

As with aubergines, cropping is more reliable in a greenhouse, even in mild districts. Such protection is essential elsewhere. The bush-like plants, which have soft stems with a woody base, grow to about 45cm (1½ft) outdoors but to perhaps twice this height under glass. Support the taller varieties with canes and secure the growing plants to them with string.

If planted outdoors in a suitably mild district, set peppers 30cm (1ft) from a south-facing wall and leave 45cm (1½ft) between the plants. Elsewhere, the plants need the protection of a greenhouse.

Spray greenhouse-grown pepper plants with clear water to help the fruits to 'set' and also to keep red spider mite at bay. Do this every day while the flowers are open.

MAKING A START
Prepare the soil and sow the seeds as for aubergines. If you are moving them outdoors from a greenhouse, take care to harden them off gradually so that they are not subjected to a drastic change of temperature. Cloche protection is valuable once they are moved from the cold frame.

CARE OF THE CROP
In a greenhouse, spray the plants lightly with clear water at least once a day. Besides discouraging red spider mites, this helps to ensure that the fruits set. Pinch out the growing point when the plants are 15cm (6in) high, and pick off the first few flowers. Shade the glass during hot, bright weather. There is no need to limit the fruits. Once the fruits start to swell, give them a weekly feed of liquid fertilizer.

HARVESTING
Start picking when the fruits are the size of a tennis ball, and pick regularly to encourage cropping. Peppers are slow to ripen and turn red or yellow outdoors, but the green fruits have a mild, pleasant flavour. If there are still fruits on outdoor plants when frost threatens, lift the plants, complete with their roots, and stand them in a shed.

PESTS AND DISEASES
Red spider mites and capsid bugs are the most likely troubles. Grey mould may also occur.

RECOMMENDED VARIETIES
'**Antler**' F1 hybrid. Particularly hot flavour. Early, with a heavy crop.
'**Canape**' F1 hybrid. Early, with a mild flavour. A good choice for outdoors.
'**Chilli Serrano**' Extremely hot pods about 4cm (1½in) long.
'**Clio**' F1 hybrid. Only 40cm (16in) high, but bears plenty of fruits.
'**Early Prolific**' F1 hybrid. Compact, and a good choice for outdoors.
'**Gypsy**' F1 hybrid. Early, with unusually heavy yields.

The pods of this tender plant (*Abelmoschus esculentus*), also called 'lady's fingers', are often considered an acquired taste. It is worth sampling some before deciding whether to grow your own. Okra is a versatile vegetable: it may be added to stews of various kinds, steamed and braised and served as a vegetable, or it can be used to form the basis of spicy dishes, such as sweet and sour okra. A characteristic aspect of okra is the sticky 'gum' it produces when cooked, hence the term 'gumbo' to describe some okra dishes.

Okra originates in tropical Africa and therefore does best in a greenhouse as a rule. However, like aubergines and peppers, it may produce a crop outdoors in a mild area and a sheltered garden. The plants grow from 1–2.5m (3–8ft) high. The taller varieties will need some form of support.

Pick the pods of okra before they exceed 8–10cm (3–4in) in length. After this they are liable to become tough. Scissors or secateurs are the best means of severing the stalks. Use the pods as soon as possible after picking and before they become limp. Do not refrigerate, since the dry air causes rapid deterioration.

MAKING A START AND AFTER-CARE
The methods advised for sowing and growing aubergines also apply to okra.

HARVESTING
Be sure to pick the pods while they are still young and tender – no more than 8–10cm (3–4in) long. Test for tenderness with your thumbnail. Cut them with scissors or a sharp knife; do not remove the caps but leave on a short length of stalk.

RECOMMENDED VARIETIES
Two varieties listed by seedsmen are '**Long Green**' and '**Tender Pod**'; the latter is an F1 hybrid recommended for greenhouse growing only.

SOWING UNDER GLASS, pages 38–39
VEGETABLE FRUITS, pages 126–127

TOMATOES AND OTHER VEGETABLE FRUITS, page 128
PESTS AND DISEASES, pages 172–175

FREEZING VEGETABLES, pages 232–233

167

Tomatoes (*Lycopersicon esculentum*) rank high in any list of favoured garden crops, especially among greenhouse-owners. They are one of the most popular and most universally grown vegetables despite the considerable amount of time and care they entail, and despite their susceptibility to pests and diseases.

Tomatoes are versatile in their culinary use. They are one of the tastiest and most useful raw foods, for eating either on their own or in mixed salads. They are invaluable in sauces, a surplus can easily be frozen as a purée, and any unripe ones used to make green tomato chutney.

You can expect a yield of up to 2kg (4lb) from each plant grown outdoors (more from bush varieties), with perhaps double this amount from greenhouse crops. The taste of even the standard varieties is all the better for being home-grown and freshly picked, while home growing offers a much wider range of sizes, colours and flavours than the commercial product.

The choice of varieties ranges in size from the cherry-sized fruits to 'beefsteak' tomatoes that weigh around 450g (1lb) apiece. There are also pink, yellow and striped varieties as well as plum- and pear-shaped fruits. New kinds of tomato are introduced every year, and many are an improvement on the traditional choices.

Tomatoes are half-hardy plants, vulnerable to frost but well able to grow outdoors during the summer in relatively mild areas provided you choose the right variety. The flavour of outdoor-ripened tomatoes is said to be better than that of those ripened under glass though this is a matter of subjective preference. They do best in a sheltered,

Bush tomatoes, which need no side-shooting, are early to ripen but make untidy growth.

Cordons are slightly more trouble but the fruits are supported clear of mud splashes.

sunny position, such as against a south-facing wall. Results will be poor during a damp, chilly summer, however, unless you choose one of the varieties specially bred to ripen outdoors without sun.

In colder districts – and as an insurance policy elsewhere – choose one of the compact bush varieties and grow them under cloches or in a frame. For an even greater guarantee of success, and for heavier yields, grow the plants in a greenhouse.

All tomatoes need a warm start in order that the seeds germinate successfully and the seedlings develop well. In a greenhouse, localized heat can be provided in a propagator or by siting the seed trays close to a small heater. In the home, an airing cupboard and a sunny windowsill can furnish the

required warmth. From about mid-spring onward, the plants need little or no artificial warmth, so an unheated greenhouse is satisfactory. The only advantage of a heated greenhouse is that it allows earlier sowing and planting, which brings picking forward by several weeks.

Greenhouse tomatoes can be grown either in the soil border or in containers. However, the soil in a greenhouse border suffers over the years from a build-up of pests and diseases associated with tomatoes. Though it is possible to change or sterilize the soil at regular intervals, an easier solution is to use gro-bags or pots. Ring culture is also suitable for greenhouse use (see p.170). All greenhouse tomatoes are grown as cordons.

GROWING TOMATOES IN CONTAINERS

If you have a sunny patio, it makes sense to grow tomatoes in pots or gro-bags outdoors. Each tomato plant requires a 25cm (10in) pot. Place a crock over the drainage hole, followed by a layer of gravel or small stones, then fill to within 5cm (2in) of the top with John Innes potting compost No. 3, or a good peat-based compost. Insert a cane in each pot and tie the growing plant to it at intervals with soft twine, allowing room for the stem to thicken. Use new bags or fresh compost each year. Later in the season, add more compost to cover exposed surfaced roots.

If you are using gro-bags, set three plants in each bag and make only small holes for planting.

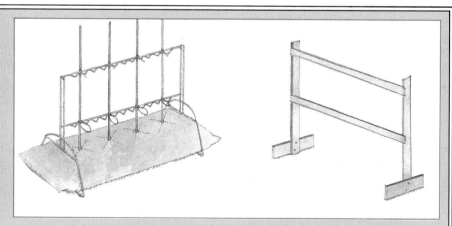

Tomatoes in gro-bags outdoors require a supporting frame for securing the canes. You can buy frames designed for the purpose.

Alternatively, it is not difficult to devise a home-made frame formed from battens and pieces of scrap timber. The support must be sufficiently stable to withstand winds and eddies once the plants are fully grown.

GROWING TOMATOES OUTDOORS

For outdoor growers, there is a choice between single-stemmed cordon types and low-growing bush varieties. In open ground, tomatoes need fertile, well-drained soil; on a patio, use either gro-bags or pots.

Prepare the soil by digging in compost or well-rotted manure during the previous autumn or winter; allow at least a bucketful to the square metre or yard. Avoid growing tomatoes near potatoes, or where potatoes were grown the previous year, since they belong to the same family and are subject to the same pests and diseases.

Plant outdoors only when there is no further risk of spring frosts; it is safe to plant out three or four weeks earlier than this under cloches or a frame. Sow the seeds approximately two months before the expected time of planting out.

MAKING A START

Sow the seeds in a pan of seed compost. After scattering them thinly, just cover with more compost. Water them in with a fine-rosed can then cover with glass and paper until they germinate. A temperature of 16–18°C (60–65°F) is needed for cordons.

If you do not have a greenhouse or a propagator, enclose the pan in a plastic bag and place it in an airing cupboard. Check daily for signs of growth from the sixth day onward. Place the pan on a warm, well-lit windowsill when the first shoots appear.

Prick the seedlings out individually into 8cm (3in) pots when the seed leaves have grown to at least twice their initial size. Hold each seedling by a leaf and ease it out of the compost with a pencil or small stick. Plant it centrally with its leaves just clear of the surface – deeper than it was previously.

Grow the plants on in gentle warmth. During good weather the sun may give sufficient heat by day but a little artificial heating will be needed at night, at least for the first few weeks.

Move the plants to a cold frame for hardening off two weeks before planting out. At the same time, rake a dressing of general fertilizer into the planting site, at 70g per sq m (2oz per sq yd), and put cloches in position if these are to be used. The ideal time to move the young plants is just before the first flower truss is visible. But delay planting if there is any risk of frost, or if the soil temperature is below 10°C (50°F).

When planting, leave 75cm (2½ft) between rows; allow 45cm (1½ft) between cordons and 60cm (2ft) between bush plants. Water the plants in and insert a 1.2m (4ft) cane alongside proposed cordons.

Avoid handling the stems when pricking out tomato seedlings into individual pots. If planted deeper than they were previously, additional roots will have formed before the plants are moved to their final positions.

Removing side-shoots from the leaf axils on the main stem is a regular task when growing single-stem cordon tomatoes. Wait until they are large enough to come away cleanly but pinch them out before they are longer than about 5cm (2in).

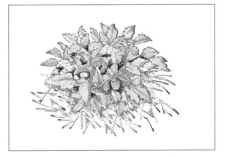

Lay either black plastic or a layer of straw beneath bush plants to help keep the fruits clean. Those close to the ground will otherwise become mud-splashed, and others may even lie directly on the soil.

CARE OF THE CROP

Spread a mulch of compost around the plants to help retain soil moisture and reduce weed growth.

Cordons require supporting and the regular removal of side-shoots. Use canes to support cordons grown in open ground; for those in gro-bags, either buy proprietary supporting frames or make your own out of wood. Outdoors, you most provide strong enough support to withstand winds.

As the cordons grow, keep the stems tied loosely to the canes and remove side-shoots as they develop in the leaf joints, once they are about 2.5cm (1in) long. Pinch them out early in the day when they are distended so that they come away cleanly. Pinch out the top of each plant two leaves beyond where the fourth truss of fruits has begun to form.

Bush tomatoes require neither support nor the removal of side-shoots; they are stockier plants, best grown sprawling on the ground. They are the obvious choice for cloches and frames. Place straw or black polythene sheeting under bush tomatoes to support the fruits clear of the soil, otherwise they will become splashed with mud.

Keep the plants watered during dry weather. Those in pots or gro-bags will probably need watering daily, or twice daily during hot weather. Give them a weekly feed with a high-potash liquid fertilizer but do not feed other plants if they are already growing well.

During a damp season, spray with Bordeaux mixture every two weeks from soon after midsummer, to guard against an attack of potato blight.

HARVESTING

Pick the fruits as they ripen by twisting them upward while pressing with your thumb against the joint in the stalk. Do not pull the tomato away from its green calyx.

If unripe fruits remain on the plants in autumn, undo the ties, lay the plants flat, with straw beneath them, and cover them with cloches. A sprinkling of slug pellets is a wise precaution. Alternatively, uproot the plants and hang them indoors, where they will ripen further.

TOMATOES

GROWING TOMATOES IN A GREENHOUSE

The early stages are as for outdoor plants, though the timing is different. To raise plants for growing in an unheated greenhouse, sow the seeds in early spring. This will give fruits for picking by midsummer.

Ring culture, a soil-less method of growing tomatoes in a greenhouse (or outdoors) that reduces the risk of soil-borne infection, is described in column three.

With adequate warmth – that is, a night-time temperature of not less than 10°C (50°F) – tomatoes can be harvested right through the year, though their growth is slower during the winter and heating costs are high. For an early-summer harvest, sow at the turn of the year and plant during late winter or early spring.

MAKING A START

If you plan to use the greenhouse border (this is inadvisable if more than one or two crops of tomatoes have already been grown there) dig it well ahead of planting time and add plenty of well-rotted manure or compost. Rake in a dressing of general fertilizer, at 70g per sq m (2oz per sq yd), a week or two before planting, then give the soil a good soaking.

Plant when the young tomatoes are 15–20cm (6–8in) tall; set them 45cm (1½ft) apart. If pots or gro-bags are used, plant as described for outdoor tomatoes. Water the plants in well but do not insert canes or a support frame.

RING CULTURE

Plant each tomato in a 23cm (9in) bottomless container or 'ring' filled with John Innes No. 3 potting compost or a special soil-less tomato compost. Place the rings on a bed of aggregate such as washed gravel, 15cm (6in) deep. Water the plants generously immediately after planting. After about ten days, when the roots have reached the bottom of the containers, water the aggregate. Keep it constantly moist but do not water the rings.

When fruits begin to form on the first truss, feed the plants once a week with a high-potash liquid fertilizer, applied to the compost in the rings.

CARE OF THE CROP

Support each plant with a vertical string; tie one end loosely around the stem just beneath the lowest true leaf and take it up to a wire fastened to the glazing bars above the row of plants. In a timber greenhouse, support the wire with hooks; for aluminium structures, use one of the patent fastenings that slot into the glazing bars. Tie the upper end of the string with a half-bow so that it is easily undone to adjust the tension.

Remove side-shoots that appear in the leaf axils when they are 2.5cm (1in) long. Water the plants regularly once the weather becomes warm – daily if necessary – so that the soil never dries out. Plants in gro-bags or pots may need watering twice a day or even more frequently. Take care that gro-bags do not become waterlogged, since they have no drainage outlet.

Tomato plants like well-ventilated, airy conditions. Ventilate the greenhouse freely on warm days, and shade the glass lightly during hot, bright weather. Damp down by spraying the greenhouse and plants lightly with water on bright mornings. The extra humidity will help the fruits to set. Always water or sprinkle early in the day, to allow the leaves to dry by the evening.

Feed the plants weekly with a high-potash liquid fertilizer once the fruits on the bottom truss start to develop.

When the plants are a metre (2–3ft) tall, cut off a few of the lower leaves to assist air circulation. Pinch out the top of the plant when it reaches the roof.

Twist the developing stems of greenhouse plants around string fixed to the glazing bars.

PESTS AND DISEASES

Pests of the tomato include aphids, potato cyst eelworms, red spider mites and tomato moths.

Among diseases and disorders commonly affecting tomatoes are blossom end rot, blotchy ripening, foot rot, greenback, grey mould, scald, potato blight, verticillium wilt and virus diseases.

RECOMMENDED VARIETIES

Greenhouse

'Big Boy' F₁ hybrid. Massive, fleshy fruits. Few seeds. (Restrict to three fruits per truss.)
'Eurocross' Early-maturing and a heavy cropper. Disease-resistant.
'Herald' F₁ hybrid. Medium-sized fruits which ripen evenly and have an excellent flavour.

Greenhouse/outdoors

'Ailsa Craig' Heavy crops of medium-sized fruits with a fine flavour.
'Alicante' Reliable producer of medium-sized fruits. Good flavour.
'Golden Sunrise' Golden fruits with an appealing flavour.
'Moneymaker' A long-time favourite. Crops heavily and reliably.

Outdoors (cordon)

'Outdoor Girl' Early, and one of the most reliable outdoor varieties.
'Super Marmande' Large fruits with a fine flavour.

Outdoors (bush)

'Alfresco' Vigorous habit; a heavy cropper.
'Pixie Hybrid' Compact habit and suitable for containers. The smallish fruits ripen very quickly.

'Red Alert' An early crop of delicious, rather small fruits.
'Roma' Elongated, plum-shaped fruits. Excellent for cooking.
'The Amateur' Heavy crops of medium-sized fruits. Long-established.
'Sub Arctic Plenty' Small to medium fruits which ripen early even without sun.

Novelties (greenhouse or outdoors)

'Gardener's Delight' Long trusses of small, exceptionally sweet fruits.
'Sweet 100' F₁ hybrid. Early-maturing crop of sweet, cherry-sized fruits.
'Tigerella' Small to medium-sized fruits with golden stripes.

USING A GREENHOUSE, pages 12–13
SOWING SEEDS OUTDOORS, pages 36–37
SOWING UNDER GLASS, pages 38–39
TOMATOES AND OTHER VEGETABLE FRUITS, page 128
PESTS AND DISEASES, pages 172–175
FREEZING VEGETABLES, pages 232–233

MUSHROOMS

Although there are hundreds of different species of mushroom growing wild, only one species (*Agaricus bisporus albida*) is cultivated. White, cream and brown varieties exist, of which the brown kind is the most vigorous and disease-resistant. The cultivation of mushrooms bears no resemblance to that of any other vegetable in the food garden. It is a fungus and obtains its nutrition in a completely different way from other crops.

There are at least three different ways to grow mushrooms. The easiest, if least adventurous, is to buy a commercial kit, as shown right. Results are reasonably reliable, provided the pack is fresh. The kit consists of a box or bucket of prepared compost which has already been 'spawned', or impregnated with mushroom fungus.

Provided you keep the compost at 10-13°C (50–55°F), and subsequently topdress it with the 'casing' supplied with the kit, you can expect to start picking mushrooms within two months, with further flushes over a two-month period.

Mushroom kits (and also spawn) are readily available from garden centres, nurseries and seedsmen. They offer a simple means of enjoying fresh mushrooms with little trouble. Instructions are provided.

The second method, which is something of a gamble, is to try growing mushrooms in the lawn. Though results are uncertain, this involves little trouble, unlike the third method – preparing your own mushroom compost and seeding it with spawn – which involves a fair amount of effort; the results are reasonably assured, however.

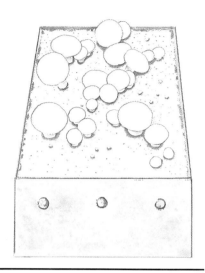

GROWING MUSHROOMS OUTDOORS

This method depends on your having a large enough area of lawn to devote a patch of it to mushroom growing; if mushrooms appear, this patch of grass will have to stay uncut for some time.

Choose an area of lawn that has not been treated with a hormone weedkiller. Pick a little-used spot so that the crop, if one appears, will not be trodden on.

At any time during the summer, cut out and remove an area of turf about 5cm (2in) deep. Loosen the base a little and work in some well-rotted stable manure before scattering some pelletized spawn on it, or else placing separate small chunks of block spawn, about the size of a walnut, on it, 25–30cm (10–12in) apart. Then replace the

For an autumn crop of mushrooms outdoors, lift a shaded patch of turf and work some well-rotted manure into the soil beneath before placing the spawn. Replace the turf. Avoid using chemical weedkillers on this area.

turf. Avoid mowing from late summer onward, which is when the first mushrooms may appear.

HARVESTING

From spawning to picking takes about two months, with mushrooms appearing in flushes, every ten days or so, for about as long again. They may be picked at the button stage or left until they open. Pick by twisting the mushroom upward – do not just pull them out of the compost.

Eat them with as little delay as possible.

GROWING MUSHROOMS INDOORS

Obtain a quantity of fresh stable manure containing plenty of straw and form a substantial heap; water it thoroughly if it is dry. Leave the heap for a week or two to heat up, then turn it weekly – outside to inside – until it decomposes into a dark, crumbly, pleasant-smelling mass.

Scoop some of this compost into containers about 25cm (10in) deep. Wooden boxes or cardboard boxes lined with polythene will serve the purpose. There will be an initial rise in temperature, but after this check daily with a thermometer until it falls to 24°C (75°F). Once is does, introduce pieces of spawn at 30cm (1ft) intervals, 5cm (2in) deep, or else mix pelletized or grain spawn with the compost by scattering it on the surface. Place the boxes in a room or cellar at 10–13°C (50–55°F) and water the compost lightly.

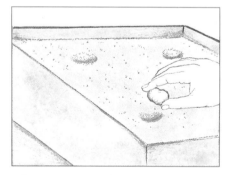

When growing mushrooms indoors, place the spawn in the prepared compost at about 30cm (1ft) spacings. Place the boxes out of direct sunlight in a room or cellar where the temperature remains fairly even.

About ten days later, when the spawn will have sent white threads through the compost, cover the surface with a layer of subsoil. This will trap warmth and moisture but, being virtually sterile (unlike garden topsoil), will not introduce spores of alien fungi. Keep this 'casing' slightly moist by occasional spraying.

HARVESTING

Harvest the mushrooms in flushes, as they appear, as for outdoor-grown mushrooms.

After picking, replace the casing each time by filling in holes left by the mushrooms. The exhausted compost provides valuable humus for the garden.

MAKING AND USING GARDEN COMPOST, pages 30–31
TOMATOES AND OTHER VEGETABLE FRUITS, page 128

The risk of attacks from pests and diseases can be cut down by nourishing the soil well and keeping it free from weeds, as well as sowing and transplanting your vegetables at the correct time and in the most suitable weather conditions.

Both commercial pesticides and organic treatments are suggested where an alternative exists. The commercial pesticides (□) are described by their chemical names. The organic or more homely remedies (△) are those recommended by the Henry Doubleday Research Association (HDRA), a leading advocate of organic gardening.

BLACKFLY
Sap-sucking aphids found mainly on broad beans but also on other vegetable crops.
□ Pinch out the tops of beans when in flower to deter these pests. Spray with permethrin at dusk if plants are in flower when attacked by blackfly.
△ Treat with quassia- or nicotine-based spray mixed with soft soap.

CELERY FLY
A leaf-mining pest that causes the leaves to shrivel and may check growth. It also attacks parsnips.
□ Spray with dimethoate or trichlorphon.
△ Spray with nicotine and soap.

APHIDS
The 'greenfly' that cluster on the leaves and stems of several vegetables and suck their sap may make the plants unusable. They also spread disease. (See also blackfly; root aphids.)
□ Among many commercial sprays are pirimicarb, dimethoate, permethrin and malathion. Use derris if the plants will shortly be picked and eaten. Ladybirds and hover flies feed on aphids.

CABBAGE ROOT FLY
Maggots of this fly attack roots of young brassicas.
□ Treat the soil at planting time with bromophos, diazinon or gamma-HCH.
△ Simple deterrents to the fly that lays the eggs include strips of creosote-painted blanket hung over the rows; also, small squares of carpet underlay, each with a slit, placed to cover the soil round a newly-planted stem.

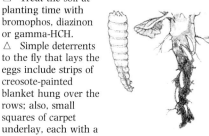

CUTWORMS
Fat, root-eating larvae, often found only by digging up a plant that has wilted and died. Brassicas are especially vulnerable, but they also attack lettuces and root vegetables.
□ Dust planting positions with pirimiphos-methyl if past attacks make precautions worthwhile.

△ Make collars for seedlings from cardboard or plastic bottles and push them at least 1cm (½in) into the soil.

ASPARAGUS BEETLE
The adults and larvae of this damaging pest attack both the leaves and stems of plants from early summer onward and can sometimes leave them bare.
□ Prompt treatment is essential. Spray plants with malathion or pirimiphos-methyl.
△ Dust with derris. Cut down the ferns and clean up the beds in late autumn so that the beetles can find no cover for the winter.

CARROT FLY
Maggots, hatching from eggs laid alongside the seedlings, tunnel into the roots of carrots, parsnips and celery.
□ Treat seed drills with gamma-HCH, bromophos or diazinon. Spray maincrop roots with pirimiphos-methyl in late summer.
△ Sow sparingly to minimize the smell caused by thinning. Spread lawn mowings thinly between rows or hang creosote-soaked strips of blanket over them.

FLEA BEETLE
Brassica and some root-crop seedlings with holed leaves are under attack from these tiny, jumping insects. Water, if necessary, to hasten plants through the vulnerable period.
□ Dust the rows with gamma-HCH, derris or pirimiphos-methyl as soon as the seedlings appear.

△ Hoe regularly and feed with a quick-acting organic fertilizer.

BEAN SEED FLY
A soil pest, worst in heavy soil, that attacks pea, bean and sweet corn seeds and seedlings.
□ Where damage has occurred before, dust seed drills with bromophos and avoid freshly-cultivated beds.
△ Wet seeds with paraffin before sowing.

CATERPILLARS
The larvae of a number of moths and butterflies cause considerable damage to leafy crops.
□ Spray or dust with trichlorphon, permethrin or derris.
△ Hand-pick if outbreaks are small.

FRIT FLY
Sweet corn seedlings are vulnerable to the fly's larvae; the damage shows in twisted, ragged leaves. Subsequent growth is affected. Greenhouse-raised seedlings are unlikely to be harmed.
□ Dust outdoor-raised seedlings with gamma-HCH.

MANGOLD FLY
Leaf-mining by the larvae results in blisters and browning of the leaves.
☐ Remove damaged leaves if only a few plants are affected. Otherwise, spray with trichlorphon, dimethoate or pirimiphos-methyl.

POTATO CYST EELWORM
Stunted growth, withered leaves and tiny tubers are symptoms of this minute but serious pest. Tiny cysts develop on the roots. Affected plants die prematurely.
☐ There is at present no treatment. Burn the haulm and tubers. Do not grow potatoes or tomatoes in the same soil for five years.

STEM AND BULB EELWORM
The pest is microscopic but the damage severe to such crops as onions, leeks and rhubarb. The foliage and stems or bulbs of affected plants become distorted and rotten.
☐ Burn infected plants. Avoid growing host plants in the same soil for at least two years. These

include beans, leeks, onions, peas, rhubarb and strawberries.

ONION FLY
Larvae burrowing into the bulbs of onions, shallots and leeks cause wilting and discoloured foliage. Plants are killed or deformed, bulbs rot.
☐ Dust young plants with pirimiphos-methyl or gamma-HCH, at the 'loop' stage and again two weeks later. Remove and burn affected plants. Growing

onions from sets reduces the risk: with no thinning, there is less scent to attract the flies.

RED SPIDER MITE
Beans and marrows grown outdoors are at risk from these minute sap-sucking insects.
In the greenhouse, the glasshouse red spider mite causes similar damage on tomatoes, cucumbers and aubergines.
☐ Control with malathion, dimethoate or derris. Use only derris if beans are shortly to be picked.

TURNIP GALL WEEVIL
All brassicas are vulnerable to attack. Swellings on the root look similar to those caused by club root disease, but they are hollow. It is not a serious pest.
☐ Where there has been trouble previously, dust the soil around seedlings with gamma-HCH or pirimiphos-methyl.

PEA AND BEAN WEEVIL
Seedlings with notched leaves are a sign of attack. Only heavy infestations are serious.
☐ Dust with gamma-HCH or pirimiphos-methyl.
△ Dust with derris, and give a fast-acting organic feed to stimulate growth.

ROOT APHIDS
Lettuces are the crop most seriously affected by these white, waxy insects that live in the soil and feed on plant roots. Beans and globe artichokes can be attacked, too. Examine the roots for signs if plants wilt and die.
☐ Remove and dispose of affected plants, watering the others with malathion or dimethoate.

△ Grow resistant varieties of lettuce – 'Avondefiance' and 'Avoncrisp'.

WHITEFLY
Cabbage whiteflies damage all types of brassicas if present in large numbers on the undersides of leaves. Control can be difficult.
A different species, glasshouse whiteflies, are troublesome on tomatoes.
☐ Spray every few days with pirimiphos-methyl, permethrin, pyrethrum or

malathion. Try using different chemicals alternately. Burn brassica stumps if the crop has been infected.

PEA MOTH
The tiny, yellow caterpillars of this pest result in maggoty peas.
☐ Spray with fenitrothion or permethrin a week after peas start to flower.
△ Spray with quassia or nicotine, mixed with soft soap.

PEA THRIPS
Mottled, distorted leaves and pods may, on closer examination, reveal tiny yellow or black insects at work. Severe attacks cause stunted growth and few flowers.
☐ Spray with dimethoate or permethrin.
△ Spray two or three times with nicotine and soap.

SLUGS AND SNAILS
Many vegetables are at risk, but particularly leafy crops in the earlier stages of growth. Slugs and snails make holes in the leaves, but also eat tubers and roots. They leave slime trails and are most active in mild, damp weather.
☐ See p.109 for suggested control measures.

WIREWORMS
These slender orange grubs, about 2.5cm (1in) long, are the larvae of the click beetle. They bore into roots and tubers of potatoes, lettuces and tomatoes and are especially troublesome in new gardens.
☐ Dig newly-cultivated land thoroughly and apply bromophos, diazinon or pirimiphos-methyl before planting.

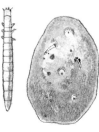

ANTHRACNOSE
Patches and spots, caused by a fungus, appear on the leaves and pods of French beans and runner beans. Damage is variable, but in a damp summer plants may be destroyed.
☐ Burn badly-affected plants. Spray others with a fungicide, such as benomyl.

BLOSSOM END ROT
A condition that occurs on tomatoes that have been given insufficient water. The fruits have a dark, sunken patch on the side opposite the stalk.
☐ Prevent by avoiding inadequate or irregular watering.

CROWN ROT
The name aptly describes this bacterial infection of rhubarb, most prevalent on heavy, wet soils. Discoloured leaves are often the first sign.
☐ Lift and burn affected plants. Replace with new ones elsewhere on the plot.

CUCUMBER MOSAIC VIRUS
A virus disease (see below) which affects cucumbers, marrows and squash. It causes mottling of the leaves and discoloured and deformed fruits.
☐ Spray against aphids, which may carry the virus. Destroy infected plants at the first symptoms.

GANGRENE
A storage rot of potatoes, which results in the tubers decaying.
☐ Burn affected tubers. Take great care not to damage tubers at lifting time, which gives entry to the spores.

GREENBACK
Greenhouse tomatoes fail to ripen around the stalk end. Scorching, coupled with a potash deficiency, are the causes.
☐ Shade the glass. Feed with liquid high-potash fertilizer.

BLOTCHY RIPENING
A disorder of greenhouse tomatoes and other vegetable fruits that may be due to uneven watering, temperature or feeding. Parts of the fruits are discoloured and fail to ripen normally.
☐ Give more attention to shading, ventilation, watering and applications of liquid fertilizer.

BORON DEFICIENCY
Celery leaves become yellow and the stems develop cracks. The roots of turnips, swedes and beetroots become discoloured inside; beetroot leaves wilt and shrivel.
☐ Apply borax to the soil at 35g per sq m (1oz per 20 sq yds) first mix it with dry, sharp sand for easier distribution.

DAMPING OFF
This fungal infection causes seedlings – indoors or out – to collapse. Seedlings are vulnerable when they are under stress from excessive moisture, overcrowding or extreme temperatures.
☐ Apply cupric carbonate or Cheshunt compound (copper sulphate and ammonium carbonate). Dress seeds with captan.
△ Improve sowing techniques: always use clean pots and sterilized seed compost.

GREY MOULD (BOTRYTIS)
A grey, furry mould appears on stems, leaves and fruits. Most prevalent in still, damp conditions.
☐ Lift and dispose of badly-affected plants. If spotted early, spray with benomyl, thiophanate-methyl or captan. After clearing greenhouse crops, fumigate with tecnazene. Give more attention to ventilation, watering and warmth.

CELERY HEART ROT
On being lifted, the insides of plants are found to be rotten. Slugs, frost damage, or careless earthing up allow access to the bacteria responsible.
☐ Take precautions against slugs, including improving drainage. Follow a rotation plan, as with other crops (see p.25). Cultivate and earth up very carefully.

CHOCOLATE SPOT
A fungal infection of broad beans, which causes brown marks on stems and leaves. During damp seasons, the fungus may take over and the plants die.
☐ Spray with benomyl when seen. Lift and burn badly-affected plants.
△ Attend to liming and feed with extra potash; increase growing space.

DOWNY MILDEW
Yellowing of the upper surfaces of leaves is combined with white, furry patches on the undersides. Cool, damp weather favours the fungi responsible; young plants of brassicas, lettuces, onions and spinach are most at risk.
☐ Remove affected leaves and spray with mancozeb. Avoid overcrowding and excessive dampness.
△ Use a copper-based spray.

HALO BLIGHT
A seed-borne fungus disease that results in yellow-edged leaf spots and stunted growth in French and runner beans.
☐ Burn affected plants. Avoid sowing any seeds that are blistered.

HONEY FUNGUS
A widespread parasitic disease. If rhubarb plants die, check for tell-tale white streaks in the rootstock and honey-coloured toadstools nearby.
☐ Burn affected roots. As the infection is persistent, use the site only for vegetables (other than potatoes) for several years; no fruit bushes or trees.

CLUB ROOT
A serious soil-borne fungal infection of brassicas. The roots become swollen and distorted, and the foliage yellows and wilts on warm days. Plants may eventually die. Especially common in acid, poorly-drained soils.
☐ Lime the soil thoroughly. Dust calomel (mercurous chloride) into drills and planting holes, or dip roots in benomyl.
△ Crop rotation and improved drainage help to prevent it being carried over from season to season.

FOOT ROT
The base of the stems of affected plants (peas, beans and tomatoes) first becomes discoloured, then rot. The fungal spores responsible may persist in the soil.
☐ Grow seedlings and container plants only in sterilized compost. If caught early, the disease may be controlled by watering with cupric carbonate or Cheshunt compound (copper sulphate and ammonium carbonate).

LEAF SPOT
Spotting and browning of the leaves, and sometimes the stems, is due to a fungal infection. Beetroots, spinach, celery and celeriac are the plants principally at risk. Leaves may fall prematurely.
☐ Pick off and burn marked leaves. Spray with a fungicide, such as benomyl, cupric carbonate or mancozeb.

MAGNESIUM DEFICIENCY

On tomatoes, the deficiency first shows as a yellowing of the lower leaves. This spreads upward, with leaves eventually turning brown. The leaves of beetroot and spinach, too, become discoloured. The trouble is often due to an excess of potash.
☐ Spray with a solution of magnesium sulphate: 230g (8oz) in 11 litres (2½ gallons) of water, with added soft soap. Spray tomatoes weekly; beetroot and spinach every two weeks.

POWDERY MILDEW

Marrows, cucumbers and related plants are particularly at risk from this fungal infection, which covers leaves and stems with a powdery coating. Dry soil is a contributory factor.
☐ Spray with thiophanate-methyl, benomyl or dinocap. Keep the soil moist.
△ Use a spray made from elder leaves.

RUST

A fungal infection that speckles the leaves of asparagus with rust-coloured spots and gives leeks and onions patches of a similar colour.
☐ Cut off and burn infected foliage. Follow a rotation plan for onions and leeks.
△ Spray with Burgundy mixture after removing infected foliage.

SPRAING

Potato tubers look normal on the outside but show discoloured rings when cut in half. The trouble is viral in origin.
☐ There is no cure. Do not grow potatoes on the same site in successive years. Avoid the variety 'Pentland Dell', which is highly vulnerable, if trouble has occurred previously.

VERTICILLIUM WILT

This fungal infection causes sudden wilting of greenhouse tomatoes, with yellowing of the lower leaves. Total collapse follows. It is most common where crops are grown for several years in the same soil.
☐ Lift and burn diseased plants. Either replace the soil for future crops or use gro-bags.

NECK ROT

A grey mould and rot of stored onions that first appears on the neck. The disease is present, but unseen, while plants are growing.
☐ Destroy affected bulbs. For the future, dress seeds and sets with benomyl powder. Ensure that bulbs are fully ripened and dry before storing.

PARSNIP CANKER

A fungal infection that causes the shoulders of roots to blacken and rot.
☐ There is no cure. For the future, follow a crop rotation programme. Apply lime if the soil is more than slightly acid. Grow the variety 'Avonresister'.

SCAB

Common scab of potatoes causes rough brown patches on the skin, but does little damage. It occurs most often on light soils. In less common powdery scab, the scabs contain powdery spores.
☐ Common scab is exacerbated by lime, so avoid planting in recently-limed soil. Work in plenty of organic matter and do not let the soil dry out.
△ Plant on a 10cm (4in) layer of lawn-mowings.

VIOLET ROOT ROT

Asparagus is especially at risk from this soil-borne fungus. Yellow or dead leaves are an early indication. Violet-coloured threads of the fungus will be seen among the roots. Carrots and seakale may also be affected.
☐ There is no chemical treatment. Lift and destroy affected plants.

VIRUS DISEASES

Virus diseases are caused by minute organisms, transmitted by insects, fungi, seeds or even by the gardener. They gain access to plant tissue through wounds.
☐ There is no cure; lift and dispose of badly affected plants. Buy seeds and plants only from reputable sources.

PETAL BLIGHT

Circular dark patches on the flowerheads of globe artichokes may eventually lead to rotting.
☐ Cut off and burn damaged heads. In future years, spray flower buds with mancozeb or zineb every two weeks until a month before harvest time.

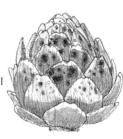

SCALD

Thin-skinned, discoloured depressions may disfigure tomatoes exposed to excessive sunshine, whether in the greenhouse or outdoors.
☐ Shade the glass in a greenhouse and maintain a more humid atmosphere.

SCLEROTINIA

A fungal disease that shows as a white mould on stored carrots, or, sometimes, while they are still growing. Damage is rapid and total.
☐ There is no cure. Burn affected roots and stick to a strict rotation scheme.

WHIPTAIL

A lack of molybdenum causes cauliflower and broccoli leaves to become narrow. Curds and flowerheads fail to develop.
☐ Spray several times with a foliar feed containing molybdenum. Prevent a recurrence by watering on a solution of sodium molybdate.

WHITE BLISTER

This is a form of leaf spot, or small white blisters, that occurs on brassicas and salsify. It is unsightly but seldom causes serious damage.
☐ Pick off badly affected leaves. If practicable, remove some plants to give others more space. Do not grow brassicas on the same site the following year.

POTATO BLIGHT

The principal fungal disease of potatoes, and sometimes tomatoes. Leaves develop brown patches and the edges curl. Before long the haulm disintegrates and the infection spreads to the tubers.
☐ Prevention provides the only real control. Spray during the first half of summer with a fungicide such as mancozeb, or one based on copper, such as cupric carbonate or Bordeaux mixture. Repeat every two weeks in damp weather.

SMUT

During hot summers this disease may infect sweet corn; it results in large 'smut balls' full of fungal spores.
☐ Cut off the growths before they burst and disperse the spores. Burn all the haulm and other material. Wait for a few years before planting this part of the plot with sweet corn again.

SPINACH BLIGHT

Caused by a virus that is spread by aphids, the leaves become increasingly discoloured and distorted.
☐ Spray to control the aphids (see p.172). Lift and destroy affected plants.

WHITE ROT

Members of the onion family are affected by this fungal disease. The leaves yellow and die. A white mould can be seen around the base of the bulb.
☐ Lift and dispose of affected soil. Do not grow onions on the same site for several years. Always dress seed drills with calomel dust (mercurous chloride) before sowing.

WIRE STEM

A fungus disease, principally of brassica seedlings, that causes discoloration and shrinking of the stems. Plants that survive remain stunted.
☐ Improved growing conditions, and the use of sterilized compost, should prevent a recurrence.

The
VEGETABLE COLOUR
CATALOGUE II

Salad plants, even more than most other vegetables, must be home-grown if you wish to enjoy them at their freshest and their best. Lettuces, spinach and chicory are all the better for being eaten with all their flavour and crispness intact. By growing your own, you can also sample the more unusual leafy crops such as rocket and corn salad, as well as the oriental vegetables and the less common herbs which are seldom available in the shops and supermarkets.

The colour plates that follow, while they cannot claim to be totally comprehensive, give an idea of the range and variety of salad vegetables, brassicas, onions and herbs suitable for growing in the food garden.

The separate entries on pages 194–223 give specific details about sowing and individual cultivation requirements, as well as recommending varieties additional to those selected for illustration.

ENDIVE
'Batavian Broad Leaved'

CELTUCE

ENDIVE
'Green Curled'

CULTIVATION DETAILS SEE PAGES 199–201

LETTUCES Selected varieties

CRISPHEAD LETTUCE
'Webb's Wonderful'
'Marmer'
'Great Lakes'

COS LETTUCE
'Lobjoit's Green Cross'
'Winter Density'

CRISPHEAD LETTUCE
'Saladin'
'Avoncrisp'

COS LETTUCE
'Little Gem'
'Dandie'

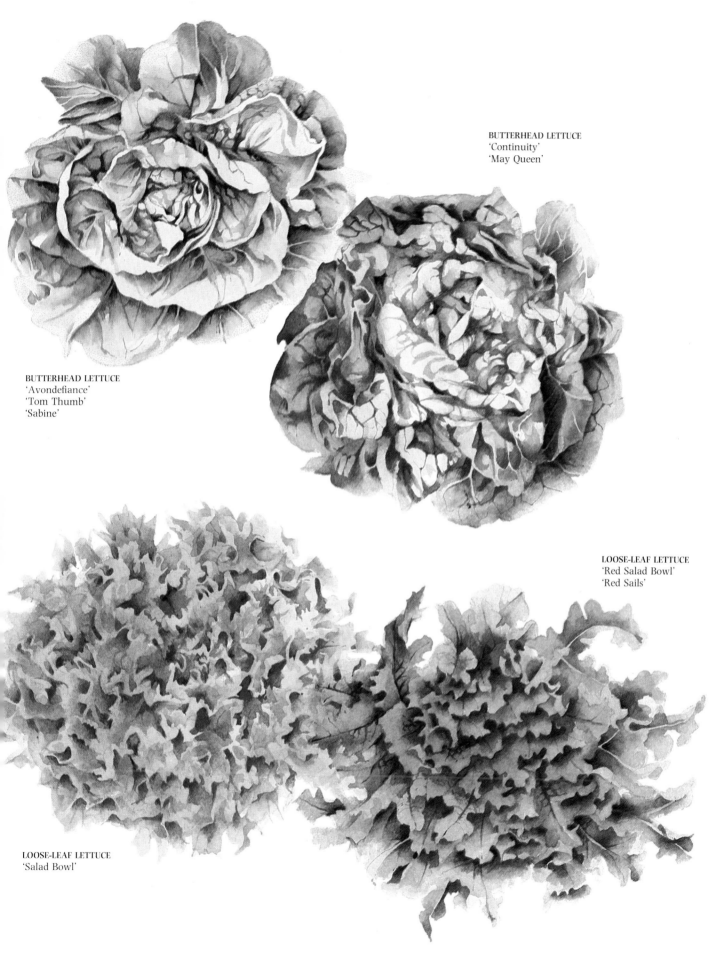

BUTTERHEAD LETTUCE
'Continuity'
'May Queen'

BUTTERHEAD LETTUCE
'Avondefiance'
'Tom Thumb'
'Sabine'

LOOSE-LEAF LETTUCE
'Red Salad Bowl'
'Red Sails'

LOOSE-LEAF LETTUCE
'Salad Bowl'

SPINACH AND LEAFY SALAD VEGETABLES Selected varieties

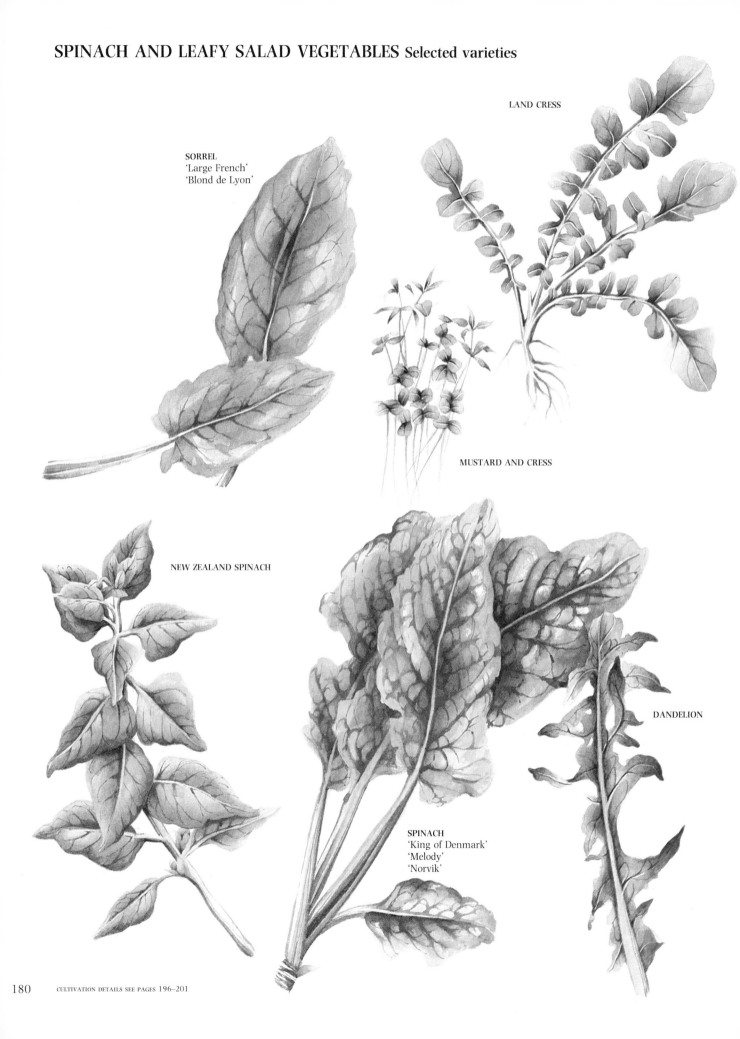

LAND CRESS

SORREL
'Large French'
'Blond de Lyon'

MUSTARD AND CRESS

NEW ZEALAND SPINACH

DANDELION

SPINACH
'King of Denmark'
'Melody'
'Norvik'

'SUGAR LOAF' CHICORY
'Sugar Loaf'
'Crystal Head'
'Winter Fare'

WITLOOF CHICORY
'Normato'
'Witloof'

RADICCHIO
'Rossa di Verona'

ROCKET

CORN SALAD
'Large Leaved Italian'
'Verte de Cambrai'

CABBAGES AND CHINESE VEGETABLES Selected varieties

AUTUMN/WINTER CABBAGE
'Celtic'
'Hawke'

SUMMER/AUTUMN CABBAGE
'Hispi'
'Greyhound'

SPRING GREENS
'Durham Early'
'Wheeler's Imperial'

SAVOY CABBAGE
'Aquarius'
'Ormskirk Late'
'Wivoy'

RED CABBAGE
'Ruby Ball'

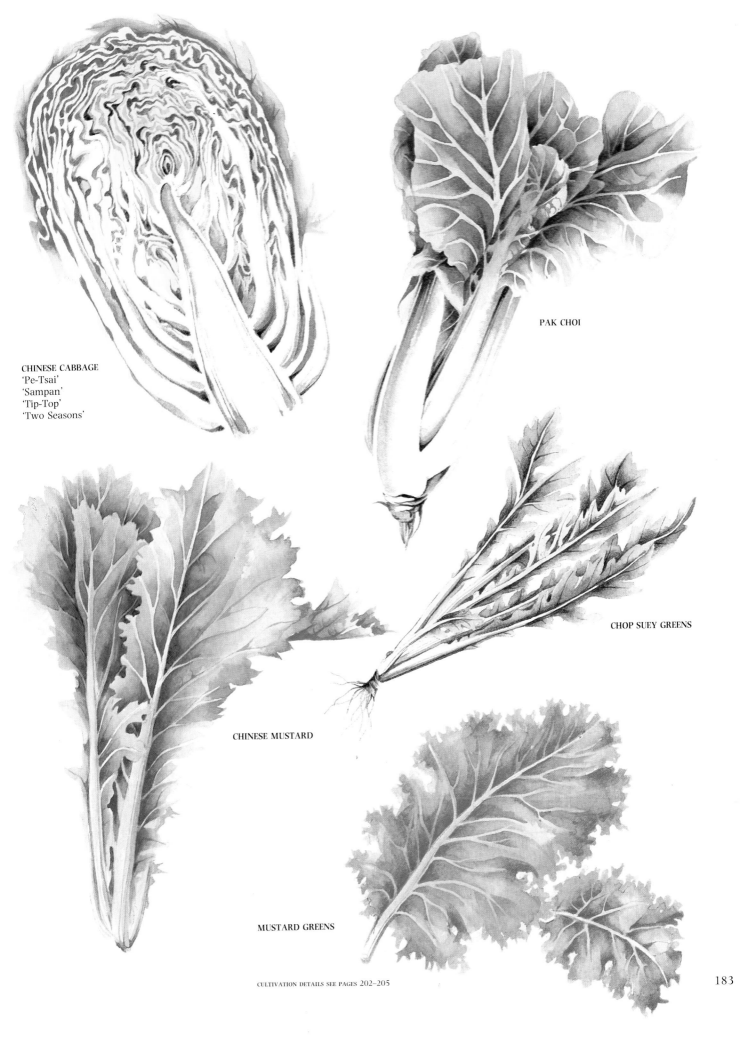

CHINESE CABBAGE
'Pe-Tsai'
'Sampan'
'Tip-Top'
'Two Seasons'

PAK CHOI

CHOP SUEY GREENS

CHINESE MUSTARD

MUSTARD GREENS

CULTIVATION DETAILS SEE PAGES 202–205

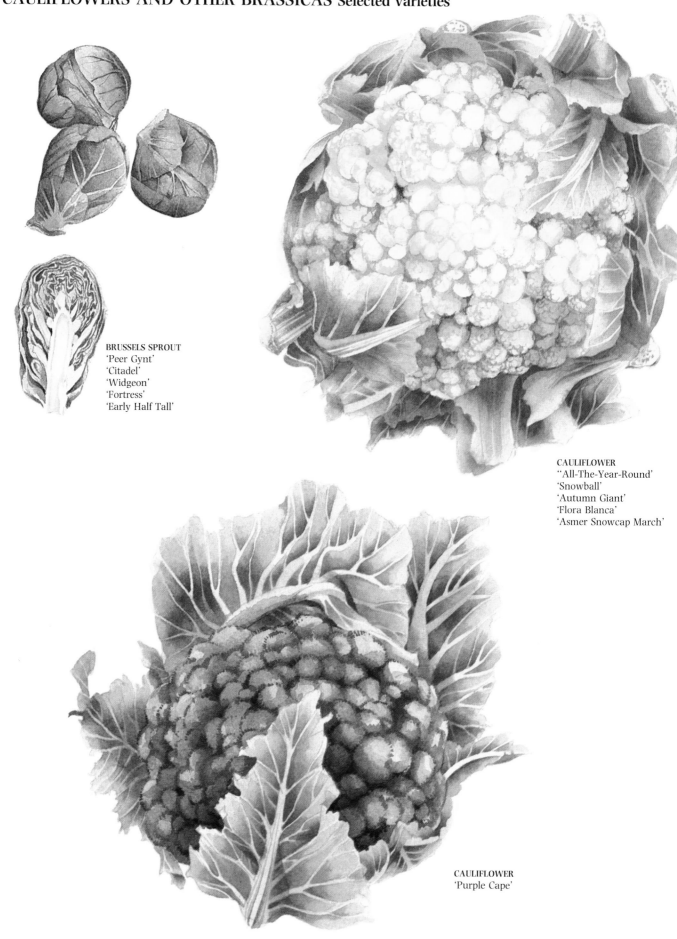

CAULIFLOWERS AND OTHER BRASSICAS Selected varieties

BRUSSELS SPROUT
'Peer Gynt'
'Citadel'
'Widgeon'
'Fortress'
'Early Half Tall'

CAULIFLOWER
''All-The-Year-Round'
'Snowball'
'Autumn Giant'
'Flora Blanca'
'Asmer Snowcap March'

CAULIFLOWER
'Purple Cape'

CALABRESE
'Autumn Spear'
'Corvet'
'Early Romanesco'
'Green Comet'
'Mercedes'

SPROUTING BROCCOLI
'Early Purple Sprouting'
'Purple Sprouting'

KALE
'Dwarf Green Curled'
'Fribor'
'Hungry Gap'
'Tall Green Curled'

KALE
'Dwarf Blue Curled Scotch'

CULTIVATION DETAILS SEE PAGES 206–211

THE ONION FAMILY Selected varieties

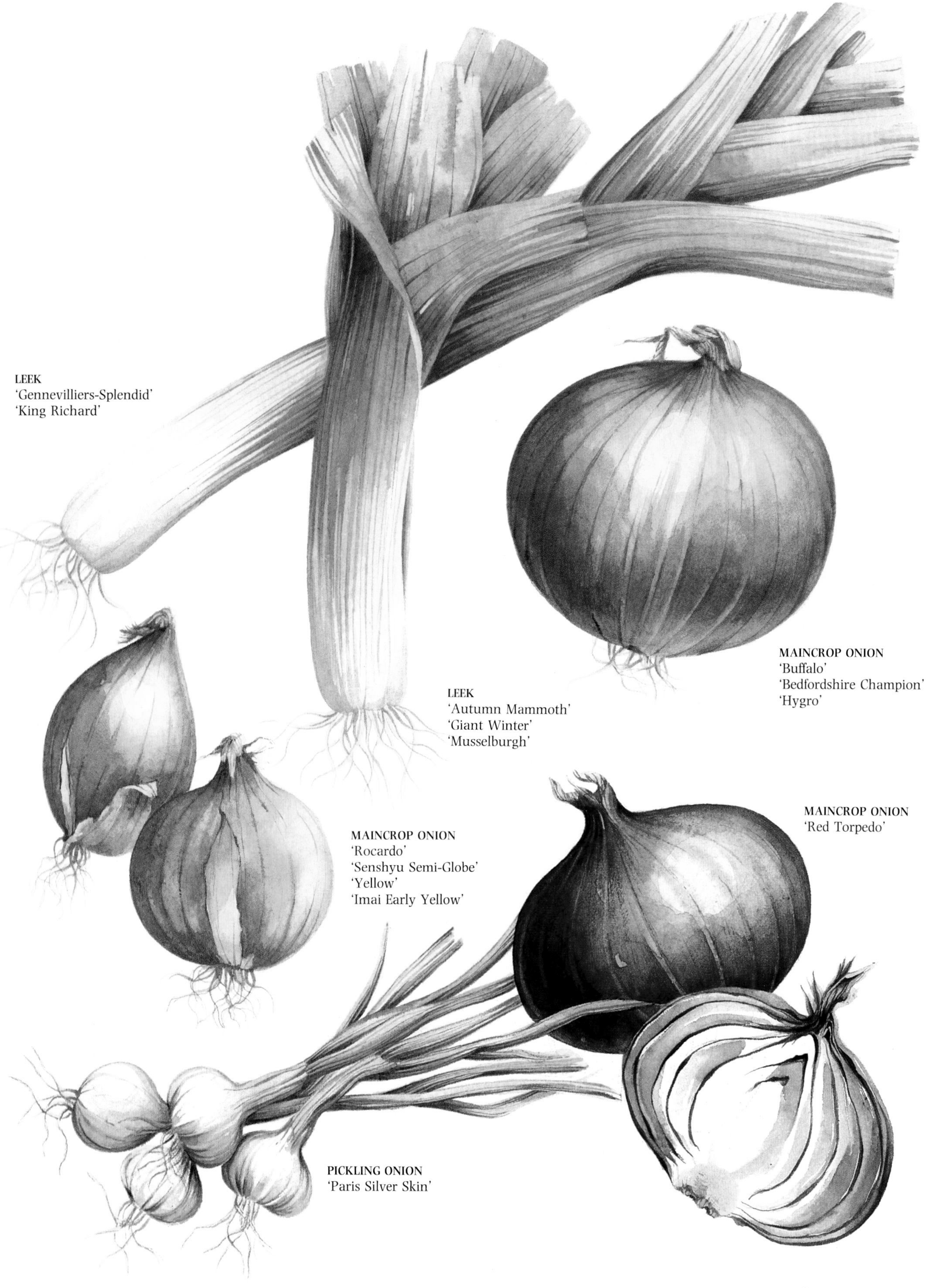

LEEK
'Gennevilliers-Splendid'
'King Richard'

MAINCROP ONION
'Buffalo'
'Bedfordshire Champion'
'Hygro'

LEEK
'Autumn Mammoth'
'Giant Winter'
'Musselburgh'

MAINCROP ONION
'Rocardo'
'Senshyu Semi-Globe'
'Yellow'
'Imai Early Yellow'

MAINCROP ONION
'Red Torpedo'

PICKLING ONION
'Paris Silver Skin'

SPRING ONION
'White Lisbon'
'White Lisbon Winter Hardy'
'Winter White Bunching'

SHALLOT
'Giant Long Keeping Red'
'Hâtive de Niort'

PICKLING ONION
'Giant Zittau'

GARLIC
'Marshalls Long Keeper'

RED GARLIC

WHITE ONION

FRESH GARLIC

CULTIVATION DETAILS SEE PAGES 213–216

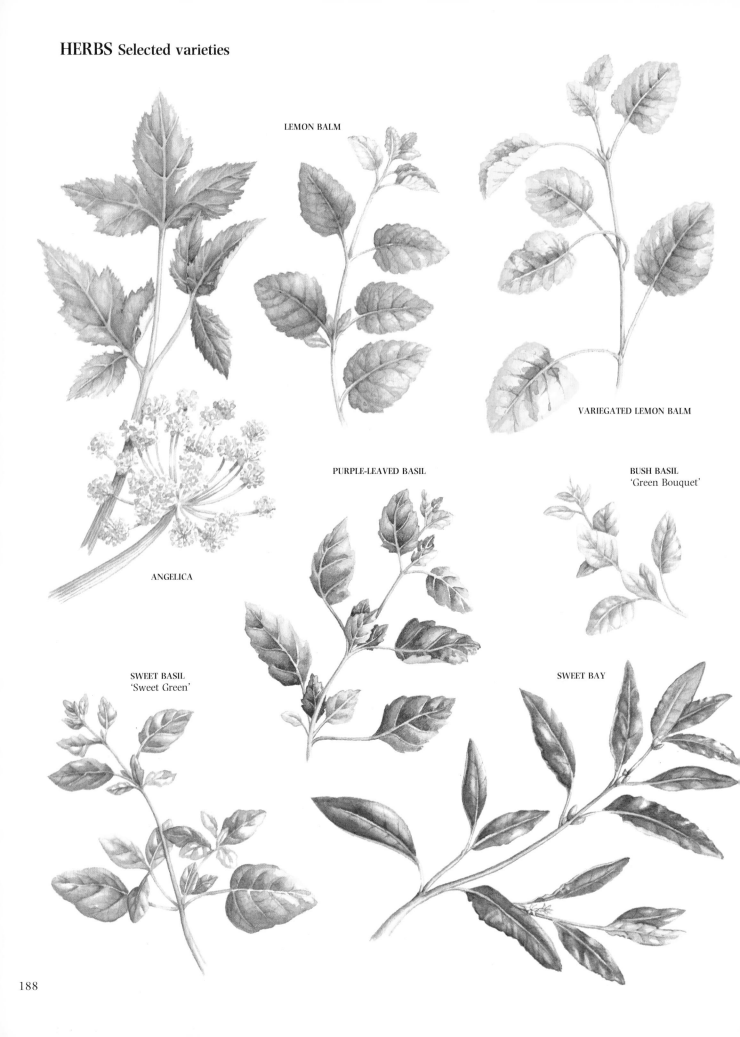

HERBS Selected varieties

LEMON BALM

VARIEGATED LEMON BALM

PURPLE-LEAVED BASIL

BUSH BASIL
'Green Bouquet'

ANGELICA

SWEET BASIL
'Sweet Green'

SWEET BAY

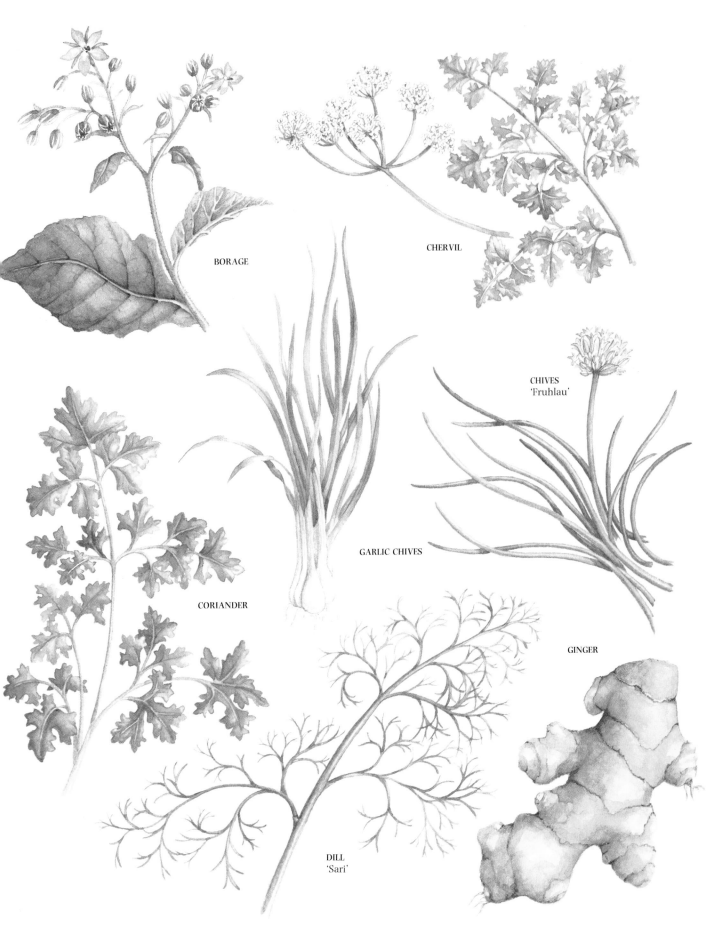

BORAGE

CHERVIL

CHIVES
'Fruhlau'

GARLIC CHIVES

CORIANDER

GINGER

DILL
'Sari'

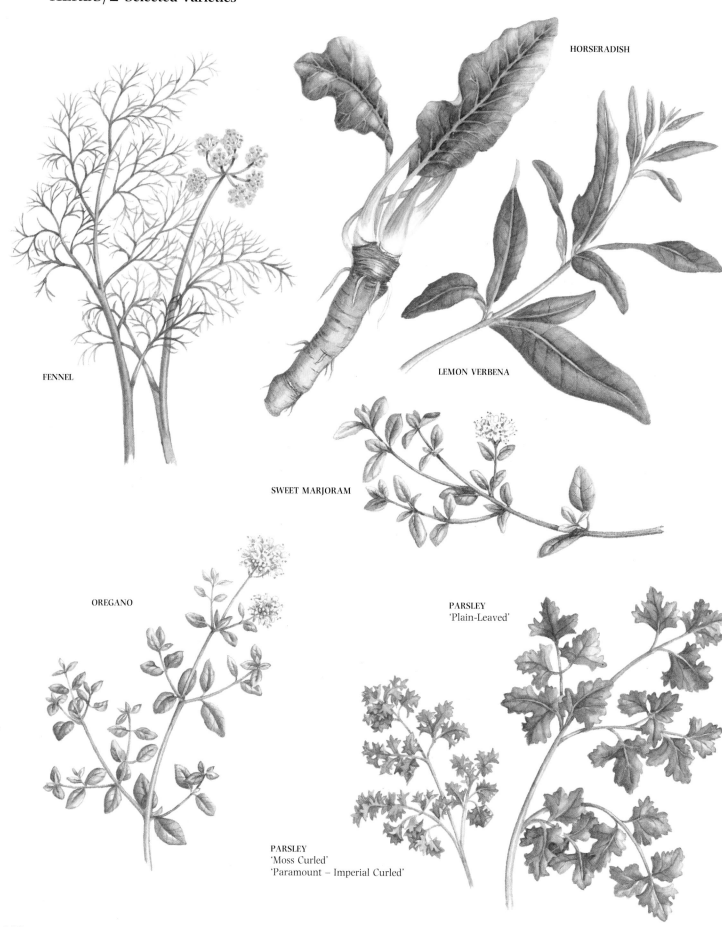

HORSERADISH

FENNEL

LEMON VERBENA

SWEET MARJORAM

OREGANO

PARSLEY
'Plain-Leaved'

PARSLEY
'Moss Curled'
'Paramount – Imperial Curled'

PINEAPPLE MINT

PEPPERMINT

SPEARMINT

SAGE

ROSEMARY
'Miss Jessop's Upright'

GOLDEN VARIEGATED SAGE

PURPLE SAGE

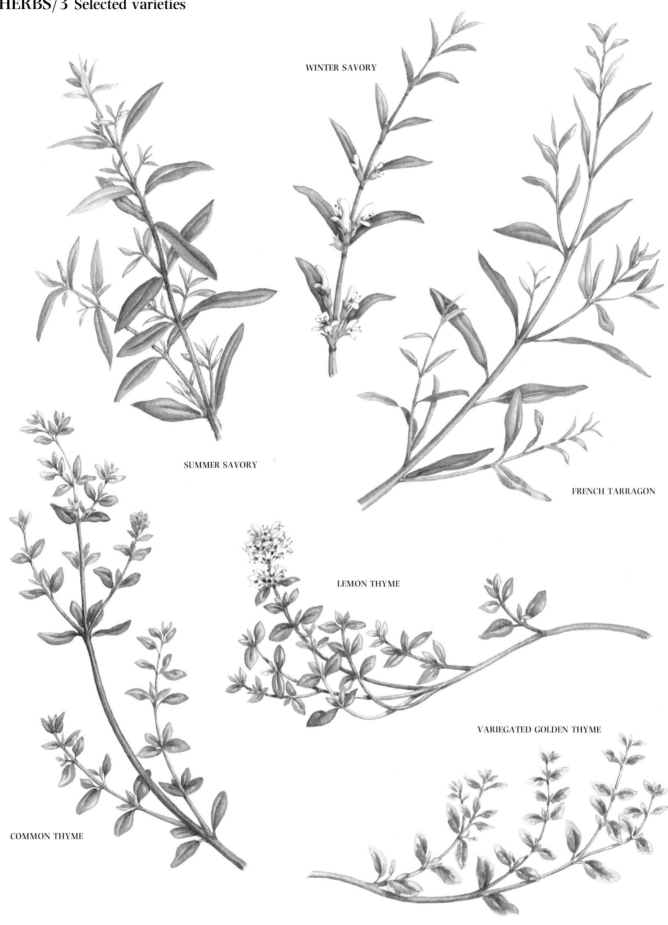

WINTER SAVORY

SUMMER SAVORY

FRENCH TARRAGON

LEMON THYME

VARIEGATED GOLDEN THYME

COMMON THYME

VEGETABLE GARDEN II

Leafy salads and herbs are the prettiest plants in any vegetable garden. They are elegant in shape and varied in the form and colour of their foliage – leaves range through all shades of green to purple, crimson and yellow. Many herbs also offer the bonus of attractive flowers to add to their aromatic foliage.

Growing salads and herbs gives the gardener the opportunity to combine the best of traditional gardening practice with the best of the new species and varieties of plants now available. The idea of the herb garden goes back to medieval times, when herbs were grown for medicinal purposes, rather than as flavourings for food as they usually are in today's vegetable garden.

Your herb garden, which might contain some of the most modern varieties of herbs, could easily be designed to reflect the ancient tradition of herb-growing, and the pages devoted to herbs in the following section give some ideas as to how this can be achieved. If your space is limited, you might prefer to grow your herbs in containers, and they respond well to this type of cultivation.

Both herbs, and the more ornamental types of leafy salad vegetables, would also make attractive additions to the flower garden. For example, you could grow rosemary and bay among your shrubs; add thyme, French tarragon, sage and lemon verbena to your herbaceous border; and edge beds and borders with chives, bush basil, red lettuce or radicchio. Beds of annuals could comfortably contain borage, dill, coriander and chervil.

Nowhere are the new additions to the vegetable garden more obvious than among the salads. As well as new types and colours of lettuce, you could try salads of European origin, such as batavia, endive or radicchio; modern varieties of lamb's lettuce; as well as dandelion, sorrel and other old-established salads that have been 'discovered' and become fashionable.

Other significant newcomers among the salads are the Oriental vegetables. Many specialist garden shops and suppliers now offer seeds of these plants, all of which are brassicas. Most of them are easy to grow, but they should be included in your plans for crop rotation.

Chinese cabbage, pak choi, mustard greens, chop suey greens and shungiku greens are among the most popular and easily-available of the oriental vegetables. Some of them, including chop suey greens, are plants with attractive – and edible – flowers, which makes them especially versatile, in both garden and kitchen.

Also included in the section that follows are the remaining brassicas – cabbages, cauliflowers, Brussels sprouts, broccoli and kale – and the members of the onion family, which supply some of the elements essential to the culinary arts. These include the onions themselves, both maincrop and salad types, and also leeks, garlic and shallots. As with other families of food plants, new varieties of brassicas and onions and their relations are appearing every year, with improvements in flavour and disease-resistance, as well as looks.

When buying seeds or plants to grow in the herb or salad garden, it is worth remembering that most herbs are sold by their species name, rather than a varietal name. So seeds of chervil, for instance, would be labelled with their scientific species name of *Anthriscus cerefolium*.

Many of the new salads, because they have not yet been highly bred, are similarly also sold by their species name, or simply even by a common name such as 'Green in the Snow', though a few named varieties are gradually becoming available from seedsmen and nurseries.

Lettuce is one of the most rewarding of home-grown salad vegetables and there is now a wide variety of different types to choose from – soft, crisp, round, red, curly – many of which cannot readily be bought.

Except in very hot climates, home-grown lettuces may – at least in theory – be enjoyed right through the year, provided there is a greenhouse for the winter crop. In practice, year-round production calls for quite careful planning and management. Consistent results depend on a suitable site and soil, on the right choice of variety for the particular season, and on care and attention during their growing period to forestall any checks in growth. These include overcrowding, sudden changes of environment when transplanting, and dryness. Summer lettuces, in particular, are liable to run to seed in reaction to any of these shortcomings. Early and late crops are especially prone to fungus diseases, and so it is important to select varieties recommended for the season.

As a rule, lettuces need a sunny and reasonably sheltered position. Partial shade will be an advantage during the summer months. Shelter is also particularly valuable for early and overwintered crops. The soil needs to be free-draining and fertile, with plenty of organic matter to hold moisture. Good drainage is vital for winter and spring crops. A neutral or slightly acid soil (pH 6.5–7) is ideal.

Cloches, a cold frame or a greenhouse will all contribute to an extended growing season and continuity of supply. The earliest plants can be raised under glass while the vegetable plot is still too wet to work.

SOIL PREPARATION

It may not be necessary to earmark a special space for lettuces since they are the ideal plant for catch-cropping (using ground left empty between crops) and inter-cropping, whereby the plants are grown between rows of slower-growing vegetables.

If lettuces are treated as a separate crop include them in the legume section of your rotation, where the soil will have been given a good dressing of manure. Dig this in during the previous autumn or winter, and afterward spread lime over the lettuce area if the soil is more acid than about pH6.5.

Two weeks before sowing or planting out, rake in a dressing of general fertilizer at 70g per sq m (2oz per sq yd). Give another, similar dressing once the crop is growing well (though leave this until early spring in the case of winter lettuces). Put these in place two weeks before sowing or planting.

SPACING

Whether sown direct or planted out, allow 30cm (1ft) between rows of lettuces in open ground, and a final spacing of 15–30cm (6–12in) between plants in the row, depending on their ultimate size. The extremes are miniature types such as 'Tom Thumb', and large crispheads such as 'Great Lakes'.

Start thinning lettuces sown outdoors as soon as possible or their quality will start to suffer. Thinning can be done in two stages, the first to 8cm (3in) apart as soon as the seedlings are large enough to handle.

MAKING A START

Lettuces germinate at surprisingly low temperatures, and they transplant reasonably well, which makes it possible to grow them almost all year round.

Sowing *in situ* is used for leaf lettuce, 'Salad Bowl' types and for summer crops where transplanting would be risky. The main drawback is that germination may be poor if the weather is unfavourable.

Indoor sowing gives good quality plants and allows more flexibility over the timing: you can plant them out as and when there is space available in the vegetable garden.

Plant most types of lettuce shallowly, especially when grown under glass, with the seed leaves just above soil level; plant cos types a little deeper.

Protected sowings for an early crop

Sow quick-maturing types of lettuce in late winter or early spring, depending on the mildness of your district: these are for cutting in late spring. Sow direct in a frame or cloches or in a box of seed compost in an unheated greenhouse, a cold frame or under a cloche, for transplanting later.

If you sow in boxes, thin the seedlings or prick them out before they become overcrowded. When large enough, plant them out in a cold frame or under cloches; keep them there until after mid-spring.

Summer lettuces in the open

Sow direct between the first half of spring and midsummer, and thin the seedlings before they can become overcrowded. Surplus seedlings may be transplanted, until late spring, if you wish.

Early winter lettuces under cloches

A sowing made a week or two after midsummer will provide lettuces for late autumn or early winter. Mildew can be a problem, so consider sowing a mildew-resistant variety. Surplus thinnings may be moved to a cold frame. Cover the remainder with cloches from early autumn.

Overwintered lettuces for winter use

Some hardy varieties will stand the winter outdoors, in mild areas. Sow the seeds in summer or early autumn. Covering them with cloches during midwinter improves their quality.

Water the plants well when they are planted out, then avoid watering during the winter months since this heightens the risk of diseases, such as damping off. Thin in two stages: thin to 8cm (3in) during autumn, but leave the final spacing until spring.

Winter lettuces in a greenhouse

Provided you can maintain a minimum temperature of around 7°C (45°F), lettuces can be sown in boxes in early autumn and subsequently planted in the greenhouse border to mature during winter.

TYPES OF LETTUCE

Cabbage lettuces

The most familiar kind, further divided into butterheads and crispheads.

Butterheads, the most widely grown, have smooth-edged leaves. This group includes fast-maturing varieties for spring sowing, hardy kinds, such as 'Arctic King', to sow outdoors during autumn for cutting in spring, and forcing varieties for frames, cloches, cold and heated greenhouses.

Crispheads have firm, crisp leaves, often with crinkled edges. They will germinate at higher temperatures and they grow a little more slowly, but are less likely to bolt. There are summer outdoor varieties and others for sowing or planting under cloches or glass.

Cos lettuces

Cos, or romaine, lettuces have an upright, slender habit, with a crisp heart in the centre of the elongated leaves. They are slower to mature than cabbage lettuces and need good soil.

Loose leaf

This type of lettuce produces masses of individual, tender leaves and no heart. Instead of cutting the whole plant, a number of leaves may be taken from several plants at a time on a pick-and-come-again basis. They last several months and are slow to run to seed.

Mixed seeds

A number of seedsmen offer packets of mixed lettuce varieties. The purpose is to spread maturity over as long a period as possible. They are well worthwhile if you need only a few lettuces at a time.

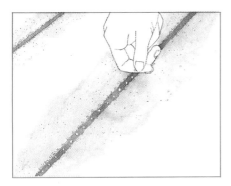

Well-spaced sowing prevents overcrowded seedlings and makes subsequent thinning a lot easier. The task is simplified by pelleted seeds, with each seed encased in a ball of soluble material.

Thin the seedlings in two stages: initially to 5–8cm (2–3in) spacings; increase the gaps a little later as the plants develop. Progressive thinning ensures that there are always plants in reserve should any of them fail to grow.

For the final thinning, alternate plants can be lifted with a trowel for planting elsewhere, until late spring. After this, warmer and drier weather makes them likely to run to seed. Water the row first so that soil adheres to the roots. Lettuces should be transplanted when they have four or five true leaves.

CARE OF THE CROP

Water transplanted seedlings in well if the soil is at all dry. After this, keep it watered during dry weather and hoe regularly. Protect young plants from birds and slugs.

HARVESTING

Lettuces remain fresh longest if they are gathered early in the morning. Pick the first ones young, otherwise the last in the row may run to seed before all are eaten. Pick hearted varieties when the first hearts form.

PESTS AND DISEASES

Potential pests include aphids, cutworms, root aphids, slugs, snails and wireworms.

Ailments include damping off, downy mildew, grey mould and lettuce mosaic virus.

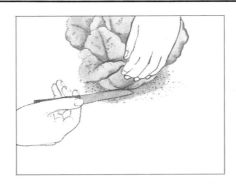

Gather hearted lettuce by cutting through the stem with a sharp knife at ground level. Do this early in the day, and keep the lettuce in a cool place until eaten. Remove stumps from the soil as the row is cleared. Alternatively, pull up the whole plant and cut off the roots.

If cos lettuces seem reluctant to form a tight heart, secure the leaves gently with raffia or string or a large elastic band. This will ensure that the inner heart, at least, becomes crisp and blanched.

LEAF LETTUCES

If you are content with leaves rather than hearts, sow closely in rows or broadcast from mid-spring and cut the crop with scissors or a sharp knife, rather than gathering individual plants. Cos lettuces are best; if you cut them about 2.5cm (1in) above the ground a second crop will grow, ready for gathering a month or so later.

First clear perennial weeds. To broadcast, scatter seeds very thinly over an area of about a square metre or yard, then scuffle them gently into the surface. Use black cotton to protect the patch from birds. To sow in rows, form shallow drills 10–13cm (4–5in) apart, and sow sparingly. Thin with care to a final spacing of about 2.5cm (1in).

RECOMMENDED VARIETIES
Butterhead + suitable for early sowing * for over-wintering only.
All-The-Year-Round' Reliable; solid hearts.
* **'Arctic King'** Compact habit; very hardy.
'Avondefiance' Resistant to root aphids and mildew. Dark green.
'Continuity' Red-tinged; fine flavour.
'Sabine' Tight, crisp heads. Mildew-resistant.
+ **'Tom Thumb'** Small, sweet and tight-hearted. Early maturing.
Crisphead
'Avoncrisp' Slow to bolt. Resistant to root aphids and mildew.
'Great Lakes' Large, dark green heads. Frilled leaves.
'Minetto' Early-maturing, with crisp hearts.
'Saladin' Large, slow-maturing. Disease-resistant and slow to bolt.

'Webb's Wonderful' Long-time favourite.
Cos + suitable for early sowing.
* also suitable for autumn sowing.
+ **'Little Gem'** Quick-maturing and compact. Fine texture and flavour.
+ * **'Lobjoit's Green Cross'** Large, crisp, dark green heads.
+ * **'Winter Density'** Intermediate cabbage/cos shape. Fine flavour.
For protected sowings
'Dandie' Ideal for a winter crop in a warm greenhouse. Upright habit.
'Marmer' Crisphead lettuce, best in a frost-free greenhouse.
'May Queen' Medium-sized lettuce for over-wintering in a frame or under cloches.
Loose-leaf varieties
'Red Sails' A decorative lettuce that remains deep red even during hot weather.
'Salad Bowl' A constant supply of tender young leaves, but no heart.

SOWING SEEDS OUTDOORS, pages 36–37
SOWING UNDER GLASS, pages 38–39

SPACE-SAVING METHODS, pages 132–133
LETTUCES, pages 178–179

PESTS AND DISEASES, pages 172–175

195

Besides the true summer and winter spinach (*Spinacea oleracea*), a variety of leafy vegetables, including spinach beet and Swiss chard, are included under this heading. They resemble spinach and can be eaten raw or used and cooked in much the same way.

Summer and winter spinach are both fast-growing annuals which are fairly tricky to grow. The main danger is that they readily run to seed in hot, dry conditions. Summer spinach may be sown from late winter until late spring to provide a succession of tender leaves from early summer onward. The seeds are round and smooth. Winter spinach is sown in late summer and harvested during the winter and into the following spring. The seeds have a rough, prickly surface.

The other crops all remain in the ground for longer than summer and winter spinach and must therefore be given a place in your crop rotation plan (see p.25). Spinach beet and Swiss chard are closely related; they are both hardy biennials and more tolerant of hot, dry conditions. New Zealand spinach is a half-hardy annual which continues to grow all summer, even on the poorest soil; it produces mild-flavoured leaves which have a spinach taste. Sorrel is a perennial herb whose leaves resemble those of spinach although their flavour is much sharper.

Both summer and winter spinach need to be sown in really fertile soil, so that rapid growth is guaranteed. A heavy soil is more suitable than a light, sandy one; if you have light soil you would do better to try one of the spinach substitutes. The pH should be about neutral. Their tendency to run to seed should be kept in check provided they have ample moisture and nourishment.

Summer spinach, especially the later sowings, should do well in partial shade. Winter spinach dislikes cold, wet conditions and requires a sheltered site, fully open to the sun.

SUMMER SPINACH: MAKING A START

Summer spinach, because it is so fast-growing, is a good catch-crop to grow on land that will be vacant for a few weeks in spring. In midsummer it can be sown between rows of vegetables such as peas or beans that will provide shade for the growing plants. Whatever your cropping plans, the soil should be dug and well-manured during the previous autumn or winter.

Sow the seeds from early spring as soon as the soil is sufficiently dry and crumbly. Two weeks before sowing, rake in general fertilizer at 70g per sq m (2oz per sq yd).

Draw the drills 1cm ($\frac{1}{2}$in) deep and, if you are sowing more than one row, 30cm (1ft) apart. It is best to sow little and often to ensure a continuity of supply. Sow thinly.

CARE OF THE CROP

Thin the seedlings as soon as they are large enough to be pulled out with finger and thumb. Leave 15cm (6in) between remaining plants. Water at the first hint that the ground may dry out. Hoe regularly and rake in another dressing of general fertilizer, at the same rate as the first, when the plants have started to grow well.

HARVESTING

When the leaves have grown sufficiently large – 8–12 weeks after sowing – start picking some from each plant. Do not pull them, which may loosen the plant roots; either cut them or pinch them off. Continue picking every week or so and take up to half the leaves from each plant.

Copious watering is essential during dry spells, otherwise the plants are likely to run to seed prematurely. Frequent soaking with a hose will ensure that the ground does not dry out, especially on light soil.

WINTER SPINACH: MAKING A START

Prepare the soil as for summer spinach; choose well-drained ground and sow during late summer or early autumn. Water the drills first if the weather is warm and dry. Leave the second fertilizer application until late winter or early spring.

It is a great help, though not essential, to cover the crop with cloches from autumn onward. The plants will grow better and the leaves will be more tender. Pick sparingly, taking a few leaves from each plant at a time.

PESTS AND DISEASES

Aphids and slugs may sometimes give trouble on spinach.

Summer and winter spinach may suffer from downy mildew, leaf spot, manganese deficiency and spinach blight.

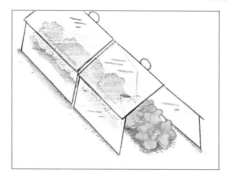

A covering of cloches makes all the difference to winter spinach. This will keep the plants growing more reliably during cold weather and will make the leaves more tender. Barn cloches are ideal for the purpose.

RECOMMENDED VARIETIES

Summer

'Bloomsdale' Leaves are deep green. Slow to run to seed.

'King of Denmark' Upright variety. Leaves are less gritty, being held clear of the ground.

'Melody' F1 hybrid. Dark green leaves, resistant to downy mildew.

'Norvak' Abundant leaves and slow to bolt.

'Symphony' F1 hybrid. Another slow-to-bolt variety, with large, dark green leaves.

Winter

'Broad-leaved Prickly' Fleshy, dark green leaves and very hardy.

'Monnopa' Hardy, bolt-resistant and mild-flavoured.

'Sigmaleaf' A dual-purpose summer/winter variety. Slow to run to seed.

This low-growing, fleshy-leaved, trailing plant (*Tetragonia expansa*) is not a true spinach. It produces mild-flavoured, spinach-like leaves and will grow on the poorest soil. It is half-hardy, however, and therefore vulnerable to frost. It may be sown outdoors during the spring, once it is safe to do so, or else sown indoors for planting out later.

New Zealand spinach continues to grow right through the summer. Its main advantage is that it does not run to seed, even in dry soil, and in this respect it offers a marked advantage over true summer spinach. Ideal conditions are provided by light soil that has been dug and manured during the previous autumn or winter.

MAKING A START
To raise seeds indoors sow in a pan of seed compost and germinate in gentle warmth – about 13°C (55°F) – a little before mid-spring. Soak the seeds for a few hours first. Cover with glass and paper until the seeds germinate.

When seedlings are large enough to handle, prick them out 5cm (2in) apart in a seed tray. In late spring, move them to a cold frame for hardening off and dress the planting site with a balanced general fertilizer at 70g per sq m (2oz per sq yd).

Plant out when there is no further risk of frost; set the plants 60cm (2ft) apart in rows 90cm (3ft) apart.

To sow direct outdoors, allow 90cm (3ft) between the drills and sow two or three seeds every 60cm (2ft). Later reduce the seedlings to a single strong plant in each of the positions.

CARE OF THE CROP AND HARVESTING
Give a second, similar dressing of fertilizer when the plants are growing strongly. Encourage growth by watering in dry weather, and by pinching out the tips of the shoots.

Pick the young shoot tips, each bearing two or three leaves, frequently, as soon as there are sufficient to be worthwhile. The older leaves become tough.

There are no named varieties. The plants are usually free from pests and diseases.

This hardy biennial (*Beta vulgaris* 'Cicla'), sometimes called 'perpetual spinach', is a form of beetroot grown for its tender leaves rather than its roots. The leaves are used like spinach, though they are somewhat coarser in both texture and flavour. An abundant crop is produced on land liberally dressed with manure or compost during the previous autumn or winter. This plant is useful over a longer period, and seldom runs to seed until its life-cycle is completed late the following spring.

MAKING A START
Sow in mid-spring, after raking in a dressing of general fertilizer at 70g per sq m (2oz per sq yd) two weeks before. Draw the drills 40cm (15in) apart and 1cm (½in) deep. Sow the seeds thinly.

CARE OF THE CROP AND HARVESTING
Thin the seedlings to 30cm (1ft) spacings. Once the plants are growing strongly, apply another similar dressing of fertilizer, and hoe this in around the plants. On poor soil, apply a dressing of a high-nitrogen fertilizer to help to promote leaf growth. Water in time to prevent the soil from drying out.

Start picking the leaves before they become too large; take a few from the outside of each plant. Pick frequently, to encourage continuous cropping, and because the leaves become coarse if left to mature.

There are no named varieties. Pests and diseases are as for summer and winter spinach (see facing page).

SWISS CHARD
Swiss chard (*Beta vulgaris* 'Cicla'), otherwise known as seakale beet, is an easily-grown member of the beetroot family. The green leaves are cooked like spinach. Their thick white leaf midribs, and the supporting stems, are cooked and eaten like asparagus.

An attractive form of this tall, vigorous plant, called ruby, or rhubarb, chard, has red stems and red-tinted foliage. It is handsome enough for any flower border.

Like spinach beet, Swiss chard is a hardy biennial and it responds to the same treatment and spacings. Sow it a little later, in late spring, and, ideally, cover with cloches during the winter. Pull the leaves, since cutting makes the plants bleed.

Sorrel (*Rumex* spp.) is a common plant, often found growing as a weed. But cultivated plants can, by removing their flowering stems, be induced to produce a continuing supply of fresh, sharply-flavoured young leaves. Those picked in the wild are likely to become tough and dry once spring is over.

The young sorrel leaves, which have a deliciously sharp, lemony flavour, can be used finely chopped in salads, preferably mixed with a blander leaf vegetable; the larger leaves can be cooked like spinach. Sorrel is also used as the basis for a number of soups and for a sharply-flavoured sauce.

In addition to the native wild plant, *Rumex acetosa*, with narrow, arrow-shaped leaves, there is a species found principally in Europe, *Rumex scutatus* or French sorrel. This has shield-shaped leaves, wider at the base, and a particularly acid flavour. Both are perennials and grown in the same way. Once established, sorrel is one of the first of the perennial plants to emerge in the spring; *Rumex acetosa* is slightly earlier.

MAKING A START
Choose a sunny situation and fertile soil which retains the moisture. In dry soil the plants will be much less productive. Sow the seeds in mid-spring in a shallow drill, and thin the seedlings to 20cm (8in) spacings. Alternatively, sow them thinly in a window box, or in a tub or large pot.

Keep the soil moist to ensure steady growth. Pinch out the flowering heads when they appear.

Once they are large enough, take a few leaves per plant at each picking. They will freeze well if there is a surplus, and it is better to pick regularly than to leave the plants untouched for long periods.

To increase your stock, divide the roots in spring or autumn, and replant the pieces at once. It is a good idea, in any case, to divide the plants every three years or so.

Sorrel is seldom troubled by any pests or diseases.

RECOMMENDED VARIETIES
'Large French' Tangy and very early.
'Blond de Lyon' Another French variety.

SOWING SEEDS OUTDOORS, pages 36–37
SOWING UNDER GLASS, pages 38–39

STALKS AND SHOOTS, pages 116–117
PESTS AND DISEASES, pages 172–175

SPINACH AND LEAFY SALAD VEGETABLES, pages 180–181
FREEZING VEGETABLES, pages 232–233

The diverse group of chicories (*Cichorium intybus*) includes two main kinds. The type generally classified as Witloof or Belgian chicory requires forcing during the winter to produce blanched, tightly-packed shoots, called 'chicons'. Their somewhat bitter taste is modified by the blanching process. Though forced chicory is slightly more trouble to grow, it makes a welcome change for winter salads and can also be braised and eaten as a cooked vegetable.

The other type, often categorized under the varietal name 'Sugar Loaf', looks more like a giant cos lettuce, with densely packed, crisp leaves. It is gathered, unblanched, during autumn and early winter. Its quality is improved if it can be given winter protection in an unheated greenhouse or under cloches outdoors. The inner leaves of this chicory are blanched naturally through lack of light, and are sweeter than the outer ones. The leaves may be eaten raw or cooked like spinach.

In addition to these two main kinds, there is also a group of deep red and variegated chicories, which have a dramatic appearance. They start off green but turn deep red when the weather becomes colder. Exposure to the cold also makes their taste less bitter. They can be left in the ground for winter use or else the roots lifted and forced like Witloof chicory; forcing turns them a pale pink colour and gives milder-flavoured, more tender shoots. Depending on the district in which they are grown, they may need a covering of straw or cloches in the winter, to extend their period of usefulness. They make a crisp, tasty salad vegetable.

Chicories are a good choice of salad crop since they are available during the winter, when lettuces and other salad crops are most scarce. They can be grown easily and successfully in most climate zones since they are fairly hardy and virtually free from pests and diseases. If you are short of space, you can delay planting unblanched ones until the summer crops have been cleared.

None of the chicories is particularly fussy about soil, though they do best in fertile ground and an open, sunny situation. Ground manured for a previous crop is best for forcing varieties, which may otherwise develop forked roots, but non-forcing kinds will thrive in land dug and manured during the previous autumn or winter. In both cases, apply a general fertilizer at 35g per sq m (1oz per sq yd) two weeks before sowing.

When forcing chicory indoors, lift the roots in batches, trim off most of the leaves and then plant up to four roots in each 23cm (9in) pot. Light garden soil will do, or else use peat or compost.

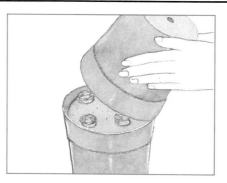

Cover the planted pot with another of similar size and stand it in a fairly warm room where the temperature is reasonably stable. Cover the top hole in the upper pot to exclude all light.

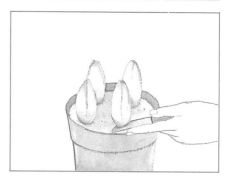

Within a month the chicons should be 15cm (6in) high and ready for eating. Cut them just above the base, and at once cover the pot again to encourage a second, if smaller, crop of young shoots.

WITLOOF CHICORY: MAKING A START AND CARE OF THE CROP

Sow seeds in late spring or early summer in drills 1cm (½in) deep and 30cm (1ft) apart. Thin the seedlings to 15cm (6in). Keep the soil moist and topdress it with a general fertilizer at 70g per sq m (2oz per sq yd) once the plants are growing strongly. Hoe regularly and remove flowering shoots to build up good roots.

FORCING OUTDOORS

This method is less trouble and gives tighter chicons, but they take longer to develop. The soil must be free-draining.

Cut off the leaves once night temperatures are almost freezing; leave stumps of about 2.5cm (1in). Cover these with 15cm (6in) of soil; set cloches over the top. Cut sparingly once blanched shoots appear.

FORCING INDOORS

Start lifting the roots in small batches from late autumn onward; discard those that are small or forked. Cut off all but 2.5cm (1in) of the leaves. Alternatively, lift them all at the same time and place them in a shallow trench (see p.44), just covered with soil.

Force only a few roots at a time, to give a continuous supply of chicons during the winter. The roots will be about 30cm (1ft) long; trim the ends first, if necessary. Then stand three or four in a 23cm (9in) pot, with damp soil or old potting or seed compost packed between them. Invert a similar pot over the top and cover the drainage hole. Place the pots in total darkness in a moderately warm room, attic or cupboard, or under the staging in a greenhouse, at about 10–13°C (50–55°F). The shoots will take about three weeks to emerge.

Cut the chicons when they are about 15cm (6in) high, just above their base. Dampen the soil and cover them again to encourage a secondary, smaller crop.

Those that cannot be eaten straight away should be wrapped in foil or kept in the refrigerator; they will become green and bitter if exposed to light.

PESTS AND DISEASES (ALL TYPES)

Though seldom affected by disease, chicory may be attacked by cutworms, slugs and snails, and caterpillars of the swift moth.

RECOMMENDED VARIETIES

'Normato' F1 hybrid forming particularly tight heads, whether forced indoors or out. 'Witloof' The most widely used variety. 'Witloof Zoom' An F1 hybrid producing chicons of uniformly high quality.

'SUGAR LOAF' CHICORY: MAKING A START AND CARE OF THE CROP

Sow seeds up to late summer, with drills 1cm (½in) deep and 30cm (1ft) apart. Place three or four seeds in stations 25cm (10in) apart and leave only the strongest seedlings, or sow sparingly for subsequent thinning; the 'thinnings' can be used in salads. Water well before sowing.

Leave the remaining plants to heart up. Keep them hoed and water as necessary to prevent drying out. Topdress with general fertilizer at 70g per sq m (2oz per sq yd) once the crop is growing well.

HARVESTING

Start cutting the heads during the autumn. They are only moderately hardy, but should last well into the winter if covered with cloches before the onset of severe frosts.

RECOMMENDED VARIETIES

'Sugar Loaf', 'Crystal Head' and 'Winter Fare' all give large, long-lasting, crips heads during autumn and early winter.

Cut through the stems of non-forcing chicories, such as 'Sugar Loaf', at soil level from autumn onward.

RED-LEAVED CHICORY

This beautiful group of varieties is also known as radicchio or Italian chicory. Sow and grow it as for 'Sugar Loaf' kinds. From autumn on, cut and eat them as the heads mature, or lift and force them as for Witloof varieties.

The red chicories are reasonably winter-hardy, but will benefit from some protection. The main risk is from rotting in damp weather. To minimize this risk, avoid overcrowding and keep the plants weed-free. If you use a frame or greenhouse, keep it well-ventilated.

RECOMMENDED VARIETIES

'Rossa di Verona' Deep red leaves; maroon and white chicons if forced.
'Treviso' Upright heads early in spring.

Endive (*Cichorium endivia*) is often thought of as a type of lettuce, since it has much the same growth habit and use, but in fact belongs to the chicory family. Its flavour is more bitter than that of lettuce, and for this reason the plants are generally blanched for a period before being eaten to make them milder in flavour.

Endive, like chicory, is an excellent winter salad crop, since it is readily available at a time when lettuces are least plentiful. It may be grown during the summer too, principally for the sake of its original taste and appearance. It is also relatively immune to pests and diseases and less likely than lettuce to bolt in hot weather.

For a winter crop it is necessary to grow the Batavian type of endive, or escarole. This is a tall plant, with broad, wavy-edged

leaves. The curly endive, a flat, lower-growing plant with frilled leaves, is less hardy and therefore more suited to summer and autumn crops. It also has a tendency to rot in damp, cold weather.

Endive is a vigorous but slow-growing crop; it lends itself to being cut successively if the roots are left in the ground after cutting. Both kinds need the same growing conditions as lettuce – that is, fertile, well-drained but moisture-retentive soil and, as a rule, an open position. However, since endive has something of the tendency of lettuce to run to seed in hot, dry conditions, spring-sown plants would benefit from a little shade.

Grow endives in soil that has been well-manured during the autumn or winter before sowing.

MAKING A START

Sow frilled varieties from spring to midsummer; the latest sowings will provide an autumn crop. Hardy, broad-leaved kinds may also be sown from spring and a late-summer sowing provides a winter crop.

Give the seedbed a dressing of general fertilizer at 70g per sq m (2oz per sq yd) about two weeks before sowing. Sow the seeds where the plants are to grow, drawing the drills 1cm (½in) deep and 40cm (15in) apart. Sow very thinly; water the drills first.

CARE OF THE CROP AND BLANCHING

Thin the seedlings of frilled varieties to 25cm (10in) spacings, and those of broad-leaved endives to 40cm (15in) spacings. Make sure that the soil remains moist, or the plants will suffer a growth check and may run to seed. Give a second, dressing of fertilizer once the plants are growing well.

Crops being grown for a winter harvest are best covered with cloches or grown in a frame or an unheated greenhouse.

It is mostly the curly-leaved endives that need blanching, since they are at their most bitter in hot weather. The broad-leaved kinds require little blanching since their central leaves are naturally crisp and pale as a result of their lack of exposure to light.

If you wish to blanch the leaves, wait until the plants are mature and choose a time when the leaves are dry. Tie them loosely with soft string, or raffia and cover each plant with a large, porous pot or similar lightproof container, with its drainage hole covered. Do not use a plastic pot, since warmth inside causes the build-up of pests and diseases. Blanch only two or three plants at a time, since they deteriorate soon after being exposed to the light. Sprinkle slug pellets around them before covering.

HARVESTING

Blanching takes a week or so during warm weather but up to three times as long in late autumn and winter. Cut through the stem with a sharp knife and use at once.

PESTS AND DISEASES

Apart from slugs and snails, there are likely to be few problems.

RECOMMENDED VARIETIES

'Batavian Broad-Leaved', 'Batavian Green' and 'Cornet de Bordeaux' are hardy broad-leaved varieties.
'Green Curled', 'Moss Curled' and 'Frisée de Namur' are curly endives suitable for summer and autumn use.

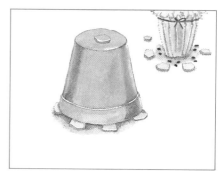

Cover each tied plant with a flowerpot, after sprinkling some slug pellets around the base. Place a few small crocks beneath the rim to allow some ventilation but cover the drainage hole to exclude light. Blanching is fastest in warm weather.

SOWING SEEDS OUTDOORS, pages 36–37
SOWING UNDER GLASS, pages 38–39

PESTS AND DISEASES, pages 172–175
CELTUCE AND ENDIVE, page 177

SPINACH AND LEAFY SALAD VEGETABLES, pages 180–181

199

Mustard and cress are almost always paired as a quick-growing salad crop; they are equally useful in sandwich fillings and as a garnish. However there are advantages to growing them separately so that the two can be mixed according to taste.

Cress (*Lepidium sativum*) has a peppery tang and you will probably use a smaller quantity of it. White mustard (*Sinapis alba*), which is the kind usually grown, has a pungent, hot taste, but some people prefer to grow the milder-flavoured salad rape (*Brassica nigra*). Cress germinates more slowly so, for a mixed crop maturing at the same time, sow cress three days earlier.

It is possible to grow mustard and cress in the garden, but more satisfactory, as a rule, to sow the seeds indoors. Outdoors, the low-growing plants become splashed with soil, although this is less likely under a cloche or in a frame.

SOWING OUTDOORS
Fine, light soil is needed; water it well before sowing. Sow at any time during the spring or summer, though choose a shaded spot for warm-weather crops. A cold frame is ideal.

Scatter the seeds closely over a small area, and press them into the surface with a short length of board. Cover with a cloche if in open ground, and leave one end uncovered. Do not allow the soil to dry out while the seeds germinate and the shoots begin to develop.

SOWING INDOORS
Place several layers of blotting paper, or kitchen paper, or cotton wool in a seed tray, or cover the bottom with peat or a peat-based compost. In each case make sure that the lining is thoroughly damp before scattering the seeds quite thickly. Press them down lightly then cover the tray with glass and folded paper. In the winter place the tray in a warm position in the house, or in a heated greenhouse.

Uncover when the seeds germinate and place the tray in a well-lit position. Allow a few more days for the seedlings to become darker green and to expand fully. Keep the lining moist.

HARVESTING
Cut the crop with scissors when the stems are about 4–5cm (1½in–2in) high, Outdoor sowings will give repeat crops.

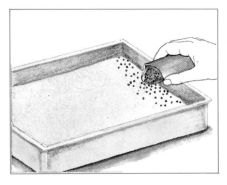

Layers of blotting paper or kitchen paper make a growing medium for mustard and cress, for the seedlings need only moisture. Place this in a seed tray or similar low-sided container.

Scatter the seeds fairly thickly, sowing the cress three days before the mustard to allow for its slower growth rate. Use separate containers for each type of seed.

Cover each tray with a sheet of glass to conserve moisture and folded paper to exclude light. Turn the glass daily to prevent condensation dripping onto the seeds. Remove as soon as they germinate.

Use scissors to harvest the mustard and cress when it has grown to about 5cm (2in) high. Discard the remains of indoor-grown plants, though follow-up crops can be expected from outdoor sowings if these are kept watered.

Land cress (*Barbera praecox*), also called American cress, has a similar hot flavour to watercress and may be used in the same way in soups, salads, for garnishing and for other purposes.

This low-growing hardy annual provides pickings as quickly as two months after sowing. It is grown in two batches as a rule, one to provide a summer crop and the other for the winter.

Land cress tolerates most types of site, although it runs to seed rapidly in hot weather. It will thrive in damp, shady positions and north-facing situations that would suit few other vegetables. It can also be intercropped between taller vegetables such as brassicas. For the best results, dig in plenty of manure or compost, well before sowing, to nourish growth and ensure ample moisture-retention.

MAKING A START
For a summer crop, sow during the spring. For a winter supply of leaves, sow in early autumn. Provided the site has been well-manured, any further fertilizer should be unnecessary.

Set the rows 23cm (9in) apart and sow the seeds thinly in shallow drills. Soak the soil first if sowing time coincides with a dry spell. Sprinkle slug pellets over the soil as a precaution against attack by these pests.

CARE OF THE CROP
Thin the seedlings to 15cm (6in) apart when they are big enough to handle. Provided the soil was kept damp, they should transplant successfully.

Keep the soil moist by frequent watering during dry spells. Autumn-sown plants will remain more active, and their leaves more tender, if they are covered with cloches during the colder months.

HARVESTING
Start picking the outer leaves when the plants are about two months old. Later, cut only young, tender shoots and leave the centre of the plant intact while it is still producing new growth.

PESTS AND DISEASES
Slugs and snails are the most frequent problem, although flea beetle is a hazard in the early stages. Disease is unlikely.

Rocket (*Eruca sativa*), or 'Italian cress', is another old-fashioned hardy annual which, like corn salad, is currently enjoying a revival of popularity as a 'new-wave' salad ingredient. It is especially useful during the winter when lettuce may be in short supply. Rocket leaves have a sharp flavour: the young leaves are best, since the older ones have a hotter, more distinctly spicy taste. The attractive flowers can also be eaten.

Rocket grows best in cool conditions. Since it is fast-growing, it can be used for inter-cropping or catch-cropping. If grown during the winter months, it is best cloched to keep the leaves tender.

MAKING A START

Prepare the soil as for corn salad and give the plant the same spacings. Sow in late summer or early autumn for a winter crop, and during spring for a summer crop. The plants run to seed easily, so provide light shade and ample moisture for spring-sown plants.

It is also possible to sow seeds very early in the year under cover, to give continuous cutting throughout the spring.

CELTUCE

Celtuce (*Latuca sativa* 'Angustana'), known as stem lettuce or asparagus lettuce, is an oriental lettuce on a long edible stem. The young leaves may be eaten raw or cooked and the stem is peeled and sliced and either eaten raw in salads or cooked like celery. The heart of the stem is crisp and crunchy, with a delicate taste.

Celtuce is grown like summer lettuce, but it usually needs a well-manured soil and plenty of moisture to do well. It makes a good autumn and winter crop from a later summer sowing.

Sow the seeds between spring and summer in shallow drills 45cm (1½ft) apart. Thin the seedlings, when they are large enough to handle, to 25–30cm (10–12in) apart.

Water the plants well. Hoe regularly between the rows to prevent competition from weeds.

Pick the leaves once they are big enough to make a worthwhile harvest. The stem will be ready to eat about three months after sowing.

This hardy annual (*Valerianella locusta*), also known as lamb's lettuce, grows wild in cornfields and has been eaten for centuries. It is currently enjoying a new popularity as an ingredient of *nouvelle cuisine* types of salad, usually mixed with lettuce. The flowers are edible too. Corn salad is also a good substitute for lettuce during the winter. Cloches will help to maintain growth during the coldest months; they will also keep the leaves more tender.

A sunny, sheltered position provides the best growing conditions. The soil needs to be well-drained and the plants will perform best if it has been dressed recently with plenty of well-rotted manure or compost.

MAKING A START

For a winter crop, sow during late summer or early autumn in drills 2cm (1in) deep and 30cm (1ft) apart. This spacing may be reduced to 15cm (6in) when you are growing crops in beds. Thin the plants when they have three true leaves to 10cm (4in) apart.

You can also sow the seeds broadcast, or in drills, in the spring and summer.

CARE OF THE CROP

Water the plants generously for the first few weeks after sowing and hoe frequently.

HARVESTING

Once there are sufficient leaves for a worthwhile picking – about three months after sowing – take a few of the largest leaves from each plant at a time.

RECOMMENDED VARIETIES

'Large Leaved Italian' Very hardy. Leaves and flowers can be eaten raw.
'Verte de Cambrai' Round leaves which are smaller and darker green.

Pick the leaves from corn salad plants little and often. Since they are quite small, this means that a number of plants must be grown in order to provide sufficient material for gathering at any one time. Wash the leaves well, since they grow very near the ground and easily become mud-splashed.

Dandelion leaves (*Taraxacum officinale*), blanched or green, make a pleasant addition to spring salads. They can also be cooked like spinach. They have a distinct, tart flavour, which is sweetened by blanching. Dandelion leaves are at their best in spring, when the leaves are young and pale green. After midsummer, they tend to become coarse and bitter, then they die back in mid-winter.

As every gardener knows, these hardy perennials grow readily in most soils and situations. However, the leaves will be more succulent if grown in a rich soil. Rather than rely on chance weeds, sow one of the cultivated strains of dandelion, available from seedsmen, which have larger, more tender leaves.

MAKING A START

Sow the seeds in late spring in drills 1cm (½in) deep and 30cm (1ft) apart. Later thin the seedlings to a spacing of about 15–23cm (6–9in).

CARE OF THE CROP AND HARVESTING

When the plants mature, cut off their flowerheads. Blanch some plants in early spring, if you wish, by covering them with a large flower pot. Either discard the plants afterward, or else allow them to recover during the rest of the summer. Alternatively, pick the leaves green throughout the spring and early summer, and leave the plants to grow from year to year.

RECOMMENDED VARIETIES

'Large-Leafed Salad' Sharp-tasting leaves for salads, which can also be blanched to sweeten them.

SOWING SEEDS OUTDOORS, pages 36–37
SOWING UNDER GLASS, pages 38–39

SPINACH AND LEAFY SALAD VEGETABLES, pages 180–181
CHICORY, pages 198–199

PESTS AND DISEASES, pages 172–175

Cabbages (*Brassica oleracea* 'Capitata') are the chief member of the brassica family and comprise several varieties. They come in various shapes – mainly round, conical and loose-leaf forms – and in a variety of colours. These include not only dark green, light green, white and red, but also those with pink, purple or bluish variegations.

Cabbage had, until recently, a poor culinary reputation, mainly on account of its strong taste and smell and because it was habitually overcooked. But many of the newer varieties have a much more subtle flavour; provided you grow these and cook them so that they stay crisp, cabbage is first-rate. Red and white cabbages can also be pickled, or grated and used as a crisp winter salad vegetable.

All cabbages are hardy and easy to grow. The cultivation methods are broadly similar for all types. The timings and crop spacings differ according to variety, however, and there are one or two other minor variations.

All cabbages need similar growing conditions. The ideal is an open site, free from shade, where there is firm, fertile, free-draining soil that contains plenty of organic matter. If the manure or compost was supplied for a previous crop, so much the better, and since cabbages follow nitrogen-rich legumes in the usual rotation or crops, this is often the case. Otherwise, work in a moderate dressing of well-rotted manure or compost some months before planting. Avoid freshly-manured ground and loose, recently-worked soil.

Sow the seeds in a separate seedbed, then set out the young plants in their final positions when they have four or five leaves. Spring cabbages may be sown *in situ*.

Spread lime over the soil surface following winter digging and before planting cabbages. This prevents the acid conditions that inhibit the growth of cabbages and other brassicas. It also helps to reduce the risk of club root disease to which these plants are prone.

TYPES OF CABBAGE: WHEN TO SOW AND HARVEST

There are classes of cabbage suited to sowing and cutting at particular seasons. By choosing an apt selection, cabbages can be harvested all year.

Spring cabbage This valuable crop matures quickly once the worst of the winter weather is over and does not grow as large or coarse as winter cabbage. Sow during late summer and plant in early autumn to provide both hearted cabbages and loose-leaf 'spring greens' the following year.

Timing is particularly important for spring cabbages. Sown too early, plants may grow too large and soft to withstand severe frosts, but sown too late, they will not have time to develop beyond the seedling stage before the weather gets colder. In cold areas, sow a week or two after midsummer to give the plants time to develop before autumn. Sow two weeks later in warmer districts.

Covering with cloches in mid-winter is worthwhile in cold areas.

Summer cabbages Sown in mid-spring, these varieties will be ready for cutting during late summer and early autumn. For an earlier crop, sow a fast-maturing variety in a frame in early spring. Most summer cabbages have round, dense heads, with only a few outer leaves.

Red cabbage This autumn-maturing type has a compact habit. It needs a long growing season to be at its best, and this involves overwintering. Sow the seeds in late summer or autumn in a seedbed and thin to prevent overcrowding. Protect them with cloches in cold districts or during a very severe winter. The following spring, plant them out.

Winter cabbages These hardy cabbages, sown during the second half of spring and ready from autumn onward, are one of the principal winter crops. There are two basic types – those, such as 'Christmas Drumhead', that have fairly smooth leaves and mature early, and crinkly-leaved savoys, which are ready some time between autumn and spring. One or two with slightly wrinkled leaves, such as 'January King', are at their best during the period up to mid-winter.

MAKING A START

About two weeks before sowing all types except spring cabbage, dress the eventual planting site with a general fertilizer at 90g per sq m (2oz per sq yd). Firm the bed and rake it into a fine tilth. When sowing in a seedbed, form drills 1cm ($\frac{1}{2}$in) deep and 15cm (6in) apart. Thin overcrowded seedlings.

Transplant the young cabbage plants from the seedbed when they have four or five leaves. The permanent site should also be firm. Use a dibber to form planting holes; set each plant in its hole and then push the dibber in again alongside it, to press soil against the roots. The spacings for different types are given below.

Water the plants in gently and provide temporary shading if the weather is hot and dry (see p.40).

To sow spring cabbages *in situ*, draw the drills 1cm ($\frac{1}{2}$in) deep and 30cm (1ft) apart. Sow thinly and later remove surplus seedlings to give a spacing between plants of 10cm (4in); they will be thinned to their final spacings the following spring.

SPACINGS

Spring cabbages Thin to leave 30–40cm (12–15in) between plants sown *in situ* or transplanted from a seedbed early in spring (see Harvesting, opposite).

Summer cabbages Allow some 40cm (15in) between rows and also between plants in a row. A spacing of 30cm in each direction is sufficient for compact varieties.

Winter cabbages Leave about 45cm (1$\frac{1}{2}$ft) between rows, and 40–45cm (15–18in) between plants, depending on variety. The large savoys need the most space.

Red cabbages Leave 60cm (2ft) in each direction.

A dibber is the best tool for planting cabbages of all types, since plants need to establish firm contact with the soil. Form a hole with the pointed end of the dibber, place the plant roots in the hole and press the soil against them.

CARE OF THE CROP

Remove any shading once the leaves have ceased to be floppy, but ensure that the soil does not dry out while the plants are developing fresh root systems. Once they are growing strongly, give summer and winter cabbages a further, similar dressing of fertilizer. Wait until spring before giving spring cabbages a topdressing.

Hoe regularly to keep down weeds; take care during this operation since cabbages hate root disturbance. Draw some soil around the stems of spring and winter cabbages. Remove dead leaves from plants and take action at once if significant numbers of whiteflies are seen.

Apply a third and final dressing of fertilizer to summer and winter cabbages about a month after the second dressing.

Cabbages need plenty of nitrogen to ensure rapid, healthy growth. If given as part of a general fertilizer, apply half as a base dressing before sowing seed, and the remainder as a top dressing around the growing plants.

HARVESTING

Start thinning out the spring cabbage rows in early spring; remove plants in pairs to leave those remaining spaced 30–40cm (12–15in) apart. Leave the smaller spacing between cabbages to be harvested as 'spring greens' and the larger between the hearted cabbages. Spring greens may be pulled from the soil but gather hearted cabbages by cutting through the stems with a knife.

For a further crop, cut a cross, about 1cm (½in) deep, in the top of the stump. The growths that will develop from each stump can be eaten as 'greens' while they are still tender.

Cut summer and winter cabbages when the heads are firm and fleshy. The flavour of savoy cabbages is said to be better after a slight frost. Red cabbages and the white Dutch winter types, such as 'Polonius', may be lifted in late autumn and stored until needed (see pp.226–7).

Dig up and burn all cabbage stumps when the crops are harvested.

PESTS AND DISEASES

The principal pests are caterpillars, cabbage root flies, flea beetles and slugs and snails.

Possible diseases and ailments are club root, downy mildew and white blister.

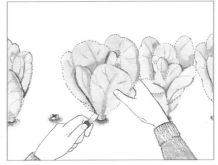

Spring cabbages can be planted close together. In early spring remove plants for eating as spring greens so that those remaining are 30cm (1ft) apart; they will grow into hearted cabbages. When harvesting, by cutting the stumps crossways with a sharp knife, four separate shoots will be induced to form.

RECOMMENDED VARIETIES

Summer/autumn
'**Derby Day**' Round-headed and early. Ideal for cold-frame sowings.
'**Greyhound**' Fast-maturing, with a conical head and good flavour.
'**Hispi**' F_1 hybrid. The earliest summer cabbage. Tender, pointed heads.
'**Minicole**' Compact white heart, maturing in early autumn.
'**Ruby Ball**' F_1 hybrid. Late-summer red cabbage with a fine flavour.
'**Winnigstadt**' Compact, pointed heads maturing in late autumn.

Autumn/winter
'**Celtic**' F_1 hybrid. Mid-winter cabbage with a large, solid head.
'**Christmas Drumhead**' Compact, blue-green heads maturing in late autumn.
'**Hawke**' F_1 hybrid. Matures in autumn; lasts for up to two months.
'**Holland Winter White**' A Dutch white variety that can be eaten raw.
'**Polonius**' F_1 hybrid. Another white cabbage, excellent for coleslaw.

Savoy
'**Aquarius**' F_1 hybrid. Compact, hybrid version of 'January King'.
'**January King**' Hardy, mid-season cabbage. A long-established favourite.
'**Ormskirk Late**' Solid heads maturing from New Year until spring.
'**Winter King**' Blue-green heads, ready in early winter.
'**Wivoy**' F_1 hybrid. Excellent quality and stands until mid-spring.

Spring
'**April**' Compact, pointed, early-maturing heads.
'**Durham Early**' Dark green, pointed heads. Occasionally runs to seed.
'**Offenham – Spring Bounty**' Medium to large pointed heads. Very hardy.
'**Spring Hero**' F_1 hybrid. Round-headed, with a good flavour.
'**Wheeler's Imperial**' Small, pointed, dark green heads.

SOWING SEEDS OUTDOORS, pages 36–37
PLANTING VEGETABLES, page 40

CABBAGES AND CHINESE VEGETABLES, pages 182–183
PESTS AND DISEASES, pages 172–175

STORING VEGETABLES, pages 226–227

CHINESE CABBAGE

Chinese cabbage, (*Brassica pekinensis*) or Chinese leaves, is a relative newcomer to the vegetable garden and has as much in common with lettuces as with ordinary cabbage. In appearance, it resembles a giant cos lettuce; in the kitchen, the leaves are used raw for salads or can be stir-fried or braised or simmered briefly.

As they are brassicas, Chinese cabbages should take their place in the rotation of crops along with other members of the brassica family. Where they differ from the other brassicas, apart from their milder flavour, is in the lack of frost-hardiness, their speedy growth and their marked disposition to run to seed. For all these reasons, it is better to sow the seeds in summer than in spring, and to harvest the crop during the autumn.

Because of the plant's tendency to bolt, it is better to sow plants *in situ* than to move them from a seedbed. The inevitable stress that transplanting causes is a significant factor in inducing the production of flowers and seeds. However, some of the more recent F_1 hybrid varieties are bred to be resistant to bolting, so these are the ones to choose for planting.

To make rapid growth, Chinese cabbages need really fertile, moisture-retentive soil. You need to dig in an ample supply of organic matter, in the form of manure or compost, some months before sowing. If Chinese cabbages are grown as a follow-up to early potatoes, peas or autumn-sown broad beans, you should give an additional light dressing of well-rotted material.

Choose a part of the plot that gets a reasonable amount of sunshine, although shade for part of the day will be an advantage in the summer months. Apply lime after the preparatory digging if a soil test shows that it is on the acid side – much below pH 6.5.

About two weeks before sowing, rake a dressing of general fertilizer into the site, at 90g per sq m (3oz per sq yd).

MAKING A START

Sow around midsummer, or a week or two later. Draw the drills 1cm ($\frac{1}{2}$in) deep and about 45cm ($1\frac{1}{2}$ft) apart, then water the soil thoroughly through a fine rose if the weather is warm and dry. Either sow the seeds very thinly, and later thin the seedlings to give 30cm (1ft) spacings, or else place them in groups of three or four 30cm (1ft) apart. In this case, remove all but the strongest seedling from each group after germination.

Sow Chinese cabbages in groups to save seed. Soon after germination, remove all but the strongest seedling from each position and leave this to grow. Seedbed sowing is unwise, since transplanting encourages bolting.

CARE OF THE CROP

More than most vegetables, Chinese cabbages need abundant moisture throughout the growing period. Dry soil means an inevitable check to their development.

Some time after thinning, and when the plants have started to grow strongly, give two further dressings of general fertilizer, each at 90g per sq m (3oz per sq yd); leave an interval of two weeks between them. Hoe each dressing in, and water generously if soil and weather are dry.

Hoe regularly to prevent competition from weeds, and scatter slug pellets in late summer to discourage those pests.

Given good growing conditions, the cabbages will usually form solid hearts without assistance. If the outer leaves seem floppy, however, it helps to tie the whole head, fairly loosely, with soft string or raffia.

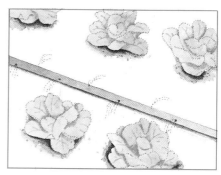

A trickle hose that waters the soil rather than the leaves is ideal for Chinese cabbages. Plants need abundant moisture in order to ensure steady growth and to minimize the risk of their running to seed.

HARVESTING

Chinese cabbages grow quickly and may be ready for picking as little as nine weeks after sowing. Cut them as they mature during the autumn. The thick midrib makes good eating, along with the green part of each leaf.

Leave the stumps in the ground and cover them with cloches, for a secondary crop of tender greens. If there are still cabbages in the ground when frost threatens, cut them, place them in plastic bags and store in a refrigerator.

PESTS AND DISEASES

The principal pests are caterpillars, cabbage root fly, cabbage whitefly, flea beetles and slugs and snails.

Diseases and ailments that may arise are club root and downy mildew.

Chinese cabbages, like the tallest types of cos lettuce, may need securing with string or raffia during late summer. Secure in two places but keep the ties fairly loose. Take precautions against slugs and snails.

RECOMMENDED VARIETIES

'**Pe-Tsai**' Slender, pale green hearts.
'**Sampan**' F_1 hybrid. Large hearts, slower to bolt than some.
'**Tip-Top**' F_1 hybrid. Large, barrel-shaped, bolt-resistant heads.
'**Two Seasons**' F_1 hybrid, resistant to bolting even if spring-sown.

Oriental vegetables' crisp texture and their subtle, interesting flavours make them excellent for eating raw in salads or for light cooking, such as stir frying. Most oriental brassicas, or 'Chinese greens', are fast-growing and are harvested in autumn and winter, when other vegetables are in short supply. Many seed companies, and specialist merchants stock the seeds.

CHOP SUEY GREENS

This edible species of annual chrysanthemum, also known as shungiku or garland chrysanthemum, is pretty enough for the flower border. It has yellow flowers and deeply cut, bright green fleshy foliage. Allowing the plants to flower is somewhat counter-productive to achieving the maximum number of tender leaves, but the flowers themselves can be eaten fresh or dried, added to soups and stir-fried dishes.

The leaves have a distinctive, aromatic scent and a slightly pungent flavour. They form a major ingredient of well-known dishes such as Chop Suey.

Shungiku leaves can be ready for picking within two months from the time the seeds are sown. This speedy growth makes shungiku a good plant for catch-cropping and inter-cropping (see pp.132–3).

Any ordinary soil will do for chop suey greens, provided it contains plenty of organic matter and retains mosture well. Choose a sunny spot for spring sowings but light shade for a summer-sown crop, because of the risk of bolting. Sow at any time between spring and autumn in rows 23–30cm (9–12in) apart; thin to 10cm (4in).

Keep the soil moist to promote rapid growth and discourage bolting. The leaves are best at about 13cm (5in) long and should be used soon after picking.

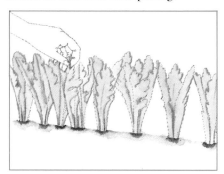

Chop Suey greens will keep growing over a much longer period if the flowering stems are pinched out at an early stage. Similarly, frequent harvesting of the leaves will help to maintain growth of tender new foliage.

LEAFY CHINESE MUSTARDS

This group includes several different hardy plants that provide good quantities of tasty winter greens when cut frequently.

'Green in the Snow' (*Brassica juncea*) This mustard grows up to 45cm (20in) tall and has fairly coarse-textured leaves with a sharp flavour; the young leaves can be shredded and eaten raw in salads but the older ones should be lightly cooked.

'Tendergreen' mustard spinach (*Brassica rapa*) This fast-growing winter crop looks like spinach. The leaves are mild-flavoured and smaller ones can be used whole in salads; larger leaves need shredding.

Japanese 'Mizuna' (*Brassica juncea 'Japonica'*) This plant has deeply-dissected, dark green fern-like leaves and looks pretty in a flower bed. It is low-growing (up to 20cm/8in) and useful for intercropping between taller plants. Cut either individual leaves or the whole heads just above ground level; the plants will resprout several times.

Mustard greens (*Brassica juncea*) This useful autumn and winter crop is especially popular in the USA. The leaves have a slight peppery tang. Small young leaves can be chopped and eaten raw in salads, and even the full-sized leaves remain tender. As with perpetual spinach, continual picking encourages the production of new leaves.

There are both smooth-leaved and curly-leaved varieties of mustard green. A dramatic-looking variety called 'Mike Giant' has huge leaves with striking purple veins.

Besides a late summer or autumn sowing, the seeds can also be sown in early spring for a late spring or early summer harvest. They have a tendency to bolt if they are planted too late in spring.

For all these leafy mustards, the principal season of use is autumn and early winter, with the main sowing made around mid- or late summer. An early autumn sowing is also worthwhile if you can spare cloches for winter protection. With rapid growth in mind, choose a spot that contains plenty of organic material. Light shade is best for a summer sowing, though the plants are generally slow to bolt.

Sow the seeds *in situ* or transplant the seedlings from a seedbed. Allow 30cm (1ft) between rows as a general rule, and thin the plants within each row to a similar distance. 'Green in the Snow' and Japanese 'Mizuna' require less space – thin the former to some 15–20cm (6–8in) and the latter to 23cm (9in) apart.

Keep the plants well watered and hoe frequently to prevent competition from weeds. Take precautions against slugs during damp weather, especially while the plants are still young.

LEAFY CHINESE BRASSICAS

This is a blanket name for several hardy, quick-growing plants also known as 'celery mustards' or 'Chinese celery'. The best-known examples are 'Chinese Pak Choi' and 'Japanese White'. The 'celery' part of their name derives from the appearance of the stems, which are thick and pure white.

The plants are compact and slow to bolt, with bright green, rounded, glossy leaves. Both the leaves and stems are edible: they are succulent and mild-flavoured. The leaves in the centre are particularly good eaten raw in salads, while the outer leaves can be used for stir-frying or be lightly braised. They are generally robust and relatively disease-free.

The soil conditions and cultivation requirements are broadly similar to those of their taller and more pungent counterparts, the leafy mustards. Being smaller plants, however, the celery mustards need a spacing between them of only 23cm (9in) in each direction.

Celery mustards grow rapidly and can be cut within five or six weeks of sowing. Though the leaves may be gathered individually, the stumps will resprout if the base of each stem is severed.

FLOWERING MUSTARDS

This group of oriental vegetables is grown chiefly for its edible flowers. Two main types are available:

Flowering Purple Pak Choi This decorative, small-leaved brassica (*Brassica campestris 'Purpurea'*), also known as 'Hon Tsai Tai', produces tasty flowering purple stalks. Both the young flowering stems and the leaves can be stir-fried or lightly braised and served with sauces or with meat or fish.

Hon Tsai Tai needs a fertile, moisture-retaining soil. It is best used as a quick catch-crop or inter-crop since it takes up little space before flowering. Sow the seeds in spring for a summer crop, in cool areas, or in autumn for harvesting in early spring. It will survive a light frost, but for added safety should be overwintered in an unheated greenhouse or given the protection of cloches outdoors. Sow the seeds in a seedbed or direct in shallow drills; transplant at, or thin to, 40cm (15in) spacings. Keep the growing plants well-watered.

Flowering Pak Choi This flowering mustard (*Brassica chinensis 'Parachinensis'*), known as 'Chinese Tsai Shim', is less hardy than the purple-flowering type, but has thicker, more succulent shoots. Sow the seeds in spring for late summer and autumn salads. Grow it in the same way, but space the plants 25cm (10in) apart. The flowering shoots can be harvested from 40–60 days after sowing the seeds.

SOWING SEEDS OUTDOORS, pages 36–37
SPACE-SAVING METHODS, pages 132–133

CABBAGES AND CHINESE VEGETABLES, pages 182–183

Brussels sprouts (*Brassica oleracea* 'Bullata gemmifera') are one of the most valuable of winter vegetables. They are remarkably hardy and are able to withstand all but the worst winter weather. By growing suitable varieties for successional cropping, they can be enjoyed from autumn right through until spring. If you grow your own Brussels sprouts, you can be sure of eating them at their best – as small, tightly-formed buttons, which taste far superior to the larger, loose sprouts often found in the shops.

Brussels sprouts have one major drawback: they occupy more space than most other crops and for the greater part of the year. Planted in late spring, they remain in place until at least the following winter. This disadvantage can be minimized by inter-cropping Brussels sprouts with faster-growing plants, such as radishes. Another partial solution is to grow a compact variety, such as 'Peer Gynt' or 'Early Half Tall', which can be planted closer together.

Choice of variety is important in other respects, too. There are early, mid-season and late types, though with overlap. Choose some carefully for a succession.

Equally important, there are 'standard' and F_1 hybrid varieties; the F_1 hybrids are noted for their heavy crops of uniform sprouts. These tend to mature over a relatively short period, whereas those on older, standard varieties develop over a longer period and are much less uniform in size and quality.

Brussels sprouts are reasonably easy to grow, provided that their basic needs are met. First, they are hungry feeders, and require really fertile soil to fulfil their potential. Choose a part of the plot heavily manured for a previous crop; if you think there may be a lack of organic matter, dig in some additional manure or compost the autumn before planting.

The ideal pH rating is 6.5, so spread lime over the dug ground during the winter if a soil test shows a significantly lower reading.

Brussels sprouts also require that the ground in which they are planted should be firm. This is easier to achieve on a heavy soil than on a light, sandy one. If the ground is loose, the roots rock, which means that plants grow less well and may fail to form tight buttons. Digging during the autumn gives the site six months to settle. At planting time, take care not to loosen more than the very top layer of soil.

MAKING A START

Choose a site open to the sun, but sheltered from strong winds. This applies both to the main growing area and to the seedbed where the plants will be raised.

Seeds sown in a cold frame or under a cloche in late winter or early spring will provide a late-summer picking, although it is a widely held belief that sprouts do not attain their full flavour until they have been subjected to frosts.

For the normal autumn and winter harvest, sow the seeds in an uncovered seedbed during the first half of spring. If you are growing more than one variety, sow these in batches over a period of three or four weeks, starting with the earliest.

Whether or not you are growing them under cover, sow the seeds thinly in a drill 1cm ($\frac{1}{2}$in) deep and leave 15cm (6in) between multiple rows. Be sure to label the different varieties accurately, since the seedlings will look almost identical.

Soon after germination, thin seedlings to 5–8cm (2–3in) spacings. If they are too close, they become drawn and spindly.

While the seedlings are growing, rake a dressing of general fertilizer lightly into the top 2.5cm (1in) of the planting site at 90g per sq m (3oz per sq yd).

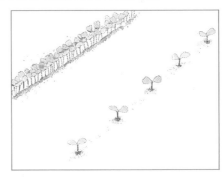

Seedlings of Brussels sprouts will grow spindly and tall if allowed to remain close together in the seedbed. Thin them to 5–8cm (2–3 in) apart as soon as they are large enough to handle, and while they are still at the seed leaf stage of development.

PLANTING OUT

Move the plants to their final positions when they are about 13cm (5in) high. Set them 75cm ($2\frac{1}{2}$ft) apart in each direction, or 50cm (20in) in the case of compact varieties. Plant very firmly, with the aid of a dibber. Use the dibber to make the planting hole first, then press it in again to firm the soil up against the plant.

Ideally, choose a wet day and transplant in the evening if possible. But if the soil is dry, water the plants in well. If planting is followed by a spell of hot, dry weather, rig up some form of temporary shelter over the plants while they develop fresh roots.

If you have plans for inter-cropping, this is the time to sow other seeds between the Brussels sprouts plants.

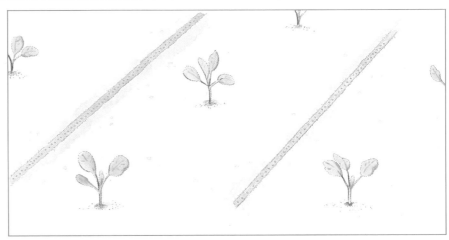

To **save space**, sow a quick-growing crop, such as lettuces, between newly-planted Brussels sprouts. If sown between the rows, or between individual plants in a row, they will mature before the Brussels sprouts have grown very large.

CARE OF THE CROP

Remove any shading once the leaves have ceased to be floppy. Keep the soil moist, however, until the plants are growing strongly. At this stage give another dressing of fertilizer at the same rate as the first, and then draw soil around the plants as a form of support. Apply a third and final top-dressing of fertilizer about a month later.

Hoe regularly to prevent weeds becoming established. If the plot is exposed to the wind, secure each plant – especially the taller varieties – to a cane. Wind-rock would loosen the roots, and lead to the formation of poor-quality sprouts.

In the autumn, take off any yellow leaves and firm the soil around each plant. Watch out for signs of whitefly and take immediate action if you see significant numbers.

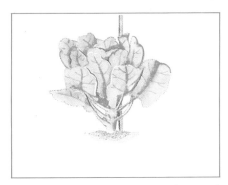

On an exposed site, Brussels sprout plants need support to prevent damage from the wind, especially if they are growing in light soil. Insert canes when the plants are half-grown, and secure the stems to these with string.

HARVESTING

Start picking sprouts at the bottom of each stem. Begin when the bottom ones are the size of a walnut, since small, tight sprouts are crispest and have most flavour. Take a few buttons from each plant by twisting them downward. Sprouts higher up the stem will increase in size to provide a succession of pickings. Remember, also, to remove any open sprouts that have not formed proper buttons.

Harvesting after a frost helps to ensure a good flavour. Mature sprouts can, in fact, be left on the plants for many weeks. Unless the weather turns warm, they will not deteriorate quickly. Once all the buttons have been picked, the plant tops themselves make surprisingly good eating.

The sprouts will form progressively on the stems, starting at the base. Pick them as they become large enough, taking a few from each plant at a time. As you do so, remove any sprouts that are poorly formed.

Dig up the stalks, since they harbour pests. Either chop them into small pieces and mix them into the compost heap, or else dry them under cover and then burn them.

PESTS AND DISEASES

The principal pests are caterpillars, cabbage root flies, flea beetles and slugs and snails.

Possible diseases and ailments are club root, downy mildew and white blister.

RECOMMENDED VARIETIES

(In approximate order of maturing)
F₁ hybrids
'**Peer Gynt**' Compact habit and early, with heavy crops of top-quality sprouts.
'**Citadel**' Produces dark green, tight, medium-sized sprouts.
'**Widgeon**' Medium-sized plants, which are resistant to mildew.
'**Achilles**' Heavy yields of medium-sized, dark green sprouts.
'**Rampart**' Tall plants, noted for their winter hardiness.
'**Fortress**' Short, very hardy plants with dark green sprouts.

Standard varieties
'**Early Half Tall**' Compact plants for an early crop.
'**Bedford – Winter Harvest**' Firm, dark green sprouts from autumn into late winter.
'**Roodnerf – Early Button**' Mid-season crop that lasts well.

SOWING SEEDS OUTDOORS, pages 36–37
CAULIFLOWERS AND OTHER BRASSICAS, pages 184–185
PESTS AND DISEASES, pages 172–175

Kale (*Brassica oleracea* 'Acephala') is one of the hardiest and least demanding of vegetables. After even the most severe winters it will produce its tender young shoots in the spring. It is often grown to fill the midwinter gap when other winter vegetables are scarce. Kale is an ideal crop for cold, wet, northerly climates since it can withstand frost and needs a lot of moisture. It will also be productive in soils where other brassicas would be less happy. Its crisp, curly or flat leaves can either be cooked or eaten raw as a winter salad vegetable.

Kale takes up a considerable amount of space in the vegetable garden, but midsummer planting allows it to follow on after a crop harvested in early summer, such as early potatoes or peas. And for small gardens there are compact varieties, such as 'Frosty', that take up no more space than is occupied by cabbages.

Some kales have curly leaves, such as 'Dwarf Green Curled', whereas others are plain-leaved, such as 'Thousandhead'. Some of the curly-leaved varieties have deep blue-green frilly leaves, which look very ornamental. The curly-leaved varieties, may be picked from late autumn onward, but the best eating from both types is provided by the young shoots that appear later in the season.

The closely-related rape kale (*Brassica napus*), of which 'Hungry Gap' is the best-known example, is sown later and produces a mass of tender shoots from early spring onward.

Provided it has good drainage, kale will grow in most soils. It needs a reasonably open situation, however, and does best in moderately-fertile ground. Land manured for a previous crop is ideal; if necessary, add lime to give a pH level of around 6.5. Like some other brassicas, it needs firm soil, so avoid digging too near to planting time.

Most kales are sown in an outdoor seedbed for subsequent transplanting. The exception is the rape kale, which resents root disturbance and therefore needs sowing in its final growing place.

MAKING A START
Sow all varieties during the week or two following the middle of spring. For a seedbed sowing, form the drills 1cm ($\frac{1}{2}$in) deep and 15cm (6in) apart. Sow thinly, and later space the seedlings to allow 5–8cm (2–3in) between plants. Dress the main site with general fertilizer at 90g per sq m (3oz per sq yd) about two weeks before the plants are due to be moved there; this should be carried out when they are approximately 13cm (5in) high.

Planting distances depend on the variety. For the smaller, compact kinds allow 45cm ($1\frac{1}{2}$ft) in each direction, but leave 60cm (2ft) between the larger ones. Water the plants in and provide shading if the weather is hot (see p.40).

Frequent watering of kale plants may be needed if warm, dry weather coincides with the earlier stages of growth. It is important to keep young kale plants growing steadily. They will recover only slowly from any checks to their growth.

When sowing rape kale, space the drills 45cm ($1\frac{1}{2}$ft) apart and place the seeds, in clusters of three or four, the same distance apart. Later, remove all but the strongest seedling from each group.

CARE OF THE CROP
Remove the shading as soon as the plants' leaves cease to be limp, but be sure to keep the soil moist while the new roots are forming. Give a top-dressing of general fertilizer, at 70g per sq m (2oz per sq yd), once the plants are growing strongly.

Hoe regularly to kill the weeds. Remove any yellow or dead leaves that appear.

HARVESTING
Pick the young leaves of curly varieties from late autumn, but never too many from one plant at a time. When shoots develop on these and other kales in late winter and early spring, pick them when they have grown to at least finger length.

PESTS AND DISEASES
The most likely pests are cabbage root flies, caterpillars, whitefly, flea beetles and slugs and snails.

Possible ailments are club root and downy mildew.

Pick the leaves and young shoots of kale a few at a time. Never strip a plant of its foliage or you may kill it. Harvesting of curly varieties starts in late autumn, of other types during the spring.

RECOMMENDED VARIETIES
'Cottagers' Fairly tall, plain-leaved variety. Masses of shoots in early spring.
'Dwarf Blue Curled Scotch' Compact, dark blue-green variety with fancy frilled leaves.
'Dwarf Green Curled' Dwarf habit; tightly curled leaves.
'Fribor' F_1 hybrid. Medium height, with deep green curled leaves.
'Frosty' Very hardy; only 30cm (1ft) high. Curled leaves.
'Hungry Gap' Lots of shoots in mid-spring when other vegetables are in short supply.
'Tall Green Curled' Hardy, large plant. Masses of curly leaves.
'Thousandhead' Plain-leaved and very hardy. Tender shoots in winter and spring.

Sprouting broccoli (*Brassica oleracea* 'Botrytis cymbosa') is grown for the harvest of tasty shoots abundantly produced during late winter and early spring. It is a tough plant which can withstand a hard winter. Purple sprouting varieties are slightly hardier than the white.

Calabrese (*Brassica oleracea* 'Italica'), also called green sprouting broccoli, lacks this hardiness but compensates with the fine and delicate flavour of its spears. It needs less space and matures more rapidly, being ready for picking from late summer.

Both types require an unshaded site and a fertile soil with a pH of around 6.5. If the ground was not heavily manured for a previous crop, dig in some manure or compost well ahead of planting. Spread a dressing of lime if the soil is too acid.

The central heads of calabrese are the first to form. Cut these before they run to seed to encourage side-shoots to form. These side-shoots will develop over a long period, often until the first frosts put an end to the growth of the plant.

The secondary heads of calabrese that form after the central head has been cut are smaller but may be quite numerous. Frequent cutting actually encourages more to form as the plant attempts to produce seed.

MAKING A START
Purple and white sprouting broccoli Sow in a seedbed about mid-spring; draw the drills 1cm ($\frac{1}{2}$in) deep and 15cm (6in) apart. Sow thinly and later thin to leave 5–8cm (2–3in) between the plants. Plant out when the seedlings are about 13cm (5in) high. Two weeks before doing so, give the planting area a base dressing of general fertilizer at 90g per sq m (3oz per sq yd). Plant very firmly, using a dibber; leave 60cm (2ft) between rows and between plants.

During dry, warm weather, water the plants in and give them temporary shading (see p.40). Keep the soil moist while the plants become established. When they are growing well, top-dress with general fertilizer at 70g per sq m (2oz per sq yd).

Calabrese Sow where plants are to grow, since calabrese transplants badly. Make the first sowings around mid-spring, with one or two further sowings in early summer for an extended harvest, or sow early- and late-maturing varieties together. Dress as for broccoli.

Draw the drills 1cm ($\frac{1}{2}$in) deep and 30cm (1ft) apart, then place groups of three or four seeds every 30cm (1ft). Later reduce each cluster to one strong seedling. Top-dress as for broccoli.

CARE OF THE CROP
Encourage the growth of calabrese, in particular, by watering before the soil dries out. Draw soil around the stems of over-wintering broccoli; tie tall plants to canes.

Sprouting broccoli is vulnerable to wind damage. If it is growing on an exposed site, draw soil around the stem to help provide extra anchorage. It may also be necessary to insert a cane against each plant and secure the stem to it with string.

HARVESTING
Calabrese first develops a single, central head. If this is cut when it is green and tightly closed, before the flower buds start to open, smaller side-shoots will then form in quick succession. Frequent picking encourages the formation of more shoots; cut the side-shoots with 10–15cm (4–6in) of stem.

Start gathering the shoots of sprouting broccoli from late winter onward, once they are about 15cm (6in) long. Keep cutting the side-shoots and do not allow any to flower, otherwise they will run to seed and exhaust the plant.

PESTS AND DISEASES
The principal pests are caterpillars, cabbage root flies, whitefly, flea beetles and slugs and snails.

Possible diseases and ailments are club root, downy mildew and whiptail.

RECOMMENDED VARIETIES
Purple and white sprouting broccoli
'**Early Purple Sprouting**' Matures during the first half of spring.
'**Early White Sprouting**' Matures during the first half of spring.
'**Late White Sprouting**' About two weeks later than 'Early White Sprouting'.
'**Nine Star Perennial**' White heads before mid-spring. Crops annually if all are gathered.
'**Purple Sprouting**' Slightly later than 'Early Purple Sprouting'.

Calabrese
'**Autumn Spear**' Plentiful green shoots throughout the autumn.
'**Corvet**' F$_1$ hybrid. Good flavour and an abundance of shoots.
'**Early Romanesco**' Matures in early autumn. Soft texture; very large heads.

'**Green Comet**' Excellent yield of medium-sized heads from late summer. Uniform.
'**Mercedes**' F$_1$ hybrid. Compact growth and very early. Medium to large heads.

SOWING SEEDS OUTDOORS, pages 36–37
PLANTING VEGETABLES, page 40

PESTS AND DISEASES, pages 172–175
CAULIFLOWERS AND OTHER BRASSICAS, pages 184–185

Cauliflowers (*Brassica oleracea* 'Botrytis cauliflora') are for vegetable growers who enjoy a challenge. Compared with most other brassicas, including cabbages and Brussels sprouts, they can prove decidedly temperamental. But successful cropping, measured by the gathering of evenly-shaped, blemish-free curds, is within the reach of anyone prepared to take a little extra trouble. And the trouble is well worthwhile if you enjoy the crisp, nutty texture and distinctive taste of this vegetable.

Two essential requirements can make all the difference between success and failure when cultivating this crop. First is the soil, which has to be firm, fertile and either neutral or only very slightly acid. It is worth taking a soil test, which should give a pH reading of 6.5–7 – slightly more alkaline than for most brassicas. The soil must also contain ample organic matter, either left over from a previous crop or else dug in some months earlier. The delay is needed in order to give the ground time to settle and consolidate. The plot should be unshaded, although a little shelter is an advantage for plants that will have to withstand the winter.

The second essential is a growing routine that avoids all possible checks to development. The conditions likely to induce a setback include leaving seedlings over-long before transplanting, and lack of water at any stage of growth. Checks due to these or other causes often lead to undersized heads or to 'buttoning', which means that part of the curd emerges prematurely through the shield of leaves.

MAKING A START
Seedbed sowings are made in the same way, whether in a cold frame or in the open. Draw the drills 1cm (½in) deep, with a space of 15cm (6in) between multiple rows. Sow the seeds very thinly and cover them with a layer of sifted soil or compost. Keep the frame lights closed until after germination, at least, then allow a little ventilation during mild weather.

Remove any surplus seedlings to give a spacing between plants of 5–8cm (2–3in). Water the seedbed carefully if a dry spell follows germination.

A week or two after the seedlings appear, give the planting site a base dressing of general fertilizer at 90g per sq m (3oz per sq yd). Rake this in gently so that you do not disturb the soil too deeply.

It is best to plant the seedlings out before they grow too large, to avoid checks to growth at the transplanting stage. Move them when they are about six weeks old, or at about the five-leaf stage. Reject any seedlings that do not have a growing point. Water the seedlings during the previous evening and transplant them as quickly as possible, no deeper than in the seedbed. Use a dibber to make the holes and then to firm the soil against the roots. Water the plants in afterward.

Cloudy, damp weather is ideal, but the dehydrating effect of warm, dry weather can be reduced by erecting some temporary shading over the plants (see p.40).

Spacing varies according to the season in which the cauliflowers will be cut. As a general rule, the later the planting the wider the space can be between plants. Leave 50cm (20in) each way between summer cauliflowers, 60cm (2ft) between autumn cauliflowers and up to 75cm (2½ft)

between winter cauliflowers.

Sowing direct is especially worthwhile for autumn cauliflowers that would otherwise have to be moved from a seedbed in high summer. Give a base dressing of general fertilizer two weeks or so before sowing, at 90g per sq m (3oz per sq yd).

Draw the drills 1cm (½in) deep, spaced to suit the type of cauliflower (see above). Water the drills if the soil is dry, then sow the seeds in groups of three or four. Later, remove surplus seedlings to leave the strongest plant at each station.

Seedlings raised in the greenhouse provide the earliest cauliflower crop of all. Prick out the seedlings individually into compost-filled or peat pots, and keep them warm and well-watered so that their growth is not checked. Harden seedlings off before planting them out.

Seedlings grown outdoors in a seedbed need to be thinned at an early stage in their growth. Failure to do this will result in lanky plants that are likely to suffer a check in growth when they are moved to their final positions.

CARE OF THE CROP

Be sure to keep the soil moist if a dry spell follows transplanting. Remove any shading material once the leaves have ceased to be limp. When the plants are growing strongly, give the site a top-dressing of general fertilizer at 70g per sq m (2oz per sq yd).

Hoe regularly to prevent competition from weeds. Continue watering, as necessary, so that the bed gets at least 5cm (2in) of water each month, either from a hose or from rainfall.

In late summer, draw soil around the stem for extra support – cauliflowers, like all brassicas, dislike wind-rock.

When each curd reaches tennis-ball size, snap about three of the outer leaves level with its top and bend them over as a protection. (This is unnecessary if the leaves are already curved over to cover the curds.) The purpose is to prevent the curds of summer and autumn cauliflowers being turned yellow by the sun.

In the case of winter- and spring-heading types, the covering helps to prevent damage due to over-rapid thawing of the curds after a heavy frost.

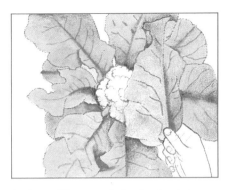

As the cauliflower curds develop, break two or three leaves over them if they are not already covered by foliage. In summer this will protect them from sun; in winter from over-rapid thawing following a frost.

HARVESTING

Cut the heads of cauliflowers when they are firm; if they are left too long, the curds break up and flowers start to appear. If a complete row of cauliflowers appears to be maturing simultaneously, start to cut some of them before they attain full size. Curds cut in the morning, while they are still damp, last the longest, but do not gather any while they are still frosted.

Cauliflowers will keep for up to three weeks if they are placed in a polythene bag and kept in the refrigerator. Alternatively, you can hang them upside down in a string bag, in a shed or in a cool place indoors.

Cauliflowers can be stored in a cool shed. If lifted complete with their roots, hung upside down, and sprayed occasionally with water, they will keep for two or three weeks.

PESTS AND DISEASES

The principal pests are caterpillars, cabbage root flies, flea beetles and slugs and snails.

The most likely diseases to affect cauliflowers are club root, downy mildew, leaf spot, whiptail and wire stem.

RECOMMENDED VARIETIES

Summer/early autumn
'All-The-Year-Round' Popular variety. Suitable for both protected and open-ground sowings.
'Alpha – Polaris' Fast-maturing, with pure white curds.
'Dok Elgon' Excellent-quality curds. Sow for an early or late autumn crop.
'Dominant' Large, firm, top-quality heads.
'Mechelse – Classic' Best sown in autumn for an early-summer crop.
'Snowball' Compact and very early. Good for protected sowings.

Autumn
'Autumn Giant – Autumn Protecting' Dense white heads in late autumn.
'Barrier Reef' Mid- to late autumn, with a compact habit.
'Canberra' Large heads in late autumn.

Curds are naturally well-protected.
'Flora Blanca' Solid white heads maturing in early autumn.

Winter
(For very mild areas only)
'St. Agnes' Matures in mid-winter. Curds may be loose.

Winter
(Spring-heading)
'Asmer Snowcap March' Very hardy. Matures in early spring.
'English Winter – Reading Giant' Matures in mid-spring.
'Purple Cape' Purple heads maturing from late winter.
'Walcheren Winter – Armado April' This variety matures in mid-spring.
'Walcheren Winter – Markanta' Matures after mid-spring.

SOWING SEEDS OUTDOORS, pages 36–37
PLANTING VEGETABLES, page 40

PESTS AND DISEASES, pages 172–175
CAULIFLOWERS AND OTHER BRASSICAS, pages 184–185

STORING VEGETABLES, pages 226–227

Leeks (*Allium porrum*) are one of the most versatile and popular of autumn and winter vegetables. They are members of the onion family but are both easier to grow and more dependable than most onions. Failure is unlikely, even in the coldest districts, since leeks can survive hard winters. They are also troubled by very few pests and diseases.

Leeks require a long, steady growing season and may occupy part of the vegetable plot for up to a year. But space for leek-growing need not be a problem, despite their long occupation of the ground, since planting distances are closer than for some other winter vegetables, such as cabbages and Brussels sprouts.

Depending on the variety, the harvest extends from early autumn until late spring. For the largest and earliest specimens, the seeds may be sown in a greenhouse during late winter, but this is of more interest to leek exhibitors than to most food producers.

Though not over-fussy about soil, leeks are most likely to thrive in fertile, well-worked ground that has not become compacted. Plenty of organic matter will help to ensure good-sized stems; this can either be left over from a previous crop or be dug in during the winter or spring before planting.

A pH rating of 6.5–7 (slightly acid to neutral) suits leeks best. The plants are most likely to thrive in a spot that is fully open to the sun.

Leeks are best raised in a seedbed for subsequent transplanting. Apart from leaving the main site free for other vegetables for a little longer, deep planting ensures that the greatest possible length of stem is blanched and made edible.

MAKING A START

Sow seeds in early to mid-spring, ideally, but be guided by soil temperature rather than the calendar. The seeds are unlikely to germinate until the soil starts to warm up. On heavy soil, which is the slowest to warm, consider sowing under cloches or in a frame. If you use cloches, wait until they have been in place for two weeks or so.

Two weeks before sowing, rake a dressing of general fertilizer into the seedbed at 70g per sq m (2oz per sq yd).

Draw the drills 2.5cm (1in) deep and 15cm (6in) apart. Sow thinly; later thin the seedlings to 2.5cm (1in) apart.

Transplant the seedlings two to three months after sowing, when they are about 15–20cm (6–8in) high. Rake a dressing of general fertilizer at 130g per sq m (4oz per sq yd) two weeks beforehand. Water the day

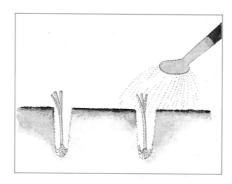

Before dropping the young leek plants into dibber holes, cut off some of the floppy top growth and also trim the roots. Water the plants in, using a watering can and rose so that some earth is washed over the roots.

before transplanting. Lift the leek seedlings from the seedbed with a hand fork.

Use a dibber to form holes about 15cm (6in) deep to take all but the top 5cm (2in) of the plants. Leave 30cm (1ft) between the rows and 15cm (6in) between plants.

Drop a plant into each hole and pour some water in: your aim should be to anchor the roots without drowning or floating the seedling. Do not replace any soil – this will crumble in during the summer.

CARE OF THE CROP

Little after-care is needed, beyond hoeing to suppress weeds and keeping the soil damp during the early stages of growth. Gradual earthing-up will ensure a maximum length of blanched stem, so during the early autumn draw soil around the developing stems from between the rows.

With the aim of increasing the length of the blanched stems, use a hoe to draw soil around them from the second half of summer onwards. Leeks are slow-growing, but continue to develop until they are harvested.

HARVESTING

Start lifting the leeks from autumn onward, when the stems are about 2cm (¾in) thick. Lift carefully with a fork and take only as many as you require immediately; leeks will keep growing during the winter, but only slowly during the coldest months. Finish lifting autumn varieties before the end of the year.

Any winter leeks that remain at spring planting time can be lifted and heeled-in in a small trench on a spare corner of the plot (see p.133), until they are needed. Harvest them before they run to seed.

PESTS AND DISEASES

Onion fly, together with stem and bulb eelworms, may occasionally prove troublesome, but seldom do.

Rust is the most likely ailment.

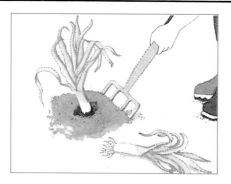

Use a fork to ease leeks out of the soil, otherwise the stems are liable to break. It is helpful to carry a knife so that the roots can be cut off on the spot, together with the soil adhering to them.

RECOMMENDED VARIETIES
Autumn-maturing
'**Autumn Mammoth – Argenta**' Late. Thick, medium-length stems.
'**Gennevilliers – Splendid**' Matures early. Long stems.
'**King Richard**' Late. One of the longest-stemmed leeks.

Winter-maturing
'**Autumn Mammoth – Snowstar**' Mid-winter. Short, thick stems.
'**Giant Winter – Catalina**' Mid-late winter. Short, thick stems.
'**Giant Winter – Royal Favourite**' Late. Large stems and very hardy.
'**Giant Winter – Wila**' Late, with thick, straight stems.
'**Musselburgh**' Mid-winter. Very popular variety, with thick stems.

SOWING SEEDS OUTDOORS, pages 36–37
THE ONION FAMILY, pages 186–187

PESTS AND DISEASES, pages 172–175

No other vegetable plays a more important role in the kitchen than the onion (*Allium cepa*). It is an indispensable ingredient of countless cooked dishes. Onions are also easy to grow and, thanks to their excellent storage qualities, a vegetable plot can keep a family supplied with cooking onions for most of the year.

At one time there was a period during midsummer when the winter-stored crop has finished and the current year's plants were still only half-grown. The so-called Japanese varieties, which mature at precisely this time, now fill this gap.

There are several types of onion, which have slightly different cultural requirements. The various types and their needs are summarized below.

MAINCROP ONIONS
There are two quite different methods of growing these bulb onions. One is by sowing seeds and the other is to plant 'sets'. Sets are immature, grape-sized onion bulbs that are readily available from seedsmen or garden centres. They are grown and harvested commercially during the summer and stored for the winter months before they are sold for planting the following spring.

Sets have a number of advantages and are probably the best choice unless you wish to grow a particular variety that is available only as seed. They present few difficulties in growing, they are pest- and disease-resistant, and they mature ahead of seed-sown crops. They are certainly the better choice for gardeners living in districts where the summers tend to be cool, short and wet.

Bolting can be a hazard, but heat-treated sets seldom run to seed. The initial cost of sets is a little higher than for seed, but the difference is slight when weighed against the greater likelihood of a successful crop of onions.

The thinnings of maincrop onions grown from seed may be used as a salad crop, like spring onions.

JAPANESE ONIONS
These straight, non-bulbous plants are used for their stems. They can be over-wintered and are grown mainly as a summer stop-gap, since they are unsuitable for keeping. They are available only as seeds, not sets and should be sown *in situ* because they are liable to bolt if transplanted.

SPRING ONIONS
These are eaten while the white stems are still immature and slender; the leaves can also be chopped and eaten. As a rule, spring onions are sown in spring for gathering during the summer and autumn. The harvest will be advanced by a few weeks if a sowing is made in late winter in a cold frame or beneath cloches.

For an even earlier crop that will be ready from spring onward, sow a particularly hardy variety, such as 'White Lisbon Winter Hardy', during mid- to late summer. In cold areas it is advisable to protect young plants with cloches.

PICKLING ONIONS
These small bulbs, used as cocktail onions or for preserving, are grown from a spring sowing. They will store like full-sized onions.

WELSH ONIONS
Welsh onions, also known as ciboules or green onions, are hardy perennial plants which resemble multi-stemmed spring onions. Their shoots or thickened stems are a useful substitute for spring onions and their leaves can be used like chives. Welsh onions may also be used to flavour cooked dishes.

Raised initially from a spring sowing, the plants may subsequently be propagated by division quite easily, since they grow together in close tufts.

SOIL AND POSITION
All onions do best in an open, sunny part of the plot, preferably with a little shelter for over-wintered crops. The ground needs to be well-drained and must be limed if a soil test gives a pH reading lower than 6.5.

Various pests and diseases, such as white-rot, are soil-borne, so it is not wise to grow onions in the same place in the vegetable garden year after year.

All types of onion need reasonably fertile soil, but seed-sown maincrop onions, in particular, require ample organic matter. Dig in a good dressing of well-rotted compost or manure – one or two bucketsful to the square metre of yard – during the previous autumn. This will give the ground time to settle and become firm. Firm soil is another requirement of onions; you may need to tread it to achieve this.

Onions sets also respond to well-prepared soil, but they will give reasonable results with rather less organic matter.

Spring onions, pickling onions and Welsh onions are the least demanding. Averagely fertile soil will do, including ground manured for an earlier crop. But all need neutral or only slightly acid soil conditions.

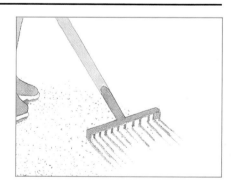

Site your onion bed in an open, well-drained and sunny place. In the autumn dig over the soil and incorporate plenty of organic matter; add lime if the soil is acid. In early spring, dress with a general fertilizer and rake the soil to produce a fine tilth. Tread the bed to firm it and rake again before planting.

MAKING A START

Maincrop onions from sets

Planting time depends on whether or not the sets have been heat-treated to deter bolting. If they have, wait until nearly mid-spring, when the soil has started to warm up. Untreated sets may be planted from early spring onward. Suppliers usually make it clear if sets have been heat-treated, and their skins are darker than those of untreated bulbs.

Give the bed a dressing of general fertilizer at 90g per sq m (3oz per sq yd) two weeks before planting. Firm the soil. Leave 30cm (1ft) between rows and 10cm (4in) between the bulbs. Simply push them into the soil, using the tip of a trowel if necessary, so that the tops are just visible.

Birds have a habit of flicking newly-planted sets out of the soil, so protect them with a humming line or with strands of black cotton criss-crossed between pegs (see p.44).

Keep the ground weed-free by frequent hoeing. Watering is necessary only during the early stages, or if the summer brings hot, dry spells.

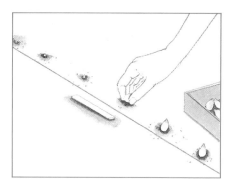

Plant onion sets so that most of the bulb is under the soil and only the tip remains visible. You will need a trowel for planting sets on firm soil, but if your soil is light and well-cultivated you should simply be able to press the sets into it.

Maincrop onions from spring-sown seeds

Sow the seeds during the first half of spring, once the ground has started to dry out and become warmer. On cold, heavy soils it is an advantage to set cloches in place in order to speed up this process. Either way, dress the area with a general fertilizer at 90g per sq m (3oz per sq yd) two weeks or so ahead of sowing the seeds.

Draw the drills 30cm (1ft) apart and 1cm (½in) deep. Sow thinly; dust the small, black seeds with flour first if it helps to ensure that you sow them thinly enough. Subsequently remove surplus seedlings to leave one plant every 10cm (4in). Provided that they were not sown too closely, the thinnings make excellent salad onions.

Alternatively, sow the seeds under glass in the winter for planting out the following spring. Sow at 2.5cm (1in) spacings in trays or pans of seed compost in mid-winter. Press the seeds just under the surface and sift a little compost over the top, then water with a fine-rosed can. Cover with glass and paper and place in an unheated greenhouse or cold frame. Remove the glass and paper once the seeds germinate.

Harden the seedlings off in early spring and plant them out three to four weeks later, once the soil has started to warm up. Firm the bed and plant them, with the aid of a trowel, 15cm (6in) apart in rows 30cm (1ft) apart. Plant them shallowly, so that the bottom of the bulb is only about 1cm (½in) below the surface of the soil.

Maincrop onions grown from seed need thinning to provide the bulbs with sufficient space to develop. Do this in stages, and use the thinnings as spring onions. Do not over-thin: small onions, which result from close spacing, store better than very large ones, and often have a better flavour.

Maincrop onions from seeds sown in late summer

Onions suitable for sowing in late summer and autumn include some hardy maincrop varieties and the Japanese varieties that can be overwintered successfully.

Sow the seeds during the last weeks of summer – at the very end in the mildest areas but up to four weeks earlier in cold districts. Two weeks before sowing, give the bed a base dressing of general fertilizer at 130g per sq m (4oz per sq yd).

Draw the drills and water them, the evening before sowing; space them 30cm (1ft) apart. Sow thinly and subsequently thin the seedlings further to 3–5cm (1–2in) spacings. Keep the drills moist during dry weather. Complete the thinning process the following spring, so as to leave 10cm (4in) spacings.

The alternative to sowing in drills is to prepare a seedbed in a sheltered part of the garden and to sow the seeds at closer spacings. Leave the seedlings unthinned over the winter, and then transplant them to their permanent positions the following spring.

In cold or exposed gardens, cover the onions with cloches from about mid-autumn onward. The bulbs will be ready for pulling from midsummer.

Spring onions

For an early crop, sow in late winter in a cold frame or under cloches. Such an early sowing under cloches will succeed only on light, free-draining soil, and provided the soil has started to warm up. It is necessary to place the cloches in position two weeks or so before the seeds are sown.

One alternative is to grow an extra-hardy variety that will stand the winter outdoors. In this case, sow in about midsummer if you live in a cold northern district, or two or three weeks later where conditions are more favourable. Or you can simply sow in spring for a summer/autumn crop.

At either season, rake in a base dressing of general fertilizer at 70g per sq m (2oz per sq yd) in advance of sowing, and work the seedbed down to a fine tilth.

Form the drills about 1cm ($\frac{1}{2}$in) deep and 15–30cm (6–12in) apart. The narrower spacing is adequate for plants grown in a bed, but more working room will be needed between rows on an open plot.

Sow very sparingly, in order that there should be no need to thin the seedlings any further until the first plants are pulled. The less thinning you have to do the better, since the smell given off by root disturbance during thinning attracts the onion fly to the site.

In cold, northern areas, cover over-wintered onions with cloches from about mid-autumn onward.

Pickling onions

Since only small bulbs are wanted, there is no need to manure the ground if it is already quite fertile. Prepare a fine seedbed, and dress with a general fertilizer at 70g per sq m (2oz per sq yd) two weeks before sowing.

Sow sparingly in drills 30cm (1ft) apart and 1cm ($\frac{1}{2}$in) deep. If the seeds are well-spaced there should be no need for further thinning. Keep the area weeded in the early stages until the fairly dense growth is able to swamp competition.

Welsh onions

Sow the seeds from spring onward in moderately fertile soil; allow 30cm (1ft) between rows and thin the seedlings to a spacing of 25cm (10in). Use the tufted plants for salads and as flavouring for cooked dishes. Lift and divide them every few years, and replant the offsets.

CARE OF THE CROP

Hoe or hand-weed between the plants to prevent competition from weeds. Water during prolonged dry weather, but stop watering as soon as the bulbs begin to ripen.

HARVESTING
Maincrop onions

Gather onions once the necks have softened and the leaves have turned yellow and collapsed. Just before this is complete, ease the bulbs gently upward with a fork to aid ripening. In a damp season, bend the onion tops over by hand also.

Harvest the crop a week or two later by lifting each bulb carefully with a fork; choose a dry day. Remove soil from the roots, then place the onions in a greenhouse or shed to finish drying.

Larger bulbs will take two weeks or more. Store the onions when the leaves are brittle. Remove any with thick necks, since they will not keep.

Store only sound, firm bulbs in netting bags or by forming ropes (see p.227). If these are hung in a cool, dry and reasonably frost-free place, there should still be onions for eating the following Easter. Inspect them frequently during the winter and remove any which have gone soft.

Spring onions

Pull the first salad onions when they are about 15cm (6in) high – about eight weeks after sowing. Leave others in the ground for up to twice as long, by which time they will have formed proper bulbs.

PESTS AND DISEASES

Onion flies may cause trouble. Possible ailments include downy mildew, neck rot, rust and white rot.

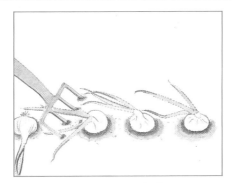

When they are nearly ready for harvesting, loosening maincrop onions with a fork helps to speed the process. This is especially useful during damp weather, when the foliage may take longer than usual to wither.

Greenhouse staging, or the bench in a well-ventilated shed, will provide ideal conditions for completing the ripening process. The stems and foliage must be completely withered before the crop is stored.

RECOMMENDED VARIETIES
Maincrop (sets)
'**Autumn Gold**' Half-round; seldom bolts.
'**Golden Ball**' Large, round bulbs that store well.
'**Rocardo**' Semi globe-shaped. Excellent keeper.
'**Stuttgart Giant**' Semi-flat bulbs, with a fine flavour.

Maincrop (spring-sown)
'**Bedfordshire Champion**' Globe-shaped; heavy cropper; keeps well.
'**Buffalo**' F_1 hybrid. Large and early; moderate keeper.
'**Hygro**' F_1 hybrid. High yield of globe-shaped bulbs. Good keeper.
'**Rijnsburger – Balstora**' Dark-skinned, globe-shaped bulbs. Excellent keeper.
'**Red Torpedo**' Red-skinned onion that stores well.

Maincrop (late-summer sown)
'**Express Yellow**' F_1 hybrid. Hardy and reliable for over-wintering.
'**Imai Early Yellow**' Semi globe-shaped, with yellow skins.
'**Senshyu Semi-Globe Yellow**' Matures ten days later than 'Imai Early Yellow'.

Spring onions
'**White Lisbon**' The favourite for spring sowing.
'**White Lisbon Winter Hardy**' Extra hardy, for late summer sowing.
'**Winter White Bunching**' For late summer sowing. Stiffer foliage than 'White Lisbon'.

Pickling
'**Giant Zittau**' Medium-sized, pale brown bulbs.
'**Paris Silver Skin**' Small, near-white bulbs.

SOWING SEEDS OUTDOORS, pages 36–37
SOWING UNDER GLASS, pages 38–39

CROP PROTECTION, page 44
PESTS AND DISEASES, pages 172–175

THE ONION FAMILY, pages 186–187
SHALLOTS AND GARLIC, page 216

SHALLOTS

Shallots (*Allium ascalonicum*) are used for pickling and as a milder, more subtle substitute for onions; they are one of the easiest crops to grow. Each offset planted in late winter or early spring will have sprouted a cluster of at least six and up to twelve bulbs by midsummer.

There are red- and yellow-skinned varieties of shallot and both types store extremely well – often for up to a year. Each year's crop provides bulbs for planting the following spring. Make sure you start by purchasing bulbs that have been certified as virus-free.

Shallots need much the same growing conditions as onions sets – that is, an open position and well-worked, firm and reasonably fertile soil that is either neutral or only very slightly acid. Light soil is certainly the best. A dressing of sharp sand worked into the top layer will make heavy soil more suitable.

GARLIC

Garlic (*Allium sativum*) is a member of the onion family grown for its unique pungent aroma and flavour. It is crushed or chopped to give a heightened flavour to almost any cooked savoury dish. Garlic is indispensable in the modern kitchen and is an essential ingredient of much Mediterranean cooking in particular. It is also said to have antiseptic properties in its raw state.

A single clove (small division of the bulb) is usually sufficient to add a distinctive flavour to a dish, so only a few plants need be grown. Each plant consists of about a dozen separate cloves. Home-grown garlic usually produces bigger, juicier and more pungent cloves than those sold in the shops.

Choose an open, sunny position and free-draining, fertile soil. Land manured for an earlier crop may well be suitable, but dig in some more manure or compost ahead of planting if you have any doubts about your soil's fertility. Spread lime if the soil is more than slightly acid – below pH 6.5.

Plant during the autumn, if possible, since this gives more time for the bulbs to ripen during the following year. However, overwintering may not succeed on heavy, wet soil and in such conditions it is better to plant in late winter or early spring.

MAKING A START AND CARE OF THE CROP

Plant in late winter or early spring, as soon as the soil will crumble. Choose medium-sized bulbs, and set them 15cm (6in) apart in rows 30cm (1ft) apart, deep enough to bury all but their tips.

Keep the soil moist while the bulbs become established. Check to see whether any of the bulbs have become dislodged, and replant them. Hoe regularly.

Around midsummer, draw some soil away from the bulbs to help them ripen.

When planting garlic, set the individual cloves 10cm (4in) apart, and pointed end upward, in holes or drills 4cm (1½in) deep, with 30cm (1ft) between rows. Hoe regularly and water during early summer.

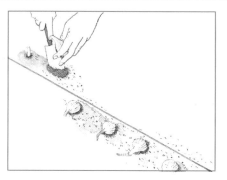

Plant shallots by digging a shallow hole with the tip of a trowel, then placing the bulb in this so that all but the tip is buried. Protect bulbs from birds until they have had time to anchor themselves with roots. This may take several weeks.

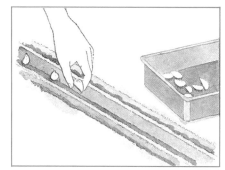

A continuous drill, formed with a draw hoe and about 4cm (1½in) deep, is a convenient way of planting garlic, and less time-consuming than making individual holes for each clove. Set cloves 10cm (4in) apart, then cover with soil.

HARVESTING

Shallots

The shrivelling of the foliage in high summer is a signal to lift the clumps with a fork and place them to dry in a well-ventilated place under cover. Once the leaves and stems are quite dead, split the clumps into individual bulbs and store these in netting bags in a cool, dry, frost-free place.

Garlic

Lift the plants with a fork during the second half of summer once the foliage has turned yellow. Spread the bulbs to dry under cover, and finally hang them in bunches once the stems and leaves have withered. They can be strung up like onions (see p.227). Choose a cool, dry, frost-free place for storage – not the kitchen.

PESTS AND DISEASES

The most likely pests of shallots are onion eelworm and onion fly. Fungus infections include downy mildew, neck rot, white rot.

Few pests trouble garlic, but white rot sometimes appears on plants.

Protect plants against birds with black cotton or a humming line.

RECOMMENDED VARIETIES

Shallots

'Giant Long Keeping Yellow', 'Giant Yellow', 'Giant Long Keeping Red' and 'Giant Red' are all good croppers and differ only in skin colour.

'Hâtive de Niort' produces large, well-shaped bulbs, but fewer in number.

Garlic

'Marshall's Long Keeper' A reliable cropper whose bulbs store well.

Shallot bulbs form in a tightly-packed cluster around the single bulb originally planted. Lift ripe bulbs, dry them under cover in a light, airy place, then break the clusters into individual bulbs before storing the crop.

PLANTING VEGETABLES, page 40
THE ONION FAMILY, pages 186–187

PESTS AND DISEASES, pages 172–175
ONIONS, pages 213–215

The seeds of many legumes and cereals, if germinated and allowed to grow for a few days, produce sprouts which can be eaten when they are between 1 and 8cm ($\frac{1}{2}$–3in) long. These sprouted seeds deserve the increased popularity they are currently enjoying, since they are extremely quick and easy to grow. The sprouting can be done at any time of year, regardless of the pressure on space in your vegetable plot, these shoots are highly nutritious, for they are rich in both protein and vitamins.

Sprouted seeds require minimum preparation before eating and are versatile in their culinary use. They may be added raw to mixed salads to give a crunchy texture, or they make a good addition to soups, stews and various Chinese dishes. Mung beans (*Phaseolus aureus*), commonly known as Chinese bean shoots, are the basis of much oriental cooking and are the best known of the sprouted seeds. The mustard and cress that many children grow is another familiar edible seed sprout (see p.200).

The sprouted seeds of most vegetables and cereals are, in fact, edible and it is remarkable how such immature plants, only days old and grown without soil, can develop such distinctive flavours. One or two sprouts, notably those of tomatoes and potatoes, are actually harmful, however. Seeds from a farm or a similar source may have been chemically dressed, which could make them poisonous. For both these reasons, buy only approved types of seed sold specially for sprouting by horticultural seedsmen or by most healthfood stores.

Remember also that, since sprouted seeds develop so rapidly, they soon pass their peak of flavour and nutritional value. After this point they may become bitter. It is best to grow small batches at intervals. The sprouts will keep for several days or up to two weeks in a sealed plastic bag in a fridge, provided that they are rinsed daily to keep them fresh.

There are two principal methods of sprouting the seeds – one in a tray and the other in a jar – and results are reasonably assured with both of them, provided a few simple rules are followed. An average room temperature (between 13–20°C/55–70°F) is usually sufficient, but a short spell in a warm airing cupboard will help one or two varieties and will also produce the blanched shoots which are whiter and crisper and, in some cases (see p.218), have a better flavour. Take care that the atmosphere is not too wet and warm, however, or the seeds will turn mouldy. Rinsing the seeds in cold water – twice a day if possible – is essential to keep them fresh; otherwise they can become stagnant and develop a sour taste.

Before starting with either method, rinse the seeds in a sieve under running water. Then cover them with tepid water and soak them for a few hours or overnight, until the seeds soften and swell up; the skins may begin to burst. Then rinse them again and let them drain.

SEED SPROUTING KITS

There are now several types of seed sprouting kit available; they can be bought from healthfood shops and some garden centres. The most useful kind has several tiers so that different kinds of seed can be sprouted at the same time.

Most proprietary kits incorporate a method of pouring water in and out without removing the seeds, which makes rinsing quick and easy.

It is also possible to buy a plastic 'sprouter cap' which fits most wide-mouthed preserving jars. The cap can be twisted into three positions, each with different sized holes. The smallest-holed position is suitable for the smallest seeds, such as alfalfa. The middle position is for seeds like mung beans and fenugreek. The position with the largest holes is for drawing off the hulls as the sprouted seeds grow.

SPROUTING IN A TRAY

This method is best for mung beans and lentils, which are eaten at an advanced stage of sprouting. Place a double layer of blotting paper, cotton wool, flannel or several sheets of kitchen paper over the base of a waterproof tray. Dampen this layer thoroughly and distribute the seeds thickly in a single layer over it. Cover the tray with glass, aluminium foil or a polythene bag and exclude all light until the seeds sprout. Keep the base moist by trickling in water at one end of the tray and pouring out any surplus at the other end. Do this daily.

For greener, unblanched shoots, move the tray to the light once seeds germinate. Either way, continue to keep the base moist until the shoots are long enough to eat. Then cut them off at the base with scissors.

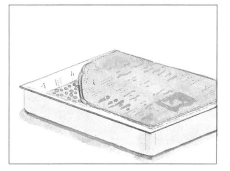

Any shallow, waterproof tray that has been lined with absorbent material is suitable for sprouting seeds. To retain moisture and exclude light, cover the tray with glass and newspaper until after the seeds have germinated.

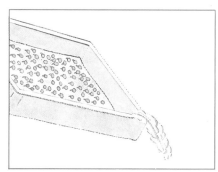

It is essential to keep the base moist until the shoots are ready. To avoid disturbing the seeds, trickle water in at one end of the tray, and tilt it so that any not absorbed by the lining material runs out of the other end.

SPROUTING IN A JAR

After soaking, pour a shallow layer (about 1cm/½in thick) of the damp seeds into a large glass jar then cover the top with a circle of muslin or other strong but porous material. Hold it in place securely with a rubber band.

Rest the jar on its side in a large bowl, and tilt it to drain off any surplus water. Place the bowl in the dark until the seeds sprout, then move them into the light if green shoots are wanted.

Both before and after the seeds germinate, rinse and moisten them once or twice daily by half filling the jar with water and swilling the seeds gently. Drain the water out through the muslin. To 'harvest' the seeds, simply pull out the sprouts when they are long enough.

The jar method is an easy alternative to sprouting seeds in a tray or a purpose-made sprouter. Place a layer of soaked seeds in the bottom of the jar, cover the top with muslin and secure with an elastic band.

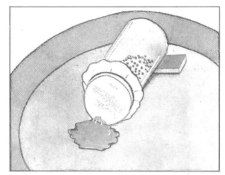

Drain off any surplus water by placing the jar on its side in a bowl, with its neck tilted down toward the muslin. Moisten the seeds with fresh water daily, and allow any surplus to drain away through the muslin as before.

TYPES OF SEED

Adzuki beans Grow in a tray or jar. Best blanched for eating when 2.5cm (1in) long. Takes 4–5 days.

Alfalfa Grow in a jar. Excellent for salads, with a sweet garden-pea flavour. Eat when up to 5cm (2in) long; let them 'green'. Takes 1–3 days.

Mung beans Grow in a tray. Best eaten blanched when up to 8cm (3in) long. Takes 3–8 days.

Fenugreek Grow in a warm place in a tray or jar. The spicy shoots are best eaten green when between 2.5cm (1in) and 8cm (3in) long. The curry flavour diminishes as sprouts get longer. Takes 3–5 days.

Wheat Grow in a warm place in a jar. Use blanched when only 1cm (½in) long. Takes 4–5 days.

Buckwheat Grow in a jar or tray and harvest when only 1–2.5cm (½–1in) long. Takes 2–4 days.

Chick peas Grow in a jar and harvest when only 1cm (½in) long. Takes 3–4 days.

Lentils Grow in a jar and harvest when 1–2.5cm (½–1in) long to eat raw or cooked. Takes 3–5 days.

Sunflower Grow in a jar and harvest after two or three days when only 1cm (½in) long, otherwise the delicious shoots become too strong-tasting. Takes 2–3 days.

TYPES OF SEED

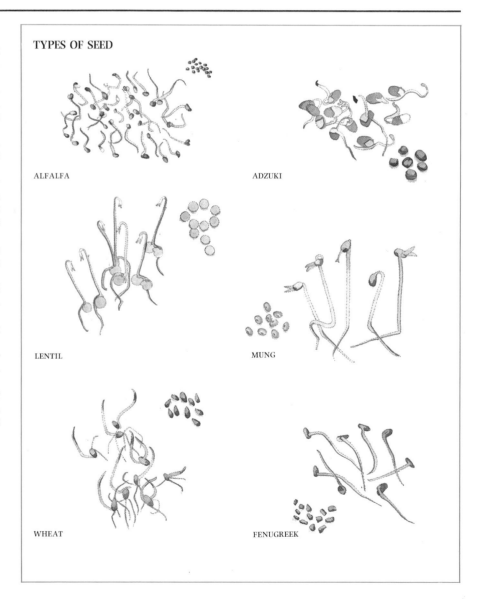

ALFALFA

ADZUKI

LENTIL

MUNG

WHEAT

FENUGREEK

It is well worth making space for a variety of herbs in any food garden. For the small space they occupy, herbs can have a considerable influence on the diversity and flavour of your home cooking, and many are decorative in themselves.

This assortment of annual, biennial and perennial plants will grow without fuss in almost any part of the garden that has free-draining soil. Some herbs, such as fennel and sage, are sufficiently ornamental to earn their place in the flower border. An alternative, especially where space is limited, is to cultivate a selection of herbs as pot plants. If these are placed on the patio they will be handy for picking in any weather. Low-growing thyme, one of the least demanding herbs, will even grow in the spaces between paving stones.

Most herbs die back in winter, except for evergreen perennials such as bay and rosemary. Some herbs, such as chervil or parsley, will grow throughout the winter provided they have the protection of cloches while others, like thyme, winter savory or marjoram, will keep their leaves if they are in pots on an indoor windowsill.

While most herbs are all the better for being used fresh, several may be dried for winter use (see p.236). The more succulent herbs, such as basil, parsley and chives, can also be frozen successfully.

Most herbs can be raised from seed or, if only one or two plants are needed, bought from a garden centre or plant nursery. Subsequently, most perennials are easily propagated by division or from cuttings, either tip cutting of non-flowering shoots or heeled cuttings of semi-ripe wood (see p.41); the most suitable method of propagation is given under the individual entries that follow in the next four pages.

GROWING CONDITIONS

Most herbs like a sunny position and free drainage. While the soil should be reasonably fertile, rich ground is seldom an advantage. Several herbs, including thyme, marjoram, winter savory and sage, like a dryish position and develop more flavour and scent when grown in poorish soil. Others, including chervil, parsley, balm, angelica and mint, tolerate light shade.

The practical purpose behind separating the plants in traditional, patterned herb beds is to prevent an incursion of the weaker kinds by their more vigorous neighbours. Bear this in mind when devising your own planting scheme. Separation is particularly important for such invasive plants as mint and tarragon. Prevent their roots from spreading, either by planting in an old, bottomless bucket sunk up to its rim in the soil, or by inserting vertical slates or a similar barrier around the plants. Alternatively, grow such herbs in a container.

GROWING HERBS IN CONTAINERS

Whether you choose pots or tubs, make sure there are drainage holes in the base before adding the compost. Use a soil-based compost, such as John Innes No. 2, for perennial herbs and either soil-based or peat-based material for annuals.

Water the herbs frequently between spring and autumn during dry weather. Peat-based compost, in particular, should not be allowed to dry out or it will be difficult to saturate again.

Topdress perennial plants each spring by removing the upper 8cm (3in) of compost and replacing it with a layer of fresh material. Feed all plants with liquid fertilizer every two weeks during the summer months when they are growing rapidly.

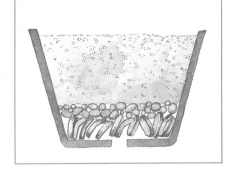

Most herbs like a free-draining soil, so ensure that the compost in containers is well-drained. Place a layer of broken crocks on the bottom, followed by a layer of gravel or other small aggregate, before filling a pot or tub with compost.

There is no need to repot perennial herbs every year, provided the container is big enough. Simply remove the top 8cm (3in) of compost and topdress with fresh compost to the same level; do this annually.

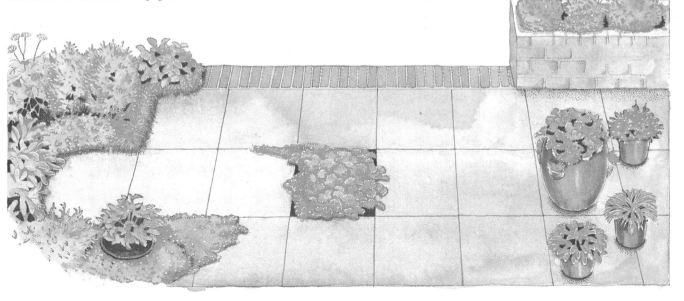

ANGELICA

A beautiful, hardy annual herb, angelica (*Angelica archangelica*) grows tall (up to 2m/6ft high), and has bright green, serrated leaves which are smooth and glossy.

The young leaves and stems can be added sparingly to salads and to flavour stewed fruits; both the leaves and root can be used to flavour fish. When candied, pieces of the ridged, hollow stem make an attractive decoration for cakes and puddings.

Sow seeds in late summer in shallow drills, preferably in a rich, moist soil; sow them in groups of three or four about 1m(3ft) apart. Harvest the leaves before the plant flowers, after which it loses its vigour. Dry them in the shade in order to preserve their colour and scent. The seeds can be collected as soon as they ripen for planting out immediately.

BASIL

There are two species of this half-hardy annual, which has a powerful, spicy flavour slightly reminiscent of cloves. It is a valuable addition to salads, especially tomato salads, and can be used in cooked vegetable, cheese or tomato dishes. It is the basic ingredient of *pesto*, an Italian pasta sauce.

Sweet basil (*Ocimum basilicum*) has much larger, stronger-flavoured leaves and grows to about 40cm (15in) high. There is also a beautiful purple-leaved variety. Bush basil (*Ocimum minimum*), also known as Greek basil, is more compact and has small, pointed leaves. It is a good choice for growing in a pot, and for bringing indoors during the winter.

Either sow under glass in gentle warmth during the first half of spring or outdoors in late spring. Space plants 15–30cm (6–12in) apart, or plant in individual pots.

Pinch out the tops to induce the plants to bush out, and pick the leaves as needed. Preserve by drying or freezing.

BORAGE

This easily-grown annual herb (*Borago officinalis*) reaches a height of 45–90cm (1½–3ft). Its young leaves, when bruised or shredded, taste like cucumber and are used to flavour salads and drinks such as wine cup. The sweet-tasting blue flowers can also garnish salads or be candied for cake and sweet decoration.

Borage will thrive in most types of soil. Sow the seeds where they are to grow – in spring for summer use and in summer for autumn use – 1cm (½in) deep and 30cm (1ft) apart, in groups of three. They will germinate rapidly. Thin to leave only the strongest seedling in each group.

BALM

The common name of this hardy perennial derives from the fragrance of its heart-shaped leaves when crushed. Lemon balm (*Melissa officinalis*) is easy to grow and is tolerant of most soils and of partial shade; it forms strong, bushy growth. There is also an attractive variegated variety.

The leaves provide a refreshing flavouring for summer drinks, including herb tea, and are a valuable addition to salads, fruit salads, and cooked savoury dishes. They may be used fresh, dried or frozen; dry them quickly to keep their colour.

Sow the seeds in a fine seedbed in mid-spring; later thin the seedlings to 45cm (1¼ft). Cut the plants back to near ground level in autumn, and cover the roots with straw if severe weather threatens. Propagate by division in spring or autumn.

BAY

This hardy, slow-growing evergreen shrub (*Laurus nobilis*) will grow to 4.5m (15ft) or more if unchecked. With pruning, it can be kept to a more compact 90cm (3ft). It is a good idea to grow a bay within the confines of a large pot or tub. The aromatic bay leaves are an essential ingredient of a *bouquet garni* and are used in many savoury dishes, and to flavour pâtés.

Buy a young, container-grown plant and set it in a sheltered spot. It can be brought indoors in winter if there are severe frosts. Pick the young leaves as needed; they are slightly bitter when fresh, but they sweeten as they dry.

Propagate by semi-ripe cuttings in late summer or early autumn.

CHERVIL

The finely-cut leaves of this biennial (*Anthriscus cerefolium*) resemble parsley and give a delicate aniseed flavour to salads, sauces and soups. Chervil is a fast-growing, hardy annual or biennial whose leaves remain green in winter; it is best grown under cover, except in mild areas.

Sow in spring for summer use, or in late summer for potting up and growing indoors during the winter. Leave 20cm (8in) between plants. Keep the soil moist during dry weather to deter bolting.

Pick the leaves before the plants flower. They may be dried if you wish.

CHIVES

Chives (*Allium schoenoprasum*) are the smallest member of the onion family and are invaluable for giving a mild, onion-like flavour to salads; they are also used to garnish soups and vegetable dishes, or may be added to cold sauces. The plant is a hardy perennial and grows in clumps of narrow, hollow, spear-like leaves, up to 30cm (1ft) tall. Chives are easily grown and will thrive in either sun or partial shade; moisture is an essential requirement.

Sow the seeds *in situ* during the spring, and thin the seedlings to 20cm (8in) spacings. Pinch off the round, pink flowerheads before they open. Cut back the leaves periodically to encourage young, fresh growth.

Lift and divide the bulbs every three years during spring or autumn. Plant them out in clumps of four or five, 25cm (10in) apart, in rich, damp soil.

DILL

Dill (*Anethum graveolens*) is a tall-growing hardy annual which reaches 1.5m (5ft) in height. Its delicately flavoured feathery leaves can be chopped in salads and are a particularly apt flavouring for fish. The seeds, and sometimes the stems, are used in pickling, especially of cucumbers.

Sow the seeds *in situ* during spring or early summer, and later thin to leave 23cm (9in) between plants. Keep the plants well-watered and weed-free. Start picking the foliage when the plants are about 10cm (4in) high; they will resprout at least once; the leaves can be used fresh or dried.

Enclose the seedheads in paper bags to catch the ripe seeds, then hang them upside down under cover. Collect and store the seeds when they are quite dry.

GINGER

Ginger (*Zingiber officinalis*) is a tropical perennial which can be grown either in a heated greenhouse, or in a container outdoors during the summer months, provided it is brought indoors for the winter. It is an essential flavouring in curries, pickles and spiced meat, fish, rice and vegetable dishes. It has a rich, pungent flavour.

Ginger is a root which you can buy in some greengrocers or at oriental food stores. When potted up, it sends up lily-like fronds as much as 1m (3ft) high and produces a spike of yellow, purple-lipped flowers. At the end of the growing season it will have produced additional bulbs for culinary use. It can be used fresh or dried or can be preserved in syrup or vinegar.

CORIANDER

Both the seeds and the young leaves of this hardy annual (*Coriandrum sativum*) have culinary uses. The feathery leaves give a spicy flavouring to soups and meat dishes, and the dried and ground seeds are a favourite (if not essential) ingredient of curries, used either whole or crushed.

Sow the seeds in spring and thin to a spacing of 15cm (6in). Germination is slow. The unripe seeds have a strange smell, which disappears once they are mature; once this smell has faded, cut off the seedheads and dry them thoroughly under cover. Rub the seeds out, then store them, either whole or ground into a powder.

FENNEL

This handsome perennial (*Foeniculum vulgare*) grows to 1.5m (5ft) or more. It may also be grown as an annual. Fennel bears a mass of feathery foliage which gives a pronounced aniseed flavour to sauces for serving with fish, as well as to salads and soups. The aromatic seeds of fennel are used in pickling.

Either start with purchased plants or sow groups of seeds 45cm (1½ft) apart during the spring and thin to the strongest single seedling. Gather the leaves and seedheads as for dill.

HORSERADISH

Although horseradish (*Amoracia rusticana*) is a hardy, long-lived perennial, it has a spreading, weed-like habit that makes it advisable to lift every part of the roots each year. They may be used raw or dried – but much of the flavour is lost during cooking. The traditional way to serve horseradish is to grate or mince the roots and use them immediately to make horseradish sauce or cream to accompany meat.

To start growing horseradish, plant 30cm (1ft) lengths of root, purchased from a nursery, at 60cm (2ft) intervals and 30cm (1ft) deep during early spring. Lift the roots during autumn; store them under cover in sand. Keep a few roots for replanting the following year.

HYSSOP

This hardy, partially evergreen perennial (*Hyssopus officinalis*) has a bushy habit and can be used to form a low hedge. It has attractive shiny leaves and purple tubular flowers and grows up to 1m (3ft). The leaves have a pungent, mint-like, but rather bitter, flavour, so use them sparingly. Their chief value is as a flavouring for soups and in cooked dishes to 'balance' fatty meats or oily fish.

Sow seeds in a seedbed during the spring, and later plant out the seedlings at 30cm (1ft) spacings in a light, well-drained soil. Set them a little closer to form a hedge, and cut off the growing tip of each plant. Use the leaves fresh or dried.

Hyssop plants should be renewed every three or four years; they may be propagated from tip cuttings.

MINT

Mint is a widely-known and easily-grown perennial herb, traditionally used in much Middle Eastern cooking, and to make mint tea. There are several different species and hybrids, but the most familiar is spearmint, or common mint (*Mentha spicata*). Other mints worth growing include apple, or round-leaved, mint (*Mentha rotundifolia*) and the decorative pineapple mint (*Mentha rotundifolia variegata*).

All species will grow almost anywhere; they prefer a semi-shaded position and damp conditions. To reduce their invasiveness, restrict them inside a buried bottomless bucket or similar container. Plant pieces of root 5cm (2in) deep and about 30cm (1ft) apart during the spring and water well until they are established. Use the leaves fresh, dried or frozen.

Propagate by lifting and dividing the roots during spring.

ROSEMARY

This hardy evergreen herb (*Rosmarinus officinalis*) of Mediterranean origin grows into a bushy shrub some 1.8m (6ft) high, though it can be kept smaller by pruning and picking. It has a strong fragrance and taste and is widely used to flavour roast meat and as an ingredient in a number of stuffings and sauces.

Rosemary likes a well-drained, fertile soil and a sunny, sheltered position. Sow the seeds in a bed outdoors, or in a pot, during spring. Thin the seedlings to 10–15cm (4–6in) apart before planting out in early summer; allow 60–90cm (2–3ft) between plants. Rosemary can also be planted as a hedge, in which case the plants should be spaced 40cm (15in) apart. Semi-ripe cuttings may be taken during the summer.

'Miss Jessop's Upright' is a recommended, ornamental variety.

MARJORAM/OREGANO

There are two main types of this Mediterranean herb, also known as oregano. The leaves of both may be used in various stuffings and as a flavouring for meat, poultry and various Mediterranean dishes.

Pot marjoram (*Origanum onites*) is a compact, hardy perennial that needs a warm, sheltered site. It may also be grown as a pot plant. Sow the slow-germinating seeds in spring and thin to 30cm (1ft) spacings.

Sweet marjoram (*Origanum marjorana*), although naturally perennial, is not very hardy and may have to be treated as an annual. It has soft leaves and a better flavour than pot marjoram, and grows twice as large, to 60cm (2ft). Sweet marjoram can either be raised from seed under glass in early spring, or sown outdoors in mid-spring where it is to grow.

PARSLEY

Parsley (*Petroselinum crispum*) is possibly the best-known of all culinary herbs. Because it is a biennial, it runs to seed in its second year, so is commonly grown as an annual. It needs moist conditions and a fertile soil; it makes a good edging to paths.

Sow the seeds in spring for use during summer and autumn, and in summer to provide tender leaves during winter. Cover the plants with cloches in cold districts or during severe weather. Sow seed in shallow drills where the plants are to grow, and thin them to about 23cm (9in). Alternatively, make the later sowing in a pot and bring this indoors before winter. The seeds are slow to germinate, so keep the soil moist.

There are two main types of parsley: the kind with curly leaves, such as 'Champion Moss Curled', and the broad-leaved variety, for example 'Plain Leaved'.

SAGE

Sage (*Salvia officinalis*) is a hardy, evergreen perennial which grows to 30–60cm (1–2ft) high. The common sage has attractive grey-green leaves, but there are also purple- and golden-leaved forms. Sage is a good flavouring for many meats, especially veal and liver, and is used in the preparation of stuffings, as well as extensively in Italian cooking.

Sage prefers a well-drained, light soil and a sunny, sheltered position. Sow the seeds outdoors or in a cold frame during the spring, and later transplant the seedlings to allow 30cm (1ft) between plants.

Sage is fairly short-lived, so propagate new plants by dividing the older ones in spring or autumn every three years. Prune the shrubs back lightly in late summer, and use the leaves fresh or dried.

SAVORY

Both winter and summer savory have fairly strong, spicy flavours that go well with peas, beans, stuffings and sauces.

Summer savory (*Satureia hortensis*) is a half-hardy annual with an erect, bushy form. Winter savory (*Satureia montana*) is a hardy perennial with evergreen leaves which has a more spreading habit.

Sow the seeds of both types in mid-spring and later thin the plants to 23cm (9in) spacings. The seeds germinate slowly. If they are transferred to pots in late summer, both types of savory can be kept on a windowsill indoors during the winter. Pick the leaves while they are young; the leaves of summer savory may be dried.

THYME

This aromatic Mediterranean herb (*Thymus* spp.) has small leaves and is extensively used in soups, stuffings and in many cooked dishes. The two most widely-grown species are both hardy, dwarf and evergreen.

Common thyme (*Thymus vulgaris*) is strongly flavoured; lemon thyme (*Thymus × citriodorus*) has a more subtle aroma. There are golden variegated forms of both species.

All thymes are sun-loving and prefer a well-drained, fertile soil. Raise common thyme from a spring sowing outdoors, and transplant the seedlings to 23cm (9in) spacings. Buy nursery-grown plants of lemon thyme in spring, and set them 30cm (1ft) apart. Renew the plants every three years or so; propagate them by division in spring. The leaves of all thymes may be dried or frozen.

Low-growing thymes will do well in crevices between paving, provided there is some soil beneath for their roots.

HERBS FOR A PURPOSE
Evergreen leaves
Bay
Rosemary
Sage

Basic culinary herbs
Mint
Sage
Thyme
Chives
Parsley

For pots and windowboxes
Basil
Borage
Chervil
Pot and sweet marjoram
Summer savory
Tarragon
Thyme

Bouquets garnis
Parsley (2–3 sprigs)
Marjoram (1 sprig)
Thyme (1 sprig)
Bay leaf

TARRAGON

This narrow-leaved, hardy perennial herb (*Artemisia dracunculus*) has a unique flavour, somewhat reminiscent of tobacco. The leaves, which are a basic ingredient of *fines herbes*, are used in vinegar-making and to flavour chicken and other white meats, as well as sauces and various cooked dishes. They may be dried or frozen.

The roots of the bushy plant are vulnerable to severe frost, so cover them with a layer of ashes, straw or bracken if you live in a cold area. Restrict the roots in some sort of surround to prevent them from spreading. Start with a nursery-grown plant and give it a well-drained, sheltered position.

Russian tarragon (*A.d.* 'Inodora') is coarser and has an inferior flavour to French tarragon (*A.d.* 'Sativa').

VERBENA

This deciduous perennial shrub (*Lippia triphylla*) can grow up to 2m (6ft). Its sweet, lemon-scented leaves can be used, chopped, in stuffings or to flavour fish and chicken, as well as jams and jellies. It can also make a refreshing tea and gives a sharp fragrance to pot pourri. Harvest the leaves at any time and store them in an airtight container; they will retain their flavour and scent for a long time.

Plant lemon verbena in a sunny position, though in a fairly dry, poor soil to keep its roots hardy. Cut the plant down in autumn and cover its roots with straw or leaves until spring if you live in a cold district. Alternatively, plant it in a pot and overwinter it indoors.

SOWING SEEDS OUTDOORS, pages 36–37
GROWING HERBS, page 41

HERBS, pages 188–192
DRYING AND FREEZING HERBS, page 236

STORING AND PRESERVING

If you store and preserve the bounty your food garden provides, you will be able to enjoy the tastes of summer all winter long, as well as the knowledge that nothing from your food garden has been wasted.

The aim of all storage and preservation is to prevent deterioration after the crops have been harvested. You should aim to harvest when they are young, full of flavour and in prime condition. Vegetables are best gathered in the morning, and fruit should also be picked early in the day. If the weather is very hot, plunge vegetables into a bucket of cold water as soon as they are picked.

Storing and preserving food entails considerable effort on the part of the gardener and/or the cook, but in some instances, nature does provide a helping hand – in the form of vegetables and fruits that will last for at least part of the winter with only the minimum of assistance. Examples include hardy roots, such as parsnips and swedes, and long-keeping apple varieties that need little more than a frost-free store.

Most other crops need more careful attention if they are to keep well, and all must be handled with care to avoid bruising. Beetroots, carrots, potatoes, onions and other main crops also need special forms of protection if they are to last throughout the winter.

Of all the preserving methods commonly practised, drying is one of the most ancient. It works successfully for many herbs, and for certain fruits, though it is less well-suited to preserving vegetables. By exposing the plant material to heat, and by driving out most of the water it contains, it becomes much more impervious to decay due to the action of bacteria and moulds.

Additional time-honoured and appealing methods of preserving the home-grown harvest include pickling, in which vegetables are preserved in vinegar, salting, jam-making and crystallizing foods in sugar.

Fruits preserved by bottling keep well – often for over a year. In the bottling process, the food is heated and vacuum-sealed. This ensures that the organisms of decay are either killed or prevented from multiplying by the absence of air. Fruits should be bottled either in their own juice or in water or sugar syrup.

Freezing is the most popular method of preserving, and works not by killing bacteria and moulds but by arresting their growth. There are very few fruits and vegetables that cannot be successfully frozen. The form in which you freeze your crop will depend on its condition, its water content, and the form in which you eventually want to eat it.

Though you may attempt always to pick vegetables and fruit for preserving when they are young and in the best possible condition, this is sometimes impossible. You might find yourself, for instance, with a large crop of raspberries soaked by persistent rainfall, or a glut of overgrown courgettes on your return from holiday. In situations such as these, you need to improvise: the raspberries can be picked and frozen as purée, the courgettes cooked as part of a *ratatouille*, then frozen.

Fruits and vegetables with a high water content, such as lettuces, melons and cucumbers, do not freeze successfully except as a purée or as an ingredient of soup. As the water in their cells turns to ice during the freezing process, the cells themselves – and thus the texture of the food – are destroyed. Other crops that do not freeze well include some of the more delicately-flavoured herbs. They retain their taste much better if they are dried.

Gentle handling is vital for fruits of all kinds, but especially those that are to be stored for some time. Most fruits bruise easily, and even the slightest damage may reduce their storage life. Set aside for immediate consumption any fruits that show signs of damage caused by pests or disease.

Freezing or bottling are the only practical ways to keep soft fruits and some tree fruits for eating during the winter (see pp.228–9 and pp.234–5). Some soft fruits, such as strawberries and raspberries, deteriorate very rapidly after being picked. Others can be kept for varying lengths of time in a refrigerator (see below).

Some of the firm-fleshed tree fruits, notably apples and pears, can be stored in their natural state for winter use, though only a minority will keep in good condition until well into the new year. The particular variety is the critical factor and their keeping qualities are outlined in the descriptions of individual recommended varieties (see p.95 for apples and p.97 for pears). Apples and pears can also be cut up and dried, as can some other tree fruits.

STORING FRESH TREE FRUITS

Apples The best conditions for keeping apples in their natural state are a cool, dark but frost-free store, where the atmosphere is fairly humid. If you have a cellar, this would be an ideal place.

Some apple-growers wrap the fruits in special oiled paper or in tissue before storing them, but others do not. Wrapped apples probably keep slightly better, but it is less easy to spot the first signs of developing rots.

Place the apples, wrapped or unwrapped, either in moulded paper trays (see p.91) or in fruit boxes with extended corner posts to support the tray above (see p.97).

Pears Store pears as for apples, though moulded paper trays are less suitable for pears because of the shape of the fruit. Pick pears for storage before they are fully ripe and check frequently for signs of ripening, since most varieties of pear remain in peak condition for only a brief period.

Peaches and nectarines The fruits will keep for up to a week in a refrigerator, It helps if the container is first lined with cotton wool.

Apricots Stored in a cool place, apricots will remain in good condition for three weeks or even longer.

Cherries, plums, mulberries and figs Eat these fruits as soon as possible after you have picked them.

Quince Stored in a cool cellar or shed, these fruits will last for about two months.

STORING SOFT FRUITS

As a general rule, the storage life of soft fruits is prolonged by cool conditions. Chill them as soon as possible, and make a good start by picking the fruits early in the day, before they have a chance to become warm.

Strawberries Eat the ripe fruits within 12 hours of picking, or within two days if the fruits are placed in the refrigerator at once. If you pick strawberries while they are only two-thirds pink, they will ripen in a refrigerator over a 10-day period.

Raspberries Pick these fruits early in the day. Any that are not fully ripe will store for up to a week in a refrigerator, but fully ripe fruit will last for only a couple of days.

Blackberries and hybrid berries If these fruits are picked dry, they will keep for two or three days in a refrigerator. Picked in damp weather, they deteriorate faster.

Blueberries and cranberries These keep for a week or so at room temperature and for up to three times as long in a refrigerator.

Blackcurrants and red and white currants Use currants as soon as possible after picking. They last a little longer if they are kept on the stalk, or 'strig'.

Gooseberries The berries may remain unpicked, without spoiling, far longer than other soft fruits. This is better than trying to keep the berries once picked.

Grapes Kept in a refrigerator, undamaged fruits remain sound for up to two months.

Kiwi fruits These fruits will store for about two weeks at room temperature, or for two or three months in a refrigerator. The close proximity of other fruits, especially apples, speeds ripening, however.

DRYING

House-dried fruits will keep for many months. This method works well for apples, pears, apricots, peaches, plums and grapes.

Lay the fruits on muslin-covered wire cake racks or on trays, with the cut surfaces uppermost. Dry them in a very cool oven at 50–65°C (120–150°F, gas mark $\frac{1}{4}$) for several hours; keep the oven at the lowest temperature for the first hour so that the skins do not burst.

When the fruits are ready they should feel springy and soft; no moisture should ooze out when you press them. Cool the fruits at room temperature for 12 hours afterward, covered with a cloth. Then pack them in boxes lined with greaseproof or waxed paper and store in a dry, frost-free place.

Apples Peel, core and cut into slices 5mm ($\frac{1}{4}$in) thick, then thread them on canes. Hang in a cool oven with the door slightly ajar for 4–6 hours.

Pears Peel, core and quarter, then drop the pieces into lightly salted water. Place in a cool oven for 4–6 hours.

Apricots, peaches and plums Use large, firm, ripe fruits as they shrink in drying. Place them on trays and dry slowly in a cool oven with the door left open. Once the skins begin to shrivel, raise the temperature to 65°C (150°F). Allow whole fruits two days to dry and halved fruits a day.

Grapes Use seedless grapes if possible. Wash, pat dry with a cloth, and dry in a cool oven for 8 hours, gradually increasing the temperature to 65°C (150°F), with the door left open.

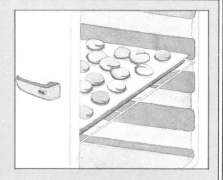

Plums and other stone fruits may be dried in a low oven. Place the fruit in a single layer on a muslin-covered tray; larger fruits are best halved and stoned first. Drying takes up to 48 hours, depending on the size and water content of the fruit. When it is ready, all the juices will have evaporated.

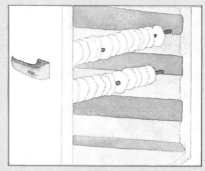

To dry apple rings, dip them in salted water to prevent them from discolouring, then pat them with absorbent paper to remove all excess water, thread them on wooden canes and hang them in a cool oven. They should be thoroughly dry within about six hours. Allow the rings to cool, then store them in airtight jars.

STORING VEGETABLES

Most vegetables keep better in the short term than soft fruits. Among the exceptions, however, are leafy vegetables such as lettuce and spinach, which should be eaten as soon as possible after gathering. Harvest them early in the day, while they are still cool and before they become dehydrated. If leafy or salad vegetables have to be kept for a while, place them in a refrigerator, then enclose them in a plastic bag once they have become cool.

Harvest and handle with great care all vegetables that have to be kept for a while. Use at once, and do not store, any that are accidentally cut or bruised, as well as those which show signs of damage from pests or disease.

STORING OUTDOORS

Some vegetable crops are winter-hardy enough to be left where they are growing until you need them. With certain qualifications, this applies to root vegetables such as carrots, beetroots, turnips, parsnips and swedes, as well as to leeks, celery and celeriac. It is also applicable to Brussels sprouts, savoy cabbages and other brassicas that mature during the colder months.

The qualifying factors are mainly to do with soil and district. Root crops fare much better, and are easier to harvest, when they are left in light, free-draining soil than in sticky clay. Crops that will survive the winter in a relatively mild climate zone may suffer frost damage in an exposed, northerly vegetable garden.

If you have a heavy soil, the best solution is to lift root crops during late autumn or early winter and store them under cover. If your winter climate is risky, protect the rows with a good layer of straw in early winter, and cover this in turn with netting pegged down to the ground (see p.159). Except in the most severe weather, this will also prevent the soil from freezing rock-hard, which would make lifting impossible.

Under adverse climatic conditions, select the hardiest varieties of brassica or grow early-maturing varieties of vegetables that are suitable for freezing for winter use.

Always lift potatoes before the winter and keep them in a frost-proof store.

STORING ROOT CROPS AND ONIONS

A safer means of storing root vegetables, provided you have the space, is in boxes in a ventilated shed or outhouse. Place the roots in layers, with slightly dampened peat or sand around them; take care not to include any damaged crops. When the winter weather is severe, place straw over and around the boxes for extra protection.

Store potatoes in paper or hessian sacks (not plastic, since they need to 'breathe'). Ensure that their skins are completely dry first; the best way to do this is to lift the tubers in the morning during a dry spell and leave them to dry on the surface of the soil for a few hours. Close the sacks and keep them in the dark in a frost-free, ventilated store. A generous packing of straw beneath, around and over the bags is the best protection against possible frost. But never cover the sacks in a way that prevents all movement of air.

Onions and garlic also need frost-free storage, but they should not be kept in the dark or they will start to sprout. Once they have been fully dried and ripened in a cool, dry place, either hang them in nylon or string netting bags, or string them up by twisting their withered stems around a length of rope or thick string.

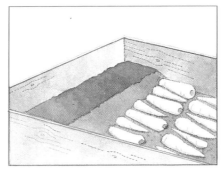

Peat is the ideal storage medium for carrots and other root crops; it should be slightly damp to prevent the crop from drying out. Store the roots in layers, with peat between each, in a frost-free place.

The solid hearts of Dutch winter white cabbages will keep for several months if placed in a net and hung in a cool but frost-free shed or cellar. Before the cabbages are stored, cut each cleanly at the base and remove the outside leaves.

> **DRYING PEAS AND BEANS**
> Dried peas, haricot beans and butter beans are all useful sources of winter protein. If you want to grow them for this purpose, choose varieties such as 'Chevrier Vert' for the half-ripened bean seeds known as flageolets, or 'Comtesse de Chambord' for the mature, ripened 'haricot' beans.
>
> Simply leave the pods on the plant, provided the weather is dry, until they are withered and dry. In damp weather, pull up the plants and hang them in an airy, covered place. Shell when the pods are withered, and leave the beans or peas spread out for a few days until they are completely dry. Store them in an airtight container.

Hessian or paper sacks allow stored potatoes to 'breathe' and permit the evaporation of moisture from around the crop. By contrast, moisture levels build up inside polythene sacks, which results in rotting. To protect the sacks from frost, stand them on straw, then pack more straw between and over them.

Tie onions to a rope by their stems and hang them in a light, dry, frost-free place. They should keep throughout the winter.

Bottling is a reliable means of preserving most kinds of fruit, with their natural flavour, colour and texture preserved intact. Bottled fruits will keep well for one to two years, after which time the quality and nutritional value of the fruit will deteriorate, though it can still be eaten perfectly safely. Except for tomatoes, bottling is far less satisfactory for vegetables. The most important requirements for successful bottling are good-quality produce and rigid adherence to the rules of timing and hygiene.

WATER OR SYRUP?
Fruits can be bottled satisfactorily in either water or syrup. The advantage of bottling fruits in syrup is that it improves both their colour and their flavour.

Prepare the syrup beforehand. Allow 450g (1lb) of granulated white sugar to every litre (2 pints) of water. Add the sugar to half the quantity of water, bring it slowly to the boil, stirring all the time, then let it boil for one or two minutes.

Add the rest of the water. At the same time, when bottling less sharp fruit (pears, cherries or strawberries), add two dessert-spoonfuls of lemon juice or citric acid to each litre (2 pints) of syrup; this will increase their acidity. Remove any scum from the surface before using the syrup.

Cherries, small plums, damsons, peaches and pears can be bottled in a brandy syrup. Make a heavier syrup, allowing 450g (1lb) of sugar to every half-litre (1 pint) of water. Add an equal quantity of brandy when the syrup is cool. Prick the fruits with a stainless steel fork so the syrup can permeate them.

BOTTLING EQUIPMENT
You will need a large preserving pan or very large saucepan with a close-fitting lid; it must be at least as deep as the jars, with space for a false bottom, and should be of sufficient diameter to hold at least three jars, allowing for a small space between them. It is possible to buy a purpose-made sterilizer, but this is expensive.

Bottling jars are available in a range of sizes and types; they come complete with tops and a supply of rubber seals. The widely-used Kilner type have flat metal or glass tops with an integral rubber ring, held in place by plastic or metal screw bands. Another popular type has glass lids, separate rubber rings and spring clip closures. The 1kg (2lb) size is the most convenient and the instructions here are for this size.

You will also need a thermometer if you are using the slow water bath method of bottling. Buy one specially made for bottling and jam-making, which reads up to 100°C (212°F).

PREPARING THE FRUITS
The small, firmer fruits, such as plums and apricots, are more successful bottled than the softer berry fruits which lose their texture easily; strawberries also lose colour.

Use only sound, ripe fruits, except for gooseberries, which are best slightly unripe. Remove all stalks and leaves and check for insects. Do not wash soft fruits, though a light rinse is sometimes necessary.

Wash stone fruits. Small plums and apricots may be bottled whole, but large ones can be packed more closely if they are cut in half and the stones removed.

Bulk quantities of fruits, such as apples, can be preserved as bottled pulp or purée, also a good way to use up imperfect fruits.

Choose baby tomatoes for packing closely in the bottle. Preserve them in brine, made by dissolving 15g (½oz) of salt in 1 litre (2 pints) of water. Alternatively, they can be puréed and bottled.

The preparation and timing of individual fruits is given in the chart opposite.

PACKING THE JARS
Wash the jars and tops in warm water; drain them, but leave them wet. Pack the fruits in carefully and tightly; use the handle of a wooden spoon but be careful not to squash the fruits. A 1kg- (2lb-) jar will hold about 550–700g (1¼–1½lb) of fruits. Pack in layers, or in concentric rings, and always fill the jars to the brim; some shrinkage will occur during processing.

Soak the rubber rings in warm water for about 15 minutes. Dip them in boiling water immediately before putting them on the jars, to make them more supple.

For the slow water bath method (see below), pour the cold water or syrup gently over the contents of the jars, causing as few air bubbles as possible. Top up the jars to ensure that the fruits are totally submerged.

Put the rubber seals and the tops in place. Secure the jars but leave screw bands slightly loose, to allow air to escape during sterilization. Spring clips allow the steam to escape without their being loosened.

STERILIZATION
Slow water bath method
It is necessary to insulate the jars from the hot base of the pan with a circular wire grill, a piece of wood, or a folded piece of cloth. Place the jars on this, with a folded cloth between them so that they do not touch.

Pour sufficient cold water into the pan to match the level of the liquid in the jars. Cover the pan with a lid and heat the water very gradually so that the thermometer gives a reading of not more than 55°C (130°F) after an hour. Aim to reach the sterilizing temperature in another half hour.

For sterilizing temperatures and times, see chart. Once the critical temperature is reached, adjust the heat so that it stays constant for the rest of the sterilizing period.

When the time is up, turn off the heat and remove the jars; place them on a wooden table or pastry board, not on stone or a similar cold surface, otherwise they might crack. Non-slip tongs will help you raise the jars far enough out of the water for the tops to grasped with a cloth.

Tighten the screw band of each bottle fully as soon as it is removed. Leave the jars undisturbed for a day; check once or twice during this period to see whether the screw bands can be tightened any further.

Quick water bath method
This is simply a faster version of the method above. For sterilizing times, see chart.

Warm the jars before filling them with the prepared fruits and pour in hot syrup up to the brim. Seal the bottles after releasing all the air bubbles, and place them in the pan, with folded cloth between them.

Add hot water to the level of the liquid in the jars and heat it slowly, so that it reaches simmering point (88°C/190°F) in half an hour. Simmer steadily for 2 to 40 minutes, depending on the fruit type. Allow an extra five minutes for larger bottles.

TESTING PROCESSED BOTTLES
After 24 hours, the contents of the jar will have cooled completely and a vacuum should have formed. To test whether the lids are securely sealed, remove the screw band or securing clip and lift the jar by its top. If it is airtight, the vacuum inside and the air pressure outside will hold it in place. Eat the contents of unsealed jars at once.

MAKING PULPS AND PURÉES
This is an economical way of preserving many fruits and some vegetables, such as tomatoes.

For pulps, simmer the prepared fruit in a little water until it is thoroughly cooked. Pour it into the hot bottles while it is boiling hot and seal them at once. Sterilize them by the quick water bath method: bring the surrounding water up to boiling point and keep it simmering for five minutes, or ten minutes in the case of tomato pulp. Remove the jars and allow them to cool, then check the seal.

To make a purée, blend and/or sieve the raw fruit or cooked pulp and sweeten and flavour or season it to taste. Sterilize the bottles as for a pulp.

Release any trapped air bubbles from the jars after filling them with fruit. This helps to create a good seal. Tapping the sides may be sufficient; otherwise, insert a knife blade very gently down the side of the jar where the air bubble is lodged.

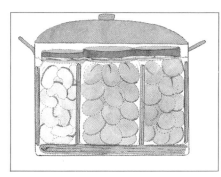

Place a piece of wood, a metal grid, a folded cloth or even a layer of folded newspaper on the base of the pan beneath the jars. To reduce the risk of cracked jars, prevent them from touching each other by inserting a folded cloth between them.

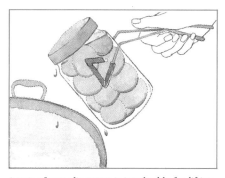

A pair of non-slip tongs is invaluable for lifting jars out of the scalding water after they have been sterilized. Place them on a wooden surface, then tighten each of the securing bands.

BOTTLING TIMES AND TEMPERATURES

Temperatures and times are critical for safe, long-term preservation. Figures are for 1kg (2lb) jars. Allow an extra five minutes for fruits in 2kg (4lb) jars (but allow ten minutes for large jars of close-packed tomatoes).

FRUIT	PREPARATION	SLOW WATER BATH	QUICK WATER BATH
Raspberries	Pick over, remove stalks.	74°C (165°F): 10 mins	2 mins
Blackberries and hybrid berries	Use only firm fruits.	74°C (165°F): 10 mins	2 mins
Gooseberries	Use unripe fruits; top and tail with scissors.	74°C (165°F): 10 mins	2 mins
Currants	Remove stalks; rinse.	74°C (165°F): 10 mins	2 mins
Blueberries	Remove stalks.	74°C (165°F): 10 mins	2 mins
Cranberries	Remove stalks; pick over.	74°C (165°F): 10 mins	2 mins
Apples	Peel, core and slice; immerse in lightly salted water to prevent browning. Rinse before packing.	74°C (165°F): 10 mins	2 mins
Dessert pears	Peel, halve and core; immerse in lightly salted water with lemon juice added. Rinse before packing.	88°C (190°F): 30 mins	40 mins
Cooking or unripe pears	Peel, halve and core; immerse in lightly salted water with lemon juice added. Tenderize in hot syrup.	88°C (190°F): 30 mins	40 mins
Quince	Peel, halve and core; immerse in lightly salted water with lemon juice added. Tenderize in hot syrup.	88°C (190°F): 30 mins	40 mins
Mulberries	Use only firm fruits.	74°C (165°F): 10 mins	2 mins
Figs	Remove stems and peel. Add ½ tsp citric acid to 1 litre (2 pts) syrup. Use equal quantities of fruit and syrup.	88°C (190°F): 30 mins	40 mins
Plums	Remove stalks, rinse and wipe bloom from dark fruits. Halve and stone large fruits.	82°C (180°F): 15 mins	10 mins / 20 mins
Peaches	Blanch for 30 seconds; cool and remove skins. Halve and stone.	82°C (180°F): 15 mins	20 mins
Apricots	Remove stalks; rinse. Halve larger fruits by cutting round stone and twisting halves apart.	82°C (180°F): 15 mins	10 mins / 20 mins
Cherries	Remove stalks. Use whole or stone and add juice to syrup. Add ½ tsp citric acid to 1 litre (2 pts) syrup.	82°C (180°F): 15 mins	10 mins
Rhubarb	Remove leaves. Trim and cut into short lengths. Soak overnight in hot syrup.	74°C (165°F): 10 mins	2 mins
Tomatoes	Choose firm, small tomatoes. Remove calyx and rinse. Bottle in brine solution.	88°C (190°F): 30 mins	40 mins

Freezing is the best way to preserve home-grown fruits, vegetables and many herbs so as to retain their colour, texture and flavour. Freezing puts the organisms responsible for decay into a state of suspended animation, but their activities are resumed once the fruits or vegetables are thawed.

Virtually all home-grown fruits may be frozen, although some freeze more successfully than others. Pears, for example, lose their flavour when frozen, while the distinctive texture of fresh strawberries does not return once the frozen fruits are thawed.

The majority of vegetables also freeze satisfactorily. There are exceptions, however, and these include leafy salad vegetables and others, such as cucumbers, with a high water content. But, in some instances, even these difficult types may be frozen if they are first cooked or made into a purée or a soup.

Successful freezing depends on following certain basic rules. Vegetables must first be blanched briefly in boiling water to halt the chemical processes taking place inside them. If they are placed in a freezer without blanching, their flavour, appearance and nutritional value all suffer, because these processes go on, however slowly, even at sub-zero temperatures, and accelerate as soon as the food is thawed.

Fruits do not need blanching, but some keep better for being packed in sugar or syrup. Detailed instructions for preparing individual vegetables and fruits are given in the charts on pp.232–3 and pp.234–5.

PICKING FOR FREEZING

Always freeze fruits and vegetables that are in peak condition. With vegetables, this means picking them while they are young and tender, and undamaged by pests and diseases, and with fruits before they become over-ripe. In both cases, it means frequent, regular picking, in small batches – daily if crops are heavy.

Processing small batches at a time is also necessary for the satisfactory operation of the freezer. The machine is able to cope with only a limited amount of unfrozen food in a day; as a rule, this should be no more than a tenth of its overall capacity.

Freeze garden produce as soon as possible after picking, before it can become dehydrated. Gather crops just before you plan to process it, but ideally early in the day.

Provided they have been prepared well and frozen in peak condition, most fruits and vegetables will last for at least a year in the freezer without noticeable loss of quality. It makes sense to use them up within this period, and to work to an annual pattern that corresponds to the growing and harvesting cycle of your crops.

PACKAGING

Efficient packaging is essential both to keep frozen foods in optimum condition and also to prevent the transmission of smells and flavours from one type to another.

Plastic freezer bags, sold in several sizes, are one of the simplest forms of packaging. Always exclude as much air as possible from the bag (suck it out with a drinking straw), then seal the neck with a wire closure. Plastic or waxed boxes and tubs make convenient storage containers, too, provided they have lids. Square or rectangular cartons make the most efficient use of space in the freezer.

Clear labelling is essential; the label should record the contents, the approximate number of portions and the date it was put into the freezer. Use a pencil, Chinagraph or a felt-tipped pen (not a ballpoint) to mark packages and labels.

You may find it helpful to keep a record of everything you put into your freezer, and to log foods in and out.

LOADING THE FREEZER

Place unfrozen foods in the coldest part of the freezer, where they will freeze with the least possible delay. Some freezers have a fast-freeze compartment for this purpose. Otherwise, turn the freezer to the coldest setting, then place the food along its bottom and sides. Most foods freeze solid within eight hours; remember to turn the freezer down again later.

When transferring foods after their initial freezing, place the packs in logical groups, and help to cut down tedious searching with the aid of coloured labels or stickers.

USING FROZEN FOODS

Allow frozen fruits to thaw quite gradually in a closed pack. Ideally, thaw them in the refrigerator for about six hours; this is especially important for fruits such as apples which discolour quickly. Frozen fruits collapse rapidly and lose their texture if they are thawed in a warm place or left for too long once thawed. If you are in a hurry, you can thaw them, still in a covered container, for about three hours at average room temperature. Fruit which is to be cooked can be put into water or syrup while still frozen, and cooked at once.

By contrast, most vegetables are better cooked straight from the freezer, without being given a chance to thaw. Sweet corn is the chief exception.

Both vegetables and fruits should be eaten soon after being taken from the freezer. They will keep less long than fresh produce. On no account re-freeze food that has been even partially thawed, except after thorough cooking.

Fruits spread out individually on a tray before dry freezing will remain separate even when packed together after they have been frozen. Raspberries and strawberries are ideal for this method, and it works well for mushrooms, too. Fruits intended for eventual cooking are better packed and frozen together.

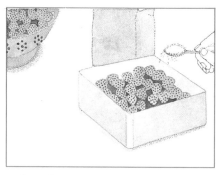

To freeze fruits in sugar, place the fruit and the sugar in layers in a rigid container. The thawed fruits will be soft and sweet, and suitable for use in a wide range of hot and cold desserts.

Rectangular packs make the best use of freezer space. To freeze puréed fruit, pour it into a polythene bag and place this in a square container. Once frozen, the bag may be removed and replaced in the freezer and the container re-used.

FREEZING FRUITS

Most fruits may be frozen sweetened or unsweetened as you prefer. There are two principle methods of sweetened freezing: using dry sugar or a sugar syrup. The choice depends on the fruit and on its intended use.

UNSWEETENED FREEZING

This method suits most berried fruits and is the least time-consuming. Dry-packed berries retain their shape better.

FREEZING IN SUGAR

The sugar method is suitable for soft fruits as well as for cherries, but remember that sugar-frozen fruits are apt to go mushy when thawed. Use caster sugar for preference, and allow 450g (1lb) of sugar to 1.5kg (3lb) of fruit. Rigid containers are needed for this method. Layer the fruits and sugar: start with fruit and finish with sugar.

FREEZING IN SUGAR SYRUP

Freezing in sugar syrup suits several stone fruits and also those that discolour easily, such as apples, peaches, plums and apricots. It brings out the flavour of figs, damsons, grapes and melons and is a good method for fruits with little natural juice.

Allow about 1 litre (2 pints) of syrup for each 1.5kg (3lb) of fruit. The proportion of white, granulated sugar to each litre (2 pints) of water is as follows:

Light syrup   220g (7oz)
Medium syrup   300g (11oz)
Heavy syrup   450g (1lb)

Bring the sugar and water to the boil and boil steadily for about a minute, stirring all the time. Allow the syrup to cool. Add lemon juice or citric acid – 1½ tablespoonfuls to 1 litre (2 pints) – when freezing fruits such as apples or peaches, which are low in Vitamin C and discolour easily.

Place the fruit in rigid containers, and leave 1cm (½in) at the top to allow for expansion. Pour enough syrup over the fruit just to cover it. If fruit tends to float, place crumpled greaseproof paper over the top before fitting the lid.

POACHING

The skins of large fruits, such as apricots, plums and peaches, will harden during freezing unless they are removed or the fruits are poached. Halve and stone the fruits, then poach them in a heavy syrup (see above) for a few minutes. Allow to cool, and then pack into rigid containers. Alternatively, skin the fruits first.

PURÉES

Purées are a suitable form in which to freeze less-than-perfect fruits, but do not use any that are bruised or well overripe.

FREEZING VEGETABLES

Most vegetables can be frozen satisfactorily and will retain nearly all their natural flavour and appearance. The chief exceptions are those that contain a lot of water, such as leafy salad vegetables, radishes, asparagus, cucumbers and members of the marrow family. Some vegetables, such as celery, tomatoes and cabbage, can be frozen but they will lose some of their texture and will be suitable for using only in cooked dishes, not salads.

It is seldom worth bothering to freeze long-lasting, winter-hardy vegetables, such as parsnips and leeks, since they are generally better left in the ground (see p. 226).

The secret of successful vegetable freezing lies in blanching. For precise blanching times see pages 232–3. Exceptions to the blanching rule are the one or two vegetables that require cooking before being placed in the freezer. Beetroots become rubbery if blanched only briefly. Tomatoes do not need blanching, but they do need skinning.

BLANCHING

Aim to complete the job as quickly as possible. Immerse the vegetables in boiling water and bring it back to the boil quickly. Aim to have the water boiling again within a minute of immersion. You will need a pan that holds about 3 litres/5 pints. Blanch only small batches at a time (never more than 450g/1lb), so that the drop in water temperature is not too great. Keep the pan on a high heat for the required time.

The same water, which may be lightly salted, can be used for several batches. A wire basket makes it easy to immerse and remove vegetables. For peas and other small vegetables that would pass through the mesh, use muslin bags, or line the basket with muslin. Keep the pan covered during blanching.

Time the blanching very carefully. If the vegetables are blanched for too long, they will lose flavour and crispness. If they are blanched for too short a time, there will be a colour change and they will lose some of their nutritive value.

Immediately after blanching, cool the vegetables rapidly in a bowl of cold water, preferably containing ice cubes, for the same length of time as blanching.

Once they are cooled right through, shake the vegetables in a colander and then quickly dry them on absorbent kitchen paper. Pack the dry vegetables in plastic bags or rigid containers. Exclude as much air as possible, seal the tops and attach labels. Overwrap onions and brassicas in an extra polythene bag to prevent strong smells spreading to other foods.

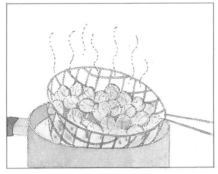

To blanch vegetables, always plunge them into water that is already boiling. Keep the heat turned up so that the water returns to the boil as quickly as possible. Blanch for the correct time – three or four minutes in the case of Brussel sprouts, depending on size.

Immediate cooling after blanching is important to prevent the vegetables from cooking and to help keep their colour. Lift the vegetables out of the water and immerse in cold water for two or three minutes. Iced water is ideal, or the water can be changed once or twice during cooling.

Pack the cooled, drained and dried vegetables into a plastic bag. Exclude as much air as possible by inserting a drinking straw through the neck of the bag, holding the plastic tight around it and then sucking out the air. Seal the bag at once with a wire twist, label it and freeze.

VEGETABLE	PREPARATION	BLANCHING TIME	SERVING
Peas	Freeze only young peas. Shell, blanch and cool. Pack in bags, or open-freeze then pack. **Mangetouts** Wash whole pods. Top and tail, then blanch.	1 minute $\frac{1}{2}$ minute	Cook for 5 minutes in boiling water. Cook for 7 minutes.
Broad beans	Shell small, young beans. Blanch, cool, then drain. Pack in bags, or open-freeze then pack.	$1\frac{1}{2}$ minutes	Cook for 8 minutes in boiling water.
French beans	Top and tail. Leave whole or cut into 2.5cm (1in) pieces. Blanch, cool, then pack.	2 minutes	Cook in boiling water for 7 minutes (whole) or 5 minutes.
Runner beans	Top and tail. Cut in thick slices. Blanch, cool and pack.	2 minutes	Cook for 7 minutes in boiling water.
Sweet corn	Avoid large, overripe cobs. Remove leaves and silks. Blanch, cool, drain and pack.	4–6 minutes	Thaw in fridge. Cook for 10 minutes in boiling water.
Artichokes	Remove outer leaves and stalk. Cut out hairy 'choke', then wash and blanch. Add 1tbs lemon juice to blanching water. Cool and drain upside down; pack in rigid containers.	6 minutes	Cook for 5 minutes in boiling water.
Asparagus	Remove woody portions and scales; wash well. Cut tips to 15cm (6in) and blanch. Cool, drain, pack in rigid containers.	2–4 minutes	Cook for 5 minutes in boiling water.
Celery	Scrub and remove strings; cut into 5cm (2in) pieces. Blanch, cool, drain and pack.	2 minutes	Braise or use in casseroles and soups.
Florence fennel	Wash and cut bulbs into pieces. Blanch and keep blanching water. Cool and drain. Pack in rigid containers with blanching water.	3 minutes	Simmer for 30 minutes in blanching water.
Rhubarb	See Fruit Freezing table (p.234)		
Jerusalem artichokes	Peel and slice. Soften in butter and cook in chicken stock. Sieve and freeze as a purée.		Make into a soup with milk and cream, season.
Potatoes	**New** Scrape and blanch. Drain and blanch. **Old** Peel and dice or cut into chips. Fry in clean fat for 4 minutes without browning. Cool and pack. Or peel and cook, then mash. Make into croquettes or duchess potatoes. Cook, then cool and pack in rigid containers.	4 minutes	Cook in boiling water until soft. Fry in deep fat. Thaw for 2 hours, then cook for 20 minutes in pre-heated oven at 180°C (350°F, gas mark 4).
Carrots	Freeze only young, tender roots. Wash, scrape and leave whole or slice. Cool, drain and pack.	3 minutes	Cook for 8 minutes in boiling water.
Parsnips	Trim and peel young roots. Dice or cut into quarters. Blanch, cool, drain and pack.	2 minutes	Cook for 15 minutes in boiling water.
Swedes	Do not freeze well.		
Celeriac	Peel, and dice or cut into thick slices. Blanch in water with 1 tbs lemon juice added. Cool, drain and pack.	3 minutes	Cook for 10 minutes in boiling water..
Radishes	Do not freeze well.		
Beetroot	Freeze only small young roots. Cook in boiling water until tender, then rub off skins. Pack in boxes, whole or sliced.		Thaw 2 hours in fridge. Drain and add dressing or re-heat briefly in boiling water.
Salsify and scorzonera	Do not freeze well.		
Turnips	Choose small, young roots. Peel, dice and blanch. Cool, drain and pack.	$2\frac{1}{2}$ minutes	Cook for 10 minutes in boiling water.
Kohlrabi	Use small, tender roots. Peel, dice and blanch. Cool, drain and pack.	2 minutes	Cook for 10 minutes in boiling water.

VEGETABLE	PREPARATION	BLANCHING TIME	SERVING
Squashes and pumpkins	Do not freeze well.		
Marrows and courgettes	Large marrows must be peeled, seeded and cooked until soft. Mash and freeze as a purée. Cut young marrows and courgettes into 1cm (½in) slices. Blanch, cool and pack.	1 minute	Reheat gently in butter. Fry in oil and butter.
Cucumbers	Do not freeze well.		
Aubergines	Use only tender, medium-sized aubergines. Peel and cut into 2.5cm (1in) slices. Blanch, chill and drain, then pack.	4 minutes	Thaw for 15 minutes and fry.
Peppers	Wash, remove stems, seeds and membranes. Halve or slice, then blanch. Cool, drain and pack.	2–3 minutes	Thaw for 1½ hours at room temperature.
Tomatoes	Wipe and freeze small fruits whole, without blanching. Or skin, chop and cook for 5 minutes in their own juice. Cool and freeze. May also be puréed before freezing.		Fry, grill or bake from frozen. Add to soups, sauces and cooked dishes.
Mushrooms	Wipe and leave whole or slice. Blanch, or sauté in butter until soft.	4 minutes	Add, frozen, to dishes before cooking.
Lettuce	Does not freeze well, except as soup.		
Spinach, spinach beet, New Zealand spinach	Avoid older leaves with thick midribs. Remove stems from young leaves and wash. Blanch only a few leaves at a time, so they remain separate. Cool, drain and press out excess moisture. Leave whole, chop or purée, pack.	2 minutes	Cook from frozen for 7 minutes in butter.
Swiss chard	Freeze leaves and stems separately. Prepare and freeze leaves as for spinach. Blanch stems in water with 1tbs lemon juice added. Cool, drain well, then pack in boxes or bags.	Leaves 2 minutes Stems 2 minutes	Cook leaves as for spinach. Cook stems for 7 minutes in boiling water.
Sorrel	Does not freeze well, except as a purée.		
Chicory	Suitable only for cooking after freezing. Trim and wash; blanch in water with 1tbs lemon juice added. Cool, drain and press out excess water. Open-freeze, then pack.	2 minutes	Thaw and cook gently in butter.
Cress and endive	Do not freeze well.		
Brussels sprouts	Choose small, tight sprouts. Wash and trim. Blanch in water with a little vinegar added. Cool, drain and pack.	3–4 minutes	Cook for 8 minutes in boiling water.
Cabbages	Crisp red and white cabbages may be frozen. Wash, shred coarsely and blanch. Cool, drain and pack.	1½ minutes	Cook from frozen for 8 minutes in boiling water.
Kale	Freeze only the youngest leaves and shoots, stripped from their stems. Blanch, cool and drain. Chop, then pack.	1 minute	Cook for 8 minutes in boiling water.
Broccoli: sprouting and calabrese	Divide into sprigs and wash carefully; soak in salted water for 30 minutes. Length of blanching time depends on thickness of stalks. Cool, drain and pack in rigid containers.	3–5 minutes	Cook for 7 minutes in boiling water.
Cauliflowers	Choose firm, compact heads. Divide into florets and wash. Blanch in water with 1 tbs lemon juice added. Cool, drain and pack.	3 minutes	Cook for 8 minutes in boiling water.
Leeks	Will stand the winter outdoors. To freeze a surplus, trim and cut into rings; wash well. Blanch, cool and drain, then pack.	2 minutes	Use within 6 months. Thaw in container, then use in soups and cooked dishes.
Onions	Peel and chop or slice. Do not blanch. Overwrap to prevent the strong smell spreading. Best stored as dry bulbs.		Thaw and use raw in salads, or add to cooked dishes.
Shallots	Store as dry bulbs.		

FRUIT	PREPARATION	THAWING AND SERVING
Strawberries	Use ripe, firm fruits UNSWEETENED Open-freeze first. Unsweetened berries retain their shape and texture best. DRY SUGAR Pack in layers with sugar in rigid container. SUGAR SYRUP Use a medium syrup. PUREE Sieve ripe fruits and sweeten to taste.	Thaw for 6 hours in fridge. Serve when barely thawed (*frappé*): strawberries deteriorate rapidly. Best used for mousses and ice creams.
Raspberries	UNSWEETENED Open-freeze on trays first. DRY SUGAR Pack in layers with sugar in rigid container. SUGAR SYRUP Use a light syrup. PUREE Sieve ripe fruits and sweeten to taste.	Thaw in fridge for 6 hours. Use in fresh or cooked desserts.
Blackberries	UNSWEETENED Open-freeze first. DRY SUGAR Pack in layers with sugar in rigid container. SUGAR SYRUP Use a heavy syrup. PUREE Sieve very ripe or less than perfect fruits and sweeten to taste. Freeze as a purée.	Thaw in fridge for 6 hours. Use raw or cooked.
Loganberries and other hybrid berries	Prepare, freeze and use as for blackberries.	
Gooseberries	Top and tail ripe fruits. UNSWEETENED Open-freeze, then pack in plastic bags. DRY SUGAR Pack in layers with sugar in rigid container. SUGAR SYRUP Use a medium syrup. PUREE Cook to a pulp with a little water. Sieve and sweeten to taste.	Cook from frozen or thaw in fridge for 6 hours to use in sauces, ice creams, fools, mousses and cooked pies and puddings.
Currants: red, white and black	Strip from stems, wash and drain. UNSWEETENED Open-freeze, then pack in bags or rigid containers. DRY SUGAR Pack in layers with sugar in rigid container. SUGAR SYRUP Use a medium syrup. PUREE Cook blackcurrants, then sieve and sweeten to taste.	Cook while still frozen or thaw in fridge for 6 hours. Use for pies, fools, mousses, summer pudding.
Blueberries	Wash and drain; crush slightly since skins tend to toughen when frozen. UNSWEETENED Open-freeze then pack in plastic bags. DRY SUGAR Pack in layers with sugar in rigid container. SUGAR SYRUP Use a heavy syrup.	Thaw in fridge for 6 hours. Best used in pies or puddings.
Cranberries	Choose firm, glossy berries and wash and drain them. UNSWEETENED Open-freeze, then pack in bags. PUREE Cook, sieve and sweeten to taste, then freeze as purée.	Cook in water and sugar while still frozen, or thaw purée in fridge for 6 hours.
Melons	Halve and remove seeds. Cut into small cubes or scoop into balls. SUGAR SYRUP Toss in lemon juice and cover with a light syrup. Pack in rigid container.	Thaw in fridge for 6 hours; use while still slightly frosted. Use in fruit salads.
Kiwi fruits	Do not freeze well.	
Grapes	Freeze seedless grapes whole; others need skinning and their pips removing, after cutting them in half. UNSWEETENED Freeze small seedless grapes whole. SUGAR SYRUP Use a light syrup for halved larger grapes.	Thaw in fridge for 6 hours. Use in fruit salads or flans.
Apples	Peel and core, then cut into thick slices. Drop at once into water containing 1tbs lemon juice, then rinse. UNSWEETENED Blanch in boiling water for 1 minute, then cool and pack. DRY SUGAR Pack slices in layers with sugar in rigid container. SUGAR SYRUP Use a medium syrup. PUREE Make this from windfalls or other unsound fruits, and with varieties that tend to go mushy when cooked. Cook with a little water and a little sugar until soft.	Cook from frozen for pies and puddings. Use purée for sauces and puddings.

FRUIT	PREPARATION	THAWING AND SERVING
Pears	Not recommended for freezing unless peeled, quartered, cored and cooked until tender in light syrup. Cool, then freeze pears and syrup together.	Thaw for six hours in fridge. Use in cooked desserts or mousses.
Quince	Peel and core, then cut into segments. Cook gently in a light syrup for 20 minutes. Cool, then pack slices and syrup in small, rigid containers.	Thaw for 6 hours in fridge. Use in small quantities with other fruits.
Mulberries	Freeze as for blackberries.	
Figs	Choose sweet, ripe figs; remove stems and avoid bruising. UNSWEETENED Open-freeze, on trays, then pack in strong plastic bags. SUGAR SYRUP Use a light syrup, to which 1tbs lemon juice has been added. Freeze peeled or unpeeled.	Thaw in fridge for 6 hours. Can be served as a dessert, in syrup.
Plums	Halve and remove the stones. Avoid varieties with tough skins, or scald the prepared fruits for 1 minute in boiling water. Drop into water containing 1tbs lemon juice. Drain and dry. UNSWEETENED Pack into rigid container. SUGAR SYRUP Use a light syrup.	Thaw in fridge for 6 hours, in closed pack. Use immediately, since the colour is quickly lost.
Peaches and nectarines	Peel the fruits under cold running water. Halve and stone them, then dip them into water to which you have added 1tbs lemon juice. Peaches discolour readily, so you need to work quickly. Leave in halves, or slice. DRY SUGAR Pack in layers with sugar in a rigid container. SUGAR SYRUP Use a light or medium syrup to which you have added 1½tbs lemon juice to each litre (2 pints) of syrup. PUREE Sieve or liquidize very ripe fruits and sweeten to taste. Add 1tbs lemon juice to every 450g (1lb) fruit.	Thaw in fridge for 6 hours. Use, nearly thawed, in fresh or cooked desserts.
Apricots	Peel, halve and stone. Drop into water containing 1tbs lemon juice. DRY SUGAR Pack halved fruits in layers with sugar in a rigid container. SUGAR SYRUP Peel the fruits, cut into slices and cover with a medium syrup. PUREE Sieve very ripe, stoned and sliced fruits, or put them in a liquidizer. Sweeten to taste, and add lemon juice at 1tsp per 450g (1lb) to prevent browning.	Thaw in covered container for 6 hours and use in fresh or cooked desserts.
Cherries	Chill in water for 1 hour to firm them, then remove the stones. UNSWEETENED Open-freeze, then pack in rigid container. Cherry juice remains liquid when frozen. DRY SUGAR Pack fruits in layers with sugar in rigid container. SUGAR SYRUP Use a medium syrup, to which you have added 1tbs lemon juice, for sweet cherries. Use a heavy syrup, also with lemon juice added, for sour cherries.	Thaw in fridge for 6 hours and use uncooked or in pies or cooked desserts.
Rhubarb	Wash, trim and cut the stalks into 2.5cm (1in) lengths. UNSWEETENED Blanch pieces in boiling water for 1 minute, then drain, cool and pack. SUGAR SYRUP Use a medium or heavy syrup. PUREE Cook to a pulp in a little water then sweeten to taste.	Cook from frozen, or thaw purée in fridge for 6 hours.

All herbs are better for being freshly gathered, but there are several months of the year when picking is not possible for most species. Apart from evergreen herbs such as bay and rosemary, and any perennial or biennial herbs over-wintered indoors in pots, from autumn onward it is necessary to rely on what was preserved the previous summer.

Herbs can be either dried or frozen for winter use; they will be unsuitable for use as a garnish, however. Remember that the flavour of dried herbs is more concentrated, and you need use only half the quantity specified for fresh herbs in a recipe. Both methods of preservation are easy and straightforward.

FREEZING HERBS

This means of preserving retains the flavour of herbs well, though they will become limp on thawing. Frozen herbs are best used within six months. The best results are obtained with young, tender growths which have been picked fairly early in the summer, before the plants come into flower. The most suitable herbs for freezing are the tender-leaved species such as basil, mint, chives and parsley.

Freezing whole

Pick young shoots, or sprigs, and pack them in plastic bags. It is a good idea to place plastic bags in a rigid container afterward, to enable them to be found easily and to avoid undue crushing in the freezer.

It is essential to package frozen herbs in a really airtight fashion, to ensure that their aroma does not permeate other foods in the freezer. Mint is especially penetrating. Seal plastic bags carefully, and reseal them well if some of the contents are removed and the rest returned to the freezer.

Frozen herbs can be used to flavour soups, casseroles and sauces without thawing: simply crumble them into the dish before cooking.

Freezing in water

This is a convenient way to freeze all kinds of leafy herbs. Strip the leaves from the stalks and chop them finely. Place a layer of pieces in the compartments of an ice tray and top them up with water. Put the tray back into the freezer, or the ice compartment of a refrigerator, to freeze.

When the cubes are hard, empty them into a plastic container or polythene bag and seal tightly. Label, and place in the freezer. Take several cubes out at a time and put them straight into the pan or dish with the ingredients they will flavour. If you are using the herbs for an omelette or a dish in which you do not want the extra water, thaw the cubes out first in a sieve so that only the chopped herbs remain.

DRYING HERBS

The leaves of herbs have maximum flavour and aroma while they are young and soft, before the flowers develop on the plant and the leaves become tough. This is the time to gather the shoots and young stalks of herbs for drying; choose a warm, dry day, if possible, and pick them early in the morning before the sun reaches them.

Pull off any damaged or diseased leaves and tie up the sprigs in bunches. Strip larger-leaved herbs, such as sage and mint, from their stalks, then tie these together. There is no real need to blanch herbs for drying, although immersing them for a few seconds in boiling water helps them to retain their colour. Shake off excess moisture, and dry them on absorbent paper.

Hang the bunches, leaves downward, to dry in a well-ventilated, dry, fairly warm place, such as a shed, airing cupboard or a conservatory. If you wish, you can wrap them in muslin or thin paper bags to keep the dust out while they are drying. Drying will take between five and fourteen days, depending on the amount of warmth and humidity and the type of leaf.

Alternatively, spread the individual sprigs or leaves on a bench or tray, well spaced out. A tray can be placed in an airing cupboard, over a radiator or in the warming drawer of an oven. Turn the leaves every day or so to ensure even drying. They will dry out completely in two or three days.

Although natural air-drying is the best means of preserving herbs, the leaves can also be dried in an oven, set to the lowest temperature and with the door ajar. Place the blanched leaves on a covered tray and turn them after half an hour; they will be dry in an hour. This method is suitable for the leaves of sage, mint and parsley, stripped from their stalks.

Whichever method you use, once the leaves are thoroughly dry and crisp enough to crumble when touched, remove the hard stalks and leaf midribs and crush the leaves. Store the herbs, carefully labelled, in airtight tins or jars in a cool place. Place glass jars in a dark cupboard. Dried herbs will retain their flavour for about a year.

You may care to make up some *bouquets garnis*, each consisting of three sprigs of parsley, a bay leaf, a shoot of marjoram and a sprig of thyme. Tie the herbs together and dry them; leave them intact after drying, but enclose each bunch in a small muslin bag. Tie the neck around their stems and store the bags in an airtight container.

To gather the seeds of herbs such as dill, fennel and coriander, pick the flower-heads when they are fully ripe and hang them upside down to dry in an airy place. Enclose them in a bag to catch the seeds.

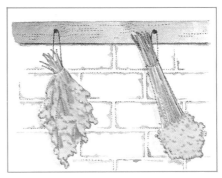

Small-leaved or feathery herbs, such as marjoram, fennel or chervil, can be tied in bunches and hung upside down to dry in an airy place. Leaves of herbs, such as sage and mint, should be first stripped from their stems and tied together by their leaf stalks.

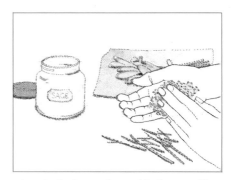

When the herbs are thoroughly dry, crumble them between your hands and store them in an airtight container such as a screw-top jar. Dried herbs have twice the pungency of fresh herbs: use only half the quantity in cooking.

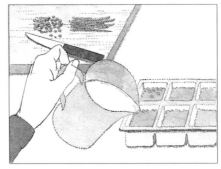

Freezing finely-chopped herbs in the compartment of an ice tray is a convenient method of preservation. Top them up with a little water before freezing, and simply drop the frozen cubes into the pan or dish when cooking. Freeze measured amounts, such as a tablespoonful at a time, for convenience.

HERBS, pages 219–223
FREEZING FRUITS AND VEGETABLES, pages 230–231

INDEX

Numerals in **bold** type refer to main entries.
Numerals in *italic* refer to illustrations.

ADDRESSES OF SUPPLIERS

It is advisable to send a large stamped addressed envelope to the following general and specialist suppliers for their current catalogue or list. Some suppliers make a small charge for their catalogue.

FRUIT TREES AND BUSHES

Chris Bowers & Sons
Whispering Trees Nurseries
Wimbotsham
Norfolk PE34 8QB
Tree fruits, soft fruits and strawberries; wide selection of hybrid berries and unusual varieties

Buckingham Nurseries
28 Tingewick Road
Buckingham MK18 4AE

Deacon's Nursery (CFS)
Godshill
Isle of Wight PO38 3HW

Highfield Nurseries
Whitminster
Gloucester GL2 7PL

Laurels Nursery
Benenden
Cranbrook
Kent TN17 4JU
Tree fruits, soft fruits and herbs

Ken Muir
Honeypot Farm
Rectory Road
Weeley Heath
Clacton-on-Sea
Essex CO16 9BJ
Soft fruits, strawberries, grapes, kiwi and asparagus

Scotts Nurseries (Merriott) Ltd
Merriott
Somerset TA16 5PL
Soft fruits, grapes, tree fruits and herbs

VEGETABLES

Chiltern Seeds
Bortree Stile
Ulverston
Cumbria LA12 7PB
Oriental and unusual vegetables

Samuel Dobie & Son Ltd
P.O. Box 90
Paignton
Devon

S. E. Marshall & Co. Ltd
Wisbech
Cambridgeshire PE12 2RF

Donald Maclean
Dornock Farm
Crieff
Perthshire PR7 3QN
Salad vegetables and unusual potato tubers

W. Robinson & Sons Ltd
Sunny Bank
Forton
near Preston
Lancashire PR3 0BN
Unusual tomatoes, onions and celery

Suttons Seeds
Hele Road
Torquay
Devon TQ2 7QJ

Thompson & Morgan
London Road
Ipswich
Suffolk IP2 0BA

Unwins Seeds Ltd
Histon
Cambridge CB4 4LE

HERBS

John Chambers
15 Westleigh Road
Barton Seagrave
Kettering
Northamptonshire NN15 5AJ

Duncan Ross
Poyntzfield Herb Nursery
by Conon Bridge
Black Isle
Ross-shire
Mail-order herb plants

Suffolk Herbs
Sawyers Farm
Little Cornard
Sudbury
Suffolk CO10 0PF
Italian salad plants, herbs, oriental and unusual vegetables

HORTICULTURAL ASSOCIATIONS

Royal Horticultural Society
80 Vincent Square
London SW1P 2PE

Henry Doubleday Research Association
National Centre for Organic Gardening
Ryton-on-Dunsmore
Coventry CV8 3LG
Information on organic methods and mail-order suppliers of seeds for oriental, salad and general vegetables and herbs for organic gardeners. Also suppliers of safer pesticides, organic fertilizers, green manures, etc.

The Soil Association
86–88 Colston Street
Bristol BS1 5BB
Books, leaflets and technical papers on compost-making, nutrition and gardening by natural methods.

Northern Horticultural Society
c/o R.E. Shersby
Harlow Car Gardens
Harrogate HG3 1QB

National Vegetable Society
c/o W.R. Hargreaves
29 Revidge Road
Blackburn
Lancashire BB2 6JB